Religion and Politics in Contemporary Iran

RELIGION AND POLITICS IN CONTEMPORARY IRAN:
CLERGY-STATE RELATIONS IN THE PAHLAVĪ PERIOD

SHAHROUGH AKHAVI

State University of New York Press
Albany

Published by
State University of New York Press, Albany

© 1980 State University of New York

All rights reserved

Printed in the United States of America

For information, address State University of New York Press, State University Plaza, Albany, N.Y., 12246

Library of Congress Cataloging in Publication Data

Akhavi, Shahrough, 1940–
    Religion and politics in contemporary Iran.

    Includes bibliographical references and index.
        1. Islam and politics—Iran.   2. Ulama—Iran.
    3. Iran—Politics and government—1941–1979.
    I. Title.
    BP63.I68A36   297'.197'70955   79-22084
    ISBN 0-87395-408-4

10 9 8 7 6 5 4 3

For Elaine, the Bird of My Heart

CONTENTS

ACKNOWLEDGMENTS

Research on this book was made possible by the senior coordinators of the Islam and Social Change project at the University of Chicago: Professors Leonard Binder of the Department of Political Science and Fazlur Rahman of the Department of Near Eastern Languages and Civilizations. I would like to thank them for the opportunity to investigate the problem of religion and social change. I gratefully acknowledge, too, the financial support of the Ford Foundation in carrying out this project.

While in Iran, I received the cooperation of a number of persons who were willing to provide access to written materials, and although it is not possible to list them all here, I would specifically like to mention Mr. Hasan Mahjūb, research specialist on religious affairs of the Senate Library; Mr. Iraj Afshār, Director of the Library of Tehran University; and Dr. ʿAbd al-Husayn Hāʾirī, Director of the Majlis Library.

I also am grateful for the encouragement, cooperation and support of individual academics, members of the clergy, friends and relatives. I hope that I have done justice to their counsel and wisdom and spared them any embarrassment for whatever faults this book may contain. These, of course, I must and do assume as my own responsibility.

My gratitude to Professor Michael M. J. Fischer of the Department of Anthropology at Harvard University is due to his having read earlier drafts of the manuscript with a critical eye and for his generous willingness to make suggestions of conceptual and factual nature. In addition, our informal discussions never failed to suggest to me new insights into the problematic of religious structure, organization, culture and ideology in the context of the political process. I would like to express my thanks, additionally, to four anonymous reviewers of this monograph, a number of whose suggestons has been incorporated into the final draft. Mr. Manoochehr Mohammadi, Ph. D. candidate in the Department of Government and International Studies at the University of South Carolina graciously made available to me copies of tracts, manifestos and other information disseminated by the clergy and their supporters in the 1978–1979 period. And Professor Abdulaziz Sachedina of the Department of Religious Studies at the University of Virginia provided inestimable help in the transliteration of Arabic and Persian words and phrases.

GLOSSARY

ᶜAbbāsids: the caliphs who ruled the Islamic community from 750–1258 A.D., from their capital, Baghdad.

ahl al-bayt: descendents of the prophet through his cousin, ᶜAlī ibn Abī Tālib.

Akhbārīs: a school established in 1624 A. D. that held the *mujtahid* to be an invalid feature of Shīᶜism and minimized the clergy's role.

akhlāq: ethics, a subject taught in the theological colleges.

ākhūnd: a low-ranking clergyman, usually a derogatory term.

aᶜlamīyyat: the principle by which a clergyman may claim deference from his colleagues; lit. the quality or characteristic of being most knowledgeable.

ᶜ*aqā* ᵓ *id:* lit. "beliefs;" ideology.

ᶜ*aql:* reason.

ᶜ*atabāt:* the Shīᶜī shrine towns of Najaf, Karbalāᵓ, Kāẓimayn and Sāmarāᵓ in territorial Iraq.

awqāf: (sing. *vaqf;* Arabic sing. *waqf*): religious endowments.

āyatullāh: lit. "sign of God," a title conferred by his followers upon a distinguished *mujtahid.*

al-amr bi al-maᶜ rūf: the injunction "to command the good."

anjuman: society, organization.

Bahāᵓīs: the followers of Bahāᵓullāh, a religious leader who led a movement in the early 1860's that broke with Shīᶜism and saw him as the manifestation of God on earth.

barakah: blessing, a gift of grace.

bayirīyah: waste lands.

dabīristān: a secular secondary school.

dabistān: a secular primary school.

dānishgāh: a secular university.

falsafah: philosophy, a subject not frequently taught in the theological colleges.

faqīh: a Muslim jurisprudent.

farmān: a rescript or edict.

fatvā: an authoritative opinion issued by a *mujtahid* on a matter of law.

Fidāᵓīyān-i Islam: a militant fundamentalist organization established in 1945 with the aim of restoring the pure Islam of the prophet.

fiq: Islamic jurisprudence.

hadīth: a saying attributed to the prophet.

harām: conduct prohibited under Islamic law.

haram: the sanctuary of a shrine.

hawzah-yi ʿilmīyah: a center of religious education.

hijrah: emigration, the archetype of which was that undertaken by Muhammad in 622 A. D. from Mecca to Medina.

hikmat: wisdom; (*hikmat-i ilahī:* theology).

hukūmat: government.

husaynīyah: a place where mourning for Imām Husayn occurs.

ʿibādāt: the rituals of Islam by which to worship God.

ijāzah: diploma enabling a clergyman to exercise *ijtihād.*

ijtihād: independent judgment in the interpretation of Islamic law.

ʿilm: knowledge.

ʿilm al-ghayb: esoteric knowledge, the possession of which renders the *imāms* infallible.

imām: one of 12 preternatural souls who descended from the prophet through his cousin, ʿAlī, the first in the line. Considered the "proofs of God," their outstanding piety, knowledge and chastity are said to enable them to transmit God's light to believers.

Imām: the messiah, whose advent will inaugurate the age of justice in the world.

imāmat: the institution of the rule by the *imams.*

intizār: the principle of awaiting the return of the hidden *Imām.*

Ismāʿīlīs: a Shīʿī sect the followers of which believed that the oldest son of the sixth *Imām* (Jaʿfar al-Sādiq), that is to say, Ismāʿīl, was the legitimate seventh *Imām:* hence, they are known as "seveners."

ʿismat: chastity, a quality attributed to the *imams.*

Ithnā ʿAsharīyah: a Shīʿī sect, dominant in Iran, the followers of which believed that the younger son of the sixth *Imām,* that is to say, Mūsā al-Kāzim, was the legitimate seventh *Imām.* The Ithnāʾ ʿAsharīyah (lit. "twelvers") believed that the line of *imams* extended to 12, the last of whom will return to this world as the Mahdī to establish a reign of justice.

jihād: a holy war conducted on behalf of the Islamic community.

kalām: theology.

khālisah: state lands.

khān: a tribal chief; a general title of respect.

Khawārij: an early schismatic puritanical movement that rejected claims to inherent superiority by the members of the prophet's tribe.

khilāfat: the caliphate of Islam.

khums: lit. "one-fifth," signifying that proportion of annual income Muslims are expected to contribute as a tax to the religious authorities.

madrasah: the traditional theological college or seminary of the Islamic sciences.

Mahdī: the messiah, whose return will inaugurate the age of justice in this world. For "twelvers," the 12th Imam; for "seveners," the son of the seventh.

Majlis: the Iranian parliament; a council.

majhūl al-tawlīyah: the principle in Islamic law where the guardian of an endowment is declared to be unknown.

makrūh: conduct discouraged under Islamic law.

maktab: an elementary religious school.

mantiq: logic, one of the traditional subjects in the theological college.

ma' rifat al-rijāl: biography, a sometime subject in the theological college.

marja'-i taqlīd: "source of emulation" the highest rank among the *Shī'ī* clergy.

marja' īyat: the principle that *Shī' ah* should emulate a living eminent *mujtahid* in matters of law.

mashrūtīyat: the Constitutional Revolution of 1905-1909.

mavāt: dead lands.

mazhab: a school of thought, creed, or sect.

milk: private property.

mudarris: teacher, especially in the theological college.

muftī: a religious official of the *Sunnī* rite with the authority to issue authoritative opinions in matters of Islamic law.

mujtahid: a *Shī'ī* clergyman who, by dint of his eminence in learning, may issue authoritative opinions in matters of Islamic law.

mullā: a lower-ranking clergyman, typically a preacher; also a generic term signifying a clergyman.

muta' azzir al-masraf: the principle in Islamic law whereby the proceeds from an endowment may not be used in the manner originally prescribed in the deed.

mutavallī: administrator of a school, shrine or other endowment made for religious purposes.

Mu'tazilites: the "rationalist" movement in medieval Islam that held it was possible to know God through the exercise of reason.

al-nahy ' an al-munkar: the injunction "to forbid evil."

nā' ib al-tawlīyah: an administrative official who oversees a shrine on behalf of the ruling Shah.

Pahlavī: the dynasty that ruled Iran between 1925-1979.

qādī: a judge.

Qājār: the dynasty that ruled Iran between 1785-1925.

Qur' ān: the sacred book of revelations uttered by the prophet, Muhammad, and codified in the reign of the third caliph, 'Uthmān (ruled 642-656 A. D.)

rawzah khvānī: recitation of narratives of the lives of the *imāms.*

rivāyat: a narrative or tradition.

rūhānīyat: the generic term for the religious institution in Iran.

Sadr: The highest administrative official appointed amongst the clergy by the Shah in the Safavid state.

Safavids: the rulers of the Safavī dynasty that ruled Iran from 1501-1722.

sahm -i imām: one-half of the annual income tax (*khums,* q.v.) paid by Muslims to the *marāji̇̄̇ -yi taqlīd* for the upkeep of mosques, student stipends in the theological colleges, faculty salaries, etc.

sayyid: a direct descendent of the prophet.

sharī̇ ah: the religious law of Islam.

shar̊ : canon law.

shaykh: an elder; a wise leader.

Shaykh al-Islam (pl. Shuyūkh al-Islam): an official appointed from the ranks of the clergy to serve in each of the major cities of Iran by the Shah.

Shī̇ ah: the partisans of ʿAlī ibn Abī Tālib, the cousin of the prophet.

Shī̇ ī: of or pertaining to the *Shī̇ ah.*

shūrā: a council.

shūrā-yi fatvā: a council of eminent *mujtahids* whose duty would consist in the collective issuing of authoritative opinions in matters of Islamic law.

shuʿ ūbīyah: the movement of Persian scribes and writers in the Medieval period that sought to denigrate Arabic culture and who held a skeptical view of the world.

sultān: a secular ruler of the Islamic community.

Sunnah: the tradition of the prophet's behavior and practice; also, those adhering to the legitimacy of the caliphate of Abū Bakr, ʿUmar, ʿUthmān and the rule of the Umāyyad dynasty.

Sunnī: of or pertaining to the orthodox branch of Islam, based on the principle of electing the successor to the prophet.

tabdīl bi al-ahsan: the principle in Islamic law whereby an endowment may be alienated on grounds of improving it.

tafsīr: commentary on the *Qurʾ ān,* among the most intellectually demanding subjects taught in the theological colleges and therefore rarely offered in recent times.

taqīyah: the principle of prudent dissimulation of belief for the purpose of safeguarding the *Shī̇ ī* community from annihilation.

taqvā: piety.

tārīkh: history, a subject sometimes taught in. the theological colleages.

tawlīyat: administrative guardianship of an endowment, school or shrine.

taʿ zīyah: a passion play enacting the tragedy of Imām Husayn on the battlefield of Karbalāʾ.

tullāb (sing.: tālib): students of the Islamic sciences in the theological college.

ʾulā al-amr: lit. "those in authority"; the leaders of the community; the clergy.

ʿulamāʾ (sing.: ʿālim): the learned men of the religious law of Islam.

Umāyyads: the dynasty that controlled the caliphate, with its seat in Damascus, during the period 661–750 A. D.

ummah: the Islamic community.

ʿurf: customary law.

usūl: the principles of Islamic jurisprudence.

Usūlī: a school established under the leadership of Āghā Muhammad Bāqir (Vahīd) Bihbihānī (1705–1803) that insisted on the doctrine of *ijtihād,* the necessity of the role of the *mujtahid* and a broader role for the ʿ*ulamāʾ* in society (cf. the Akhbārīs, q.v.)

valāyat (Arabic: *walāyah*): allegiance to the rule of the *imam*s; their rule on the basis of their ability to interpret the holy law, especially its esoteric meanings.

al-wukalāʾ al-ʿāmm: the notion that the ʿ*ulamāʾ* collectively are the deputies of the *imam*s.

zulm: oppression, often associated with the rule of tyrannical secular rulers, especially the Umayyad Caliph, Yazīd, whose army massacred Imām Husayn and his followers on the battlefield of Karbalāʾ in 680 A. D.

A NOTE ON TRANSLITERATION

The transliteration of Arabic and Persian words follows closely the system adopted by the Library of Congress and the Middle East Studies Association of North America. The one exception to this is that the letters normally designated by a diacritical dot located underneath d, h, s, t and z appear here without the benefit of the diacritical mark. In all other respects, however, the standardized form for transliteration has been employed. Proper names are not italicized, while common nouns are; and words such as Shah, Islam, Iran, and Allah have so entered into English usage as not to require italicization.

PREFACE

This study is based on research carried out for the Islam and Social change research seminar at the University of Chicago, under the coordination of Professor Leonard Binder and Professor Fazlur Rahman. The field research was carried out in 1975, and supplemental research and writing of the manuscript was undertaken while participating in the seminar during the half year between January and July 1976. Further revisions were made between 1976 and 1979. A separate but related monograph has been written by Professor Michael M. J. Fischer, Department of Anthropology at Harvard University. This work will be published soon by Harvard University Press. Fischer is interested in the social anthropology of Qumm and the culture of the religious institution. My interest is in the political relationship between clergy and state in the twentieth century, with special emphasis on the Pahlavī period (1925-1979).

The focus of the research seminar was the impact of social change upon Islam. We faced the task of studying the responses of the religious institution to phenomena of social change in various societies in which Islam constituted the dominant religion. Apart from Iran, specialists were appointed to investigate religious adaptation and response in Morocco, Egypt, Turkey, Pakistan and Indonesia. It was hoped that the impact of change on the Islamic educational system could be brought into focus as much as possible. Given the "negative rewards" administered by the regime at that time for research into the political sociology of the religious schools as a result of their centrality for political protest, it seemed appropriate to adjust the research strategy. This monograph accordingly evolved into an analysis of clergy-state relations in their larger context.

Whatever strategy is ultimately adopted by the researcher, one of the key challenges is the attitude of many Shī'ī adherents that to understand the role of religion in society it is enough to describe it and the key concepts that underpin it. Here, it may be well to recall the admonition by Geertz that the description of the tenets and institutions of Islam according to what they are ideally supposed to consist in tells us too little about "what sorts of beliefs and practices support [it] under what sorts of conditions."[1] In the present case, the chief interest should be to identify the pressures of increasing secularization in the society and the response to these pressures by the leadership in the religious institution.

The chapters in this study tell a story. In this sense, then, it comprises a historical investigation of shifts in orientations, practices and thoughts within the broad time-frame of this century. It is hoped that it fills in some gaps in our all too little knowledge about politics and religion in 20th century Iran. The study, as noted, does not confine itself to religious higher education. There is, to be sure, material here that does examine the *ulamā* (clergy) orientation to educational matters. But by and large the effort is to study the clergy's competition and cooperation with the state in the overall processes that affect the shaping of decisions and policies regarding education, ideology, ethics, and matters of social justice as a whole. The story of what has been happening to the *madrasah*s (theological colleges) over the last half century or more is there. But the behavior of the religious leadership toward government programs in various public policy domains is also deemed an important part of the study.

Chapter one introduces the problem of the origins of the Islamic community; evolution of its institutions, conflicts within Islam over succession and the structure of authority; the emergence of the *Shī*ʿ *ī* and *Sunnī* systems. In the process an attempt is made to distinguish the standing, in more recent times, of the clergy in Iran from that in both Turkey and Egypt. The chapter also contains an exposition of the main elements of the *Shī*ʿ*ī* juristic and political theory. The argument, as laid out in this introductory chapter, provides the reader with the framework for placing into appropriate perspective the analysis in the substantive five chapters that follow.

Chapter two explores the state-religion relationship in the Iranian setting before the accession of the second Pahlavī Shah in 1941. Sections of this chapter deal with the confrontation between the old dynasty (Qājār) and the constitutionalist movement (of which the clergy comprised a crucial part), early developments in the transformation of the educational system of the country, and a host of administrative juridical and other statutes and regulations passed during the rule of Riza Shah. The argument is presented that the latter had attempted to win and consolidate political power in the early twenties by developing links with the ʿ*ulamā* ; and further, that after his coronation (December 1925), he virtually abandoned his relations with them and embarked on a series of measures intending to secularize the society. Critically, the ʿ*ulamā* were systematically harrassed or removed from their previous positions in the social structure; and the access they once had to the imperial court was cut off, so that they were denied their earlier ability to influence the Shah's practice of juggling the various social forces against one another in the quest to maintain his authority and rule. Since Iran historically had been a patrimonial bureaucratic empire with the usual center-periphery problems,[2] each autonomous element (tribe, clergy and aristocracy) had to be placated by the monarch. The modernization program of Riza Shah (regnabat 1925–41) severely undermined the status and power of the clergy; to a lesser extent eliminated tribal opposition to his rule; and touched least of all the power and position of the aristocracy.

To be sure, the displacement of the ʿ*ulamāʾ* from their former position in society was not a linear development of decline. Nor still did Rizā Shah play a unique role in bringing about this state of affairs. To some extent he reinforced trends and policies that antedated his arrival on the scene. Yet withal, the impact of secularization is mainly associated with him, a fact that time and again emerges in discussions with Iranians of the older generation.

Chapter three examines the period between 1941-1958, a period in which the clergy regained its confidence and certainly equalled, if it did not surpass, the influence of the state in public life. In retrospect, it becomes clear that the clergy had never been completely disestablished in the preceding years. The re-emergence of the ʿ*ulamāʾ* as a political force is reflected in their ability to ignore some of the edicts and laws that had made it difficult for them to function (for instance, the Uniformity of Dress Law, which contained onerous provisions that had to be met before the clergy could be exempted); or to secure the annulment of others (e.g., the ban on passion plays outside the confines of mosques and the proscription of pilgrimmage to Mecca). In a more informal, but perhaps more significant manner, the clergy simply gained in deference and rectitude as far as public opinion is concerned. This seems of cardinal importance when one recognizes that the Iranian clergy in this time did not fashion any new institutions to adapt to the changing functions of education, welfare, law, administration, etc. in the encompassing society. In other words, it seems to be the informality of the structure of clergy relations with the masses and the state that provides the context for their regained autonomy. Practically speaking, this long seventeen year period, on the basis of available information, witnessed little, if any, change in the organizational structure of the Iranian religious institution.

The occupation of the country by foreign armies, the crisis with the Soviet Union over the presence of the Red Army in the Northwest, and British insistence on keeping control of the Anglo-Iranian Oil Company no doubt greatly assisted the ʿ*ulamāʾ* cause. This may be explained by the signal role of the religious leadership in earlier protest movements against British power and influence. In general, an intense antiforeign orientation has historically accompanied the political activity of the Iranian religious establishment. For example, in Qājār times officials of the court or members of the aristocracy were commonly identified in the public consciousness as pro-British, pro-Russian or pro-French; although this pattern was not completely absent in the case of the ʿ*ulamāʾ*, rarely did the charge against a clergy leader that he was a creature of foreign influence appear or (even more rarely) gain widespread credibility.

The Shah's position in this period became somewhat analogous to that of monarchs in earlier times in the sense that the forces that had traditionally composed the periphery but had been "integrated" into the nation-state between 1925-1941 now became unstuck. Tribal restiveness plus the assertiveness in parliament of the landed grandees showed that the center would not hold. To this was added a new element: the social stratum of urban intelligentsia, professionals and bureaucrats—products of the modernizing policies and the needs of Riza Shah.

The ʿ*ulamāʾ* in the late forties and in the fifties are examined in terms of a highly simplified typology based on orientations to certain public policy issues then current, such as direct participation by the clergy in politics, female suffrage and enfranchisement, the role of communism in a *Shīʿ ī* society, the acceptability of the ideology and tactics of militant *Shīʿ ī* fundamentalism, and so forth. Caveats are entered to avoid treating the ʿ*ulamāʾ* as a monolithic social stratum. The split in ʿ*ulamāʾ* ranks among those who supported Prime Minister Musaddiq (and this element itself was internally divided), those opting for political quietism, and those supporting the Shah should be instructive in this respect.

The dominant faction among the clergy—termed the "conservatives" in this study and headed by Ayatullāhs Burūjirdī and Bihbihānī—apparently sought to reconcile Musaddiq and the Shah, but without success. After the overthrow of the Prime Minister the Shah sought to forge an alliance with this faction to help him gain legitimacy in the eyes of the politically important nationalists within the *nihzat-i millī* (or nationalist movement).

Such developments are further explored within the framework of the anti-Bahāʾī campaign of 1955. It is apparent that the state, needing clergy support for internal purposes (i.e., defeat of the communist movement and of the militant fundamentalist Fidāʾīyān-i Islam, both of which were clamoring against Western influence in the country) moved to implement anti-Bahāʾī measures which earned it widespread international opprobrium. Ultimately, the state was led into a confrontation with representatives of the ʿ*ulamāʾ* over the Bahāʾī issue. A review of the Majlis (parliament) debates in this period clearly highlights the leadership role of the clergy in the persecution of the Bahāʾīs.

The government's interest in an alliance with the Burūjirdī-Bihbihānī (majority) faction among the ʿ*ulamāʾ* seemed also to have been dictated by the need for domestic approval of—or at least acquiescence to—regime policies regarding Iran's joining a foreign alliance, the Baghdad Pact; and allowing foreign oil companies and countries to continue to have a dominant role in petroleum operations.

The self-confidence of the clergy began to erode, however, in the late 1950's. Chapter four discusses the early conflicts between state and religion over plans for female suffrage and land reform, the suspension of parliament by the Shah and the defeat of the political opposition by the latter. During the demonstrations of 1962-1963, the clergy did not have the linkages with the nationalist movement that it had established in the early 1950's and was to bring about in the late 1970's. Āyatullāh Khumaynī was not known to the Tehran-based National Front, and Āyatullāh Tāliqānī at that time still had not developed his reputation to the extent necessary to aggregate members of the clergy into a coalition with the National Front. The discussion rejects the charge made by the regime that clergy opposition to the Shah's "White Revolution" centered on its allegedly "reactionary" character. It also undertakes a content analysis of the editorials of the leading Tehran daily on the regime's view of the "proper" role of the ʿ*ulamāʾ*, and concludes with an analysis of the obverse side of that argument as spelled out in an important essay by Muhandis Mihdī Bāzargān. As spokesman for the socially active clergy, Bāzargān states the maximalist position for political involvement by the ʿ*ulamāʾ* . And while he himself is not a professional clergyman, his relationships with the ʿ*ulamāʾ* were such as to lend them a degree of authenticity not normally accruing to a layman's observations.

Chapter five examines the two major reform movements of the early sixties and the late-sixties and early seventies. It also documents the continuing bureaucratization of power, in particular in connection with the role and activity of the Endowments Organization. The two reform movements were different in nature, even while in each case their leaders worked on the same interfaces of religion and politics. In the case of the Monthly Religious Society, a group of socially conscious members of the clergy took the lead to reform the religious institution from within. In the case of the movement led by Dr. ʿAlī Sharīʿatī, a more conscious effort to apply the concepts of sociological analysis to the reforming of the religious institution was made. In addition, Dr. Sharīʿatī's hostility to the procedures and conclusions adopted by the orthodox clergy leadership led him to insist on the requirement of eliminating their domination over the centers of religious education in the country. The state's penetration of the religious institution by administrative and bureaucratic means, as well as through the use of the intelligence services, is highlighted in this chapter. The years between 1964–1977, then, are the peak period in the power of the state and represent the nadir of ʿ*ulamāʾ* influence in public life.

Chapter six seeks to analyze inter-clergy relations during the period covered in the preceding chapter. It also reviews the main themes in Āyatullāh Khumaynī's book, *Islamic Government* (1971), especially the important concept of *valāyat-i faqīh*. The book's main purpose, of course, is to argue that doctrinal justification exists for the purpose of creating an Islamic state in the absence of the *Imām*, whose messianic return to this world from occlusion is believed to be the starting point for the establishment of Islamic justice on earth. Along the way, Āyatullāh Khumaynī's criticism of monarchy, the behavior of quietist clergymen and the general state of decay of the religious institution are an important concomitant of the argument for an Islamic government. Finally, the differential perspectives of the two grand *āyatullāh*s of Iran in the revolutionary period (Āyatullāh Khumaynī and Āyatullāh Sharīʿatmadārī) are examined in an effort to indicate in a tentative manner the alignments among the clergy leadership both in the past and, perhaps, in the future.

A final short chapter briefly recapitulates the main themes in the book and suggests several propositions concerning social change in an Islamic state. The entire story of clergy-state relations in the Pahlavī period is yet to be written. Under the conditions of the new order, there is no doubt that information will be made available to the scholar—or the scholar may be able to generete his data through various methods—that could not have been secured in the previous period. This will inhere if only because the new regime will wish to inform the public about the nature of behavior and policy of the system it replaced. We will, therefore, happily be able to enhance our knowledge about the extent and process by which the clergy was led to the brink of becoming a déclassé stratum in Iranian society. It is my hope that the present work will make a modest contribution in laying the foundation for the future studies which will certainly follow. If I have helped to raise some of the issues which will point the way for future scholarship, then the effort will have been justified. In that spirit, I look forward with great excitement to the coming research of colleagues that will build upon, amend and transcend what I have had to say here!

CHAPTER ONE

INTRODUCTION

PRELIMINARY REMARKS

A study of the linkages between politics and religion may strike the imagination as somewhat out of place in the late twentieth century. However, in the particular case of Iran the relationship between the two continues to be of great importance. An understanding of the linkage will contribute to our larger understanding of social change in the country. Although the Pahlavī period was one of rapid secularization in many spheres of life, the current religious reaction to Pahlavī policies well indicate the abiding power of religiously inspired ideas and movements.

The proper analysis of the subject of religion and politics in twentieth century Iran necessitates a recapitulation of certain elements of the social history of the early Islamic community (610–661 A. D.); the significant divergence in that community between the Sunnī ("orthodox") and Shīʿī ("heterodox") branches of Islam; the structure of religious thought and organization; and the evolution of institutional and constitutional features of government and administration.

The early period of the Islamic community consisted of a time when the prophet, Muhammad, experienced the visions and revelations of Allah's commands, began his missionary activity, attempted to recruit followers, painfully built a local and then regional reputation in Western Saudi Arabia, and spearheaded a drive to overcome the tribal opposition to him in the crucial trading city of Mecca. Following his death (632 A. D.), his associates united themselves under a successor, or caliph, and these were responsible for the outward thrust of the Islamic community into Syria, Egypt and Iran. The first four caliphs were known as the "rightly guided ones", and it was during their tenure that the later deep schisms established their primal roots. With the death of the fourth of these religious-secular rulers in 661 A. D. the early period of the Islamic community came to an end.

The decade of political rule exercised by Muhammad between the years 622–632 A. D. was one of charismatic authority. As such, it featured little in the way of administrative development.[1] The social organization of daily life in Mecca

1

and Medina during the prophet's lifetime apparently had only the most rudimentary trappings of officialdom of either a religious or secular nature. Yet, the *outlines* of a political organization were clearly established after 622 A. D., the year that Muhammad and his followers trekked to Medina to arbitrate a tribal feud (marking the first year of the Muslim calendar). In this connection, it is worth citing the remarks of H. A. R. Gibb:[2]

> Externally, the Islamic movement assumed a new shape and formed a definite community organized on political lines under a single chief. But this merely gave explicit form to what had hitherto been implicit. In the mind of Muhammad (as in the minds of his opponents) the new religious association had long been conceived of as a community organized on political lines, not as a church within a secular state.

The coextensiveness of religious and political communities in Islam is a theme to which we will return. It is a motif that weaves like a red thread through the fabric of Islamic history and will become particularly relevant in considering the problem of politics and religion in contemporary Iran.

EVOLUTION OF THE ISLAMIC COMMUNITY

The death of the prophet left the community unprepared. His companions rallied to choose a successor from among themselves. The choice was based upon the principle of collegial selection. Because the institutional structure of the community was so simple, the process of election was not a complex matter. The companions consisted of those who joined him in the difficult days in Mecca in the first ten years of preaching, plus those who made the dramatic 200 mile journey to Medina. During the rule of the first four calips (632-661 A. D.)— sometimes also termed the era of the patriarchal caliphate—the revelations of Muhammad were codified into the holy book of Islam, the *Qur' ān*. Because a number of the prophet's close associates memorized his words, the *Qur' an* came into being and became the foundation for Islamic law, since it constituted the direct sayings of Allah.

A second foundation of the law was that of the tradition of the prophet's behavior and practice, together with his statements apart from the *Qur' ān* (termed the *Sunnah*). Taken together, these twin sources of law, *Qur' ān* and *Sunnah*, sufficed for some time as regulatory principles of community life and members' conduct. As the community evolved, however, the need for new structures and procedures became increasingly evident. The *Qur' ān* was immutable, to be sure. And the *Sunnah* was passed on from generation to generation in both written and oral form. But, as might be expected, it did not take long for contending positions on various matters to arise, with their adherents finding validating referents in the same source. Therefore, it soon became imperative to find a consensus to interpret varying points of law. We will discuss below the emergence of a stratum of professionals charged with precisely this task. At this juncture, it is well to note the early development of disputes in the ranks of the community whose arbitration more and more required a cadre of qualified individuals to make determinations on points of law. In short, it became no longer possible to meet each occasion of conflict in interpretation on an *ad hoc* basis.

Before we discuss the evolution of the professional stratum of religious leaders, however, it is apposite to focus on another kind of dissensus in the community: rebellion. Among the early schisms, those of the Khawārij, based largely in Iraq, and the *Shī'ah* are the most significant. The more minor of the two dissident movements, that of the Khawārij, had to do with their rejection of any claims to inherent superiority by the members of the prophet's tribe, the Quraysh. They professed a completely egalitarian ethos, underlain by a puritanical streak vehemently opposed to what they regarded to be the dynastic secularism of the caliphate. They did not combine in great numbers, and the orthodox leadership easily contended with their defection.

The *Shī' ī* leadership rejected the principle of electing the caliph from among the prophet's companions. They contended that Muhammad's kin had a prior claim to the mantle of leadership. They regarded the succession to the caliphate by the first three incumbents of the office as illegitimate, although they held their counsel and did not initially openly challenge the prevailing arrangements. When the fourth Caliph, 'Alī ibn Abī Tālib, acceded to the office, the *Shī'ah* rejoiced that their claims had finally been requited. However, the assassination of his predecessor by disgruntled tribesmen clouded 'Alī's claims. It is a measure of irony that his own partisans had only the remotest of connections with the assassins of the third caliph. In the event, his tenure was beset with turmoil and sedition, and ultimately, he, himself, fell victim to murder.

A second point of contention between the *Shī' ah* and the *Sunnī* majority consisted in the formers' belief in the institution of the Imāmate. The latter refers to the institution of rule by the descendents of Muhammad through his cousin, 'Alī. This indicates the belief of the *Shī' ah* that the office of the *Imām* is superior to that of the caliph and has constituted the linchpin of the *Shī' ī* theory of rule. Adherents of the particular variant of Shī' ism in Iran hold that there have been twelve *imāms* in history, including the first *imām*, 'Alī. Further, the *Shī' ah* regard the Imāmate as a guarantee of salvation through the shining example of the twelve (or seven or eleven in variant forms) descendents of the prophet. Unlike the *Sunnī* believer, who holds that the community *as a whole* is infallible,[3] the *Shī' ī* follower attributes infallibility to the *imāms*, alone.

The evolution of the history of Islamic society after the historic split between the orthodox and heterodox factions is largely a matter of social organization and governmental institutions. As the public finances, administration and law of the community of Islam (*ummah*) crystalized, the power of the ruling institution, that is, the caliphate, increased. It must be remembered that the caliphate evolved out of a framework of the Meccan tribal system, centered more specifically on the Quraysh clan. The early example of rule by charismatic authority could be followed only to a limited extent by the prophet's successors. In a word, the transfer to them of the prophet's *barakah* (charisma) was partial. The end of the "golden age" of early Islam ended with political power reposing in the relatively well-to-do merchant oligarchy of the Quraysh *shaykh*s (elder leaders). This oligarchy relied to a large extent on the support of the garrisoned tribal forces in Syria, Iraq, Yemen and elsewhere.

The Umāyyad period (661-750) of the Islamic caliphate marked a turning point in Muslim political history. It involved the appointment, as caliphs, of the relatives of the third caliph. The years of Umāyyad rule ushered in an era of Arab kingship.[4] The dynastic feature of this caliphate consisted not so much in the direct passing of office from father to eldest son (inasmuch as the succession passed more frequently to collateral line cousins or to brothers) as in the monopolization of the office by the family of Abū Sufyān. The earlier period, characterized by solidarity and feelings of tribal equality, now gave way to another which spawned a succession of increasingly autocratic rulers. The onset of Arab kingship involved the evolution of patrimonial forms of rule, in which the crucial question was to maintain the unity of the collective community:[5]

> The Community, which as time went on became predominant in Islam as the 'Sunnite' was probably most clearly represented in the Syrians. The Community was to hold sway over a single unified state; political and social superiority was vested in adherence to the Community; religious data were considered as they affected the realization and universality of the Community; exclusion of the non-Arabs from government was axiomatic and at this time hardly even discussed.

That the *Umāyyad* caliphate brought about the formation of new governmental institutions is suggested by the fact that the "patriarchal period" created only an incipient political organization embedded in tribal military structures; though it proved indispensable for the phenomenal outward thrust of Islamic armies, this putative political organization "was furnished with no administrative organs for other purposes."[6] Gibb argues that the energies unleashed by the Arab military forces exhibited a degree of concentrated power rarely, if ever, seen in that part of the world. Yet, for all of that, this power (which was, after all, brought into existence by the revelation and its attendant doctrines) did not initially have to compete with other "centers of power" in the community. The only social institution created by the doctrine for the first century was government. Thus, the tradition of Arab kingship begun in the Umāyyad caliphate must be understood in terms of a stark choice open to the members of the community: either allow government to exert its concentrated power or permit anarchy. The argument about the first century of the Islamic community is not that the Umāyyads inherently lusted after power. Rather, it must be that there existed no possibility of delegating or relegating the power of the ruling secular institution (i.e., the government) to some other entity. In effect, the government that evolved in the early and Umāyyad caliphates had a monopoly of power because it was the only coherent social organization.

This guaranteed a paradoxical situation in which a professedly egalitarian body of thought and doctrine was advanced by an increasingly powerful governmental apparatus. The later formation of social strata, together with their organizations and networks, therefore must be viewed in the light of this early trend. It explains to some extent why it was that challenges to the power of the central ruling institution were rarely successful. If one adds to this the doctrinal position that resisting even tyrants was harmful to the larger and long-run interests of the community (because it could lead to anarchy and the opportunity for infidels to destroy the *ummah*), then the historical position of the ruling institution becomes the more formidable.

The logical conclusion of these considerations is that despite the fact that in Islam religion and state are merged in a theoretical sense, practically speaking the overweening power of the governmental authority was the constantly operating factor; the result: centralization, absolutism, autocratic behavior.

While all this was taking place, what had become of the *Shī'ī* collectivity within the *ummah?* The only—and abortive—challenge they mounted to the Umāyyad caliphate occured in 680. Thereafter, the dominant theme of *Shī'ī* jurisprudence became the cautious dissimulation of belief in the face of over-whelming pressure to disguise one's allegiances to Shī'ism.[7] Reflecting on the practical side of this doctrinal point was the inability/unwillingness of *Shī'ī* adherents to form their own communal institutions outside of the *Sunnī* fold. Unlike the Khawārij who held the *Sunnī* to be in excommunication from Islam, the *Shī'ah* evolved a jurisprudence which was, in important respects, not all that different from the *Sunnī*. We have already, to be sure, indicated the central dispute over the succession and *Shī'ī* belief in the Imāmate as an institution. But we must not lose sight of a very important point: that until the last quarter of the ninth century (i.e., after the disappearance of the twelfth *Imām* in 874), since the death of 'Alī ibn Abī Tālib in 661, there was no extensively recognizeable *Shī'ī* community that could be said to be following any of the eleven *imāms*.[8] *Shī'ī* organization and institutions and political theory therefore came after the occulta-tion of the twelfth *Imām*.

Shī'ism never became the thought and practice of the Caliphate, although *Shī'ī* states were established in Egypt in 969; Tunisia in 909; Bahrayn in the early 900's. Also, such towns in this period as Kūfā in Iraq, Qumm in Iran, and Aleppo in Syria came under *Shī'ī* influence.[9] The Buwayhid princes who con-trolled Baghdad and parts of Iran around 945 tolerated *Shī'ī* ideas but professed the orthodox, or *Sunnī,* interpretation of the faith and pledged allegiance to the ʿAbbāsid caliphs of that time.

Furthermore, rifts within the fabric of Shīʿism arose, with the more revolutionary-activist element becoming known for their deeds in such far away places as India, Spain and Iran (known as the seveners, or Ismāʿīlī faction). Egypt, more centrally located in the world of Islam, was an Ismāʿīlī state between 969–1171. Yet another, Zaydī, form of Shīʿism emerged in Yemen in the late 9th century.

The *Imāmī* (twelver) creed of Shīʿism that eventually succeeded in Iran was therefore late in evolving its political structures and thought. Its *practical* political traditions (as expressed in organizational structures and processes and functions) were, prior to its establishment as the "national religion" of Iran, therefore those of the *Sunnī* Umāyyads and ʿAbbāsids.[10] It will be recalled from the earlier discussion that power became centralized and monopolized by the government in the first century of Islam. The ʿAbbāsids rapidly affirmed and consolidated this trend as a result of the influence that Persian Sassanid traditions of statecraft, hierarchy and bureaucracy had on ʿAbbāsid officialdom.

In 1501 a millenarian charismatic movement burst on the scene in northwest Iran and conquered state power on behalf of *Imāmī* Shīʿism for the first time in the long history of *Shīʿī* evolution. The structure of Shīʿism after the establishment of a centralized Iranian state under the Safavid Dynasty will be examined below. Here, it is only necessary to point out that the *Shīʿī* ʿ*ulamāʾ* could at long last begin to have the kind of input into, if not domination over, public order and government that the Sunnī ʿ*ulamāʾ* had begun to exert many centuries previously.

THE ʿULAMĀʾ AND POLITICS

The word, ʿ*ulamāʾ* (sing. ʿ*ālim*) means the learned men of the religious law of Islam. It is a term that refers to those who "know," since the root word from which it is derived means knowledge. The existence of these religious leaders of the community dates back to the early days of Islam. Muhammad, Islam's prophet, was both the spiritual and temporal ruler of the small Islamic community in Mecca and Medina. Upon his death, the community leaders gathered to choose a successor, and in this choice the learned men played a decisive role. The sources of their knowledge, of course, were *Qurʾān, Sunnah, Hadīth* (as already mentioned). These three elements were compiled, aggregated and codified in the Arabic language in the years following Muhammad's death.

It is fair to say that the ʿ*ulamāʾ* derived their status in the early Islamic community from their participation in the selection of the caliph and from their codification and interpretation of the religious law. To the extent that evidence exists, it is possible to fix in historical time the point at which the ʿ*ulamāʾ* may be seen as having a corporate status and interests to advance and defend. In a preliminary way, we have already implied that for the first century the ʿ*ulamāʾ* did not evolve their own corporate standing (in the sense of a professional grouping, ranking or status group). The *Qurʾān,* it is true, refers to the ʾ*ūlā al-amr,* "those who are in authority," meaning the spiritual leaders of the community. But in the early decades of Islam these scholars of religion were so busy laying out the details of ethical behavior within the context of a spectrum of obligatory, recommended, permitted, disapproved, prohibited actions that they did not evolve an institutional structure of their own until a good deal later. If the ʿ*ulamāʾ* can be said to have had an identity, it was as guardians of Allah's words and hopes for an ethical community of believers in this world. They thus controlled public worship. As exegetes of Islamic theology they were extremely influential, even though they did not have a monopoly in this sphere. As participants in the political system, "[t]hey exercised an effective—but never decisive—pressure in the realms of public order and government."[11]

Existing scholarship seems to point to the creation of a stratum of the ʿ*ulamāʾ* with its own corporate identity in reaction to three movements prevalent in the eighth century: Manicheanism; Shuʿūbism; and Muʿtazilism. The first was an extreme ascetic view of man and his relationship to his God; the second was a social movement of the secretaries, scribes and other functionaries of the growing patrimonial structure of empire who roundly denounced the "primitive" Arab culture in favor of the Persian and ultimately invited the faithful to a skeptical view of the world and man's role in it. The third was a form of rationalism which scandalized the orthodox because it held that it was possible to know God through the application of reason, and that one could impute rational motives to Him and seek to know them through the same process.

It was in response to these challenges to the orthodox interpretations that the ʿ*ulamāʾ* truly began to initiate their own professional roles, structures, processes and functions as a social force in society. The rout of Manichean, Shuʿūbī and Muʿtazilī positions logically led to the expulsion of the adherents of these movements from positions of influence in the caliphate. The orthodox ʿ*ulamāʾ*, in an effort to guarantee the perpetuation of their own positions, "[g]radually ... brought almost all education under their control, and worked out and implemented curricula to realize their own intellectual and spiritual ideals."[12]

The victory of the ʿ*ulamāʾ* over their rivals has been characterized as the triumph of the adherents of the charismatic authority of the community, as opposed to the adherents of the charismatic authority of the single leader.[13] Since the ʿ*ulamāʾ* were understood to be the wise leaders of the community, they understood themselves to be, as a collectivity, infallible (even if not in a theoretical sense, at least in a practical sense), by logical extension of the *hadīth* attributed to the prophet that "my community shall never agree upon error."

Yet, there were those members of the ʿ*ulamā*ʾ who, because they were attracted to Khārijī, Rāfidī or *Shīʿ ī* thought, abjured the notion of the charisma of the community. They placed principal emphasis upon the charisma of the *Imām*. The ranks of these learned men were perhaps not so badly divided as Watt makes them out to be.[14] "*Imāmī* doctrine on the Imāmate in its basic conceptions was formulated in the time of the *Imām, Jaʿfar al-Sādiq* (d. 765)."[15] Therefore, the account of al-Hasan ibn Mūsā al-Nawbakhtī (d. 922) concerning the differences between twelver *Imāmī* and other forms of Shīʿ ism is not so much the watershed for the formation of *Shīʿ ī* that Watt suggests when he says that twelver *Imāmī* doctrine became "widely accepted by moderate Shʿites" in the early part of the 10th century.[16] But however one views the problem of time frames, most scholars appear convinced that the more "revolutionary" forms of Shīʿism had succumbed to what may be termed quietism sometime during the 9th century.

Early *Shīʿ ī* jurisprudence and theology naturally acclaimed the words and deeds of ʿAlī and his descendents. It agreed with the *Sunnī* view that all power is contingent upon Allah's will, and that therefore all power is delegated by Allah to a succession of inferior agencies, including the prophet, the caliphs (for *Shīʿ ī* theologians, the *imām*s), and the officials appointed by the caliphs.[17] They did not, however, have to wrestle—as did the Sunni ʿ*ulamā*ʾ—with the ambiguities of community infallibility. That is, in the last analysis the community did not exercise judgment and power; individuals did. The twelver *Imāmiī Shīʿ ī* insistence on judgment and power supremely located in the person of the *Imām* nicely resolved the dilemma.

Yet, despite clarification of doctrine on the theoretical side, it was to be another six hundred years until central state power would be exercised in the name of Shīʿism. In the meanwhile, the destruction of the ʿAbbāsid caliphate at the hands of the Mongols occured (1258). It is not to diminish the dreadful force of the Mongol onslaught into the Middle East heartland to say that the caliphate had been in decline for centuries previously. Although the original Islamic conception of the community was that it constituted a theocracy, the passage of time led to a further and further separation of theory and practice. With the phenomenon of the migration of Turkish tribes from Central Asia came the increasing practice of "amirate by seizure," rather than by appointment through the caliph. In time these episodes of sultanistic behavior on the part of the military princes suceeded in eroding the caliph's power. Toward the end of the 10th century and thereafter caliphs increasingly resigned themselves to post-facto appointment of governors and satraps. The latter less and less heeded them, apart from ritualistic invocation of their names at Friday prayers. The jurists, for their part, had to interpret the intolerable infringement on caliphal power. In an inelegant attempt to put the best face on what was, after all, a devastating development, the leading ʿ*ulamā*ʾ evolved the doctrine of necessity. According to this reasoning, seizures of power by secular rulers were justified by reference to the chaos that would ensue if caliphs were to join the issue and challenge the dissident *amīrs*. It was better to preserve the domestic tranquility than invite anarchy, and when things reached the stage of local warlords actually assuming caliphal titles, the theologians kept pace with such developments, as well. Again, as with, for example, al-Ghazalī (d. 1111), these at bottom unlawful appropriations were adjudged to be necessary after the fact.

The situation was transformed after the collapse of the ʿAbbāsid caliphate through the seizure of power in 1312 by yet another in a long line of Turkish tribal leaders. In the next two hundred years the household of this prince expanded its domains into Europe, including the conquest of the Byzantine capital itself. Calling himself both *sultān* and caliph, and mobilizing resources in such a way as to fashion formidable military victories, the Ottoman ruler alleged that he was fulfilling the mission of the prophet and caliphs of the Umāyyad and ʿAbbāsid periods. Although the ʿ*ulamāʾ* under the Ottoman Empire were well respected by the ruler, they had become, for the most part, the guardians of the law. Certainly it could not be said of them that they continued to be (as their predecessors of centuries earlier had been) the sole bearers of the collective wisdom of the community; nor were they any longer, in effect, the repository of the community's charisma. Too much had changed for this to be the case. As *qādīs* (or judges) they held important administrative and legal positions in the empire. But the state had the same advantage that the Umāyyad state had over any other institutuion (and, in the Umāyyad case, it will be recalled that no rival social organization to the caliphate existed): i.e., it held the reins of power. Thus, we see that despite Islam's continuing insistence on the coextensiveness of religious and political spheres, in fact the ruling institution had ended by placing the weight of power in its hands and limiting the power of the religious institution to that of constraining the will of the ruler from arrant excesses. And while the power of constraint must not be underestimated, yet it is a far cry from the power to generate or create policy on internal initiative.[18]

In the meantime, *Shīʿī* theory, as evolved by al-Kulaynī (d. 939) and Ibn Bābawayh (d. 991) appeared headed in the direction of bridging earlier Islamic conceptions of the caliphate and Greek conceptions of the philosopher-king. There thus emerges in the *Shīʿī* theory of government the germs of the idea of monarchical absolutism.[19] But we must be careful not to ascribe to "mainstream" *Shīʿī* thinking the ideas of extremist factions on the margins of the movement. Shīʿism may be said consistently to have mistrusted the exercise of power by secular rulers in the absence of the *Imām*. Therefore, the *Bāṭinī Shīʿī* position that absolute monarchy constituted a necessity in the *Imām*'s absence and hence the absolute monarch was "alone the true vicegerent of God"[20] must not be construed as the general *Shīʿī* conception. When writers in the thirteenth century, such as Najm al-Dīn al-Rāzī and Fakhr al-Dīn al-Rāzī, wrote of the king as the shadow of God on earth, they did so from the point of view of Sūfism or on behalf of temporal patrons in search of legitimacy from the religious side. Such individuals placed a premium upon ability over knowledge, a direct contradiction of classic Shīʿī insistence that the Imām's leadership depends upon his ʿilm (knowledge), piety and justice. One can readily detect the pre-Islamic Persian influences emanating from the theory of statecraft and kingship in these arguments.

Now, it is true that a number of Shīʿī thinkers evolved the theme, after the establishment of the Safavid state in 1501, that the Shah was representative of the Imām and, as such, was the shadow of God on earth. But, as Lambton puts it:

> The Shīʿī jurists . . . guarded against the assumption of infallibility by temporal rulers by maintaining that the Imamate was a universal authority in the things of religion *and of the world,* belonging to a person, *which distinguished it from the dominion of judges and vice-gerants.*

Lambton, to be sure, says in the next breath that "But in practice this distinction tended to be forgotten."[21] Nonetheless, since we are dealing with matters of doctrine, the fact that practice negates theory on this issue must not make us lose sight of the refusal by many members of the Shīʿī ʿulamāʾ to give the king *carte blanche* in matters of social justice and equity.

In this connection, as Algar points out,[22] for Shīʿī Muslims the doctrine of walāyah—obedience to the rule of the Imām—stands out above all other obligations of the faith save those of the profession of faith in the unity of God and in the prophecy of Muhammad. Shīʿī belief holds that continuity with the rule of the Imām is vouchsafed by the authoritative interpreters of the religious law. Shīʿī Muslims hold that the highest ranking members of the clergy in effect possess the key to right conduct by their superior knowledge and ability to deduce "ordinances according to logical proof."[23]

This, then, permitted the clergy, through their highest ranking members, to exert a powerful influence in the social life of Shīʿī Muslims. This can be appreciated if it is understood that Shīʿī Muslim doctrine contends that all matters of social reality are inevitably and invariably affected by considerations of religious law.[24] Since guidance as to practice is a *sine qua non* in Shīʿism, and since those not learned in religious law are prohibited from engaging in discursive and deductive reasoning from basic principles to specific details (*ijtihād*), it follows that a guide (or guides) must be available for each generation until the return of the Imām. This individual(s) is (are) the "source of emulation" (*marjaʿ -i taqlīd*) and the focus of allegiance of the general population as to matters of social conduct and interaction.

In establishing the bases for the emergence of the clergy in Shīʿī Islam, it becomes very important to distinguish the doctrinal, as opposed to the practical, aspects of this group's authority. In his recent essay, Eliash[25] posits that the clergy's authority did not derive from their having received an appointment *ex ante* from the *imāms*. He contends that the supposition that it had secured such an appointment in the suggested manner was a misconception by Algar, Binder and others. In denying the thesis of *ex ante* appointment Eliash traces the tradition cited by Binder as

> attributed to the *Imām* Ja'far al-Sādiq, who said that all those who might act as judges over the Muslims and interpret the law. . . . The Shī'ite *'ulamā'*, acting as the general agency until the hidden *Imām* reveals himself, perform the functions of the *Imām*.

Eliash shows that in fact the tradition, as located in the four great books of *Shī'ī* traditions, is a very technical appointment of the judges in cases of arbitration. The text of the tradition, cited by Binder but analyzed by Eliash in its context, indicates that the community has as much appointive power over judges in matters of arbitration as the *Imām*, himself. Moreover, it becomes clear that the members of the community—and more specifically those members of the community who have a matter to litigate, and therefore require a judge—are entitled to dismiss the judge if the latter is shown to be following unsound traditions. The point is that the *imāms* did not prepare the way for the clergy to become their agents or deputies; instead, the clergy gradually assumed among their own ranks that they were, indeed, the deputies of the *imāms* (although they have never pretended to the *Imām*'s *barakah*, his infallibility, or his *'ilm al-ghayb* (esoteric knowledge). In this process of assumption, a confrontation between the *Akhbārī* school and the *Usūlī* school materialized after 1722 A. D. The former held that no need existed for religous scholars to exercise independent judgment in matters of law; the sacred texts were sufficient. By contrast, the *Usūlī* position maintained the need for *mujtahids*—i.e., those exercising such independent judgment—in view of what they saw as inevitable conflicts in interpretation. Such a debate in *Shī'ī* ranks took place relatively late in time (the early 18th century). We see, then, that the clergy evolved its authoritative position in the community not on the basis of doctrinal legitimation by the *imāms* but rather as a natural process of historical evolution in which the need for interpreters of the law as applied to concrete matters of litigation could not be denied; and somehow the *'ulamā'* came to act on their own as though *ex ante* appointment from the *Imām* in fact has occured.

The consequences of this development for clergy-state relations was great: the *Shī'ī 'ulamā'*'s historic autonomy from the state is due to its insistence upon *ijtihād*—a right they invidiously juxtapose against the *Sunnī* rejection of the principle and the *Sunnī* clergy's consequent powerlessness. The *Usūlī* triumph led logically to the reaffirmation of the concept of *marja'īyyat-i taqlīd*, a precept and practice referring to the religious guidance proferred by those grand *mujtahids* of the age, who combined in their persons a rare mixture of extreme erudition, justice and piety. Iranians have historically had a choice among a few individuals who have attained the rank of *marja' -i taqlīd*. Throughout the modern period such persons have therefore accrued great influence and significant political power over the centuries. Ultimately, the informal network of assistants, religious students, bazaar merchants and common believers that these individuals came to supervise provided a social base of support that has proven notably immune to state efforts to penetrate and dismantle.

For an appreciation of the arguments that the *'ulamā'* were to raise in the second half of the twentieth century in Iran it is critical to understand the evolution of the clergy's position as outlined above. The protest movement led by the clergy in the nineteen sixties and seventies attacked what this social force interpreted as the King's wilful attempt at the appropriation of the *Imām's walāyah*. Moreover, the *'ulamā'*, who, by early *Qājār* times (beginning of the 19th century) had come to acknowledge themselves as the general deputies (*al-wukalā' al-'āmm*) of the *Imām*, were to view the King's efforts as intended to reduce their status to nothing more than that of the *Sunnī* clergy. *Shī'ī* Muslims have caricatured the *Sunnī* religious leaders as purely passive ratifiers of old truths, as mere dogmatists without any creative power of innovation. Whether or not they are right in all of their allegations about their rival clergymen, the *Shī'ī 'ulamā'* definitely attribute the distinctions between the two streams of Islam to the matters that have been reviewed in the last few pages.

Now, the injunction in the *Qur'ān* that those in authority should command the good and forbid the bad (*al-amr bi al-ma'rūf wa al-nahy 'an al-munkar*) forms the centerpiece of the *Shī'ī* theory of government. *Sunnī*s view this more as a moral, rather than a political, precept. To *Shī'ah* it grants the possibility to protest, albeit not in any categorical sense. Moreover, this doctrinal principle should be seen alongside of Shī'ism's genesis in rebellion, leading one to expect greater recalcitrance by Shī'ism to constituted secular authority than is the case among the *ahl al-Sunnah*. If one adds to this the centuries on end of experience as a minority faith (*mazhab*) to which *Shī'ī* historiography dolorously refers in terms of martyrdom, persecution and the tragedies of the *ahl al-bayt* (descendents of the prophet through *'Alī*), the notion of political activism—at least in the negative sense of protest and opposition—is reinforced. A sort of vicious cycle is at work here: *Shī'ī* opposition to the appropriation of rule by the *Sunnī* caliphs results in the latter's discrimination against them, which in turn leads to a response of resistance, and this in its course brings forth retribution, triggering increased opposition, and so on.

It is, of course, not true that all *Shī'ī* history, or even most of it, is studded with rebellions. Only the first and third *Imāms* have been regarded by the *Shī'ah* to have actively resisted the power of the *Sunnī* caliphate. Nonetheless, the *Shī'ī* theory of the state, which may be associated as originating with *al-Kulaynī's* authoritative *al-Kāfī fī 'Ilm al-Dīn* (*The Sufficiency Concerning the Science of Religion*) consists of a "relentless refusal to make legitimate any Muslim government established after the death of the Prophet, except that of the first *Imām*, ʿAlī ibn Abī Tālib.'' [26]

Specifically, the twelver *Imāmī Shīʿī* theory of the Imāmate has made the *Imām* the practical equal of the prophet, even though Shīʿism accepts that the holy law in theory forbade the status of prophecy to the *Imām*. It is in the *Shīʿī* insistence that the *imāms* are the replacement (*qāʾim maqām*) of the prophet that one finds the inability to follow the *Sunnī* tradition—especially notable after al-Māwardī (d. 1078)—of vesting the temporal power with divine sanction. For the *Imām* is the infallible, omniscient agent of God who carries the news of His commandments to men. Without the *Imām* men could not know what God wants of them, they being too insignificant in their knowledge, His light being inaccessible to mere mortals. Whereas for the *Sunnī* sects, the *Qurʾān* and the *Sunnah* are the proofs of God, to the *Shīʿah* it is the *imāms*—pure souls—who are the proofs; they are necessary, each one for every historical age, for the guidance of the society because the *Qurʾān* and *Sunnah* are susceptible to erroneous interpretation by evildoers.

Yet, Shīʿism is inevitably forced to consider two different contexts: (1) that existing before 874 A. D., a period when the *imāms* were visibly present on earth, and consequently a time when the question of delegation of authority did not arise; (2) the period following 874 and extending to the end of time, a period in which the *Imām* has gone into hiding and therefore when the delegation of authority becomes problematic. The theocratic order that existed under ʿAlī and still anticipated under the other *imāms* may be viewed as an unattainable ideal upon the start of the greater occultation: that is, after the death of the fourth in a series of four agents through which the hidden *Imām* is said to have maintained indirect contact with believers in this world. To be sure, the government of the *Imām* is held up as an example to try to approximate, but there is no illusion that the ideal can be realized. In the absence of the *Imām*, therefore, twelver Shīʿism accepts the existence of a temporal ruler as a necessity for order and prosperity, even if it denies his legitimacy in the ultimate sense. And, in an apparant paradox, this leads to *de facto* support for the temporal ruler because he is the guarantor of the commonweal. The stability and well-being of the believers which the king undertakes to promote provides what may be termed the contextual framework within which the fortunes of the *Shīʿī* community are to be advanced.

The temporal ruler is thus destined, according to the *Shīʿī* theory, to ''satisfice'' or ''muddle through'' in his effort to organize the social order and establish social justice. Since he cannot secure legitimacy for his rule (but only try to defend the legitimacy of the *Imām*'s rule among his subjects), he can merely hope to retain his incumbency by fostering the general good in terms of what is obligatory, prefered, permitted, discouraged or prohibited.

The centralization of Safavid power and the creation of an Iranian state in which twelver *Imāmī* Shīʿism became the official religion led to a tendency among the ʿ*ulamāʾ* to acquiesce in the enlargement of the sovereign's authority on the grounds that order and tranquility were being served. The ʿ*ulamāʾ* even became vehicles for the allegation that the Safavid monarchs directly descended from the prophet through Imām Mūsā al-Kāẓim. It is true that the Safavid dynasty brought with it the subordination of the religious institution to the state. It is also true that the religious strata (ʿ*ulamāʾ*, *qādīs*, *sadrs*, *shuyūkh al-Islām*, et. al.) more or less helped this process along by accepting positions in the administration. But from the standpoint of doctrine,

> No process . . . was devised to authorize the power of the temporal ruler. No *Shīʿī* thinkers arose to do for the *Shīʿī* theory what Māwardī and Ghazālī had done for the *Sunnī*. Whereas the *Sunnī* theory recognized that kings were necessary for the prestige and continuance of Islamic government, pious *Shīʿīs* looked rather for one who would establish the Kingdom of Heaven on earth and bring an end to all the evils of the world.[27]

The vehicle for the practical supremacy of the state over the religious institution consisted in the King's appointment of the *Sadr,* who was the King's chief administrative aide in matters of religion. Law, education and tax/revenue matters lay in the hands of professionals in the religious institution. The *Sadr* occupied a position at the top of the pyramid of offices and roles in that institution.

In this structure, the clergy made no pretension to be the replacements of the *Imām;* neither, as we saw earlier, do they claim to be the administrator of the *Imām*'s social justice in the broad sense of that concept (as opposed to the *particular* appointment of judges to arbitrate *particular* issues). Rather, their distinction in society is rooted in their superior knowledge of the law which permits them to render informed judgments upon it. Their strong support for the Safavid monarchy is to be explained by that dynasty's success in overcoming what in its beginnings was a parochial, mystical movement of one of the Sūfī orders in northwestern Iran; and its establishment of a more "legitimate" religious foundation for the society. To the extent that the ʿ*ulamāʾ* harbor deep suspicion and hostility against any mystical tendencies, the Safavid achievement in restituting Shīʿism won their admiration against what must have been initial reservations. Yet, the clergy then faced the dilemma that, as participants in the political success of empire building, they permitted their own cooptation into the state system. In a word, they became "wards" of the state, or at least its dependents.

The Afghan invasion in the early 1720's brought about the collapse of Safavid power. The next 70 years or so witnessed a time of troubles, including the attempt to reimpose Sunnism in the country. With the advent of the Qājār dynasty (1779-1925), the ʿ*ulamāʾ* began in practical terms to reassert their independence from the state. Lambton argues that the Qājār shahs continued to be called the "shadow of God on earth," but they did not pretend to be the descendents of the prophet and the *imāms*. She says that the *Imām's* "mantle... devolved upon the *mujtahids*."[28] (the highest ranking scholars and teachers of religious law.)

Another factor also contributed to the strengthened position of the ῾*ulamā*᾽ *vis-à-vis* the King under the Qājārs: the weakness of the dynasty in the face of increasing European power and domination of the country. More and more did the religious forces in the country mobilize their resources in the attempt to check the rising influence of what they viewed as the infidel aliens to divide the community of true *Shī῾ī* believers. Accordingly, they began increasingly to participate, to commit themselves, in the strictly political arena.

On the whole, then, the ῾*ulamā*᾽ in Iran may be seen as trying to maintain the unity of the religious and political institutions in the face of the disappearance of the *Imām* and the rise of temporal government. Despite the latter, the *Shī῾ī* ῾*ulamā*᾽ have never relinquished the claim that the *Imām* is fully entitled to government and to rule.[29] Temporal authorities, for their part, have sought to work against the above-mentioned effort of the ῾*ulamā*᾽ and have been assisted in this by: (1) the willingness of the ῾*ulamā*᾽ to serve in administrative positions in the empire; (2) the tendency toward extreme bookishness and scholasticism on the part of some of the leading ῾*ulamā*᾽; (3) the fear that involvement in politics could lead to the disruption of the society and open the possibilities for foreign dimemberment of Shī῾ism. In the end, Qājār autocracy and tyrannical behavior led the clergy to throw caution to the winds, and they began to agitate against the dynasty's claims to rule. ῾*Ulamā*᾽ opposition took the twin forms of legal and constitutional protest and direct involvement of religious leaders in demonstrations, strikes, taking sanctuary, etc. The first form of protest was represented by the *fatvā* (religious opinion) issued by Āyatullāh Hasan al-Shīrāzī in 1891 against smoking tobacco in opposition to the British-held monopoly on tobacco); (2) the constitutional treatise by one of contemporary Shī῾ism's then leading spokesmen, Āghā Shaykh Mīrzā Muhammad Husayn al-Nā᾽īnī entitled *Admonition to the Community and Exposition to the Nation* (1909). A major point of this work was to admonish the nation's religious leaders to play a corrective role in society to amend the excesses of the political officials by means of right guidance.[30]

The position of the ῾*ulamā*᾽ in the twentieth century in Iran has been given legal expression and underpinning in the Constitution of 1906/1907. Election of members of the clergy to the early parliaments further reinforced the position of religious leaders as representatives of the people—a calling which they had claimed historically at any rate. Statutory legislation, such as the original and later election laws, sealed the process of bestowing legal recognition and sanction on the clergy as one of the "ranks" (tabaqāt) of society. The ῾*ulamā*᾽, it is true, were faced with a dilemma over the constitution. On the one hand, they were averse to the notion of sovereignty residing in the people; the reason for this is their long-held belief that sovereignty may be delegated only to the prophet and to the *imāms*. On the other side was the belief that the arbitrary rule of the Qājār shahs could and should be tempered by the grant of a constitution which made their decisions contingent upon the agreement of the people. They thus compromised by insisting on the provision of a principle calling for the creation of a committee of their members to advise the monarch. This committee would somehow represent the *Imām*'s concept of social justice and the people at the same time. Of course, there was no question of infallibility enjoyed by the top-ranking members of the *'ulamā'* serving on this committee of five people. Instead of a creative and innovative function, it was envisaged that the committee would exercise a protective and maintaining function: protecting and maintaining the holy law from bad decisions.

The constitutional period, 1905–1909, witnessed a remarkable participation by the clergy in day to day events. It mattered not which side, pro- or anti-Shah, the religious leaders supported: the point is that they participated. It is certainly true that, in their participation, the *'ulamā'* were pursuing what might appropriately be termed a "class" interest. Limitation of the court's power meant an increase in their own in the game of "grand manipulation"[31] played by Qājār monarchs *vis-à-vis* the tribes, landed aristocracy and clerics. And it is further true that some of the *'ulamā'* had close links to the big merchant elements of the bazaar, a number of whom were trying to develop capitalist relations and become large-scale entrepreneurs unhampered by economic restrictions placed on them by the crown's practice of awarding concessions to foreigners or minorities.[32] Too, the *'ulamā'*'s links with the landowning elements have often been noted, although specific data is lacking in the literature about the nature and extent of these. But if these points are admitted, it is not to deny that the aspirations of the Iranian clergy to temper secular authority in the absence of the *Imām* was also served.[33]

THE *SUNNĪ* DEVELOPMENT IN TURKEY AND EGYPT

In order to place the foregoing into context, it will be fruitful to compare the evolution of the religious institution in *Sunnī* systems with that in *Shī'ī* Iran. Contemporaneous with the establishment of Safavid power in Iran the Ottoman Empire was at the height of its glory. The Ottoman *sultāns* had, in the 14th century A. D., laid claim to the title of caliph of Islam. They thereby prevented the Mongol conquest from extinguishing this critical institution and worked to maintain the unity of theory and practice of Muslim government. It is generally recognized that the fate of the *'ulamā'* in Anatolia and Egypt, two key areas of

Ottoman rule, evolved in the following manner: cooptation of the clergy by the state; state subsidization of ʿ *ulamāʾ* activity; greater formal organizational development of the ʿ *ulamāʾ* as a social force than in *Shīʿī* lands.

In his work on the politics of religion Donald E. Smith summarizes what he calls the "organizational variables of clerical groups". By reference to these variables and to the indicators underlying them, one can seek to distinguish the situation in Iran, Egypt and Turkey. His variables include:[34]

1. Corporate identity, as indicated by recruitment: vêtements and paraphernalia of dress; residential patterns; ascetic orientations.

2. Corporate complexity, as shown by forms of hierarchy; bureaucratization; structure of clerical intra-communications; methods of arriving at policy on doctrine; theological innovation; procedures of disciplining errant behavior.

3. Corporate autonomy, as evinced by budgetary separation from government allocations; methods of electing officials and promotion/demotion to positions within the clerical institution; impact on education, justice, etc.

4. Corporate integration of the laity, as suggested by such things as parish organization; clerical control of non-clerical bodies in the society at large; clerical influence over the lay constituency, including such negative influence as threat of excommunication, etc.

Smith is trying to detect differential patterns of response to modernization in different third world cultural frameworks. Hence, he seeks to juxtapose and contrast Buddhist, Hindu, Catholic and Muslim religious forces. There are, therefore, many areas of similarity between *Sunnī* and *Shīʿī* Muslim organizational variables relative to the wide differentials one expects and does find among Buddhism, Hinduism, Catholicism and Islam. For example, recruitment patterns certainly do not differ in theory; and in practice, the pattern of recruitment from *rural* areas into a religious institution that is essentially *urban* in terms of its power base is similar for both *mazhab*s. In addition, although the *Shīʿī sayyid*s (direct descendants of the prophet) among the ʿ *ulamāʾ* wear black, rather than white, turbans, this is not a critical distinction. The clergy of both schools, too, do not markedly differ in their residential patterns: some live in the *madrasah;* others live within the precincts of the mosque; yet others have their own private apartments or even houses. Muslim clergy as a whole, moreover, combine in their aversion to celibacy as a way of life. For them, having a family is an important value in their culture.

On the other hand, there are differences in curricula in the schools that *Sunnī* and *Shīʿī* ʿ *ulamāʾ* administer and teach in. One of the major differences, here, is in the authenticity of *hadīth* to which each version of Islam subscribes. The *Shīʿah* believe that there is an undeniable and ineluctable continuity between the sayings of the prophet and those of the *imāms*. This is reflected in the great number of *hadīth* that appears in the four great *Shīʿī* codices of al-Kulaynī, al-shaykh Sadūq, and Nasīr al-Dīn al-Tūsī which are either rejected entirely by the *Sunnī* clergy or considered unsound and hence not reliable in interpreting the law.

Another great difference consists in organization. One can say that because of the greater degree of cooptation of *Sunnī* '*ulamā*' by the state, the degree of formal organizational coherence is greater in *Sunnī* Turkey and Egypt than in *Shī*'*ī* Iran. This paradox may be explained by the practice of the state in *Sunnī* societies of providing the administrative and financial support for religious institutions. Thus, al-Azhar, the ancient seat of Islamic learning in Cairo, has been regulated by the government since 1952 through the cabinet ministry for al-Azhar affairs. There is no equivalent of this for, let us say, the Madrasah-yi Fayzīyah, the largest and most important theological school in Iran and located in the city of Qumm. Rather, the Iranian state has never been able to bring the '*ulamā*' under its full control in this manner. This is so despite what has been said above concerning the appointment of religious figures as judges, administrative officials and scribes in the Safavid and Qājār periods. For its part, the clergy in Iran, left to its own devices, has evolved only an informal organizational structure. Symptomatic of this state of affairs is that the Iranian '*ulamā*' handles questions of documentation and registration in a manner that is difficult for outsiders both to obtain and analyze systematically. The registers (*dafātir*) of student enrollments, for instance, are maintained among the different major religious leaders, and there exists no encompassing central office for the maintenance of documentation. While the sociologist of religion in the Ottoman Empire has recourse to the Central Archives of the Empire, his colleague engaged in similar research in Iran does not have access to such materials there.

With respect to developments in 20th century Turkey, it is, of course, true that Ataturk, the founder of the first Turkish Republic (1922–1960), separated the religious and state institutions. On 1 November 1922 the Turkish parliament passed a resolution rejecting the notion of sovereignty reposing in a singly individual and attributed it, instead, to the people as a whole. On the 3rd of March 1924 the regime abolished the caliphate; together with it went "the whole hierarchic organization", including the "ancient office of the Shaykh al-Islam and the Ministry of the Sharī'ah (holy law)." Ataturk's policy entailed "closing the separate religious schools and colleges, and, a month later, abolishing the special *sharī'ah* courts in which theologian-judges had administered the Holy Law."[35]

The frontal attack on Islam in Turkey went further, to the "abolition of religious education, the adoption of European civil and penal codes, the nationalization of pious foundations . . . and eventual elimination of the power of the '*ulamā*'."[36] The expunging of any mention of Islam in the 1928 Constitution gave clear indication of the disestablishment of the religious institution in Turkey.

Curiously, the formally constituted '*ulamā*' proved less of an opposition to

Ataturk's secularization policies than did the mystical orders, guilds and brotherhoods. This has been explained both in the Turkish and Egyptian contexts in terms of the oppositional role of the brotherhoods in Islamic history.[37] The Turkish regime moved vigorously against the mystical convents and lodges, their properties and their assets through cabinet decrees and parliamentary legislation in the fall of 1925. And Article 163 of the Criminal Code of 1926 proscribed religiously-based political parties.[38]

Ataturk's government replaced the office of Shaykh al-Islam and Ministry of Religious Affairs and Pious Foundations with a Bureau for Religious Affairs and a Directorate-General for Pious Foundations. The Prime Minister had authority to nominate the head of the Bureau for Religious Affairs, and the latter, in turn, had charge of administering religious institutions, appointing and terminating religious officials, censoring speeches made by *mullās* (lower level clerics). The Directorate-General administered the now state-owned pious foundations and controlled payment to all religious officials. As this process evolved "the bureaucratization of the *'ulamā'*, begun by Mahmūd II (1808-1839) . . . reached its logical conclusion. Islam had been made a department of state; the *'ulamā'* had become minor civil servants.'"[39]

Religious revival became an open issue of debate within the Turkish Grand National Assembly (parliament) in 1946. Lewis notes that religious education in the fourth and fifth grades was made optional, then mandatory, by 1950. Also, along with the general loosening of Ataturk's Republican People's Party's hold on politics in the late 1940's, there occured a greater willingness on the part of the Turkish clergy vociferously to present their demands for greater religious sentiments through the agents of competing political parties. This occurrence in Turkish politics has not stopped since 1950, and the state's disestablishment of Islam continues to inhere. It is a situation which one leading scholar of Turkish society and culture has called a "Cultural Revolution.'"[40]

Egyptian modernizing elites did not effect an institutional separation such as that which occured in Turkey. Instead, another pattern of secularization, milder in form, perhaps, has come about: progressive encroachment by the state into domains traditionally dominated by religion. The experience in Egypt, ever since Muhammad 'Alī Pāshā (ruled 1804-1849) destroyed the old Mamlūk power elite, has involved the steady erosion of *'ulamā'* political power and influence. At the same time the government has rationalized access to facilities and sponsored capital construction of strategic religious institutions—such as al-Azhar. This gives the clergy the trappings of prestige and power but not the substance. One of the sources of the weakness of the Egyptian *'ulamā'* vis-à-vis the state has been their aversion to the brotherhoods, guilds and voluntary associations of that type. These, as already noted, have historically constituted agencies of at least potential opposition to the state. In this sense, the *'ulamā'* have foregone the possibility of forging at least a tactical alliance with the mystical Islamic orders.

Indeed, the Egyptian clergy have, in terms of behavior, actually acted as allies of the state in this connection.

In Egypt Berger summarizes that the mosque remains an enclave beyond the purview of the state (except for the governmental mosques, or some 17 percent of the total of all Egyptian mosques in 1962.) As such, the mosque constitutes an arena for pious worship and devotion. On the other hand, "religion as an institution of social control [of the population] is still centered on governmental agencies."[41] In short, the mosque ʿ*ulamā*ʾ are somewhat independent of the state, especially given the fact that most of such mosques are private establishments. But insofar as many members of the ʿ*ulamā*ʾ exercise "functions [which] relate to doctrine, religious law and central administration," they do so "through governmental agencies."[42] In twentieth century Egypt the history of religion-state relations has led to the proliferation of state-operated religious institutions and processes. This has resulted in greater availability of information about the number and structural conditions of religious establishments, the social background of mosque employees and salaried personnel, levels of education, pay scales, mosque attendance data, and so on. This information, as might be expected, is provided through the Ministry of Awqāf (pious foundations). While it would be wrong to suggest that the religious institution consists of nothing more than an appenage of the Egyptian state, it must be conceded that regime policies, both before and after the 1952 revolution, have continued to render the ʿ*ulamā*ʾ and their organizations into instruments of government programs

> to buttress nationalism, socialism and the one-party 'popular democracy'. In this effort the regime has followed two policies. First, it has put the somewhat autonomous religious institutions and associations of the people under the supervision of the Ministry of Waqfs. Second, it has transferred such governmental power as can be exerted over religion from the traditionalist Ministry of Waqfs to other agencies more responsive to the new goals. In making religion an instrument of the state, the government has also sought some genuine reforms in religious organization and practice, following a long tradition of such efforts; but this goal has been clearly secondary and progress toward it rather limited.[43]

At the turn of the century a vital movement of Islamic reform centered in Egypt. It was associated with the philosopher-jurist, Muhammad ʿAbduh (d. 1905) and his colleague, the political activist, Jamāl al-Dīn al-Afghānī (d. 1897). The movement was carried forward in the twenties and thirties by two of ʿAbduh's disciples, one Rāshid Ridā, a "conservative" and the other, ʿAlī ʿAbd-al Rāziq, a "liberal". ʿAbduh had attempted to reconcile Islam and reason and criticized the rigidity that had overtaken the religious institution over the centuries. But he ultimately failed in showing the compatibility between science and faith in the sense that the search for an internally consistent Egyptian ideology of modernization incorporating Islam continues to elude Egyptian leaders. In the meanwhile, the defenders of Islam have steadily given ground in Egypt until perhaps the last one or two years. Such a process is rooted as early as 1873, with Khedive Ismāʿīls introduction of the Mixed Courts—a development which "the ʿ ulamāʾ did not protest" and to which al-Azhar acquiesced.[44]

Despite vigorous defense of the unity of religion and state as a necessity in Islam by such people as Ridā and the leadership of the militant fundamentalist movement known as the Muslim Brotherhood, it has been the more radical critique of this unity by ʿAbd al-Rāziq and his followers that appears to have had the upper hand in that country during the last two generations. In brief, the radicals have stressed the need to separate "church" and state, arguing that the caliphate was a completely alien institution to the mission of the prophet. This mission had nothing to do with the setting up of a political order, being restricted purely to matters of ethical piety and spiritual devotion. Hence, it is maintained, the separation of religion and politics is legitimated by the prophet's own wishes not to comingle the two. Needless to say, this argument has come in for stinging criticism on the part of the clergy and conservative defendents of "Islamic nationalism" in the Arab world.[45] Yet, even though governments in Egypt have not actively worked to spread this radical view, the effect of their behavior in social policy would seem to be the same as if they had done so. In his explicit words of praise for Ataturk's separation of religion and politics, ʿAbd al-Rāziq wanted to lay the basis, in Egypt, of institutional separation à la turque.

Nonetheless, because no series of laws have been passed in Egypt of the magnitude and scope of those that emerged in Turkey, the Egyptian situation has remained ambiguous. This has permitted the state steadily to encroach on the religious sphere, as may be seen, for example, in the regime's annexation (indimām) of the best mosques; and its construction of a science college attached to the venerable al-Azhar, thus diluting its quintessentially religious identity. It is true that the 1971 permanent constitution ratified under the presidency of Anwār Sādāt makes Islam the official religion of the state. Yet, apart from the consideration that we may not speak of the "laicization of society", it is not clear exactly what this reference to Islam means in actual policy.

In the case of Iran, there has been far less development along the dimensions of hierarchy and bureaucratization. The closest approximation one has is the notion of the hawzahs (centers of Shīʿ ī learning) which are very loosely associated with one another through the informal network of clergy relations. The independence of the mujtahids from one another as well as from the state is legendary. The budgetary separation from the state is in marked contrast to the situation in both Turkey and Egypt. And the chief influence of the government in making appointments and dismissing personnel is in the sphere of shrine administration in such areas as Ardabīl, Qumm, Tehran, Mashhad, Ray, Shīrāz—in which cities mosque properties historically were endowed on behalf of the crown. From the point of view of theological innovation, the Iranian ʿ ulamāʾ did not experience a movement of Islamic reform like that of the *salafīyah* in Egypt. Belatedly, in the early sixties, a revival of Shīʿism occured with an emphasis on fresh interpretations of the role of religious leadership, methods of education in the theological seminaries, the relationship of doctrine and reason. In an apparent paradox, it has been argued that the lag in theological innovation in Iran is due to the dependence of the clergy for financial security on the largesse of the citizenry through the *sahm-i imām*. The latter term is a reference to that half of the 20 percent annual income of every good Muslim which is earmarked for the religious institution. Now, owing to the deeply conservative tendencies of the Iranian masses, they will object to meaningful attempts at reform; they have the powerful sanction at their disposal of simply withholding or threatening to withhold the *sahm-i Imām*. In Egypt, however, so the argument runs, the ʿ*ulamāʾ* do not have to depend on the narrow-minded masses for their financial security. They are therefore free to speculate and advocate the modernization of the religious sphere.

It is evident that the Iranian *Shīʿ ī* experience in the 20th century ought to be considered in the light of past Islamic historical development, the evolution of Shīʿism over time, and the respective experiences of *Sunnī* and *Shīʿ ī* clergy in history. Without placing the ʿ*ulamāʾ* experience since 1925 into such a contextual framework, it would be difficult to appreciate that experience in its full sense. In the pages that follow we shall seek to lay out the bases for the relationship between religion and state in terms of: the ʿ*ulamāʾ*'s role in the constitutional revolution of 1905–09; involvement in politics in the nineteen teens and twenties; educational reform and impact on the religious institution, military and legal innovations and ʿ*ulamāʾ* response; shifts in the law on endowments and the disestablishment of clergy status; revival of ʿ*ulamāʾ* power in the 1940's; religion-state *entente* in the 1950's; conflict and further attenuation of ʿ*ulamāʾ* power in the early sixties; the reform movement of the early and mid-sixties; the bureaucratization of power and penetration of the religious institution by the state; the reform effort of the late sixties and early seventies and continuing state-religion confrontation; the revolutionary events of 1978–1979, with an inquiry into the basis for clergy unity and disunity.

CHAPTER TWO

CLERGY-STATE RELATIONS BEFORE 1941

THE EXTREME INTERPRETATIONS

In a press conference held in January 1971 the Shah declared his desire to separate religion from politics. In this statement of intent, he was expressing the position of the Pahlavī dynasty from its very origins, granted the intention had not always been so clearly articulated over the years. In fact, he not only had separation in mind; he held out the likelihood that the state would create its own religious cadres to rival those of the legitimate religious institution:[1]

> It is not improbable that we may create a religion corps in the future so that if some of the students of the religious sciences have to perform their service, they can do it [within the framework of this corps]. Just as we say religion must be separated from politics (and a few years ago we saw the results of mixing the two), and just as we are insistent in that respect... so, too, we encourage the people to piety and religion. No society is truly stable without religion.

Needless to say, the Shah's insistence in separating religion and politics did not lay the issue to rest. Instead, it registered the intent of the secularizing regime to confine the influence of the ʿulamāʾ to the domain of personal status and what Muslims refer to as the ʿibādāt (rituals of worship). But, while not stating their views so forthrightly, Iranians, many Iranians, especially clergymen, yearned to preserve the linkages that the Constitution of 1906 sanctified concerning the primacy of Imāmī Twelver Shīʿism in public life.

A sampling of the literature published in the 1960's reveals a determination to refute the idea of separation of religion and politics. Among the better known of these refutations is a public lecture by Engineer Mihdī Bāzargān, Iran's first revolutionary Prime Minister who at that time was an intellectual, dissident and advocate of the social and political interfaces of religion and public life. In this lecture, entitled "The Boundary Between Religion and Social Affairs,"[2] Bāzargān made a clear and decisive call for the intervention of religion into political matters by urging ʿulamāʾ participation in finance, administration, maintaining security (hifz-i amnīyat), and, in a word, government.

It may be objected that these are the sentiments of a layman whose views find no resonance among the members of the clergy. But Āyatullāh Khumaynī is only the last in a series of clergymen who have in the last two decades been sounding this theme. Thus, Sayyid Hādī Khusrūshāhī, for many years the mutavallī of the Madrasah-yi Āzarbāyjānīhā in the bazaar in Tehran and currently the head of one of the capital city's revolutionary committees, argued strongly in his book, Two Religions (1964): the separation of religion from politics amounts to a violation of the tradition set by the prophet; yet, he lamented that "regrettably [the thesis of separation] is gaining all the more currency."[3]

Almost a decade earlier, the present leader of the Tehran clergy, Āyatullāh Sayyid Mahmūd Tāliqānī, forcefully iterated that Shīʿism has always stood for the principle that "rulership belongs to Allah, alone [inna al-hukm illā li Allāh], which he then renders in Persian as va hukūmat tanhā barāy-i khudāvand ast. Tāliqānī, like Khusrūshāhī, emphasized the dual role of Muhammad as prophet and statesman.[4] Equally forthright on the issue of clergy involvement in politics as both natural and legitimate was the argument of Sayyid Murtazā Jazāʾirī in a public lecture in 1962 in which he averred that all of Iran's social ills may be traced to the continuing failure of the ʿulamāʾ to take a definitive position of the issues of the day.[5]

These views found their practical expression in the actual participation of a number of religious leaders in the parliament. In the more recent period in the nation's political life the chief example of such involvement was Āyatullāh Mīr Sayyid Abū al-Qāsim al-Kāshānī (d. 1962). This individual, whose reputation has been resuscitated by the revolutionary regime after seventeen years of obscurity, had risen to the position of Speaker of the Majlis (parliament) in 1952–53 and acted as the quintessential power broker qua clergyman.[6]

It must be said, however, that a very considerable number of ʿulamāʾ have abjured politics. The leading Shīʿī religious dignitary in this century, Āyatullāh Muhammad Husayn Burūjirdī (d. 1961) maintained a cool aloofness from political invovement (at least at the national level), an aloofness from which he deviated only at the end of his life over the question of land reform. As a consequence, the Pahlavī shahs did not face a united front of the senior clergy in this debate over the role of religion in politics. In some cases, clergy passivity permitted the Court to adopt a much more uncrompromising position than it might otherwise have taken. Due to internal cleavages among the clergy there exists no unique ʿulamāʾ concept of the linkages between politics and religion, even though those who chose to do so could find doctrinal legitimacy in the principle of walāyah (in Persian, valāyat).[7]

THE GENESIS OF POST-CONSTITUTION RELATIONS

' *Ulamā*' involvement in the constitutionalist movement (1905-1911) represents a striking demonstration of the idea that the boundaries between religion and politics overlap in Iran. Most of the religious leaders sided with the "freedom seekers." After an initial victory against the Shah, the latter recouped against the constitutionalists with the help of the Russian forces. Nonetheless, the Shah's triumph in turn was converted into a defeat and the Shah's departure from the throne in favor of the more docile Ahmad Shah. The developments throughout the late 18th and the entire nineteenth century that led to the clergy's confrontation with the state have been analyzed in the detailed study by Algar (Ch. I, note 22 q.v.). His analysis sets the increasing power of the '*ulamā*' throughout the Qājār period against the backdrop of far greater weakness of the clergy relative to the state in the Safavid period (1501-1722).

The religious leadership active during the constitutionalist era made full and active use of the familiar slogans and phrases which their predecessors had hurled against the shahs of the 19th century: tyrannical, impious, corrupt, unjust. Such political activism on the part of the 19th century '*ulamā*' stands in significant contrast to the participation of the clergy in state administration as subordinates of secular officials and secular incumbencies throughout the Safavid era. And although the Akhbārī-Usūlī conflict, to which reference was made in a previous chapter, did take place in that era, nevertheless the clergy devoted almost no attention to defining relations between the religious and secular institutions. Instead, they seemed far more intent in elaborating doctrine as to more purely religious matters. By the end of the 18th century, however, the clergy had revitalized itself as a social force and had successfully argued its role as the *sarparast* or *vaṣī* (guardian) of the believers; and, as such, they partook, even if partially, in the *valāyat* of the *Imām*.

At the time of the constitutional revolution, consequently, the clergy stood poised both to articulate grievances and to lead the struggle against the monarchy's tyranny. The effete quality of the power of the Shah during the period 1905-1921 led to a situation of anarchic conditions in many parts of the country. This timespan has been described as an interlude dominated by "the power of foreigners, the bad example of greedy leaders, the breakdown of the religious institution and the morality it should have upheld. . . ."[8] The clergy's position was that if breakdowns had become the order of the day in the society as a whole, this was attributable not to the turpitude of the religious leadership but to the rapacity of foreign influence in alliance with the royal court and its administration. Yet, the clergy was not wholly united in its search for an appropriate response to the difficulties which they identified as facing Iran at that time. The division among the clerics over support for the constitutionalist movement rested on different perceptions of the concept of sovereignty. The pro-monarchist faction, led by the eminent Shaykh Fazlullāh Nūrī, objected to the idea that sovereignty ultimately reposed in the nation. His rationalization rested on the grounds that sovereignty belonged to Allah alone, and, at his will, was successively relinquished to the prophet, the imāms and, finally, to those learned enough to render judgment in matters of law. There was no place in this arrangement for the masses to exercise sovereignty.

On the other side were Sayyids Muhammad Tabā'tabā'ī, 'Abdallāh Bihbihānī and Hasan Mudarris. These men were unable to compete with Shaykh Nūrī's erudition—a serious drawback on most occasions in inter-clergy rivalries. But, in conjunction with the secular reformers, the triumverate succeeded in fact in drafting Article 35 of the Supplementary Fundamental Law, which stated: "Sovereignty is a trust confided (as a Divine Gift) by the people to the person of the King."

The clergy's power may be seen in the fact that Article 1 of the Constitution stipulated that Imāmī Shī'ism was the religion of the state. Additionally, the 'ulamā' prevailed in their wish to create a five-member board (Article 2) to review parliamentary legislation.[9] The membership of the board would consist of individuals appointed from among of the top religious leaders themselves. Although for the remainder of the Qājār, and throughout all of the Pahlavī, period this organ never came into existence to exercise the broad discretionary powers awarded to it, the revolutionary government in its draft constitution has stressed the importance of such a body (Articles 142–147).

The configuration of forces in the 1905–21 interlude included: (1) the Court, supported mainly by the Russians, but also by some 'ulamā' and aristocracy; (2) the constitutionalists, especially in Tabrīz, Rasht, Isfahān; (3) the rebellious tribes, notably the Bakhtīyārī in the central and west-central part of the country. The political activities of these groups must be viewed in the framework of the dislocations caused by World War I. Though the War was not fought on Iranian territory; it still brought serious hardship to the country and led to fear of foreign dismemberment of Iran. At the same time, the foreign powers, too, were badly shaken. In Russia, civil war had broken out. The British position was not so weak, but the revolt in Iraq—especially in the southern areas of that country—had caused them some security problems in the Persian Gulf region, and the Iranian Majlis's repudiation of the 1919 Treaty of Alliance with the United Kingdom also suggested a weakening of British power.

Freed from external pressure for the time being, but plagued by internal unrest, the country experienced wide-spread chaotic conditions. Only the Cossack Brigade, which Nāsir al-Dīn Shah (ruled 1848–1896) had ordered the Russians to establish in 1879, remained by 1921 as a reliable military force for the monarch. Its commanding officer, Rizā Khān, began his rapid rise in the government at this point. His strategy included support of those whom he thought were best able to

(1) modernize the country; (2) promote his own career; (3) free Iran of external control; (4) establish order (these points are not necessarily in order of priority as he saw matters).

In the pursuit of these objectives, what relationships did he establish with the *ʿulamāʾ*? His early relationship to them was qualified by the fact that the latter could serve him in all four objectives. But, as he also knew, they could, as well, hinder him in some of these.

Re-establishment of order in the country undoubtedly served the interests of the religious leaders and tapped a deep sentiment among them for stabilization. The "time of troubles" since the beginning of the tobacco crisis of 1891–92 seemed to be dragging on interminably. There must have been those among the religious forces who were yearning for quieter times and a return to more strictly religious duties. It is these, after all, that comprise the mainstay of clergy activities.

In 1920 a *mujtahid* who had been resident in Arāk (a town in Western Iran) by the name of Shaykh ʿAbd al-Karīm Hāʾirī Yazdī, journeyed to the shrine city of Qumm, some 90 miles south of Tehran. It is standard practice for Iranian clergymen to move from locality to locality in response to requests sent them by the local inhabitants to take up duties in their area and generally provide guidance in matters of prayer, arbitration, social welfare, moral leadership, instruction. Hāʾirī had undergone the normal training and education of *mujtahid*s in the *Shīʿī* holy places (*ʿatabāt*) in Iraq. Although these areas were in a state of increasing politicization during the period between 1890–1914, he seems to have prefered strict non-involvement in political matters. Hence, when matters became extremely agitated in Najaf (the site of Imām ʿAlī's tomb), Hāʾirī took himself to Iran between 1914–20 and settled in the region of Arāk.

It is not clear why he went to Qumm in 1920; nor is it known why he chose that year in particular to do so.[10] In any case, not long after taking up residence there, British authorities in Iraq expelled the *Shīʿī* leadership in Najaf. Two of them— Shaykh Muhammad Husayn al-Nāʾīnī, and Sayyid Abū al-Hasan al-Mūsavī al-Isfahānī—elected to come to Iran and finally ended up in Qumm. This incident outraged the Iranian religious forces and their mass followings among the bazaar merchants, artisans, guilds members, peasants. The Iranian *mujtahid*s urged their government to break relations with London over British policy in Iraq and the resultant humiliation of the *Shīʿī āyatullāh*s.

Hāʾirī's attitude was apparently very ambivalent. There is no doubt that inwardly he was scandalized by the insult visited upon the exiled *marājiʿ-yi taqlīd* (sing. *marjaʿ-i taqlid:* lit. source of emulation; the most authoritative and supreme rank among *Shīʿī ʿulamāʾ*) The sources differ, however, as to his behavior in fact. Was he outwardly friendly to his newly arrived colleagues? Was he discretely aloof?[11] One interpretation, if his behavior led him to maintain a prudent distance from the *marājiʿ-yi taqlīd,* would be that his chief concern was to protect his fledgling experiment of transforming Qumm into a flourishing educational center (*hawzah-yi ʿilmīyah*). Too frank a position of support for the Najaf visitors might have caused the British to pressure Tehran to close down his schools and disperse his teachers and students. A more cynical view would suggest that Hāʾirī had good rapport with Rizā Khān, whose lead he was following in the matter. And at this stage Rizā Khān could not affort to offend the British.

In his duties as Minister of War Rizā Khān had little opportunity to affect the relationship then existing between the Qājār state and the ʿ*ulamāʾ*. That relationship was antagonistic because of the continuing Qājār policies that adversely influenced their status: (1) the establishment of a new secular school system, dating back to 1851, which broke the clergy's monopoly in this field; (2) the numerous concessions granted to foreigners during the 19th century; (3) the growing orientation of Iranian culture to Western models; (4) the Qājār failure to protect that country's territory, Dār al-Islam, from foreign occupation and annexation; (5) the government's poor response to economic crises, such as inflation, the rapid increase in the cost of living, and price rises in staple commodities, notably sugar and grain; (6) the personal extravagance, corruption and repression of the court.

After becoming Prime Minister but before his coronation as Shah (i.e., between October 1923 and December 1925), Rizā Khān pursued a policy of alliance with the ʿ*ulamāʾ* which bore fruit for his own career. By 1920 the British were prepared to impose a League of Nations mandate over Iraq. However, upon reconsideration produced by the widespread internal rebellion in that year, it was decided that the establishment of a monarchy, a limited form of constitutional government and an allinace with the United Kingdom would better serve the purpose. The preparations for elections to the parliament precipitated a crisis with the Iranian ʿ*ulamāʾ* in the ʿ*atabāt*. Led by Isfahānī and Nāʾīnī the religious leadership condemned the elections, and the two *marājiʿ* issued *fatvā*s forbidding participation in them by the masses. This created a direct confrontation between the ʿ*ulamāʾ* and the British, who, as we have seen, thereupon ordered the departure of the former. As mentioned Isfahānī and Nāʾīnī made their way to Qumm, where they arrived in August 1923.

Their residence in Iran engendered competition between the ruling monarch, Ahmad Shah, and Rizā Khān. Each, on different occasions, visited Qumm and paid his respects to the *marājiʿ*. They, for their part, tried to persuade the Shah and the Prime Minister to conduct *jihād* against Britain. While holy war stood in first order of priority for the ʿ*ulamāʾ*, keeping the exiled *mujtahid*s in Iran until after the elections in Iraq represented the chief British objective. Between these two demands, Ahmad Shah and Rizā Khān jockied to gain the confidence of both the clergy and the British. Both political figures needed the ʿ*ulamāʾ* as allies. Yet, neither could afford to antagonize the British. It was in this context that ideas of republicanism began to take shape, as the Iranian language press outside the country (notably, *al-Habl al-Matīn* from Calcutta and *Irānshahr* from Berlin) and some internal publications began to agitate for a secular state.

Now, the ʿ*ulamāʾ*'s position seemed to be that the monarchy should be preserved on grounds that it was the most suitable form of government for Iran. It was impossible to overlook the connection between republicanism and Western political development; this undoubtedly comprised an important factor in the calculation of the Iranian religious leadership. True, Islam does not demand monarchy; indeed, the tragedies that befell the early *Shīʿah* have been explained by its leaders in terms of the corruptive effects of the Umāyyad dynasty. Yet, the seeds of doubt as to what republicanism held out for the future of religion in Iran were too firmly embedded in the clerical consciousness to permit a cool-headed appraisal of its merits.

Since Rizā Khān was strongly suspected of harboring republican views and intent on leading the country along the path of Kemalist Turkey, Ahmad Shah tried to capitalize on the ʿ*ulamāʾ*'s fears of Kemalism. He promised them a speedy end to the humiliation inflicted on the *Shāʿ ī mujtahids*. If Rizā Khān had, for his part, been at all interested in republicanism, he now gave to believe the opposite and took action to imprint this orientation in the public consciousness. Thus, he journeyed to Qumm and met with Āyatullāhs Hāʾirī, Nāʾinī and Isfahānī. These individuals thereupon sent a telegram to the ʿ*ulamāʾ* of Tehran stating the collapse of the republican idea:[12]

> There have been expressed certain ideas concerning a republican form of government which are not to the satisfaction of the masses and inappropriate to the needs of the country. Thus, when His Excellency, the Prime Minister . . . came to Qumm . . . to say goodbye [to the exiled *mujtahids*], we requested the elimination of this rubric [of republicanism], the abolition of the above-mentioned expressed ideas and the proclamation of this to the whole country. He has accepted this. May God grant that all people appreciate the extent of this act and give full thanks for this concern.

For his part, Rizā Khān issued the following proclamation in response to the wishes of the three leaders of Shīʿism:[13]

> It has become clear from experience that the leaders of the government must never oppose or contradict the ideas of the public, and it is in keeping with this very principle that the present government has avoided impeding the sentiments of the people, no matter whence they may derive. On the other hand, since my only personal aim and method from the beginning has been and is to preserve and guard the majesty of Islam and the independence of Iran, and fully to watch over the interests of this country and nation, assuming anyone who opposes this method to be an enemy of the country, and striving mightily to repel him; and determined to continue, henceforth in this method; and inasmuch as at present the thoughts of the masses have become divergent and the minds poisoned, and since this confusion of

thought can produce results contrary to what lies at the bottom of my heart: i.e., to preserve order and security and to stabilize the foundations of the state; and insofar as I and all the people in the army have, from the very beginning, regarded the preservation and protection of the dignity of Islam to be one of the greatest duties and kept before us the idea that Islam always progress and be exalted and that respect for the standing of the religious institution be fully observed and preserved: thus, when I went to Qumm to bid farewell to the [exiled *mujtahids*], I exchanged views with their excellencies regarding the present circumstances. And we ultimately saw it necessary to advise the public to halt the [use of] the term, republic. Rather, everyone should spend his efforts to eliminate the impediments to the reforms and progress of the country, and to help me in the sacred aim of consolidating the foundations of the religion, the independence of the country and of the national government. It is for this reason that I advise all patriots of this sacred aim to avoid calls for a republic and to unite efforts with me to achieve the supreme objective upon which we are agreed.

Having thereby placated the ʿ*ulamāʾ*, it remained for Rizā Khān to forge more positive links with them by gaining their support for his government. This support came not from Qumm but from Najaf, whence Isfahānī and Nāʾīniī had repaired in late April 1924. Rizā Khān had played a significant role in facilitating their return, although it is true that the British and Iraqi government authorities were predisposed to their resumption of residence in the holy cities. Shaykh Nāʾīnī sent a letter to the Prime Minister of Iran thanking him for the military escort he had provided the exiled ʿ*ulamāʾ* for their return journey. Further, as demonstration of his appreciation, Nāʾīnī sent along with his letter a revered picture of Imām ʿAlī, together with the sword reputedly used by the third Imām's brother, Hazrat ʿAbbās on the battlefield of Karbalāʾ in 680 A. D. (scene of the martyrdom of ʿAlī's second son, Husayn).

Despite this strong manifestation of support by Nāʾīnī for Rizā Khān, the ʿ*ulamāʾ* of Tehran seemed to have been offended by the entire episode and regarded the dispatch of the portrait and the sword as a British trick. They accordingly boycotted the ceremonies at the Shrine of Shah ʿAbd al-ʿAżīm, a shrine some eight miles to the south of Tehran. Undaunted, Rizā Khān moved to follow up his advantage in his relationship with Nāʾīnī by paying a visit to Najaf in January 1925. There, it appears he made a concerted effort to win the support of Isfahānī and Nāʾīnī in an attempt to block the return from Europe to Iran of Ahmad Shah. The trip to Najaf became all the more attractive an idea after the publication by *al-Habl al-Matīn* of a manifesto attributed to Isfahānī and Nāʾīni and dated a couple of months earlier for October 1924. The two *marājiʿ* never repudiated authorship of this manifesto, which unmistakably endorses the government of the Prime Minister, Rizā Khān:[14]

It should be specified for all the Muslims that those who revolt against the Islamic government of Iran are like those who fought against the prophet during the battles of Badr and Hunayn. Such people are those to whom the Qur'ānic verse [about polytheists] is applicable. The punishment for polytheism is death [in this world] and torture in the hereafter; therefore, it is obligatory for us to inform the people not to deviate from this Muhammadan circle [the government of Rizā Khān] which gives currency to Islam. Those who oppose this command will be considered infidels willing to destroy this religion, and consequently it is necessary to anathemize them according to the rules and proofs of the *Qur'ān*.

Out of this complex series of developments the following points emerge: (1) monarchy was important to the *'ulamā'*, although not in its Qājār form; (2) Rizā Khān was keenly aware of the power of the *'ulamā'*, and actively solicited its use on his behalf; (3) the Iranian clergy in Iraq backed the Tehran government with a view to the latter's help against British plans to expand its colonial influence in that country; (4) Shaykh 'Abd al-Karīm Hā'irī Yazdī stood aloof from these developments as a hedge against political repression against his efforts in Qumm; (5) the Tehran *'ulamā'* seem to have been suspicious of Rizā Khān as a possible instrument of British policy. Although the reason for their suspicion was misplaced, in retrospect they were correct in their assessment of his purely tactical orientation to Islam. It may be that Rizā Khān sensed this opposition, as manifested not only in their avoiding the ceremonies at Shah 'Abd al-Ażīm in June 1924, but also the campaign led by some of them—especially Sayyid Hasan Mudarris—against his mounting the throne.

A final remark is in order concerning the continuity of *'ulamā'* participation in politics throughout the 1905–1925 period. Although attention, here, has been given to the last five years of this time span, with an emphasis on Rizā Khān's tactical maneuverings and clergy behavior, one must not lose sight of the fact that the clergy led the agitation against the Shah's autocracy consistently throughout the 20 years. The Iranian *mujtahids* resident in the *'atabāt* appeared to hold the key to rebellious activity in Iran. In the earlier time—around 1905–1909—the Najaf senior *mujtahids* were Ākhūnd Mullā Muhammad Kāżim Khurāsānī, Hājjī Mullā 'Abdallāh Māzandarānī, and Hājjī Mīrzā Husayn Hājjī Mīrzā Khalil al-Tihrānī. The *fatvā*s issued *ad seriatum* by these luminaries of the faith had their roots in the classic *fatvā* issued in 1891 prohibiting tobacco consumption. And while the government sought to shed doubt on the authenticity of that *fatvā*, it could not continue to allege the forgery of the numerous authoritative opinions issued by the Najaf leadership against the crown's policies in the 1890's and afterwards. The linkages forged by this leadership with the Tehran clergy (especially Shaykhs Tabā'tabā'ī, Bihbihānī and Mudarris), as well as its contacts with Āyatullāhs Nā'īnī and Isfahānī, were a constant source of worry to the Qājārs. It is a measure of their power that Rizā Khān was obliged to consult with them and cultivate their support in his efforts to rise to the top.

Yet, what could the clergy expect from the victory of Rizā Khān? One answer must be that they anticipated the application of the constitutional provisions concerning Shīʿ ism and public policy. Perhaps nowhere was the challenge to the religious institution as significant as in the area of education. It will be useful to examine the clergy's action in matters of education as a kind of microcosm of the religious leadership's social standing. Educational reforms in the Ottoman Empire and in Egypt had led to the introduction of new institutions, facilities, techniques. They had the potential of seriously eroding the cultural hegemony of the ʿulamāʾ in those societies, and certainly the same applied in the case of Iran. Indeed, innovations in education in the 19th century had already distressed a number of religious leaders, who calculated that these were part of a grand strategy of the Western states to dismantle Shīʿism. The ineptness of the Qājār monarchs led the ʿulamāʾ to make educational reform one of the leading accusations against the dynasty's tyranny against Islam.

EARLY EDUCATIONAL CHANGES

Already in 1851 the reforming minister, Mīrzā Taqī Khān Amīr Kabīr had played a formative part in the establishment by the government of the Dār al-Funūn (Polytechnic School). This institution was the first Iranian academic unit that was not administered by the Shīʿ ī ʿulamāʾ. Nine years later the Ministry of Science, the forerunner of the Ministry of Education, was established in the Prime Ministry of Mīrzā Husayn Khān Sipah Sālār in 1860. The creation of the Ministry is definitely attributable to the Sipah Sālār because he drew up ''the decree to reorganize the Iranian cabinet along the lines of that of France'' while the ruler, Nāsir al-Dīn Shah, was away in Europe.[15]

The Dār al-Funūn's curriculum included natural science, military science, higher mathematics and foreign languages. The subject matter of the traditional madrasah received no attention in the course of study of the Polytechnic. By the end of the 19th century, the government had established three other schools: one of these was the School of Political Science, affiliated with the Ministry of Foreign Affairs and designed to train diplomats; the other two were military schools.[16]

After the assassination of Nāsir al-Dīn Shah in 1896, the government under his successor Muzaffar al-Dīn Shah (ruled 1896–1906), proceeded to establish a number of new schools. The new Shah allocated 6,000 tumans (a unit of currency) per year for the administration of five such schools, but in 1908–09 the Ministry of Education submitted a bill to parliament to convert these into state schools and grant free education to one-half of the combined student enrollment.[17]

These hesitant steps early in this century were matched by the efforts of individuals who felt the need to break away from the old-style maktab (elementary religious school) and madrasah education. The most notable experiment was the Rushdīyyah Madrasah in the city of Tabrīz. The establishment of this school in 1897[18] had provoked intense opposition among the city's 'ulamā'. According to one source, there were approximately 100 maktabs and madrasahs in Tabrīz at this time.[19] The clergy leadership of Tabrīz appeared to see in the Rushdīyyah the beginning of the erosion of their power over the education of Iranian youth.

Just as the reforming ministers, Amīr Kabīr and Sipah Sālār, inaugurated such education policies in the 19th century, so, too, did Mīrzā 'Alī Khān Amīn al-Dawlah throw his prestige behind the establishment of the new schools. By 1906 fourteen elementary schools of the new type existed in Tehran, and by 1911 the number had increased to 123.[20] Now, when compared to the number of the old-type schools in the capital such a number is not great. Yet, given the Amīn al-Dawlah's anti-clergy disposition the 'ulamā' had reason to suspect that the government would try to undermine their cultural influence through a gradual policy of expansion of the new schools. The violence with which the population reacted to the early experiments with these new schools has been well described in the memoir literature. The reformers were accused of Bahā'ism, a charge that has always carried serious consequences for those so termed (see Chapter 3 for more on the Bahā'īs). The people responded to the clergy's appeals against cooperating with the new schools, especially to statements that their children would become corrupt and encouraged to stray from the precepts of Shī'ism.[21]

The curriculum of the new schools did include religious subjects, but the difference between them and the old schools was marked. In the latter the emphasis was on learning the fundamentals of writing and reading the Persian language, penmanship, memorization of simple verses and vast amounts of the Qur'ān, plus, in some cases, a smattering of geography and an old method of accounts known as siyāq. The new schools, however, attempted to approach the education process by way of a new methodology or at least with new and different books. 'Īsā Sadīq, who was later to go on to become one of the country's distinguished men of letters and frequent Minister of Culture, reports on the books he read while attending the new-type schools: Madrasah-yi Adab and Madrasah-yi Kamālīyyah. These schools were under the administration of Sayyid Yahyā Dawlatābādī, who was a modernizer unhappy with the hegemony of the unreconstructed traditionalists over education. At the Madrasah-yi Adab, Sadīq's work consisted, at the first grade level, of: (1) Kitāb-i Ta'līm-i Atfāl (Book on the Teaching of Children) by Miftāh al-Mulk; (2) Kitāb-i Hājj Mīrzā 'Alī Khān Amīn al-Dawlah Sadr-i A'zam (The Book About Hājj Mīrzā 'Alī Khān Amīn al-Dawlah Sadr-i A'zam), by Hājj Mīrzā Yahyā Dawlatābādī; (3) "two or three other books," including a short work on geography.

If we compare these readings to those he undertook in one of the old-type schools, to which he was transferred when his parents decided that they could no longer withstand the public ostracism directed at them for sending their child to a new school, we note a major shift of emphasis: the reading becomes exclusively religious. The books read at the Madrasah-yi Nasr al-Dīn (1901-1902) were:

> *Kitāb-i Amthilah**
> *Sharh-i Amthilah**
> *Sarf-i Mīr**
> *Kitāb-i Abū Nasr Farāhī*
> *Risālah-yi Marjaʿ al-Taqlīd***

> *These are short works, in the Persian language, in morphology, compiled by Mīr Sayyid Sharīf Jurjānī (lived in the 14th century) and a staple of elementary-level instruction in the traditional school.
> **A practical treatise on Muslim behavior written by a *marjaʿ al-taqlīd* as a guide for the conduct of those following him.

As a result of his brother's persuasive tactics with his parents, they allowed Sadīq to return to one of Dawlatābādī's new schools. He was there enrolled for some five years, and the curriculum became much more diverse:[22] The books and subjects studied at the Madrasah-yi Kamālīyyah (1902-1907) were:

> *Kalām Allāh-i Majīd bā ʿAmal i Tajvīd* (apparently, a book of recitations from the *Qurʾān*)
> *Kitāb-i Bidāyah:* section on *sharʿīyyāt*, a primer on *fiq* (?) or the science of jurisprudence
> *Gulistān* (the classic of Persian literature by Saʿdī, d. 1291)
> *Tārīkh-i Muʿjam* (a history, by Fazlullāh Husaynī)
> *Sīyāq-i Chahār ʿAmal-i Aslī* (accounting)
> *Khatt-i Nastaʿlīq* (calligraphy)
> *Qawāʿid al-Jallīyah*, Vol. I (Arabic morphology)
> *Qawāʿid al-Jallīyah*, Vol. II (Arabic syntax)
> *Hāshīyah-yi Mullā ʿAbdallāh* (logic)
> *Kalām: Al-Bāb al-Hādī ʿAshar*, by ʿAllāmah ibn al-Mutahhar al-Hilli (13th century)
> *Jughrāfīyā-yi Muqaddamātī* (elementary geography)
> *Hisāb-yi Yak Dawrah* (arithmetic and mathematics)
> *Hindasah-yi Daw Maqālah* (plane geometry)
> *Tārīkh-i Mukhtasar-i Iran* (short history of Iran)
> *Jabr va Muqābalah-yi Yak Dawrah* (algebra)
> *Farānsah* (French language, based on *Favāʾid al-Tarjumān*, by Mukhbir al-Saltanah al-Hidāyat)
> *Lecture Courante* (French language book by Muhandis al-Mulk)
> *Lecture d ʿÉlocution* (French oratory book by Muhandis al-Mulk)
> *Dastūr-i Zabān-i Farānsah* (French grammar, by Muhandis al-Mulk)

Such a course of study prepared Sadīq for the Dār al-Funūn, which he, in turn, followed up with studies in France. The pattern related by Sadīq no doubt was a common one among the scions of the upper strata who were sending their children off to be educated in the secular schools.

The *ulamā* anger with the new schools extended to all segments of the religious leadership, including those who had fought in the forefront of the battle for the constitution: Sayyids Tabāʾtabāʾī and Bihbihānī.[23] Their opposition indicates that the clergy's role in the constitutionalist movement cannot facilely be interpreted to have been a modernizing one. Yet, there did exist a few individuals with close ties to the religious institution, if not themselves clergy, who were both constitutionalist and modernist (defining the latter in its broad sense of seeking a revitalization of Shīʾism by eliminating formalism, obscurantism and intentional unwillingness to adapt to social, economic and political change). In general the "clergy" at that time may be divided into three groups. First, are the unregenerate orthodox who were both anti-consitutionalist and anti-modernist; examples are Shaykh Fazlullāh Nūrī, Mīrzā Abū al-Qāsim Imām Jumah of Tehran, and, perhaps, Sayyid ʿAlī Akbar Tafrashī.[24] A second group of "moderates" supported demands for a constitution and parliament but were against cultural reform; these include the Najaf dignitaries: Mullā Ākhūnd Muhammad Kāẓim Khurāsānī, Mullā ʿAbdullāh Māzandarānī, Hājjī Mīrzā Husayn Khalīlī Tihrānī, and Āghā Shaykh Muhammad Husayn al-Nāʾīnī; it also includes the four Tehran *mujtahid*s: Sayyids Tabāʾtabāʾī, Bihbihānī, Mudarris and Mīrzā Hasan Āshtīyānī (the latter had been largely responsible for mobilizing the people of Tehran in obedience to the appeals of Āyatullāh Mīrzā Hasan Shīrāzī in 1891). A third group, the "modernists," are represented by Sayyid Yahyā Dawlatābādī and Mīrzā Hasan Rushdīyah.

Ironically, the *ulamā*'s overwhelming support for the constitution helped in the long process of attenuation of clergy power in educational matters. Article 19 of the Supplementary Fundamental Laws of October 1907 stipulated.[25]

> The foundation of schools at the expense of the government and the nation, and compulsory instruction, must be regulated by the Ministry of Science and Arts, and all schools and colleges must be under the supreme control and supervision of that Ministry.

In pursuance of this, the Education Law of 1911, in its articles 15 and 16, stated:[26]

> Article 15: *Maktab*s and *madrasah*s are of four types: (1) elementary schools in the villages and (2) those in the cities; (3) high schools; (4) higher institutions of learning.
> Article 16: Each of these four types of schools will have its own program, under the direction of the Ministry of Education.

Ten years later the Ministry of Education submitted, in 1921, an enabling bill to the Majlis authorizing the creation of a Higher Council of Education

(Shawrā-yi ʿĀlī-yi Maʿārif). Ratification of this bill paved the way for the Ministry, through this Council, to implement the broad discretionary powers assigned
to it by the constitution and by the statute of 1911. Significantly, the centralization of educational affairs envisaged by the earlier acts was thereby quickly
applied to the religious schools of the country. The key Article 14 of the 1911
Law stated:[27]

> Article 14: Out of regard for organizing the affairs of the religious schools, and in
> an effort to promote the advancement of religious studies, a council, under the
> supervision and oversight of the Minister of Education shall be formed under the
> following arrangement.
>   a. Three ʿulamāʾ of the highest rank
>   b. Two mudarrisūn [teachers] of maʿqūl and manqūl [the transmitted sciences
> and the intellectual sciences, respectively]
>   c. Two mutavallīs [administrators] from the leading religious schools.
> Branches of this council shall be created in the capitals of the provinces and
> governorates in accordance with special legislation.
> Annex: Membership in the above committee shall be without remuneration.

The specific prerogatives of the Higher Council of Education included curriculum supervision, institution and appraisal of examination procedures, oversight and evaluation of texts, mediating conflicts between religious and secular
schools, appraisal of qualifications of those seeking to establish new schools,
licensing of teachers, securing revenue produced by gifts and religious grants,
the purpose of which was disbursement for educational development and progress.[28]

From the foregoing, then, it may be seen that the restrictions on ʿulamāʾ power
often associated exclusively with the rule of Riżā Shah actually preceded it. And,
in many ways, the actions of that monarch consisted of carrying on the work of
the earlier reformers. To say as much is not to deny that secularization became
intensified with the accession of the new ruler. But it would be misleading to
neglect the preparatory work of the leaderships in the earlier era, without which
secularization would have met with even greater difficulties than it did after
1925.

The ʿulamāʾ must not be viewed as having suffered these numerous reversals
without any objection or, more importantly, resources to sustain them. Many
provisions of the Constitution as contained in the Supplementary Fundamental
Laws of October 1907) bear witness to the sources of clerical influence. The
substance of articles one and two have already been reviewed. Article 18 proclaimed for free education and acquisition of knowledge, provided its pursuit and
attainment did not contravene the sharīʿah. Article 20 declared the freedom of
the press, in conformity with the sharīʿah. Article 21 stipulated the right of free
association to be dependent upon the stand of such organizations toward Islam.
Article 27 affirmed the right of religious courts to carry on their activities, while

article 39 commanded the sovereign to "promote the Ja'farī doctrine" of Islam and "to seek help from the holy spirits of the Saints of Islam to render service to the advancement of Iran.[29]

Statutory legislation embodied in the Education Law of 1911 and the Press Censorship Law of 1922, further underscore sensitivity to the status of the ʿulamā' in society. Thus, instruction in the Islamic sciences was made mandatory in the secular schools, while simultaneously minorities were denied instruction in their faiths at such schools, according to articles 7 and 17 of the former law. The Censorship Law vested the ʿulamā', through the appointment of a mujtahid by the Ministry of Education, Awqāf and Fine Arts, with the power of censorship of articles and books judged inimical to Shīʿism.[30]

These guarantees did not ultimately prevent the entropy that befell the religious institution in the next sixteen years after the coronation of Rizā Shah. It is probable, however, that in their absence the weakening of their power would have occured much more rapidly than was actually the case.

MILITARY CONSCRIPTION AND LEGAL REFORM

The legacy left by Rizā Shah was one deeply antithetical to the ʿulamā''s interests and authority. The May 1925 Conscription Law was passed during the last months of his tenure as Prime Minister. This law badly weakened the authority and prestige of the Iranian religious institution, inasmuch as it gave the state discretionary power to decide who could be exempt from military service. In effect, it permitted the state to draft into military service those elements among the ʿulamā' whom it felt were acting against the regime's policies. The relevant article of the Military Conscription Law of 6 Khurdād 1304 H. sh./28 May 1925 is article sixteen:[31]

> People who are exempt from military service by virtue of their status [include] those with diplomas from Iranian or foreign institutions of higher education and resident and non-resident religious sciences students in the religious colleges. [The latter] shall be exempted from post-graduate conscription if they meet the following conditions: (a) they have the ijāzah-yi ijtihād [diploma attesting to their having attained the rank of mujtahid]; (b) they have no occupation save that of student and have certification as a student of the religious sciences from a mudarris [teacher] or mutavallī [administrator of a religious school] who themselves are exclusively engaged in religious studies; (c) they have passed an annual examination which is geared to the level of learning that the student has achieved.
> NB. The government shall appoint the examination board from among specialists [in the religious sciences].

The timing of the Military Conscription Law is all the more interesting in view of the concordat which Rizā Khān had just concluded with Āyatullāh Nāʾīnī in the previous months; and also his rapprochement with the Qumm and Najaf *ʿulamāʾ* over abandoning the idea of a republic. Why should he take such a calculated risk? The only possible answer is that the centralized army was more important to him at this time than a possible defection of the clergy leadership.

Apart from the issue of military conscription into the newly created national army a number of issues set the clergy at loggerheads with Riza Khan/Shah. They may here be listed in summary fashion: (1) the 1926 reform of the judiciary, beginning the demise of the *sharʾ* (religious courts, under the reforming Justice Minister, Dāvar; the uprising of the Isfahān *ʿulamāʾ* over state restrictions placed on the cultivation of poppies and opium production in 1924; (3) the exiling of Āyatullāh Bafqī (who had originally invited Shaykh ʿAbd al-Karīm Hāʾirī Yazdī to Qumm in 1920) from Qumm to Shah ʿAbd al-ʿAżīm in 1928; (4) the Law on the Uniformity of Dress, which eventuated in a telegram of protest by Hāʾirī to Rizā Shah in 1928; (5) the law on the examination of religious students and the licensing of religious teachers of 1928 (amended in 1942); (6) the law of 1931 on the establishment of a syllabus for the religious schools; (7) the new laws on the authority and prerogatives of the Endowments Department of the Ministry of Education of 1934; (8) the establishment of the Faculty of Theology in 1935 as one of the four constitutive colleges of Tehran University; (9) the crisis and fatalities at the Shrine of Imām Rizā in Mashhad in 1935. Apart from these formal actions, the regime sustained a day to day practice of harrassment concerning efforts to conduct moralistic passion plays, public homilies, pilgrimmage to shrines, etc. Together, the formal and informal measures expressed the government's objective of intimidating the clergy and placing them plainly on the defensive.

The *ʿulamāʾ*'s standing in society derived from the several roles that the clergy played in daily social life. Being the source of emulation (*taqlīd*), the highest ranking religious leaders concentrate in their own hands a variety of specific social functions. Algar has cited a *hadith* imputed to the prophet of Islam: "The *ʿulamāʾ* are guardians of those who are without protector; and in their hands is the enforcement of divine ordinance concerning what has been permitted and prohibited."[32] Such functions ranged from the safekeeping of funds entrusted to their care, custodianship over the affairs of orphans and widows, collecting alms, certifying documents, dispensing sums in the interests of the religious institution from revenues collected from the faithful, and the like, to a multitude of matters of legal administration. Law was so central to their functions that the mere suggestion that a fundamental law based on positive law might be contemplated was sufficient to stimulate deep-rooted opposition by the orthodox circles among the clergy. Even those members of the religious stratum who could reconcile the creation of a corpus of man-made law with the antecedent sacred canons of Islam were unhappy with the uneasy synthesis worked out between them.

In the ideal the *Shīʿī* community had already provided for a distinction between customary (*'urf*) and canon (*shar'*) law. *'Urf* jurisdictions consisted of matters affecting the state and its administration, while civil and personal status law constituted the domain of canon law. "In practice, however, the unstable governments of Iran had defaulted nearly all judicial authority to the *shari'ah* courts."[33]

In the context of past overwhelming clerical influence in legal matters affecting the family, property and commerce, a new civil code was introduced by Dāvar, the new Minister of Justice, in 1926. It was a measure of the respect that Rizā Shah originally had for the power of the *'ulamā'* that the judicial reforms introduced in the early part of his rule were labelled "temporary". Article two of the Supplementary Fundamental Laws, moreover, clearly had stipulated the illegitimacy of laws passed by the parliament that contravened the *shari'ah;* therefore, it was deemed expedient to soften the impact of Dāvar's reforms by imparting to them the shibboleth of "provisional."

Notwithstanding the regime's original prudent attitude in this affair, the civil code ratified by the parliament on 8 May 1928 was "in effect . . . a secularization of the *shari'ah.*"[34] The only satisfaction the *'ulamā'* might have derived from this law was that it terminated the capitulatory privileges long enjoyed by foreign powers in the country. Yet, the requitement of religiously-based grievances on this count was more than counterbalanced by later developments, especially after 1932, which thoroughly shook the foundations of the religious institution.

The permanent Law Concerning the Registration of Documents and Property of 17 March 1932 divested the *shar'* courts of the function of registration of documents such as affidavits, powers of attorney and property titles. This represented a major defeat for the clergy because a major share of the total annual income earned by *mujtahids* and *mullas* derived from their role as registrars. Henceforth, secular courts and offices would exercise this function.[35]

Another important step toward secularization was to make it impossible for *'ulamā'* to sit as judges in the courts of law. The Law of 27 December 1936 specified:[36]

> 1. [Judges must hold] a degree from the Tehran Faculty of Law or a foreign university, attesting to three years or more of legal study.
> 2. Former judges of the Ministry of Justice who do not possess such a degree must pass special examinations in Iranian and foreign law in order to remain in the employ of the Ministry, and, at any rate, may not rise above the rank of six on an eleven point promotion scale.

The regime's limitation of the jurisdictions of the *shar'* courts came in the Law of 30 November 1931. This statute prescribed that "only the state courts and the office of the Attorney General" could approve the referral of a case to a religious tribunal. The latter could only take up matters related to marriage, divorce and the appointment of trustees and guardians. The activity of the *shar'* courts came

under the supervision of the Attorney General. Neither could the *shar'* courts
pronounce sentence, being limited only to the determination of innocence and
guilt in the narrow range of issues that served as their field of competence. Only
state courts could pass sentences. Too, they were permitted the right of review of
decisions made by *shar'* courts.[37]

Dismantling of *'ulamā'* power in the field of law may be said to have been
achieved by the late thirties. Opposition by the *'ulamā'* to changes in the elec-
toral law (1951, 1962) was still to occur, and personal status jurisdiction, to
which the *shar'* courts were confined after 1940, was also later to become a
contested field as changes in divorce and marriage statutes were introduced from
above. But as far as the structure of legal power of the clergy is concerned, the
major defeats came in the third decade of this century.

'ULAMĀ' REACTIONS AND FURTHER EDUCATION LEGISLATION

It may now be useful to consider the matters of the insurrection of the *Isfahān*
'ulamā' of 1924 and the exiling of Āyatullāh Bāfqī in 1928. The earlier incident
came to pass at a time when Rizā Khān was engaged in making an alliance with
the religious leadership. This insurrection did not enjoy the support of Qumm, as
Shaykh 'Abd al-Karīm Hā'irī declared his neutrality.* His apologist explains that
he wanted to save his *madrasah*s and the effort to make Qumm a leading center
of *Shī'ī* learning—an explanation that is very likely true. The same source
stresses, nevertheless, that the insurrection was not merely a local affair involving only its leader, Hājj Āghā Nūrullāh Isfahānī and his close companions, on the
one side; and the military officials of Isfahān, led by Mahmūd Khān Amīr
Iqtidār. It was a popular movement and enjoyed the support of numerous elements of the Isfahān clergy. This is significant in view of the then important role
of that city in the religious institution in the country. Why did Nūrullāh's march
on Qumm not catch fire and spread to other cities? It *did* attract the sympathy of a
variety of social strata: clergy, guilds, merchants, artisans. These forces, clus-
tered in central Iran and, numbering "several thousands", marched on to the
holy city. Yet, after two months residence there, and eventually due to Nūrullāh's sudden illness and death (under suspicious circumstances) the movement
languished and dissolved. The *'ulamā'* in Nūrullāh's camp claim the Court
divided their forces through bribes and arrant mendacity.[38]

Dawlatābādī, however, attributes the failure to the adeptness of the Amīr
Iqtidār. This individual himself had attended religious schools and knew many of
Isfahān's religious leaders personally. More, he understood their mentality in a

---

*Hā'irī knew Nūrullāh, since, according to Tihrānī, *Tabaqāt A'lām al-Shī'ah*, III, p. 1162, Nūrullāh
had had dealings in Qùmm during Hā'irī's tenure there.

way that most military officers could not have appreciated. The presence of the large military garrison in Isfahān had already apparently demoralized very many of the conservative religious leaders. And through skillful use of informants, his support of the new secular schools, and his seemingly enlightened rule—thereby not alienating the inhabitants to the conservative clergy—Iqtidār "was able easily to close the doors of the institutions and homes of the clergy in the city."[39]

Now, the leading family of Isfahān had the *tawlīyat* (administrative guardianship) over the Masjid-i Shah, the city's chief mosque. This was the family of Hājj Shaykh Muhammad Bāqir (d. 1883), of which Āghā Nūrullāh was, in 1924, the head. This connection may be significant in view of the fact that Ayatullāh Nāʾīnī had spent his young studenthood studying in Isfahān under the aegis of Bāqir and had witnessed Bāqir's many cruelties and deceptions while he was the city's leading *ʿālim*. Bāqir had instigated a revolt of the townsmen against a rise in grain prices at the time of the governorship of Żill-i Sultan Qājār. Yet, having fomented the uprising, he then failed to join or lead them.[40] Nāʾīnī was, as we have seen, a *marjaʿ-i taqlīd;* and he was, in 1924, in contact with Qumm and the neutral Hāʾirī. Nāʾīnī's failure to take sides in the Nūrullāh affair might therefore have been colored by his earlier experiences with Nūrullāh's father, Bāqir.

The land holdings of the Bāqir family in the Isfahān region were extensive. Accordingly, Āghā Nūrullāh was a very wealthy *ʿālim* whose accumulation of property and money had reached such proportions that he gradually had relinquished his involvement in purely religious duties and left these up to the senior Isfahān clergyman, Mīrzā Husayn Fishārikī. Nūrullāh's allies, too, were, according to Dawlatābādī, "[in] the majority . . . landowners and benefit[ed] from the liberalization of opium production." Yet, restriction, not liberalization, was government policy. Before the march on Qumm finally occured, the Isfahān *ʿulamāʾ* had staged a sit-in at the post and telegraph office and issued statements and sent telegrams around the country. Street demonstrations broke out, and police opened fire, wounding a number of people. Fishārikī had been dragged by the demonstrators into the middle of the protests at the governor's house, where the tumult had broken out. Dawlatābādī does not mention Nūrullāh's role in these specific demonstrations. If he had at all played an ambiguous role, it would have been the more vindication for Nāʾīnī not to have supported him.

In the event, the protest over opium production served as a pretext for Amīr Iqtidār thoroughly to defeat the Isfahān *ʿulamāʾ*. It may well be that the clergy had not had a prayer in the struggle, since opium had by then become, as Dawlatābādī suggests, an international issue too important to be decided by local political forces with a stake in its production. But the specific issue of restriction of production is of less interest for present purposes than the fact that the administration could thus deal the clergy of one of the country's most important cities a blow from which it did not recover.

The matter of the expulsion of Āyatullāh Muhammad Taqī Bāfqī from Qumm is a curious episode in clergy-state relations. It is difficult to know whether or not it merits the attention that one of the historians of Qumm gives it. For all the gravity that this chronicler attaches to the incident, it is difficult to uncover other references to it in the literature on the lives of the Iranian ʿ ulamāʾ or the memoir and biography material.

The crisis arose allegedly over the offensive behavior of the ladies of the Court inside the courtyard of the shrine of Hazrat Maʿsūmah (the sister of the eighth Imām), Āyatullāh Bāfqī's sternly worded admonitions against them, and the descent upon the city by Rizā Shah and his chief military aide, Taymūr Tāsh. Surrounding the shrine with artillery and armor the Shah is reputed to have sent Taymūr into the sanctuary to rout the ensconced Bāfqī. Deliberately striding in with his boots and thus violating the sanctity of the shrine, Taymūr upbraided the unfortunate Bāfqī with excoriation and dragged him by the beard out of the *haram* (sanctuary). His ultimate fate was imprisonment for six months and exile to Shah ʿAbd al-Aẓīm, where he is reported to have died in mysterious circumstances—perhaps by poisoning—in 1944.[41]

If this be a true account, one would have thought that a protest would have been lodged somewhere by the ʿ ulamāʾ. Yet, they seem to have been silent on this matter. Neither Dawlatābādī, Mustawfī nor Āghā Buzurg-i Tihrānī refer to this event. Avery, however, has the following account, although the date has been switched from 1925 to 1928:[42]

> Early in that year the queen, his [the Shah's] Consort and mother of the Crown Prince, inadvertently let her veil slip to show part of her face during a ceremony in the Shrine Mosque at Qum. The officiating preacher denounced her for it. The Shah was in Qumm the next day with two armored cars and a party of troops on call. He entered the mosque without taking his boots off and thrashed the *mullā*. He also ordered the arrest and removal of three criminals who, in accordance with ancient procedure, had taken sanctuary in the mosque precincts.

Despite the mutations the story has undergone, the kernel remains. Hāʾirī's silence once again must be noted.

In the course of gradually encroaching upon the ʿ ulamāʾ 's status and power, the broad strategy the government pursued was to give the state administration the authority to define the jurisdictions of the religious institution. Thus, the Law on Military Conscription vested a *lay civilian* board of examiners with the discretionary power to decide if a religious student's claim for exemption was merited. The judicial reforms of Dāvar gave the *government* the right to decide what matters could still be adjudicated in the religious (*sharʿ*) courts.

The Uniformity of Dress Law of 6 Day 1307/27 December 1928 was in the same spirit. Article two specified the strata of society eligible for exemption from its provisions: *viz.*, the mandatory abandonment of traditional garb for Western dress for men; and the removal of the veil for women.

Article 2: The following eight categories [of individuals] are exempted from the law;

1. *Mujtahids* who have received the *ijāzah* from one of the marāji'-*yi taqlīd* who are pursuing a religious calling.

2. Those engaged in matters of the holy law in the villages and rural areas, [who will be exempted] upon the passing of a special examination.

3. *Muftī*s of the *Sunnī* faith who have the *ijāzah* to issue *fatvā*s from two other *Sunnī muftī*s.

4. *Muhaddithūn* [relators of traditions] who are licensed by two *mujtahids*.

5. Preachers who have pulpits.

6. Religious students in *fiq* and us*ūl* [jurisprudence and the principles of jurisprudence] who have passed an examination geared to their level of study.

7. Teachers of *fiq*, *usūl* and *hikmat-i ilahī* [theology].

8. Non-Muslim Iranian clergymen.[43]

Among the *Shī'ī* clergy only the *mujtahids* remained free of the burden of proving their exempt status before secular councils or examining boards. Notwithstanding, the language of the clause makes it clear that even *mujtahids* would have to have diplomas from living *marāji'-yi taqlīd*, so that some harrassment accrued to them, as well. Rural *mullā*s, by far the largest segment of religious institution in the country, were vulnerable through the requirement of examination. The religious studies students faced this obstacle, too, although they presumably were better prepared to pass an examination since they were still in a milieu in which assiduous preparation for lessons was a necessity of every day life. Preachers had to demonstrate that they had a *bona fide* pulpit in an established mosque; this ruled out itinerant sermonizers—again a large component of the '*ulamā*' stratum. With the passage of the Law the great mass of the Iranian clergy was placed on the defensive. The Law had its greatest implications for the *madrasah* system, because upon its promulgation harrassment of the students became legitimate activity on the part of the officials of the regime. Such official harrassment on a wide scale engendered numerous incidents involving arrests and bloodshed. These, in turn, finally led the cautious Hā'irī to protest these indignities.

About a month after the Law's passage, an administrative decree surfaced which further stiffened the requirement for the students and teachers at the *madrash*s to prove their status. This decree, dated 3 Bahman 1307/25 January 1929, provided:[44]

Article 14: The religious students mentioned in paragraph 6 of Article 2 of the [Uniformity of Dress] Law are considered those who have been continually studying *fiq* and *usūl* and to whom the Ministry of Education shall, by special administrative decree, have given a diploma attesting to their status as students of the religious sciences [*tullāb*]

Article 15: Teachers of *fiq* and *usūl* and *hikmat-i ilahī* as mentioned in paragraph seven of Article 2 of the Law are considered those who have been given the diploma of instruction from one of the *marāji̇ʿ -yi taqlīd* or by the Ministry of Education, and who have continually been teaching.

This further tightening of control by the Ministry of Education over matriculation and graduation of students, together with the certification of teachers (considering the difficulty of getting the few *marāji̇ʿ -yi taqlīd* to issue diplomas to teachers) constituted a frontal attack on the self-selection process within the religious institution.

When the yearly observances (known as ʿĀshūrā) of the martyrdom of the third *Imām* came to pass that year, the population of the city of Qumm reached its peak. The police exerted, during this time, a great deal of pressure on the religious establishment. Part of the harrassment entailed the surrounding of the town's major *madrasah,* the Fayzīyah, and preventing student egress from its precincts. It also involved roughing up the *tullāb* on city streets and stripping them of their traditional clothes. A delegation of Tehran bazaar merchants and guildsmen, led by one of that city's ʿ*ulamāʾ*, was in town on the customary pilgrimmage. This group apparently solicited Hāʾirī's view of the Dress Law. While not willing to go as far as to issue a *fatvā* enjoining against compliance with its provisions, Hāʾirī sent a telegram to Rizā Shah expressing his concern. Most of the text is unavailable, but the fragment cited by Rāzī is indicative of the pressure to which Hāʾirī was responding:[45]

> Although I have up to now not interfered in any [political] matter, I hear that steps are being taken that are openly contradictory to the Jaʿfarī path and the law of Islam, [in the face of which] it is difficult for me any longer to restrain myself and remain tolerant.

However, the regime paid no attention to this protest, and further government involvement in the affairs of the *madrasah*s continued without abatement. Notable among these was the decree of 15 Isfand 1307/7 March 1929 on the Examination of Religious Students and Identification of Teachers of the Religious Sciences. This 11-article decree may be summarized as follows: Ministry of Education examining boards would sit in the major towns the first month of every spring to test students in Persian and Arabic language and literature; *fiq; usūl;* and logic. These exams were to be geared to an officially approved curriculum of studies. The examining board, a civil body, would consist of two specialists in literature and three experts in *fiq* and *usūl.* The local office of the Ministry of Education in the appropriate city would be free to appoint any members of the ʿ*ulamāʾ* stratum to serve as examiner.

Additionally, examinations were to be administered to candidates wishing to earn a certificate of teaching in any of the above subjects at the *madrasah*s. Students were to be issued certificates each year upon passing the yearly examination, and these certificates were to serve as the basis for the drawing up of the yearly examination. Persons wising to sit at these examinations were required to prove their status as religious studies students based on affidavits from a teacher or the *mutavallī* of the *madrasah*.

Finally, teachers were to be identified as such on the basis of their meeting the following criteria: (1) possession of a diploma from a *marja'-i taqlīd*; (2) evidence of five years of teaching experience; (3) successful passing of examinations in *fiq*, *usūl* and *hikmat-i ilahī;* (4) possession of a certificate from the local Office of Education.[46]

A steady stream of such regulations facilitated the work that the regime set for itself in reducing the number of students and teachers in the religious schools. Whereas before the new statutes and ordinances any one could—and did—declare himself a *talabah* (student of the religious sciences), and teachers needed no certification from central authorities, now these things could no longer be regulated from within the religious institution. Indeed, they had to be contested in what virtually amounted, in many cases, to adversary proceedings. This was, as far as the regime was concerned, the whole point. The local Office of Education in any city could, by denying a passing grade on an examination to students or withholding certification to teachers, sharply restrict the scope of activity of any *hawzah-yi 'ilmīyah* that it wished. Indeed, the attenuation and virtual shriveling of the *hawzah*s of "Khurāsān, Tehran, Tabrīz and Isfahān'"[47] can be attributed to policy in keeping with these decrees and laws in the thirties. Further regulations issued by the Endowments Organization, as we shall see, made the administration of the *madrasah*s increasingly subject to government oversight and supervision. It is owing to these laws on *awqāf* (pious endowments) of 1934 that the Endowments Organization, by 1973, was financially aiding approximately 80% of all the *madrasah*s of the country and exercising the *tawlīyat* over probably at least one-third of them.[48] In general all of these administrative and statutory acts may be interpreted in the light of the desire to expand the secular school system and diminish the activity of the *madrasah*s in the broad public policy area of education.

Another step in the direction of central government control came on 21 Farvardīn 1309/28 February 1930, when the Department of Education and Instruction of the Ministry of Education issued the following examination schedule for the religious schools. Taking *fiq* and *usūl* as one category and *hikmat* (philosophy' as another, the schedule listed the required books on the basis of three levels (*rutbah*) and three or four grades (*darajah*). The levels evidently correspond to the traditional cycles of religious education: (1) introductory (*muqaddamāt*); (2) intermediate (*sutūh*); (3) and higher (*khārij* or *'ālī*). The schedule is as follows:[49]

It bears emphasis that the passage of this new examination schedule, as well as the earlier decrees discussed already, represent an indication of regime intent.

LEVEL I OF RELIGIOUS STUDIES, DIVIDED INTO THREE GRADES

Book	First Grade or Year	Second Grade or Year	Third Grade or Year
*Sharāyiʿ [al-Islam]** (*Fiq*)	From beginning to *mazāra ʿah*	From *mazāra ʿah* to *at ʿimah & ashribah*	From *at ʿimah & ashribah* to end of book
*Maʿālim [al-Dīn]*** (*Uṣul*)	From beginning to *nawāhi*	From *nawāhi* to *matlab sādis fi al-akhbār*	From *matlab sādis* to end of book
*Hāshiyah [Mullā ʿAbdallāh]**** (Logic)	From beginning to *maqsad thāni*	From *maqsad thāni* to *qiyas*	From *qiyās* to end of book
*Gulistān*****			
*Bustān*****			

FIQ and USŪL

*by Najm al-Dīn Abū al-Qāsim Muhaqqiq Hillī (13th century)
**by Hasan ibn Zayn al-Dīn, Shahid-i Thānī (16th century)
***by ʿAbdallāh Yazdī (15th century)
****by the national poet, Saʿdi al-Shīrāzī (13th century)

LEVEL II OF RELIGIOUS STUDIES, DIVIDED INTO THREE GRADES

	Book	First Grade or Year	Second Grade of Year	Third Grade or Year
FIQ and USŪL	Sharh-i Lumʿah* (Fiq)	From beginning of ta-hārat to end of vaqf	From matājir to end of liʿān	From ʿatq to end of book
	Qawānīn** (Usūl)	From beginning to nawāhī	From nawāhī to qanūn-i chahār az ʿumūm va khusūs	From qānūn chahār to chapter 6.
	Sharh-i Sham-siyah*** (Logic)	From beginning to juzʾī va kullī	From juzʾī va kullī to ahkām-i qazāyā.	From qazāyā to end of book
	Mutawwal****	From beginning to ahwāl masnad	From ahwāl masnad to ījāz va itnāb	From ījāz va itnāb to end of book
	Nahj al-Balāghah†			
	Kalīlah wa Dimnah††			

*by Shahīd-i Thānī
**by Mīrzā Abū al-Qāsim Muhammad al-Gīlānī (19th c.)
***by same author
****by Najm al-Dīn Dabīrān Kātibī Qazvīnī
†The book on the sermons and wise sayings of Imām ʿAlī ibn Abī Tālib
††An Arabic literary classic of anecdotes of kingship as cast in the animal world.

47

LEVEL III OF RELIGIOUS STUDIES, DIVIDED INTO FOUR GRADES

	Book	First Grade	Second Grade	Third Grade	Fourth Grade
FIQ AND USŪL	Makāsib* (Fiq)	makāsib muharramah to beginning of bay'	from bay' to sharāyit 'iwazin	from sharāyit to khayyār khāmis	from khayyār khāmis to end of book
	Rasā'il* or	from beginning to dalīl insidād	from dalīl insidād to part 2 of asl-i barā'at	from asl-i barā'at to beginning of tanbīhāt istishāb	from tanbīhāt istishāb to end of book
	Kifāyah al-Usūl** (Usūl)	from beginning to bahth nawāhī	from nawāhī to end of Volume I	from beginning of Vol. II to the principle of lā zarar	from the principle of lā zarar to end of book
	Sharh-i Manzūmah*** (Logic) Kalilah wa Dimnah	from beginning to qazāyā	from qazāyā to istiqrā' va tamthī	from istiqrā' va tam-thil to end of book	No examination in logic

*by Shaykh Murtazā ibn Ahmad Amīn Ansārī (c. 1864)
**by Ākhūnd Mullā Muhammad Kāzim Khurāsānī (d. 1911)
***by Hājjī Mullā Hādī Sabzīvārī (19th c.)

LEVEL I OF RELIGIOUS STUDIES, DIVIDED INTO THREE GRADES

HIKMAT

Book	First Grade or Year	Second Grade or Year	Third Grade or Year
Sharāyiʿ [al-Islam] (Fiq)	from beginning to muzāraʿah	from muzāraʿah to aʿimah wa ashribah	from aʿimah wa ashribah to end of book
Maʿālim [al-Dīn] (Usūl)	from beginning to nawāhī	from nawāhī to matlab sādis fī al-akhbār	from matlab sādis fī al-akhbār to end of book
Sharh-i Shamsīyah (Logic)	from beginning to juzʾī wa kullī	from juzʾī wa kullī to ahkām qazāyā	from ahkām qazāyā to end of book
Gulistān			
Bustān			

LEVEL II OF RELIGIOUS STUDIES, DIVIDED INTO THREE GRADES

HIKMAT

Book	First Grade or Year	Second Grade or Year	Third Grade or Year
Sharh-i Lumʿah (Fiq)	from beginning of tahārat to end of vaqf	from matājir to end of liʿān	from ʿatq to end of book
Sharh-i Manzūmah (Logic)	from beginning to qazāyā	from qazāyā to istiqrāʾ va tamthīl	from istiqrāʾ va tamthīl to end of book
Mutawwal	from beginning to ahwāl masnad	from ahwāl masnad to ījāz va itnāb	from ījāz va itnāb to end of book
Nahj al-Balāghah			
Kalīlah wa Dimnah			

49

LEVEL III OF RELIGIOUS STUDIES, DIVIDED INTO THREE GRADES

	Book	First Grade or Year	Second Grade of Year	Third Grade or Year
HIKMAT	Sharh-i Manzūmah (Hikmat)	from beginning to ilah-iyāt bi al-ma'nī al-akhass	from ilahiyāt to tabi-'iyyāt	from tabi'iyyāt to end of book
	Shawāriq [al-Ilhām fi Sharh-i Tajrīd al-Kalām], Vol. I*	from beginning to mas'alah khāmis 'ashar	from mas'alah khāmis 'ashar to fasl thānī	from fasl thānī to end of book
	Asfār [al-Arba'ah]**	from sifr awwal to minhāj thālith	from minhāj thālith to marhalah rābi'	from marhalah rābi' to awwal tabi'iyyāt
	Sharh-i Ishārat***	fi al-wujūd al-dhihnī	fī al-quwwah wa al-fi'l	last third
	Kalīlah wa Dimnah	first third	second third	
	Tārīkh-i Bayhaqī****			

*by 'Abd al-Razzāq Lāhījī (17th c.)
**by Mullā Sadrā Shīrāzī (11th c.)
***by Ibn Sīnā (10th & 11th c.)
****by Abū al-Fazl Bayhaqī (11th c.)

Information concerning the implementation of these regulations and the actual behavior of Ministry of Education officials, *mutavallīs*, teachers and students at the *madrasah*s exists only in the form of scraps and fragments. Nonetheless, a correlation of the decline in number of religious students on a national level with the dates of the issuance of these decrees indicates that they did have a generally constrictive and restrictive effect as far as the system of religious education is concerned. (For the date, see the appendixes.)

In Bahman 1312/January–February 1934 the Ministry of Education announced its permanent curriculum of studies for the intermediate and higher cycles in the theological colleges. Each cycle, consisting of six grades or years, contained a variety of subjects, not all of which, by any means, were to be found in the traditional curricula of the religious schools. This program of studies represents a modest attempt to secularize the curriculum of Iran's *madrasah*s by calling for the study of such subjects as composition, dictation and history in the intermediate cycle, while the program of studies for the higher cycle stays well within the frontiers of traditional *madrasah* education, it does underscore two subjects which had been on the decline in the last few decades: commentary on the *Qur'ān (tafsīr)* and biography (*ma'rifat al-rijāl*).[50]

Program of Studies for the Intermediate Cycle
for Religious Studies Students

First Year
1. Persian language: Reading select pieces of prose, poetry; attention will be given to the meanings of language and comprehension, using Sa'dī's *Gulistān* and *Bustān*.
2. Composition: Easy composition.
3. Dictation: Spelling drills.
4. Morphology: Divisions of the verb; radical letters only, derivative verbs, intransitive and transitive verbs; active and passive voice; strong and weak radicals; principles of weak letter permutation and substitution and contraction of two letters into *tashdīd*. Using the book, *Sarf-i Mīr*
5. Syntax: The sentence; words; parts of speech; inflection; agreement; accusative and genitive; nominative *tanwīn;* etc. Using the book, *'Awāmil*.
6. *Fiq:* Main topics of the *sharī'ah*; ablution; fasting; prayer. Using the *Risālah 'Amalīyah* of one of the *marājī' al-taqlīd*.
7. Accounting: Short course, using the book by Rāhnamāh, entitled *Kitāb Mutavassitah*.
8. History: Outline history of Iran; history of Islam, the prophecy and the life and death of the prophet.

Second Year
1. Persian language: For these three subjects perfecting the first
2. Composition: year's study, using the book, *Kitāb-i*
3. Dictation: *Marzubān Nāmah va Munsha'āt*

4. *Fiq:* Remaining major topics of the *sharīʿah.*
5. *Morphology: Completing the first year's study, using the book, Sharh-i Tasrīf* [by Saʿd al-Dīn Masʿud ibn ʿUmar Taftazānī (14th c)?]
6. Syntax: Using the book, *Hidāyah va Anmuẓaj* [by Jārullāh Abū al-Qāsim al-Zamakhsharī (12th c.)?]
7. Accounting: Completion of the previous year's study; the same book.
8. History: History of Islam and the biography and personality of the prophet; Iranian history.

Third Year
1. Persian Language: For these three subjects,
2. Composition: the book *Kalīlah wa Dimnah*
3. Dictation:
4. Morphology: Completing the study of the previous year, using the book, *Sharh-i Niẓām,* [by Niẓām al-Dīn Hasan Nayshābūrī.]
5. Syntax: Completing the study of the previous year, using [the commentary on the *Mughnī al-Labīb,* by Jamāl al-Dīn ibn Yusūf (14th c.), commentary by Jalal al-Din] al-Suyūtī.
6. Logic: Using the book, [*Risālah-yi*] *Kubrā* [by Sayyid Sharīf Jurjānī].
7. History: Outline history of Iran; Islam; conquests by the caliphs; the holy wars of Imām ʿAlī.
8. Literature: First part of *Majānī al-Adab*
9. *Fiq:* Using the book, *Ghāyat al-Quswā*

Fourth Year
1. Morphology: Remainder of *Sharh-i Niẓām.*
2. Syntax: Remainder of Suyūtī.
3. Logic: Using the book, *Hāshīyah Mullā ʿAbdullāh,* from the beginning to *mabhath qazāyā.*
4. *Fiq:* Using the book, *Sharāyiʿ* [*al-Islam*], to the end of *zakāt.*
5. Literature: Second part of *Majānī al-Adab.*

Fifth Year
1. Syntax: Using the book, *Jāmī:* chapter one—*Mughnī*
2. Logic: Using the book, *Hāshīyah Mullā ʿAbdullāh,* from *qazāyā* to end of the book.
3. *Fiq:* From the beginning of *Sharh-i Lumʿah* through the first third.
4. *Usūl:* Using the book, *Maʿālim* [*al-Dīn*], until *matlab rābiʿ.*
5. Literature: Third part of *Majānī al-Adab.*
6. Rhetoric: Using the book, *Mutawwal:* the first third.

Sixth Year
1. *Fiq: Sharh-i Lumʿah,* second third.
2. *Usūl: Maʿālim* [*al-Dīn*], from *matlab rābiʿ* to the end of the book.
3. Logic: *Shamsīyah.*
4. Rhetoric: *Mutawwal,* second third.
5. Literature: *Nahj al-Balāghah.*
6. Astronomy: Short Course.

Program of Studies for the Higher Cycle
for Religious Studies Students

First Year
1. *Fiq: Sharh-i Lum'ah*, last third.
2. *Usūl: Qawānīn*, Vol. I, first third.
3. Literature: *Āmalī-yi Sayyid Murtazā, Tahdhīb al-Kāmil.*
4. Rhetoric: *Mutawwal*, last third.
5. *Usūl-i 'Aqā'id: Sharh* [sic], chapter 11.

Second Year
1. *Fiq: Kitāb-i Tahārah*, by Murtazā al-Ansārī.
2. *Usūl: Qawānīn*, second third.
3. Literature: Continuation of *Tahdhīb al-Kāmil.*
4. Commentary: *Muqaddamāt-i Tafsīr-i Sāfī* [by Mullā Muhsin Fayz Kāshānī (11th c.)]
5. *Kalām: Sharh-i Tajrīd-i 'Allāmah* [Hasan ibn Yusūf al-Hillī (13th c.)].

Third Year
1. *Fiq: Makāsib Muharramah*, by Murtazā al-Ansārī.
2. *Usūl: Ras'il*, from beginning to *dalīl-i insidād.*
3. Commentary: *Majma' al-Jawāmi'* [by Abū al-Fazl ibn Hasan Tabarsī (12th c.)]
4. Biography: *Khulāsah al-Aqwāl*, by 'Allāmah [sic].

Fourth Year
1. *Fiq:* From beginning of *Matājir* to *sharāyit-i 'iwazīn.*
2. *Usūl: Rasā'il*, from *dalīl-i insidād* to *istishāb.*
3. Commentary: *Majma' al-Jawāmi'*, second quarter.
4. Biography: *Khulāsah al-Aqwāl*, part two.

Fifth Year
1. *Usūl. Rasā'il*, from *istishāb* to end of book.
2. *Fiq: Matājir*, from *sharāyit-i 'iwazīn* to *khayyār khāmis.*
3. Commentary: *Majma' al-Jawāmi'*, third quarter.

Sixth Year
1. *Fiq: Matājir*, from *khayyār khāmis* to end of book.
2. *Usūl: Kifāyah al-Usūl*, Vol. 2.
3. Commentary: *Majma' al-Jawāmi'*, to end of book.

A brief comparison of this curriculum with the works that were read in Mash-had's largest school, the Madrasah-yi Fāzilīyah, in the years between 1918–1925[51] indicates similarity in the basics but also some interesting differences. The Fāzilīyah students read much more and much more widely. The consequence of this is substantial to the extent that the official curriculum that has just been outlined was meant by the regime to be both the minium and the maximum that was to be taught in the theological seminaries. If the regime was intending the curriculum as a maximum program of studies, then clearly it would mean the matriculation and graduation of 'ulamā' with inferior knowledge. The Ministry of Education's program for the twelve years called for the students to read seven works in fiq; four works in usūl; three works in logic; one work in rhetoric; one work in kalām (theology); one work in biography; four works in literature and parts of two others; three works in morphology; four works in syntax; one work in religious tenets (usūl-i 'aqā'id); and two works in Qur'ānic commentary.

The Mashhad students, by contrast, read the following works: six works in morphology; 13 works in syntax; thirty works in literature, not including readings of the Egyptian and Lebanese contemporary press and unnamed Dīvāns (collections of writings) from the Ghaznavid (977–1186) and Saljūqid (1038–1194) eras; seven works in Qur'ānic commentary; eight works in philosophy and logic; sixteen works in ethics, prayer and sermonizing; four works in fiq; four works in usūl; one work in traditions (hadīth); one work in kalām; and various authoritative opinions (fatvās) issued by mujtahids through the ages.

The list of works in fiq and usūl is surprisingly short, although the books mentioned by the author of this article on the Mashhad madrasahs in these fields include three of the four authoritative codices of Shī'ī jurisprudence. None was prescribed in the original nor in entirety by the official curriculum of the Ministry of Education. These codices were: al-Kāfī fī 'Ilm al-Dīn, by Muhammad ibn Ya'qūb Kulaynī (d. 940); Man La Yahduruhu al-Faqīh, by Muhammad ibn Bābūyah Qummī (d. 991); and Kitāb al-Istibsār, by Shaykh Nasīr al-Dīn Tūsī (d. 1068). It is almost certain that such works on jurisprudence as those written by Muhaqqiq Hillī (d. 1277) and Shaykh Murtazā al-Ansārī (d. 1864) were read in Mashhad, and that these writings were among those collectively included by Gunābādī in an offhand statement of "books dealing with fiq and usūl and other religious subjects. . . ."[52]

In any case, it is possible to check the official curriculum against the listing of subjects taught in the madrasahs compiled in 1938 by Muhammad Tāhir Tabarsī.[53] He cites 15 works in fiq (not including the commentaries upon them) and 17 in usūl (excluding commentaries). Such a range is entirely commensurate with the centrality of these two subjects in the curriculum of the traditional theological colleges of Iran.

Yet, the question suggests itself again concerning the intention of the government in imposing its curriculum. Was this program meant to be a minimum thereby providing the madrasahs the option of offering more substantial fare? This might have been the case, based on the argument that too many able-bodied young men in the country, with only the smatterings of an Islamic education, were at large; and these were needed in the growing requirements for labor by a modernizing regime.

By contrast, did the government intend to restrict religious instruction within a narrow compass and thus force the madrasahs to graduate incompetents, with the obvious long-term adverse effects this would have on the religious institution?

If so, then this would have been an expensive policy to oversee. Yet, we are told that[54]

> the government of Iran at that time [i.e., at the death of Shaykh ʿAbd al-Karīm Ḥāʾirī in 1936] intended the dispersion of the educational establishment in Qumm and the fragmentation of the unity of the religious sciences students. It used various methods to eliminate that educational center: it arrested students collectively and individually, threw into prison innocent greybeards and youngsters; forced their conscription into the army; and exerted great pressure on them. . . .

Or, rather, did the regime seek to rationalize and modernize the curriculum, weeding out the excess accumulation of studies the relevance of which had long since disappeared? This must be doubted since it would have led to a revitalization of the religious institution. Evidence about the regime's policies was too overwhelming in the direction of eviscerating that institution. Yet, on one level, the argument about "modernizing" the religious school curriculum seems plausible if the elimination of the more populist or "folk" aspects of religion is seen as a "modernizing" thrust. The absence of numerous prayer and sermon books (*rawzah*) from the government curriculum may be contrasted to their presence in quantity in the Fāzilīyah school in Mashhad. It is possible to read too much into this discrepancy, but perhaps the explanation lies in the attempt by Riżā Shah to discourage the more populist manifestations of religion (*rawzah khvānī*—narrative accounts of the lives and experiences of the *imāms*.[55]

THE *AWQĀF* LAW AND THE LATE RIŻĀ SHAH PERIOD

Although the government administration of religious endowments (*awqāf*) extends back to the Safavīd period (1501–1722), "the existing administrative structure of *awqāf* definitely begins after the consolidation of the constitutional revolution."[56] In part two, chapters one and five of the famous book of government organization in the Safavid period, the *Tadhkirah al-Mulūk*,[57] references are made to a Daftar-i Mawqūfāt, i.e., an Endowments Bureau; and its director was entitled the Sadr al-Sudūr (also variously called the Mustawfī al-Mawqūfāt and/or the Vazīr al-Awqāf. This individual had been invested by the Safavid monarchs with broad power to superintend the dispatch to the Daftar of accounts by the *mutavallīs* and other functionaries involved in matters of religious endowments, the auditing of such accounts, the registration of properties, etc. But after the Afghan invasion, the accession Nādir Shah, the interlude of the Zand Dynasty and the assumption of power by the Qājārs (that is, from 1722–1785), the extent and number of religious endowments declined markedly.[58]

Information on the administration of *awqāf* under the Qājārs is scarce. It may be said as a general principle that the clergy was able to restore its institution after its eclipse throughout the 18th century. It was done doctrinally in the Usūlī victory over the Akhbārī school under Muhammad Bāqir Bihbihānī (d. 1803)—a victory which, as already mentioned, affirmed the position of *mujtahid*. The clergy triumph was in terms of involvement in social affairs, especially in the second half of the century.[59] They cannot readily have done so without improvement in their economic condition. This in turn meant, in likelihood, an improvement in the state of *awqāf*, at least in the Isfahān and Āzarbāyjān regions. Browne[60] states that the Amīn al-Dawlah (1844–1904) served as the head of Awqāf in 1880, so we know that it persisted as a department of government. Nevertheless, it was not until 1911 that the rationalization of the administrative structure of endowments was attempted. The Civil Code of 1928 contained a number of articles in reference to religious endowments, and six years later the Parliament passed the Endowments Law of November 1934. By virtue of this last legislation, the jurisdiction of the Department of Endowments within the Ministry of Education was broadened. This bore consequences for the *madrasah* system and began a period of intervention, subsidization and direct control over an increasing number of religious schools that persisted to the end of the reign of Muhammad Rizā Pahlavī (ruled 1941–1979).

The key sections of the Law of 3 Day 1313/25 November 1934 and the Administrative Statute of 13 Urdībihisht 1314/5 May 1935 pertain to the following principles of land tenure law: (1) *majhūl al-tawlīyah* (i.e., the administrator of the *vaqf* is unknown); *muta' azzir al-masraf* (i.e., the prohibition of using the proceeds from the endowment in the manner originally prescribed in the deed of endowment); (3) *khīyānah* (i.e., dereliction of duty by the administrator or agent of the endowment).

In the interpretation of the applicability of these principles to a given public endowment, the Department of Endowments was vested with the right to initiate litigation and to remain immune from the payment of court and legal fees in the process. It is within the context of this general principle that the enhanced power of the state with respect to *awqāf* should be interpreted. It is true that in the Afshār (1732–1750) and the late Qājār period state absorption of awqaf and private appropriation of endowments constituted major themes in land relations. For this reason, the developments insofar as public *awqāf* since 1934 are concerned do not comprise a sudden departure from the past. Yet, the legal changes of the mid-thirties were an important instrument in the policy of a consciously secularizing dynasty. This being the case, it is significant that not very many new endowments were deeded in the two decades following World War II.[61]

The salient features of the Law and Statute may be summarized accordingly: all public endowments judged to have no administrator or an unknown administrator were to be directly administered by the Endowments Department of the Ministry of Education. Further, the Department was empowered to exercise "full supervision (*niẓārat-i kāmil*) over all public endowments, irrespective of the status of their administration. The assumption by the Department of the direct administration of a public endowment empowered it with the right to request registration, contest registration, initiate court proceedings as plaintiff and enter the court as a third party on behalf of a litigant. These rights also applied in cases where the Department was not the administrator. Further articles mandated the duty of the Department to protest the attempt to convert endowments into private property—a common tendency over the last century. In cases where endowments were liable to sale in conformity with the provisions of the Civil Code, the Department exercised the duty of approving (and consequently, of enjoining against) such sales. It may be added by way of explanation that although in theory they are inalienable, endowments could be transferred under certain circumstances, as under the principle of *tabdīl bi ahsan* (i.e., transfer for the sake of improvement).

Article eight of the Law authorized the Department legally to proceed against corrupt or derelict administrators of public endowments. The final operational article provided for remuneration for the direct administration of public endowments by the Department as follows: failing a deed of endowment, a *vaqf* was to be administered by the Department in exchange for the latter's receiving 10 percent of the net revenue yielded by the property; in instances where the property consisted of hospitals and *madrasah*s the remuneration was to amount to 3 percent of the net revenue. In certain instances where the Department did not exercise direct administration but played a supervisory role, the respective remunerations would be 5 percent and 2 percent.

The modality for the implementation of the Law was contained in the Administrative Statute. Of notable significance is article 12, specifying the areas of Department oversight: revenues, expenditures; registration of property, contesting claims, initiating legal proceedings; approving or rejecting applications for long-term leases; and "comprehensive supervision over all matters related to the interests of the endowment." And article 19 explicitly affirmed that oversight in the matter of the budget meant the power of approval or rejection of budgets submitted to the Department by the administrators of endowments throughout the country.

Significant, too, were a number of articles (41–45) affecting properties in cases where the purpose of the endowment was unknown (*majhūl al-masraf;* where the proceeds could no longer be used for the purposes originally stipulated in the deed (*muta῾ azair al-masraf*); and where properties were endowed for purely charitable purposes (*vaqf bar mabarrāt mutlaqah*). The revenue from the above categories of endowments was to be deposited in a trust account in a bank and was, at the end of each year, to be disbursed in the following manner, less the standard administration/supervision fees as indicated above:

1. The construction of *dabistān*s (secular primary schools)   40%
2. Purchase of school supplies and clothes for needy students   10%

3. Aid for public welfare, the common good, the Red Lion and Sun Society   20%
4. Public education   10%
5. Publication of "useful" books   10%
6. Unanticipated expenses   10%

Remaining articles covered the investigative powers of the Department of Endowments. These provisions (articles 56–73) empowered the Department to exercise discretionary authority to arbitrate disputes among administrators; identifying a property as an endowment or as private property; finding whether an endowment has an administrator or declaring the position vacant; determining that the administrator is unknown (by rejecting credentials submitted before it); determining corruption and dereliction; issuing binding restraining orders against suspected administrators; appointing temporary and/or permanent administrators.[62]

Through the application of the power assigned to the Endowment Department and its successor, the Endowments Organization, by legislation and administrative decree the government succeeded in taking over a number of religious schools. While this did not mean the destruction of the schools, it certainly provided the regime with at least an instrument to discipline their officials, teachers and students. Similarly, the extensive authority permitted by these regulations established a strong presumption of dereliction from the government side. Revelations of the transfer of some choice lands under the administration of the Endowments Organization were made in the aftermath of the departure of Shah Muhammad Riza Pahlavī. Such revelations indicated that properties had been made over to entertainers, public personalities and members of the Court.[63]

The seeds for these developments were sown some fifty years earlier, however. Rizā Shah had often insisted that the intellectuals of the age could no longer be, as had been the case in Iranian history, the ʿ ulamāʾ. Their art and their craft was incapable of answering the difficult social and economic issues of the times, he believed. Yet, even Rizā Shah had needed the clergy in the beginning of his rise to power. There is also evidence of his capitulating to the ʿ ulamāʾ on rare occasions. Apparently, for example, the Military Conscription Law of 1925 originally contained no provision for exemption of the clergy. However, a delegation of religious leaders from Qumm met with him and petitioned for the insertion of the exemption. The Shah's concession included the further promise "to preserve the greatness of Islam and the ʿ ulamāʾ leadership" so that "in carrying out their convictions and intentions, as well as in distributing the sacred religious texts, they would not meet with any obstacles."[64]

A more typical reflection of the regime's relationship with the ʿ ulamāʾ, nonetheless, is the disturbance in 1935 at the shrine of Imām Rizā in Mashhad. The Shah apparently had been impressed by the Turkish law forbidding the wearing of the brimless hat. He thereby decreed that males must weared brimmed hats, which were disliked by Muslims because they prevented them from touching their heads to the ground in prayer. Attempts by local police to apply the law in the sanctuary of the shrine in Mashhad led to an ugly incident in which officials fired on a crowd that had developed and had staged a sit-in. Many hundreds either lost their lives or were wounded, both in the mosque precincts and even within the sanctuary itself. The government undertook an inquiry and convicted and then executed the nā'ib al-tawlīyah (administrator) of the shrine. Such measures failed to erase the impression held by the clergy and their supporters among the masses that the government's real intention amounted to the shutting down of the religious centers.[65] On the whole, the Shah's legacy in the matter of clergy-state relations was that of a ruler who sought to prohibit the public enactment of passion plays, narratives or even mourning for the death of contemporary marājiʿ-yi taqlīd;[66] rather than a ruler who received petitions of redress from the clergy, solicited their support in establishing order and stability, and sought their spiritual guidance, as mandated by the Constitution.

The ʿulamāʾ's capacity for active protest against Riżā Shah's efforts was confined to the behavior of Āyatullāh Hasan Mudarris in the Majlis. But even he was silenced when he was arrested in the fall of 1928 and exiled to eastern Iran. Indicative of the entropy of the religious institution in its relationship to the state was the devastating decline in Majlis deputies with clergy background:[67]

> Whereas the ʿulamāʾ constituted forty percent of the deputies in the Sixth Majlis [1926–1928], and around thirty percent in the Seventh [1930–1932], the Eleventh Majlis which met in 1937 did not include even a single well-known and important figure from the ʿulamāʾ.

Events would show that if Riżā Shah's successor differed somewhat from him in the tone with which he addressed religious issues (at least prior to 1963), he, too, felt that the clergy were a retrogressive force in the context of his "White Revolution."[68] The lines of conflict between this Shah and the ʿulamāʾ would not be sharpened until some eighteen years into his reign. In the meanwhile, as we shall see, his relations with the ʿulamāʾ began with accommodation and the need for support—not unlike the situation in the early part of his father's rule.

CHAPTER THREE

REVIVAL OF 'ULAMĀ' INFLUENCE AND CLERGY-STATE ALIGNMENT: 1941–1958

ACCESSION OF MUHAMMAD RIZĀ SHAH AND 'ULAMĀ' REASSERTION

Upon the abdication of Rizā Shah in September 1941, the organization of the clergy had reached a debilitated stage. The *madrasah*s, according to the data, were suffering the consistent application of the secular policies and legislation discussed earlier. The economic devastation brought on by the second World War and the military occupation of the country by the Allies had severely affected the financial solvency of these schools, so heavily dependent on revenue from the lease of endowed properties. The political system faced pressures from several directions at once: fissiparous tendencies among the tribes in key provinces; requisitioning of natural resources by the occupying armies; factionalism among the politicians in the capital; bureaucratic breakdown; incipient class conflict among the strata that had been engendered by the modernization program of the previous Shah.

Yet, the seeds of the growth of ' *ulamā*' influence lay in these difficulties, and especially in the dramatic rise of foreign influence in the forms of western culture and communism. Thus, by 1951 the *mujtahid*s again were intervening in politics in a major way and issuing *fatvā*s decreeing the nationalization of the Anglo-Iranian Oil Company (AIOC). There may be no doubt that this development marked the highest point of politicization of the clergy's role in society since the Constitutional Revolution. Such is the case even though the traditional scholasticism and bookishness of the religious leadership characterized the behavior of the sole *marja'-i taqlīd* of the time: Āyatullāh Muhammad Husayn Burūjirdī (d. 1961).

Politicization of clergy ranks derived in large measure from the ideas and actions of Sayyid Abū al-Qāsim Kāshānī (d. 1962). This quintessential political activist and agitator, who had studied with the "constitutionalist" 'ulamā' of Najaf in the early part of the century—namely, Mullā Muhammad Kāżim Khurā-sānī and Shaykh Husayn Khalīl Tihrānī, q.v., *supra*—saw his role as guardian of national and *Shī'ī* interests against British imperialism. But Kāshānī's political maneuverings became politically significant only after the end of WW II, since the British authorities had arrested him in 1942 under the charge that his behavior was inimical to British war policies. Thus, the resurgence of the clergy and the religious institution rested on more than his contributions.

The initial signs of comeback effected by the *'ulamā'* were observed in a reassertion of what may be termed a *Shī'ī* public morality or culture. Clerical leaders demanded the repeal of the ban imposed by Riżā Shah on publicly held passion plays (*ta'zīyah*s) and narratives (*rawzah khvānī*). This was accompanied by a return of the veil in city streets. Their agitation succeeded in causing the dismissal of the governor of Khurāsān province, who had from the beginning been condemned by the *'ulamā'* as the instigator of the 1935 Mashhad incident. A further capitulation by the regime came in its declaration that the injunctions and prohibitions associated with the observence of the holy month of Ramażān would be applied in government offices. The regime was also pressured to lift Riżā Shah's proscription of the pilgrimmage to Mecca, although strained relations between Iran and Saudi Arabia delayed this until 1948.[1]

Despite the chaos accompanying the occupation of the country by foreign troops, the regime did seek to implement internal policies. In November 1943 the Majlis ratified an amendment to Article 14 of the Education Law of 1911. On the face of it this represented a major effort to force the *madrasah*s to adapt themselves to the social changes that had developed in Iran since the *mashrūtīyat* (Constitutional Revolution). It is not clear what particular group within the regime was responsible for this amendment, since written reference to it is scanty. On balance, it is safe to say that the then *nā'ib al-tawlīyah* of the Madrasah-yi 'Ālī-yi Sipah Sālār, a certain Muhsin Sadr, played a guiding role.[2] Among *madrasah*s the Sipah Sālār was unusual since the original deed of endowment of this institution stipulated that the property would be vested in the Crown. Conditions in Qumm, Mashhad and Najaf in 1943 were so bad that it might be that the Sipah Sālār was one of the few theological colleges that was functioning normally.

Although by its language a potent call for modernization of the *madrasah* system on a national basis, the amendment apparently remained a dead letter because of unrealistic assumptions. Convincing the seminary administrators in outlying areas of the country, regions beyond the reach of the central government, seemed too ambitious a hope. Indeed, the net effect of the amendment may have been confined to Tehran: to goad the Sipah Sālār administration to reform itself. This attempt at reform itself only began in a hesitant manner as late as October 1949 when the Shah attended opening ceremonies observing the occa-

sion of the change of name of this school to the Dānishgāh-i Rūhānī-yi Īrān
(Religious University of Iran). It is not clear how this institution after 1949 was
intended to relate to the Faculty of Theology of Tehran University, one of four
faculties established in 1934 in that University under the rule of Riza Shah.

Excerpts from the amendment to Article 14 of the 1911 Education Law follow:[3]

> Article 14: With a view to organizing the affairs of the religious schools, and in an
> effort to advance and perfect the religious sciences, a council under the supervision
> and oversight of the Minister of Education shall be formed, as follows:
>
> a.) The council shall consist of ten members: two foremost members of the
> ʿulamāʾ; one outstanding teacher of the intellectual [maʿqūl] sciences; one out-
> standing teacher of the transmitted [manqūl] sciences; the nāʾib al-tawlīyah of the
> Madrasah-yi ʿAli-yi Sipah Sālār; a mutavalli of one of the country's religious
> schools; and four of the country's leading scholars.
>
> b.) Selection of the council members shall rest with the Minister of Education in
> consultation with the nāʾib al-tawlīyah of the Madrasah-yi ʿĀlī-yi Sipah Sālār.
>
> c.) The council shall, with the agreement of the Minister of Culture, prepare and
> ratify its own constitution and regulations, as well as the program of studies, the
> necessary rules and conditions for the selection of teachers, evaluation of the
> studies of the students, the method of examinations and granting of certificates and
> diplomas.
>
> d.) In addition to the intellectual and transmitted sciences and their branches and
> fundamental principles, the council is entrusted with adding other subjects of study
> which are appropriate to [the needs of] the era and necessary for the programs of
> each and every religious school, and especially for the Madrasah-yi ʿĀlī-yi Sipah
> Sālār.

It may be possible that the new regime wished to replace the madrasah system
of Qumm with one more centrally directed from Tehran. Since Shaykh ʿAbd
al-Karīm Hāʾirī's death in 1936, a triumvirate of clergymen was guiding the
affairs of the Qumm seminaries. Of these individuals, none really had the prestige of Hāʾirī. These men—Āyatullāhs Sadr al-Dīn Sadr (d. 1953), Muhammad
Taqī Khvānsārī (d. 1952) and Muhammad Hujjat Kūhkamarahʾī—inevitably
presided over a diminishing student enrollment after the death of Qumm's doyen
clergyman. Did the government intend to create the Iranian equivalent of Egypt's
great Islamic university, al-Azhar? The issue must remain inconclusive. The
most that can be said is that the reform was meant to combine a number of
strategies: prevent the rapid spread of clergy autonomy in the wake of the exile of
Riza Shah, given the new Shah's equal commitment to modernization; offer the
ʿulamāʾ an earnest of the government's concern with religious issues in order to
gain the support of the religious institution at a time when domestic allies were
difficult to secure; demonstrate to other Muslim countries that Iran could boast a
strong Islamic institution of higher learning at a time of growing nationalism in
the Middle East region.

But it was to prove difficult to contain clergy strivings for greater independence. Early in 1948, a group of fifteen *mujtahids* signed a *fatvā* forbidding
women from shopping in the bazaars and markets without wearing the veil. This
move, which would have been unthinkable in Rizā Shah's time, merely elicited a
feeble request by Prime Minister Hakīmī to Āyatullāh Muhammad Mūsavī
Bihbihānī (the son of 'Abdullāh Bihbihānī who was active in the constitutional
period), the leading Tehran *mujtahid*, to prevent illegal demonstrations and to
curb attacks on women in public places on the part of religious zealots. Some
segments of the press, including the long-established daily, *Ittilā' āt*, and *Mardum, Żafar* and *Īrān-i Mā*, attacked the *fatvā;* and the Society of Iranian Women
condemned it as a "deprivation of all women's rights."[4]

Any attempt to locate the '*ulamā*' leadership on a spectrum of orientations to
public policy would have to be constructed on the basis of individual issues.
Thus, on the question of joining political parties and political partisanship a
number of the clergy had run for parliament and sat in the Majlis. This was not
the path advised by a number of the Qumm '*ulamā*' and their allies in Tehran:
most notably Mīr Sayyid Muhammad Bihbihānī. On other issues, such as the
relatively "safe" question of women's rights, however, the '*ulamā*' seemed
united in their opposition to female enfranchisement. One notable exception to
this was Āyatullāh 'Alī Akbar Burqa'ī (about whom see below).

For the religious leadership in the late forties and early fifties the following
issues were most significant: (1) women's suffrage; (2) joining political parties
and "intervening" in politics; (3) the nationalization of the AIOC and the destruction of foreign influence; (4) Bahā'ism and the anti-Bahā'ī campaign;
(5) the subject matter published by the press; (6) orientations toward the militant
fundamentalist movement, Fidā'īyān-i Islam; (7) communism and left-wing challenges to the clergy (by and large considered identical in the minds of the
'*ulamā*'). The category of "intervention" in politics lacked a clear definition.
The implication seemed to be that clergymen would not engage in the mechanics,
tactics and strategies of political partisanship through affiliation with the
emergent political parties. Otherwise, the expression of opinion on any of the
other items listed above involved one in political matters.

Clergy pressure, under the leaderships of Burūjirdī and Bihbihānī, forced
Prime Minister Musaddiq to withdraw the bill on the women's vote which he had
mooted in late 1952.[5] But political activism was another matter. A large conference convened to discuss this provocative issue was held in Qumm in February,
1949. Āyatullāh Burūjirdī specifically invited some 2,000 or so members of the
clergy to attend the session, held in the city's largest *madrasah*, the *Fayzīyah*.
The members adopted a firm non-interventionist position which prohibited all
members of the clergy from joining parties and trafficking in politics. It mandated that opposition to this resolution by clergymen would result in a withdrawal
of recognition of the offender's status as a professional in the religious

institution—a kind of *Shī ī* excommunication that presumably Burūjirdī and the Qumm establishment would implement.[6] Kāshānī's manifest failure to abide by the spirit and letter of the Qumm proceedings of February 1949 is of great interest in an attempt to calculate the structure of inter-clergy relationships at this time.

It may be rejoined that the promulgation of a spate of *fatvā*s by numerous *mujtahid*s in the early 1950's suggests that few of the *Shī ī* leaders were willing to take seriously the proscription of the Qumm conference. Yet, in retrospect the latter seemed geared to the need felt by the religionaries to prevent factionalism and partisanship within their ranks. *Fatvā*s urging nationalization could readily be accommodated within the jurisdiction of the *mujtahid*s to promote the interests of the Islamic community.

The legitimacy of this attitude and praxis rested on the precedent set by Hājj Mīrzā Hasan Shīrāzī's authoritative opinion against the tobacco regie of 1891. Ultimately, it implicated one of the most "political" pillars of Islamic obligation, *jihād* (sacred war against the enemies of Islam). *Fatvā*s were issued on all sides, including the ʿatabāt, Tehran and the provinces. Āyatullāh Burūjirdī seemingly abstained, presumably fixed upon serving the intent of the 1949 resolution. An example of the *mujtahid*s' behavior may be seen in the case of Āyatullāh Muhammad Taqī Mūsavī Khvānsārī. He released his *fatvā* in response to interrogatories submitted to him by a number of merchants in the central bazaar in Tehran. It is an instance of the more political Kāshānī setting an example and thereby requiring a response among his colleagues, since he had already come out in favor of nationalization. Khvānsārī's opinion cited the *hadīth* attributed to Muhammad: he who, upon waking without concerning himself with the affairs of the Muslims is not himself a Muslim. The faithful had no choice but to unite and cleave to the position advanced by Kāshānī as to nationalization of the AIOC, declared Khvānsārī.[7]

The leftist movement at this time attracted a far smaller number of the religious leaders. To be leftist on social issues was to be communist in the eyes of the major religious leaders of the time. Even had they privately held more flexible ideas about the left, these leaders definitely denounced them in their public statements. The pages of the main Tehran daily from time to time published indignant denunciations by the clergy against what they perceived to be "atheistic hooliganism" in the context of the numerous incidents involving the ʿulamāʾ and the left. Among such incidents were the disorders at the Masjid-i Shah in the Tehran bazaar in late May 1952. Upon this occasion one of the country's most popular preachers, Abū al-Qāsim Falsafī was allegedly prevented from speaking and set upon by a crowd of leftist demonstrators whom, we are told, he only narrowly escaped.[8]

Regrettably, there is no simple way of determining what "leftism" (*chap girī*) meant in the context of these disorders. Certainly the press accounts ought not to be taken at face value, including those that appeared to be critical of the clergy's orthodoxy. Leftism could be a code word or a term of opprobrium against the anti-clericalism of the Iranian nationalist thinker, Ahmad Kasravī. Or alternatively it constituted a convenient ideological term that could be used to tar the socialists. Shorn of its ideological connotations, leftism typically emphasizes a redistribution of social productivity; egalitarianism with regard to access to positions of power; enfranchisement of social forces; a widening of the scope of choice; state intervention in the economy with a view to encouraging workers' councils, loosening stratification and providing for social and economic needs; and promoting a more cosmopolitan orientation to cultural development.

In trying to explain contemporary events in terms of the concept of leftism, one must take the precaution of distinguishing the ideological and analytical aspects. For example, potentially most explosive of all the incidents pitting "leftists" against the clergy in the late forties and early fifties was the Burqaʿī affair in Qumm in January 1953. It occured at a time of intense infighting and coalition building on the part of the political leaders of the time. The Prime Minister's foreign policy was highly popular, but domestic policy proved otherwise. Prime Minister Musaddiq's National Front coalition depended heavily on leftist support, which in this context means support from those favoring a clean break from the country's ties with the West, sharply curtailing the power of the Shah, and redistribution of wealth. Now, Āyatullāh ʿAlī Akbar Burqaʿī had the reputation of a leftist, a charge which his rivals sought to buttress by pointing to his membership in the Iranian branch of the front organization, the International Partisans of Peace. Burqaʿī himself hailed from Qumm, to which he was returning for a visit after a long absence. During his stay, large crowd rioting broke out. Numerous students suffered wounds in the battles that raged within the Madrasah-yi Fayzīyah. Insults were allegedly directed against Āyatullāh Burūjirdī by Burqaʿī's partisans, and ultimately this led to the intervention of Prime Minister Musaddiq.[9]

In consequence of these developments the prestige of Qumm's religious establishment rose markedly, with adverse implications for the government. The regime's embarrassment did not translate automatically into a setback for Musaddiq, inasmuch as the Prime Minister personally was exonerated from charges of blame levelled by the ʿ*ulamā*ʾ at the regime. Yet, this "defeat" for the "leftists" increased the burden of the pro-Musaddiq faction, dependent as it was for a major portion of its support on the leftist elements in society and the state administration.

The Buraqʿī affair well encapsulates the tensions involving ʿ*ulamā*ʾ and state at this time. Most of the public policy issues mentioned above were at stake. Burqaʿī stood for female enfranchisement, had entered a political movement, was identified as a leftist; perhaps he was charged or suspected of harboring an internationalist social ethos because of his membership in the International Partisans of Peace movement. Such vague internationalist attachments probably would have made it simpler to see in Burqaʿī's inclinations and actions the seeds of an incipient Bahāʾism. He could not compete with the most accomplished ʿulamāʾ of the times; yet he did have a scholarly side to him in the form of some 10 published essays on the lives of the imāms and translations of Arabic language works.[10] Yet, Burqaʿī was viewed in religious circles as perhaps the obverse of Kāshānī: an activist with leftist leanings. The commonality between them consisted in their demand for nationalization of the Oil Company. But whereas Kāshānī could marshal formidable forces among the masses and among his colleagues—some of whom reluctantly provided it to him—Burqaʿī's clerical supporters were few, indeed. His main ally in religious circles was Shaykh Husayn Lankarānī, Majlis deputy from the northwestern town of Ardabīl during the 14th-16th sessions of the Majlis.

The clergy had its problems with activists on the right, as well. In this connection, the activities of the militant fundamentalist Fidāʾīyān-i Islam movement (established in 1945) provide another dimension for analyzing clergy-state relations. The ʿulamāʾ leadership disliked and distrusted the Fidāʾīyān because of the movement's implicit—and occasionally explicit—attacks on the clergy's stewardship over religious affairs. Although we lack details of interactions between the ʿulamāʾ and the Fidāʾīyān, it may reasonably be inferred that the two were on bad terms with each other. The ʿulamāʾ felt that the Fidāʾīyān were undisciplined agitators whose behavior had brought the reputation and prestige of the religious institution into disrepute. It may be conjectured that the attempted assassination of the Shah at Tehran University on 4 February 1949 was a precipitating cause for Āyatullāh Burūjirdī's call for the Qumm Conference later in that month (20-21 February). As has been shown, the main result of that gathering was to condemn political activism by members of the clergy. An additional cause of strain between the ʿulamāʾ and the Fidāʾīyan was the social status differential between them. The ʿulamāʾ constituted itself as a semi-closed elite, with tight-knit intermarriage patterns linking families together. The Fidāʾīyān was an unabashedly mass organization. Promoting the interests of its own institution against those of the Fidāʾīyān represented an important aspect of the clergy's motivations and behavior. And although the ʿulamāʾ status could be attained by individuals from the most humble backgrounds, once high rank was achieved, a strong presumption for the development of family ties through marriage appeared to be an operating factor in the cementing of clergy solidarity.

An example of family ties is provided by the Sadr, Āshtīyānī and Bihbihānī families of Āmul, Isfahān, the ʿatabāt and Tehran. In late 1950 the press carried the obituary of Āyatullāh Hājj Āghā Yahyā Husaynī Sadr, a relative of the famous Sadr al-Dīn Sadr who shared authority in Qumm with Āyatullāhs Hujjat Kūhkamaraḥʾī and Khvānsārī between 1936-1946; and also related to the revered Hasan Sadr (d. 1935). The Sadr family was and continues to be among the most influential of ʿulamāʾ families, with branches in the region of Āmul (in the direction north northeast of Tehran, near the Caspian littoral), in the shrine areas of Iraq and the city of Isfahān. The deceased *'ālim*'s first wife was related to Shaykh Murtazā Āshtīyānī, the son of the famous Mīrzā Hasan Āshtīyānī (d. 1901) and who was, in 1975, the *mutavallī* of Tehran's most well-known *madrasah:* the Marvī. His second wife was the sister of Āyatullāh Muhammad Bihbihānī, who himself was the son of the constitutionalist leader, Mīrzā 'Abdullāh Bihbihānī (d. 1910). The product of this second marriage was the birth of Ja'far Bihbihānī, about whom more will be said below.[11] Such an alliance between the Sadr family (Sadr al-Dīn was a nephew of Hasan, and Yahyā seems to have been a cousin of Sadr al-Dīn) to the two most powerful clergy families of Tehran (Āshtīyānī and Bihbihānī) strike the observer as an important alliance formation among the religious leadership.

Given these lineage allegiances, the resources which the *'ulamā'* could wield are very extensive. An organization such as the Fidā'īyān, being outside of this network, could only hope to make an impact upon the professional clergy leadership through association with an important one of their members who himself did not have such marital affiliations as to place him in the bosom of that leadership. Such an individual was Kāshānī. Now, it is true that very early in his career as a spokesman for the *Shī'ī*-led uprising in Iraq in the nineteen teens Kāshānī's credentials were in good order. Upon his arrival in Iran in 1919, he bore a letter of introduction from the great Abū al-Hasan Isfahānī (d. 1946) to the *'ulamā'* of Tehran in which Isfahānī had called him ''a pillar of the nation and religion, a support for the *mujtahids....* ''[12] But he apparently sacrificed erudition for political involvement, and this led to the decline in his prestige as an *'ālim* among his colleagues. Therefore, Kāshānī could, at most, be a bridge between the Fidā'īyān and the *'ulamā'* in a short-term tactical coalition to expel British and foreign influence generally from the country. As events were to show, however, Kāshānī and the Fidā'īyān would part ways as early as March 1951. This marked the rapid decline in the Fidā'īyān's influence; but Kāshānī continued to play a key role in Iranian politics by providing and denying important political support to Prime Minister Musaddiq's National Front coalition between 7 March 1951 and 19 August 1953.

Kāshānī throughout seems to have been more popular among the second echelon and lower ranking members of the clergy: the mosque and itinerant preachers. An indicator of the coolness in relations between Burūjirdī and Kāshānī, for example, is that Kāshānī failed to stay as overnight guest at the lodgings of the sole *marja'-i taqlīd* during his various trips to Qumm. The reasons for his political activism must be partially sought in the precedent set by his father in the uprisings in Iraq, which lasted from 1914–1920. His father's death in the service of *jihād* against the British must have fed Kāshānī's deep and bitter hatred of British colonialism. His teachers in the cycles of religious studies through which he matriculated and graduated in the holy cities of Iraq were among the most distinguished of the age. As already mentioned, they thought very highly of him and were quite prepared to introduce him in such terms to their Iranian associates upon his arrival as an exile in Tehran in February 1921.

There are suggestions of the rapid development of friendship between him and Rizā Khān at this time, but his relations with the future Shah soon were eclipsed as a result of apparent intrigues among Rizā Khān's circle of advisers.[13] We do not know much about his activities during the next twenty years, but he apparently chose not to join ʿAbd al-Karīm Hāʾirī's Qumm *hawzah yiʿilmīyah* (educational center). After the Allied occupation and exile of Rizā Shah, Kāshānī resumed his political activity. His political mobilization efforts in the mid-to late-forties were well received by the fledgling Fidāʾīyān, the creation of which coincided with this resumption of Kāshānī's agitation against foreign control. The little we know about the membership of the Fidāʾīyān-i Islam suggests that its active participants hailed from south Tehran, where opportunities for education were limited and impoverishment proportionally great.

Both Kāshānī and the Fidāʾīyān-i Islam stressed Islamic solidarity and appeared to minimize the *Shīʿī* features of religion in Iran as an implicit consequence. The ʿ*ulamāʾ* elite could not have objected to aspects of the Fidāʾīyān-i Islam's guiding principles as such, since some of these called for the application of the *sharīʿah* as promised in the Constitution of 1906/1907; and the implementation of rule under a wise and just leader. Yet, the Fidāʾīyān demand for a return to the purity of thought and practice of the prophet suggested that the ʿ*ulamāʾ* would lose their *raison d'être*. And, of course, the tactics of assassination did not meet with clergy approval.

Now, the attempt on 4 February 1948 against the life of the Shah had led the government to exile Kāshānī to Lebanon. He was also suspected of having had a hand in the assassination of ʿAbd al-Husayn Hazhīr, former Prime Minister and then Minister of Court. Hazhīr's alleged Bahāʾism and his Anglophile orientation provoked the wrath of the movement, leading to his murder on 4 September of the same year. The final incident in this chain was the killing of Prime Minister Rāzmarā on 7 March 1951. Again, the incumbent's pro-British attitudes in the matter of the AIOC, in the context of Iranian nationalist demands for nationalization, led the Fidāʾīyān to decree his assassination. The death of the Prime Minister, together with the passage the next day of the parliament's law to nationalize the Oil Company, was the "high water mark" of Fidāʾīyān fortunes.

During this three year period of turmoil (February 1948-March 1951) the conections between Kāshānī and the Fidāʾīyān in the deaths and attacks were strongly suggested but never proved to the point of complicity. The Fidāʾīyān, we are told, sought to assist Kāshānī by appealing to Āyatullāh Burūjirdī to help in securing the government's approval for Kāshānī's return from exile in Lebanon.[14] Among the *quid pro quo*s performed by Kāshānī were his public expressions of delight at the assassinations, as well as his engineering the release of the assassin of Rāzmarā in November 1952.

The Kāshānī-Fidā'īyān relationship collapsed immediately after the installation of Muhammad Musaddiq as Prime Minister as a result of Fidā'īyān demands for a share in executive power. Kāshānī's rebuff of these demands led to bitter recrimination against him by the movement, which now began to direct its vituperations against both the Āyatullāh and the new Prime Minister. The attacks on Musaddiq derived from Fidā'īyān perceptions that he was primarily a modernist too heavily influenced by Western ideas and especially "leftist" currents. Yet, the government did not have much trouble with the movement and succeeded in 1951 in arresting its supreme guide and executing him. The complex situation was further complicated when Kāshānī, who was the Speaker of the Majlis, broke with Musaddiq over the latter's demand for extraordinary powers from the parliament in March 1953. This split is of great interest because of the failure of the eight-man ' ulamā' contingent in the parliament to side with Kāshānī in his confrontation with the Prime Minister. In fact, they stood with Musaddiq on this issue.[15] The reasons for this are not clear, but they might have had to do with suspicion of his intentions and a desire not to weaken the government at a time when the British were forcing a test of strength on the oil question.

During the last six months of the Musaddiq government Kāshānī's power was not very secure. In the chaotic three days of 16–19 August 1953, when the Shah departed the country and then returned under the aegis of the Western sponsored *coup d'état* against Musaddiq, Kāshānī is said to have played a minor role in mobilizing the crowds of south Tehran as against the larger part played by other members of the clergy, especially Āyatullāh Muhammad Bihbihānī.[16]

Through the late 1940's and early 1950's one may identify, in summary, the following groupings or factions among the religious elements: (1) the Burūjirdī-Bihbihānī network, representing the ' ulamā' elite; (2) the Fidā'īyān-i Islam; (3) Kāshānī and the non-elite members of the clergy professional stratum; (4) the parliamentary contingent of clerics, who can be said to stand apart because of their willingness to back Musaddiq as against the Burūjirdī-Bihbihānī distrust of the Prime Minister and as opposed to the Kāshānī split with the latter; (5) the miniscule Burqa'ī-Lankarānī alignment, by far the politically weakest of all. During these developments, the role of the Shah was minimal in the give and take of politics of the time, except in his defensive attempts to protect his prerogatives from Prime Minister Musaddiq. Indeed, the very significant support the Burūjirdī-Bihbihānī bloc extended to him was critical in the aftermath of the downfall of Dr. Musaddiq on 19 August 1953, as critical, indeed, as *during* his fall.

But before dealing with the post-1953 developments, it remains to discuss the case of the administration of the shrine in Qumm. This episode occured just prior to the Burqaʿī affair already discussed. The issue was joined between the government and the Qumm establishment when the government decided to change the administrator of the shrine under the rule known as *majhūl al-tawlīyah*, q.v. Although this act does not appear on the face of it to have constituted an attack on the *hawzah* of Āyatullāh Burūjirdī, it nevertheless was perceived as a provocative attempt by the regime to interfere in religious affairs. In early November 1952 rumors of the intended change in administrator led to sit-ins at the post office of the city. Women were dissuaded by the military authorities from joining the menfolk of the town in these protests. Prime Minister Musaddiq had concluded that he would have to declare martial law in Qumm. According to the press the protestors included bazaar merchants and peasants and thus represented a mix of urban and rural elements. On 7 November the Department of Endowments in Tehran announced that it had changed the administrator of the shrine and replaced him with a professor of law at Tehran University. The next day it was reported in the press that the people had abandoned their sit-in on the advice of Āyatullāh Kāshānī. On the 13th, the Minister of Culture, Āzar, met with Kāshānī and the newly appointed *mutavallī*. The latter, wearing the vestments of a member of the clergy, presented Kāshānī with a scroll reportedly containing the signatures of a number of Qumm shopkeepers and merchants supporting his candidacy. It was announced by the Minister—who had jurisdiction over *awqāf*, it will be recalled—that the new appointee would take over his duties in Qumm on 21 November.

The importance of this case lies in the determination of the government to sustain its right to change the administrators of *awqāf* in accordance with the Awqāf Law of 1934. Dr. Sharvīn, the Director of the General Department of Awqāf, explained that an inquiry into the state of finances of the shrine in Qumm had uncovered irregularities. The incumbent *mutavallī*, Mr. Tawlīyat, had failed to produce evidence of his appointment to the post, said Sharvīn. The latter riposted that all shrines in the country are headed by individuals who had received their appointment by the ruling Shah. But Mr. Tawlīyat's file had failed to show any imperial *farmān* (decree) of appointment. Moreover, the administrator of the shrine in Qumm, declared the Endowments Department, had failed to send annual financial reports for a number of years. And Sharvīn alleged that the assets of the shrine were being wasted and consumed illegally, according to the Department's audit report. For these reasons, therefore, the government was committed to a change in the administration. The government was therefore appointing a five-man committee to supervise the transfer of the assets of the shrine to Mr. Mishkvāt, the new appointee.[17]

Mr. Mishkvāt did not set out for Qumm until 7 December, however. Apparently, Kāshānī had been persuaded of the suitability of the new appointee, and he sent a telegram to Āyatullāh Sadr al-Dīn Sadr of Mishkvāt's departure from

Tehran for Qumm. The government, nevertheless, expected trouble and, as a precaution, strengthened the number of security forces in the city.[18]

Yet, Tawlīyat seems to have had the last word in this conflict, since he came back to his office shortly afterwards.[19] Once again, one can only surmise the cause of this dénouement. We know that among the ʿulamāʾ Kāshānī ended by backing Mishkvāt, although he may have been ambivalent in this support, judging from his role as intermediary between the sit-in demonstrators in Qumm and the Endowments Department. The problem may have been caused by Tawlīyat's dereliction, but in that case one must still account for the fact that someone decided it was time to hold him to account for his negligence. Why did Kāshānī send his telegram to Sadr al-Dīn Sadr? It can be conjectured that he was trying to avoid dealing with "the Āghā," as Burūjirdī was often called. Did the latter hold any special brief for Tawlīyat? Was this one of those cases where patrons seeking to provide benefits to their clients, come into conflict with one another?

The rejoinder to these lines of argument is that Sadr al-Dīn Sadr was the logical individual to receive the Kāshānī telegram, since he had been appointed as one of the five persons to serve on the transfer committee. Still, one could reply that Sadr could have refused the appointment had he felt that Tawlīyat should remain. And Burūjirdī's silence is very interesting. If the government charges against Tawlīyat's abuses were true, then it was not for Burūjirdī to air grievances. But if he supported Tawlīyat, he could reasonably have maintained his silence. Otherwise, he ought to have joined the regime and Kāshānī in demanding a change. In fact, the hawzah-yi ʿilmīyah, led by Burūjirdī, did not openly take a position on the Tawlīyat-Mishkvāt dispute. Of course, Burūjirdī, irrespective of how he may have felt regarding the legitimacy of the government's case, may have harbored suspicions that this was a front behind which the regime meant to lay hold of some of the revenues of the shrine with a view to dispensing these within the secular educational system. It will be recalled that the Awqāf Law of 1934 held open the possibility of doing so in certain circumstances.

The Tawlīyat affair and the Burqaʿī crisis closely followed upon the enfranchisement of women question. Burūjirdī's phone call to Prime Minister Musaddiq at the height of the Burqaʿī crisis was an attempt to let the Iranian leader know that Qumm was no longer to be taken for granted in the scheme of things. "Qumm, after all, is not like Sāvah or Dāmghān," (provincial towns in Iran) Burūjirdī is reported to have told Musaddiq. In a speech to the Majlis, the deputy from the holy city, Tawlīyat,* echoed Burūjirdī's words: Qumm has not received due attention from the Court or from the government as befits its stature within the Shīʿī faith. The government's negligence, it was maintained, was particularly

---

*Tawlīyat evidently was simultaneously the mutavallī of the shrine and MP from Qumm.

consequential in view of mounting leftist influence in the city. Such influence was allegedly contributing to the decay of public morality among the citizens. Yet, complained the deputy, the regime's only response in the face of such provocations was to add to the strength of the city's security forces.[20]

It was against this backdrop of increasing self-assurance and assertiveness on the part of the clergy leadership that ʿulamāʾ-state relations in the post-1953 period must be viewed. Ironically, the government called for, and received, ʿulamāʾ backing for its policies of compromise and dealing with foreign powers and influence; this was precisely one of the issues that had so exercised the religious leadership in the immediately preceding period. It may be that the clergy was willing to make this sacrifice in exchange for what it believed was the temporal authority's concessions on internal matters related to the growth of the religious institution inside the country. At any rate, the relationship appeared to be not dissimilar to that existing around 1921 to 1925. The main difference seemed to be that whereas Rizā Khān wanted to modernize while eliminating actual foreign presence in Iran, Muhammad Rizā Shah sought to do so while shoring up this presence.

CONTINUED RISE IN CLERGY INFLUENCE IN THE ZĀHIDĪ PERIOD, 1953–1955

In seeking to work out his relations with the religious elements after August 1953 the Shah naturally chose the Burūjirdī-Bihbihānī faction. It was the majority element, most respected among the professional clergy and, not insignificantly, it had already indicated its readiness to mediate among quarreling social forces in the interests of order and security. It was a choice, too, dictated by the utter unreliability of Kāshānī, the implication of the Majlis contingent of the ʿulamāʾ in policies associated with Musaddiq, and the decidedly minority status of the "leftist" clergy. As for the remaining grouping—the Fidāʾīyān-i Islām—certainly the Shah had no wish to attempt to establish rapport with the very movement that had been assassinating his officials. With the acquiescence of Burūjirdī and Bihbihānī, indeed, the government crushed the Fidāʾīyān with an intensity not unlike its elimination of the Communist (Tūdah) Party.

In the 1953–1958 period the ʿulamāʾ withdrew to their mosques and madrasahs. If in 1952 the student population of Qumm was around 3,200, in early 1956 it was estimated to have reached 5,000.[21] The reasons for this efflorescence of religious education in the mid-1950's have to do with the enhanced legitimacy of the religious calling. The religious institution, after all, had conducted a search for Iranian cultural identity in the previous decade. From its point of view this search had uncovered positive results in a context of psychological and social rejection of the Western model of modernization.[22]

If Qumm stood as the center of this Shīʿī resurgence, no doubt that Mashhad had also undergone a reawakening under the direction of Āyatullāh Hājj Mīrzā Ahmad Khurāsānī Kafāʾī (d. 1971). This individual, who was the son of Ākhūnd Mullā Muhammad Kāzim Khurāsānī (q.v.), had made his mark as leader of the Mashhad resistence to Soviet occupation forces in the WW II period. According to one of his biographers, his efforts in spearheading the creation of some 260 "religious committees" to protest Soviet occupation "prevented Khurāsān from suffering the same fate as Āzarbāyjān." Kafāʾī superintended the functioning of the 15 or so theological colleges in Mashhad during the 1950's and 1960's.[23]

But the center of Iranian Shīʿism by this time had clearly shifted to Qumm. The government's relations with the city since the mid-thirties had alternated between long-periods of studied neglect, the harrassment of the religious institution, and extension of flood relief in the disastrous years of 1933-35. The town did undergo some change in the form of the spread of secular education there, in the guise of the Rushdīyyah Schools, (q.v.). One of these had been established in 1934 when Hājj Hasan Rushdīyyah himself personally came to the city to supervise it (perhaps at the behest of Rizā Shah). This school remained under his helm until his death in 1944.[24] During the next decade, marked by Burūjirdī's domination of the hawzah, there cannot have been any significant growth in the secular school system there. Qumm became an institution unto itself, a domain where the national government leadership went to pay its respects on a regular basis. In the next few years, it was Qumm that was exercising a studied neglect of Tehran and Tehran that seemed in need of wooing Qumm.

Of course, the Court already had its own coterie of ʿulamā', in the persons of the Imām Jumʿah of Tehran, Hasan Imāmī, and ʿAllāmah Vahīdī,* a teacher of fiq at the Sipah Sālār mosque and madrasah, and other "loyalists." A person like Dr. Hasan Imāmī had moved into the clerical profession from the law, in which he had been trained and earned a doctorate at the University of Geneva in the 1930's. Upon the death of his father, the incumbent Imām Jumʿah of Tehran, in 1945, he himself accepted appointment to the post by the Shah. Such appointment was in accordance with established practice dating from Safavid times. While in this position Imāmī had gone on record a number of times in favor of the stand that "religion must be separated from politics and must, at the same time, adjust itself to contemporary circumstances."[25] In so declaring, Hasan Imāmī's views were similar to those of Āyatullāh Burūjirdī in regard to the necessity of maintaining a distance between religion and politics. Imāmī, however, became the target of an assassination attack in 1951, probably organized by the Fidāʾīyān-i Islam, and this seems to have reduced him to quietism.

Individuals such as Imāmī could not have enjoyed the confidence and/or

---

*Vahīdī, who had received the ijazah-yi ijtihad and studied with eminent ʿulamā' in Najaf, was to become the naʾib-i tawlīyah in the 1970's.

respect of the Burūjirdī-led ʿ*ulamā*ʾ elite. Yet, the latter did not demur from entering into a tactical alignment with the government-connected clergymen to combat republicanism and secularism among the opposition forces in society. In the meanwhile, the elite could always satisfy itself that the injunction against political involvement comprised a sure method to deny movements led by such mavericks as Burqaʿī and Kāshānī from stirring up dissension and disorder.

As a matter of fact, Kāshānī began protesting at once against the new appointments which General Fazlullāh Zāhidī, the Prime Minister after 19 August 1953, had made to the Ministry of Culture, the National Gendarmerie and the National Police Force. But his protests were to no avail, and it is one of the remarkable features of this period that a man of Kāshānī's reputation in national politics could have sunk so rapidly into obscurity.[26]

An open sign of siding with the Shah after August 1953 was out of the question for the cautious Burūjirdī. This explains his failure to respond to Prime Minister Zāhidī's letter urging him to mediate between the regime and the various social forces of the country and thus help to heal the wounds of the past.[27] But, on the other hand, both Burūjirdī and Bihbihānī were available for more discreet cooperation, as witness their role in agreeing to try to mediate the conflict between Musaddiq and the Shah in April 1953 over the role of the monarchy in contemporary Iranian politics.[28] Tacit cooperation in the post-August 1953 era would not have been offensive to them.

Between September 1953 and August 1955 Āyatullāh Bihbihānī's name appeared very frequently in the press in a reversal of the previous practice of daily coverage of Kāshānī's doings. In late September 1953 a summary of Bihbihānī's interview with the French news agency appeared in the leading Tehran paper in which he stressed the importance of Islamic teachings for the nation's well-being; and he praised the regime's commitment to the technical education of the peasantry.[29] A few days later Bihbihānī's trip to Mashhad, touted ostensibly as a pilgrimmage to the shrine of Imam Rizā but doubtless also to coordinate views with Āyatullāh Kafāʾī and his colleagues on the clergy's role under the new regime, received extensive treatment in the press. The list of dignitaries on hand to receive him upon his arrival spoke volumes of this cleric's great influence in national politics.

Before his departure Bihbihānī had sent a telegram to the Shah urging him to implement the promise of Prime Minister Zāhidī to ban the manufacture and sale of alcoholic beverages. In deciding on this public means of communicating with the Shah, Bihbihānī was merely following up on a series of private discussions he had been having with regime officials, the last of which had been with the Minister of Labor, over cultural and educational questions.[30]

The Shah's reply to Bihbihānī contained expression of his "endless joy" at hearing about the Āyatullāh's impending trip to Mashhad and solicited the latter's aid in prayers at the tomb of Imām Rizā to aid him in governing the country and requiting the needs of the poor.[31] One is struck by the eager, effusive tone in the Shah's message, as well as his tactically alert reference to a subject close to the clergyman's heart: help for the impoverished faithful. As for the banning of liquor the Shah replied that he had submitted the bill to the cabinet for its presentation to the Majlis.

At approximately the same time as these developments, Āyatullāh Muhammad Alī Hibat al-Dīn al-Shahrastānī, a leader of the *mujtahids* in the ʿ*atabāt*, made what he termed a purely private trip to Iran. It would be an error to take this statement at its face value, given Shahrastānī's background and connections. It may reasonably be argued that Shahrastānī's role was to convey assurances to the Iranian people that the great *mujtahids* of the shrine cities in Iraq approved of the current regime in Tehran. Additionally, his journey may be interpreted as one during which he would seek to coordinate strategy and tactics with the ʿ*ulamāʾ* elite in Iran itself.

Shahrastānī's grandfather, Sayyid Mihdī ibn Abū al-Qāsim Shahrastānī, was a contemporary of the legendary Sayyid Mihdi Bahr al-ʿUlūm (d. 1801). The line led to Ismāʿīl Sadr al-Dīn, a minister in the court of Shah Tahmāsp I (ruled 1524–76). The family possessed extensive land holdings in Karbalāʾ (Iraq) and the Isfahān region. Branches of the family resided as well in Najaf, Kāẓimayn (both in Iraq), Kirmānshāh and Hamdān (two cities in Western Iran). The extent of the landholdings in the family qualified it as aristocratic; and, we are told, Ismāʿīl Sadr al-Dīn endowed so much land as *vaqf* in his time that despite the depredations to which they were subjected over the centuries by avaricious *mutavallī*s, the remaining properties at mid-twentieth century were yielding "millions" of *tuman*s [a unit of Iranian currency[to be disbursed for religious purposes.

As for Āyatullāh Shahrastānī, himself, we know that he did not avoid involvement in politics; rather, he seemingly cultivated contacts with the kings and rulers of Iraq in the inter-war period. He served as an official in the Ministry of Education during this time. Moreover, he headed the High Court of Cassation of the Jaʿfarī Rite. This activist clergyman had, additionally, traversed much of the Islamic world and had established extensive contacts in many Muslim nations.[32]

He now found himself on one of his several journeys to Iran, in the course of which he made certain pronouncements on the state of affairs. Alleging that he had always been removed (sic) from politics, he did express his regrets over the events that had overtaken Iran during the last two years (i.e., the tenure of Prime Minister Musaddiq). Because of his eminent standing, he was received by the Minister of Court; he also gave to understand that he expected an audience with the Shah. It is not surprising that his views should be sought on internal politics. Again, he suggested his ignorance of its details but offered that every where and in all his rounds with the ʿ*ulamāʾ* in Iran he had heard things that were "entirely in praise of the Shah."[33] Such expressions of support were of critical importance to the new government and uncertain Shah. On balance, these developments involving Bihbihānī and Shahrastānī suggest an ongoing consolidation of ties between clergy and state that bespoke an accommodation between them in the years following 1953. In this the government agreed to certain educational reforms involving greater Islamic instruction in the secular schools. It also acquiesced to the anti-Bahāʾī predispositions of the clergy in 1955. The ʿulamāʾ resources which they made available for the government consisted in the public statements already reviewed, as well as the more substantive use of their influence in generating anti-communist feeling in Iran. The crushing of the Tūdah Party in 1954 and 1955 had the wholehearted approval of the clergy. And advanced word that the Vatican was intending to host a Conference to Combat Communism in 1956 and hoped to invite the Iranian clergy to send a delegation were favorably received by Burūjirdī and Bihbihānī.[34]

THE ANTI-BAHĀʾĪ CAMPAIGN

Nowhere, however, does the clergy-state relationship articulate itself so sharply as in the issue of the anti-Bahāʾī campaign. Bahāʾism is a movement stemming from a schismatic break from Shīʿism in the first half of the 19th century. Because it broke from Shīʿism, rather than having antedated it (as had been the case for Judaism, Zoroastrianism and Christianity), it has been the target of fierce hatred on the part of Shīʿī true believers. In 1843 Sayyid ʿAlī Muhammad Shīrāzī (d. 1849) declared himself to be the Bāb (gate) to the hidden Imām. Thereby, he immediately precipitated a confrontation with the ʿulamāʾ, who disputed with him on doctrinal grounds and showed his knowledge to be deficient. The clergy vehemently countered his claims in practice, as well, causing his physical punishment and recantation. Initially, certain state officials appear to have extended their protection to the Bab—presumably on grounds of rivalry with members of the clergy—but later the government assented to his execution in Tabriz in 1849 in view of an internal rebellion that was engendered by his spreading influence.

Bahāʾism followed from Bābism as a convert to the Bāb's teachings, one Bahāʾullāh, declared that he was the manifestation of God on earth. Although he was in exile in Baghdad when he made this declaration (1863), his movement centered in Iran, where it threatened the ʿulamāʾ, who stood to be eliminated as a social entity if it were to triumph. Not only that, but the claims Muslims have made that, as the last revealed religion, Islam is consequently the most perfect—than which there is to be none superior—were called into question by Bābism/Bahāʾism. There is some record of ʿulamāʾ conversion to Bahāʾism in the mid-19th century; but in the main they execrated it. And, in a development presaging the 1955 anti-Bahā'ī campaign, it was they who took the initiative against Ba-hā'ism and tried to force the state to adhere to their position.[35]

A final element that served to render Bahā'ism suspect is the implication in the message it conveys of *universal* love and understanding. In this sense, the movement appears to be subscribing to a supra-national creed. The clergy has interpreted this as catering to foreign interests and needs, a serious development in their eyes which can only serve those seeking to destroy *Shī'ī* society in the manner of British and Russian efforts of the 19th and 20th centuries.

Yet, although such was the general orientation toward Bahā'ism on the part of the clergy, one must still ask why these events broke out in May–June 1955, which that year coincided with the holy month of Ramazān. One hypothesis holds that some elements of the *'ulamā'* were feeling a newly acquired self-confidence and therefore "wanted to make a horse deal between themselves and the Shah."[36] In line with this is the thinking that the government encouraged the campaign to distract attention from more serious problems, including acute economic difficulties.[37] Beyond this lay the difficulty the regime faced in harnessing the nationalist movement that had supported Musaddiq. It is not unlikely that the regime hoped that the clergy had become the legatees of the nationalist movement *sans* Musaddiq and his associates. Then, too, orchestrating a movement against the unpopular Bahā'īs could serve the useful purpose, from the viewpoint of the regime, of obscuring the fact that the negotiations with the Western Consortium of oil companies over the distribution of revenues of the National Iranian Oil Company (NIOC) were going to lead to disbursements to Iran that would be at an unsatisfactorily low level for the nationalists. Finally, there was the pending question of Iran's entry into the Baghdad Pact (actuated in October 1955). It would not be easy to accomplish this in the face of nationalist agitation; therefore, giving the *'ulamā'* headway on the Bahā'ī question seemed an appropriate means to secure their acquiescence, if not support, for a policy of foreign entanglement. Of course, this argument also inhered in the case of the NIOC-Consortium negotiations.

On 9 May 1955 the press carried the text of telegrams from Āyatullāh Bihbi-hānī to Āyatullāh Burūjirdī and the Shah in which he congratulated them both on the destruction of the dome of the Bahā'ī center in Tehran and its occupation by the military. Bihbihānī went as far as to call the Iranian army *artish-i Islam* (the army of Islam). Assuring the Shah that this action would elicit the most fervent support for him on the part of the faithful, Bihbihānī urged that henceforth the anniversary of that day be observed as a religious holiday.[38]

On the same day appeared Āyatullāh Buūjirdī's letter of thanks to the popular preacher, Abū al-Qāsim Falsafī. The gist of the letter was Burūjirdī's appreciation of the services Falsafī had rendered to Islam and also to "the independence of the nation and the preservation of the position of the monarchy, the state, the army and all the people of the nation. . . . '' The Bahā'īs, complained Burūjirdī, had developed good organization and expended vast amounts of money which unknown sources had contributed to them. For the hundred years of their existence, he lamented, the Bahā'īs had tirelessly propagandized against Islam, "which, of course, is a cause of the unity of [our] nationalism." And now, he charged, they were "secretly working against the monarchy and the state." He also attacked the Bahā'īs for what he alleged to have been an atrocity committed against an old lady and her children. Noting that the perpetrators of the deed were still at large, Burūjirdī drew the conclusion that the Bahā'īs consequently enjoyed "complete influence in the government." In closing, he expressed the hope that a general purge of Bahā'īs from all government positions would be implemented.[39]

Bihbihānī's allusions to the Iranian military as the army of Islam and Burūjirdī's remarks about the monarchy and Islam as the basis of Iranian nationalism were hardly fortuitous in the context of clergy-state relations. Burūjirdī served notice that he meant to equate the weakening of Islam with the enfeeblement of the country's independence and the power of the monarchy in his reply to Bihbihānī: Bahā'ī agitation had as its sole purpose to attack Islam and, therefore, to undermine "the independence of the country and weaken the position of kingship. . . . ''[40]

The Shah's reply to Bihbihānī affirmed the close bonds that the clergy had suggested existed between Shī'ism and kingship to the extent that he vowed that he would be faithful to his duty to propagate the laws of Islam of the Ja'farī rite in Iran, in accordance with the Constitution. However, the Shah made no reference to his personal feelings about the Bahā'īs and the current disorders in which they were allegedly implicated by the ' ulamā'.[41]

The next day the Shah met with five ' ulamā' who doubtless were representatives of Burūjirdī and Bihbihānī. These clergymen presented a petitition on behalf of their leaders which summarized the grievances already reviewed. At this gathering the monarch, pressed again to make his position public, declared that he had instructed the government to deal with the Bahā'ī issue in a way that would be satisfactory to both the ' ulamā' and the public. In the meanwhile, the representatives of the clergy had also been in touch with the cabinet and submitted its views to the government ministers directly.

Simultaneous to the meeting between the Shah and the five religious leaders, Sayyid Ahmad Safā'ī, a rūhānī deputy in the Majlis from the town of Qazvīn, was submitting a resolution to the parliament. This four article bill declared the illegality of the Bahā'ī sect and others like it because of their attacks on the security of the state; provided for a two to ten year prison term for those found guilty of membership; stipulated the sequestration of Bahā'ī property and its transfer to the Ministry of Culture, which would be empowered to disburse it in the construction and establishment of religious schools and Islamic propaganda;

expressed the commitment of the government to purge all Bahāʾīs from the regime and state administration.[42]

In Qumm, numerous visitations to Burūjirdī's home were reported. To be sure, it was Ramazān, and such contacts always increase at such periods of the year. But the reporters of the newspaper, *Ittilāʿāt*, suggested that the traffic of *ʿulamāʾ* to the home of the *marjaʿ -i mutlaq* was unprecedented. The request for an interview with Burūjirdī was turned down, but they learned that "the Āghā" was urgently pushing for the destruction of Bahāʾism and the seizure of their assets, which were to be used for the construction of *madrasahs* and mosques. His only reservation was that these steps be taken in an orderly way, without the shedding of blood.[43]

As these events were unfolding the government ministers were meeting behind closed doors to find an appropriate solution to the problem presented by the vehemence of the *ʿulamāʾ* assertions about the Bahāʾīs. The regime faced the dilemma of requiring clergy support for its internal and foreign policies but not wishing to lose control over events and be castigated by international opinion for its complicity in the anti-Bahāʾī campaign.

In assessing the government's behavior two points bear stressing: (1) the regime proceeded through administrative decrees, rather than by parliamentary legislation (as embodied in Safāʾī's draft bill; (2) it had to call off the anti-Bahāʾī measures short of the steps the *ʿulamāʾ* had hoped would be adopted. It did so because of international pressure and certain internal exigencies, to be mentioned below. The advantage of dealing with the matter administratively was that this provided the government with greater leverage than other means. The adoption of the Safāʾī bill as law, on the other hand, would have given the issue an air of finality to it that might have been, at best, inconvenient and, at worst, seriously damaging to the country's prestige. The repeated assertions by the Shah, the Prime Minister and other officials that this matter would have to be handled within the limits of the law[44] show that there was a concern about the dubious legality of depriving Bahāʾīs of their civil rights (article 1 of Safāʾī's draft) and seizing their property.

A fascinating feature of these developments, therefore, was that the clergy was consistently leading the way, and the government was holding back. It is clear that the regime did not want to take a decisive stand and tried throughout not to expose itself. This becomes evident on examination of the parliamentary proceedings of the priod. The *ʿulamāʾ* manifestly created the issue. The regime, presented with it, tried to take advantage of it for its own purposes. But the government constantly tried to minimize its participation in the anti-Bahāʾī effort. The significance of the *ʿulamāʾ* assertiveness in the face of government caution for future relations between clergy and state is that the religious elite entered the 1958-1963 confrontation with the regime in possession of a self-confident view of its influence in public policy. Even if they had not won all the points in 1955, the religious leaders obviously had managed to rivet the government's attention to their demands in general and gain its respect in the public policy arena.

On the day of the announcement that the Bahā'ī center in Shīrāz had been closed and put under military occupation (17 May 1955) the Minister of Interior met with Majlis deputies in a closed session of the parliament. Although the gathering took place *in camera,* a summary of the proceedings was published. Asadullāh ʿAlam, the Interior Minister, reminded the deputies that he had already informed them of the government's view that existing legislation sufficed to deal with the crisis. Therefore, it did not view with favor attempts at writing new law. ʿAlam's statement constituted a clear rebuff to Safāʾī and, hence, to the Burūjirdī-Bihbihānī coalition in whose name Safāʾī had been agitating. ʿAlam vowed that the government had already implemented and would continue to implement the existing laws to keep Bahāʾī propaganda "tightly" in check. He then read to the gathered deputies the text of a draft decree that he purposed to send to all the country's provincial and city governors in pursuance of the government's decision to put down all anti-religious manifestations and demonstrations.

Faced with the objection that the words Bahāʾism and Bahāʾī failed to appear in his draft and needed to be interposed so that the Ministry of Interior officials would clearly know where their duty lay, ʿAlam replied: the deputies should be assured that the governors and military authorities were well-apprised of their functions and knew precisely what to do, when and if the orders were given. Then, he elaborated the regime's reservations with regard to the further demands concerning a purge of Bahāʾīs from the machinery of state and the sequestration of their property. On the question of the purge, he noted, its implementation would have to proceed within the limits of the law; yet, he gave his word that the government did intend to move forward on this matter. Respecting sequestration of property, ʿAlam cautioned, it would have to proceed in any case with a view to "the laws of the country, international law, and preserving the prestige of the kingdom." Such statements well embody the minimalist position that the government had decided to adopt. In short, by refusing to specify the Bahāʾīs by name, by referring to the need to observe the law, and by invoking the matter of national prestige, ʿAlam seemed really to be telling the deputies that the government would not be stampeded into blanket endorsements of ʿ*ulamāʾ* demands.

Safāʾī, who was present, then protested that he had received a message from Āyatullāh Burūjirdī to submit legislation to proscribe the Bahāʾī sect, and this is the reason for his having introduced the four-article bill a few days earlier. At this point, Dr. Shāhkār, a French trained lawyer and layman, intervened to declare his satisfaction with regime efforts up to that time. But he proposed an amendment to the ʿAlam draft decree which he felt would obviate the government's anxieties over international repercussions and the need to proceed on the basis of legality:

The formation of sects which, *under the guise of religion,* spread disorder, and which have adopted the name of Bahāʾism *in order to implement political objectives* is proscribed, inasmuch as their existence is illegal and the cause of the dissolution of order and security; and since they contradict the true religion of Islam. In accordance with the Constitution, minorities of the official[ly recognized] religions of Christianity, Zoroastrianism and Judaism shall have complete freedom within the limits of the law. [emphasis added]

The closed session meeting ended with the decision to approve the Shāhkār amendment, whereupon the deputies readied themselves to attend the coming open session of the Majlis. At that session ʿAlam made a brief statement of government resolve and intent, but he again omitted mention of the Bahāʾī sect by name.

The text of the final draft of the ʿAlam decree was published on the same day as the press published the proceedings of the closed and open sessions of the parliament. True to the government's determination, specific reference to the Bahāʾīs was missing after all, notwithstanding the formulation in the Shāhkār amendment. Now, in the closed session ʿAlam had confided to the deputies that he had called for that meeting in order to consult with them; that he purposed to hold their counsel in the highest respect; and that he was prepared to do anything which was for the good of the country. Clearly, then, ʿAlam had ultimately chosen to regard the deputies' suggestions as exactly that: counsel and advice which he could use or reject, according to his own discretion.

Indeed, the final draft of the ʿAlam decree not only fell short of the ʿ*ulamā*''s demands, or even of the more moderate Shāhkār amendment (moderate insofar as the wording made it appear that the government's campaign was not against the Bahāʾīs *qua* religious sect but *qua* political movement that was fomenting public disorder); but, indeed, this final version even contained an implicit warning to the ʿ*ulamā*' and their followers that they had better not start any incidents. The decree stated:[45]

In conformity with Article 1 of the Constitution, the official religion of Iran is Jaʿfarī Shīʿism. In keeping with Articles 20 and 21 of the Constitution, anti-religious publications and the formation of societies and associations provoking religious and secular sedition and disorder are prohibited throughout the country. Therefore, in implementing the principles of the Constitution you shall take measures to dissolve those social centers which are causing religious and secular sedition and are the source of attack against security and order. Henceforth, you will take steps in all seriousness to implement this important duty with which you are entrusted in conformity with the Constitution and stop any kind of demonstrations or acts on the part of this type of groups, and which acts are prohibited by law.

At the same time, since taking steps in these matters and implementing the laws is the task of government officials, and since the intervention of individuals or groups having no responsibility will cause disorder and insecurity, therefore, it is to be remembered that you are fully empowered to take measures against any person who provokes the people to act against the security of the country, under the guise and in the capacity of struggling against deceiving sects, or [any person] who himself commits acts which produce the smallest tremor against public order and security, according to those provisions of the criminal code which anticipate such crimes.

The government's minimalist position proved too much for the clergy. Consequently, Safā'ī delivered a parliamentary statement two days later in which he underscored the regime's lack of a clear-cut policy. Since the advent of Husayn ʿAlāʾ to the post of Prime Minister (April 1955), the regime had been propagating the slogan of a war against corruption. Now, Safā'ī attempted to link the anti-corruption struggle with the Bahā'ī issue. The source of corruption in society today is irreligion, he noted. While some say poverty is its cause, and therefore a redistribution of land will go a long way toward its cure, he allowed, experiments of land redistribution to the peasants under the Musaddiq government showed only negative results: a decline in the standard of living. If irreligion is the source of corruption, the Bahā'īs constitute the fountainhead of corruption, he declared. The ʿulamāʾ and nation are grateful for the steps undertaken to date to resolve the problems created by them, but the clergy and Iranian people are looking for more decisive acts. "Don't say Mus . . . Mus . . . say Mustafā," he mused ironically. Then, more ominously: the government must deal with the Bahā'īs in the same way it has dealt with the Tūdah Party. Yet, it would not be possible to proceed in this manner on the basis of the decree of the Interior Minister, which was lamentably "brief and vague." The Constitution has been invoked as a weapon to put down irreligion, but the regime has failed to implement its provisions against the Bahā'īs, he asserted.

At this point, Mr. Jaʿfar Bihbihānī, the nephew of the Bihbihānī who had taken such a prominent place in the nation's public life since the overthrow of Musaddiq, intervened. Jaʿfar Bihbihānī was not himself a clergyman, although he obviously had close connections to the ʿulamāʾ —especially of Tehran. Evidently wanting to restrain Safā'ī from taking too extreme a position on behalf of the clergy, and thereby effectively isolating it, Bihbihānī responded: "Yes, they have, Sir." (I.e., the government had successfully implemented provisions of the Constitution against the Bahā'īs.)

But Safā'ī continued. He thanked the Shah for granting the request of Abū al-Qāsim Falsafī to shut down the Bahā'ī center in Tehran; but he insisted that a new law was necessary to destroy Bahā'ism as a movement. Āyatullāh Burūjirdī had been waging a struggle with the Bahā'īs for many years, said Safā'ī, but the regime has constantly made excuses for itself. The politicians used to say, he opined, that they were too busy with the oil question; but oil is no longer at issue. Government declarations could not escape specifically mentioning the Bahā'ī sect by name.

At this point, Safā'ī was interrupted by another deputy, Mr. Barūmand: "My dear friend, they did mention them and implemented [the law] against them." At this point, Safā'ī probably began to be persuaded that he was losing allies by persevering in these kinds of statements, so rather than belie the patent mendacity of Barūmand's rejoinder, he weakly concluded: "At any rate, they [the Bahā'īs] must be purged from the state apparatus."[46]

About three weeks later, he made a last attempt to convince the Majlis to pass his bill by introducing it in closed session. It had accumulated more than the 25 signatures necessary to bring it before the chamber, said Safā'ī. However, the Speaker of the Majlis, Mr. Sardār Fākhir Hikmat, finessed the issue by stating: "the Majlis should not take the lead in this matter." Actions against the Baha'is are not the task of the parliament, but of the state; the Majlis must not get involved in the affair. "We must, we shall, remind the government to do its duty in this regard," noted Hikmat. Parliament's role consisted of serving as the nation's conscience and behaving as gadfly should the need arise. The stand of the Speaker of the Majlis proved authoritative, and the matter was dropped.[47] However, the anti-Bahā'ī campaign was to spill over into the chamber in a totally unexpected way five days later. This episode threw into sharp relief the thoroughly explosive nature of that campaign and the passions it aroused.

The statement of Mr. Riżā Afshār, an unidentified member of the Majlis, on the need for a government of laws rather than personalized rule (hukumat-i fardī) began simply enough. The 'Alā' government had been drawing a large measure of criticism in the parliament, and Afshār's comments were thus not novel. The gist of his speech was that the will of Majlis deputies weakens noticeably toward the end of the session, when the Ministry of the Interior begins the process of calling upon the municipal anjumans (organizations) to draw up their election lists. Afshār commended a Burkean model of the role of an MP to his colleagues, noting simultaneously that "re-election fever" predominates when the commonweal ought to be uppermost in the minds of deputies. The consequence is attempts to please the Ministry of the Interior, rather than parliamentary constituencies; working in one's own interests, rather than those of the nation. Every time Majlis deputies commit themselves and their country to principles and a government of laws, up springs a handful of "weak and immature elements . . . bearded and ignorant infantiles who have lost touch with the pulse of our society. . . . " All we get from these elements are "auditory injections of such things as the "anti-corruption struggle" [the watchword of the 'Alā' regime], Afshār complained.

The remarkable reference to "bearded infantiles" was a calculated attack on the clergy, which he also attacked as "lying prophets and hypocrites" allied to certain cabinet associates. If preventing corrupt individuals from hindering the society's development is to have any meaning, then we should expect to see some ministers, senators, representatives and bureaucrats brought before the courts, Afshār exclaimed. At this point in his statement, heckling started up among some of the deputies in the chamber.

This seemed to provoke Afshār, who promptly commenced a stinging attack on the government's management of the anti-Bahā'ī attacks by the ʿ ulamā' and their supporters. The campaign had succeeded in spreading "insecurity, confusion, plunder, killing, attacks". It had "disgraced the peace-seeking peoples of Iran in the view of the outside world." Then, he emotionally delivered himself of a charge that brought down the house:

> This cabinet has toyed with the sentiments of the marājiʿ -yi taqlīd and has dealt insolently with the predilections of the . . . good people of Iran; and it has even failed to respect international undertakings and agreements . . . " [chaos in the chamber].

At this juncture, Jaʿfar Bihbihānī pounded his fist on his desk, shouting: "What has this government done? What sin has it committed to warrant these obscenities?" Dr. Jazā'irī: "These statements are not in the country's interests. They are lies and arrant mendacity."

Afshār: "This corrupt government, under the slogan of the anti-corruption campaign, has forcibly expelled groups of innocent people [from their homes] and gotten its license [to do so] from government offices, [deceitfully using] the name of the august person of His Majesty."

These further remarks of Afshār so infuriated Bihbihānī that he stood on his chair to shout, and then, on second thought, he began to rush the speaker's dais, screaming: "What are these words? What are these meaningless words?" As the tumult mounted, Jazā'irī and Safā'ī proceeded to mount their own mini-demonstrations against the speaker. Safā'ī became so agitated that his gown fell from his shoulders: "What is the religious institution to you? Who are you that you can mouth such obscenities? It is clear that Your Excellency is a supporter of the Bahā'īs. It is hideous." Other frontbench voices joined in the attack against Afshār.

Mr. Qanātābādī, defending Afshār: "What's going on? What is it to you?"

Dr. Jazā'irī: "The people know all of you, they know the thieves, the land grabbers (zamīnkhvārān) and the defenders of corruption." Safā'ī was incensed by the mention of the marāji-yi taqlīd and so pursued his attacks in that vein.

Dr. Jazā'irī: "When do you pray? When did you fast? When did you give khums (the Islamic tax on income)? What part of you is Muslim? You have spent all of your life thieving. Are you not ashamed?"

Afshār at that point asked permission to continue, but Bihbihānī shouted: "We will not give you permission to say such nonsense in this Majlis," and again he attempted to rush the speaker but was physically restrained. All the while,

Afshār's opponents continued to revile him. Sultān Murād Bakhtīyār: "Corrupt thief!"

Qanātābādī: "They are trying to terrorize the thoughts of the deputies in this Majlis. If a deputy cannot have freedom [of speech] in this Majlis, no one will have it outside."

Afshār then condemned the immaturity of the Minister of the Interior, whom he faulted for lacking exactly those qualities Persians admire in their leaders: distinction, knowledge, experience, qualification.

Safā'ī: "What are these words? What do you mean by bearded infantiles and beardless ones?" Then, Sardār Hikmat, the Speaker of the Majlis, intervened, warning Afshār that he must not speak of the Minister of the Interior in the way he had. Next, he turned to the deputies in the chamber and admonished them to hear the speaker out. When 'Abd al-Husayn Hazhīr, the late Minister of Court, had come to the Majlis and came under the fire of various deputies exercised by his pro-Bahā'ism, he, Hikmat, had defended his right to speak. Disagreement with the views of the speaker is insufficient reason to muzzle him. He then turned to Afshār and warned him against employing insulting language; to this Afshār retorted that it was the truth, not insults, that hung in the balance that day. Hikmat, for his part, invoked his authority and said that he would decide when a statement was insulting, and no one else; and Afshār had infringed parliamentary tradition.

Afshār: "Since we are determined to inspire our foreign policy with our internal policy' we are not going to turn the Ministry [of Interior] into a soccer field for young, unskilled and raw elements who, in protracted fashion, are set to dissolve the Majlis and draw up an election list for the 19th session in order to terrorize and threaten us."

Hikmat here interrupted Afshār's statements and condemned them as "all lies and pure fallacies" and "provocative." Bihbihānī chimed in that they constituted an insult against the Majlis itself. However, Afshār would not be deterred from his purpose. While noting that he had nothing personally against the Minister of Interior and was fond of him, he held that the incumbent was "unqualified in every sense of the word." Since 'Alam was a graduate of the Agriculture School of Karaj (a town to the West of Tehran), he should therefore have been posted to direct one of the departments of the Ministry of Agriculture in the provinces. He then intoned that Asadullāh 'Alam had no business being Minister of Interior, which is one of the most sensitive positions in the government. We ought to have expected Husayn 'Alā' to have understood this, he remarked reprovingly, but somehow the thought escaped him.[48]

The Interior Minister's dialogue with Majlis deputies resumed a month later when the indefatigable Ahmad Safā'ī asked the government to tell the parliament what measures had been adopted against the Bahā'īs in general and especially those against whom prosecution indictments had been handed down. In a hesitant beginning the Minister submitted his understanding that the discussion between government and legislature had been concluded to everyone's satisfaction and repeated his request of the Majlis not to intervene in the government's investigation. At this point, Mr. Mīr Ashrāfī, a landlord who had earlier attacked the ʿAlāʾ regime's "socialist" policies,[49] intervened: "Answer the question!"

ʿAlam: "The government has put a vigorous halt to all propaganda that conflict with the Constitution. Obviously, propaganda by the Bahāʾīs is not exempt from this." [Deputies: "Hear, hear!]

Shāhrukhshāhī: "Then why have they refurbished the house of Sayyid ʿAlī Muhammad, the *Bāb*, in Shīrāz?"

ʿAlam: "You have been given bad information. I can candidly declare that all propaganda centers that are contrary to the Constitution and the true religion of Islam have everywhere been identified and closed down." ["Hear, hear!"]

The Minister of the Interior repeated the government's insistence that it would deal harshly with any kind of unrest in the society, no matter what the source of stimulation of such unrest. The language and spirit of this position was to make the Bahāʾīs an unexceptional social force in the political system and therefore to remove the salience of Bahāʾī activities from the public consciousness.

ʿAlam: "But I want to say this to the Majlis. Taking steps in any matter, and particularly this one, must, in the first instance, meet the requisites of order and tranquility. ["Hear, hear!"] Therefore, the security forces and other state authorities have been given clear and strict orders vigorously to block any kind of step contravening order and to prevent measures taken under any guise that disrupt public tranquility. ["And a very good thing, too!"]

"And especially have we given orders that oppositional elements [to the government] of whatever stripe be prosecuted and punished."

Safāʾī: "But not to the point of punishing Muslims instead of Bahāʾīs!"

ʿAlam: "No, we will never do that. But establishing order and peace throughout the land and securing the people's tranquility constitutes the primary and most important duty of the state. We cannot show the slightest imperviousness to this. Therefore, I am sure that if the government deems it necessary, in this or any other connection, to take action to preserve order and peace, it will receive the support of the Majlis."

Mīr Ashrāfī: "Provided they do not shoot the people in front of the house of Sayyid ʿAlī Muhammad, the *Bāb!*"

ʿAlam: "My dear sir, they have told you the wrong things."

Mīr Ashrāfī: "Your Excellency's comments have not been convincing."

ʿAlam: "They have convinced the majority. You are in the minority. Is that my fault?"

Mīr Ashrāfī: You have brought embarrassment to this Sayyid [pointing to Ahmad Safāʾī]."

Safā'ī: "But you [Mīr Ashrāfī] have been embarrassed more [Laughter]."[50]

In spite of Safā'ī's attempts to use humor to mask his chagrin, it is clear that the 'ulamā' were not amused by these events.[51] Still, that they did not manage to influence the government to take stronger measures against the Bahā'īs should not obscure the fact that they had secured the following tangible gains: (1) the Chief of Staff of the Army and the Military Governor of Tehran had both participated in the destruction of the dome of the Bahā'ī center in Tehran, involving the government directly in the affair.[52] (2) the Minister of Culture declared in late June 1955 that religious instruction would be augmented, beginning in the fall of that year, in the public schools; particular stress was to be given to religious instruction in grades five and six at the primary level.[53] (3) The Military Governor of Tehran and the Chief of the National Police had issued proclamations concerning the closing down of movie houses, liquor stores and public music establishments during the first 15 days of Muharram (the first month of the lunar calender, during which observance of the martyrdom of Imām Husayn takes place). In previous years, such restrictions had not been given such publicity by the regime.[54] (4) The Shah had initiated ground-breaking ceremonies for the construction of a mosque on the campus of Tehran University;[55] (5) The regime had issued a constitution for a Religious Studies High School, which it intended as an integral part of the *dabīristan* (secular high school) system that had been developed under Riżā Shah, while also serving as a laboratory school for the Faculty of Theology.[56]

The members of the clergy were holding a number of meetings during early June 1955. Two key gatherings took place in Tehran. One session was held at the behest of Āyatullāh Ahmad Mūsavī al-Khvānsārī of the capital. Āyatullāh Bihbihānī accepted this invitation, the purpose of which consisted of drawing up a petition to present to the Shah "on behalf of the *hawzah-yi 'ilmīyah* of Tehran." Although no details as to what the petition addressed are available, probably the clergy elite saw this as a chance to press their advantage with the government and submitted a list of issues on which they desired action: welfare, education, upkeep and maintenance of facilities, public morality, regularized consultation with them by regime officials, etc.[57]

The second meeting took place at the initiative of a pious philanthropist, a certain Hājj Sayyid Riżā Fīrūzābādī. The importance of this conclave is suggested by the attendance of Āyatullāhs Bihbihānī and (Muhammad Riżā) Gulpāygānī; even Āyatullāh Kāshānī put in a rare appearance. Fīrūzābādī explained that he intended to use the vehicle of such gatherings in the future as a means to convey the views of the 'ulamā' to the Shah. He expressed the hope that the Shah would consent to meet with the clergy elite on a periodical basis so as to provide a better channel for the coordination of views between monarch and religious leaders.[58] The implication is that the Shah had not been paying enough attention to the latter, and it seemed important to the 'ulamā' to revert to the practice, common in Safavid and Qājār times, of routine and quotidian interaction between Shah and clergy. The practice of using the Minister of Court as intermediary apparently was an unsatisfactory one for the religious leadership, which wanted to broaden their actual contact with the ruler beyond the formal and peremptory salutations ceremonies on anniversaries that more and more were providing the occasion for meeting with the sovereign.

In neither event of these two meetings did the name of the Imām Jumʿah of Tehran come up. One might speculate that, insofar as the ruler had relied on that individual to be his clerical link with the ʿulamāʾ, Fīrūzābādī's and Khvānsārī's sessions amounted to an endeavor to consolidate clergy ties to the crown on their own terms. It would be misleading, certainly, to suggest that the ʿulamāʾ were approaching the variety of issues which have been surveyed above with a highly coordinated blueprint for action. Given the rather informal nature of the organizational structure of the religious institution, such could not have been the case. Instead, one should see these sorts of meetings as concurrent efforts to enhance the social standing and prestige of the clerical stratum. In this context, many interfaces of cooperation existed between clergy and state, as the discussion above has already brought out. And the trade offs between the two sides need not have been explicit, as is shown in the instance of ʿulamāʾ orientation to the oil question after 1953. Their failure to condemn the formula by which the NIOC and the Consortium agreed to divide petroleum revenues as a "reprehensible betrayal" of the nation's interests was no less valuable to the regime because it was *implicit* support.

On other occasions, clergy support for the regime seemed to be masked by the fact that ʿulamāʾ action was geared to a seemingly innocuous issue not related to the interests of the government and state. Yet, it could be argued that such action nicely dovetailed with such interests and thus provided an instance of clergy-state cooperation after all. A good example of this situation surfaced with the unanticipated *fatvā* issued by the *marjaʿ-i taqlīd* of Najaf, Āyatullāh Hibat al-Dīn al-Shahrastānī against mortification of the flesh during the observances of ʿĀshūrā that year. The *fatvā* declared that no religious foundation existed for the practice of cutting one's forehead, self-flagellation or other infliction of wounds to the body.[59] What seems significant about this *fatvā* is its particular timing. The annual observances of the martyrdom of Imām Husayn would nearly coincide that year with the anniversary celebrations sponsored by the regime of the defeat of Muhammad Musaddiq. Also, the Bahāʾī disturbances were still fresh in people's memories. The ʿAlāʾ government was especially concerned over the outbreak of violence, communal conflict and a generally uncontrollable situation. When Prime Minister ʿAlāʾ granted a press conference, he was asked if the regime were, indeed, worried that the ʿĀshūrā demonstrations would lead to violence. The reporter posing this question noted that ʿAlāʾ was very quick to respond, as though he had anticipated it.[60] And Shahrastānī's *fatvā* appeared about two weeks after the press conference, indicating a strong presumption of coordination between the 'ulamā' and the government. Reinforcing this suspicion was the fact that the military and security authorities announced, that same day, that any individual or individuals engaging in mortification of their bodies would be arrested. Of additional interest is the part that Shahrastānī had played in the days just after the overthrow of the Musaddiq government. It will be recalled that he had fulsome praise for the Shah and the policies of the new regime in the aftermath of the coup of 16-19 August 1953.

Perhaps the final support that must be mentioned that the 'ulamā' extended to the government was their attitude toward Iran's participation in the regional defense alliance system involving Turkey and Iraq (later to be called the Baghdad Pact). No public clergy reservations over an alliance linking the country with the hated British seem to have been raised at that time. Any regrets that they may have entertained they kept to themselves. One of the few "'ulamā'" manifestations of attitude was the parliamentary statement by the nephew of Āyatullāh Bihbihānī, Ja'far Bihbihānī, on 19 October 1955. It was inherently a difficult speech to make for this representative of clergy interests. His position skirted perilously close to the suggestion that the Islamic nation of Iran needed "Christian" support to sustain itself.

Bihbihānī's argument rested on three points: (1) the alliance was a defensive one, not aimed at commencing hostilities against any state; (2) Iran was a sovereign nation and its government had a right to enter into diplomatic agreements with any other nation-states in the international community; (3) the pact, itself, was justified, indeed foreseen, by the collective security provisions of the United Nations Charter. Bihbihānī sounded more like an international legal specialist hired by the government to represent its position than a spokesman for the 'ulamā'. Attacking Stalin and the USSR for deceit over the question of Soviet occupation of the country in the Second World War, he noted that the United Nations, the United States and the Iranian army had saved the country from falling victim to the annexationist designs of the Soviet Union.

The reference to the United States seemed motivated by this idea: the 'ulamā' need not fear foreigners; after all, they had helped the nation out in a time of stress; therefore, the idea of seeking their help in a military alliance ought not to come as a shock; perhaps if we had had such an alliance in 1945-46, Stalin would never have dared to lift a finger against Iranian Āzarbāyjān; and so on. In its fullest sense, then, the Bihbihānī speech may be seen as an attempt to clear the mind of the most xenophobic of the 'ulamā' of the simplistic notion that all foreigners were equally harmful to Islam. If it required a theoretical underpinning from Islamic argument, Bihbihānī's line of thinking presumably could have referred to the doctrine of necessity.[61]

This chapter has provided an examination of the social influence of the Iranian clergy during a period in which the power of the Shah was weak. It has demonstrated that the mutual needs of the ʿ*ulamā*ʾ and the state authorities brought the two into an alignment within which each side sought to promote its own corporate interests. It will be noted that from 1941-1953 the Shah's power was so attenuated that clergy-state relations were in fact a matter of clergy-state administration and clergy-cabinet interaction. After 1953 a more confident monarch began to make his own policy.

Although many different issues were at play in this period, those involving clergy participation in politics in the late forties and early fifties, the firm entrenchment of the Burūjirdī-Bihbihānī axis among the ʿ*ulamā*ʾ elite, and the anti-Bahāʾī campaign of 1955 effectively encapsulated the range of clergy-state relations in the seventeen year period under review. The clergy perhaps was taken by surprise at the rapid pace of developments between 1956-1958 which led to growing state power and the Court's growing insistance on *noblesse oblige*. Agrarian reform had not yet surfaced as an idea officials were taking seriously, but this was a time when the civilian planners of modernization of the calibre of Abū al-Hasan Ibtihāj (Plan Organization) and Hasan Arsanjānī (Ministry of Agriculture) were beginning to rise and/or be noticed.

Furthermore, the Shah was beginning his program to establish a secret police apparatus in the late fifties. Thus, although the clergy may not have recognized it at the time, it is the 1956-1958 period to which one must look for the seeds of the development that can be characterized as the bureaucratization of power in the 1960's-1970's.

CHAPTER FOUR

ʿULAMĀ'-STATE CONFRONTATION AND THE DEFEAT OF THE CLERGY, 1959-1963

PRELIMINARY SKIRMISHING OVER THE LAND QUESTION, WOMENS' RIGHTS, AND FOREIGN POLICY

On 13 February 1960 the highest ranking *Shīʿī* theologian, Āyatullāh Burūjirdī, wrote a letter to Jaʿfar Bihbihānī complaining about the land reform bill drafted by the government in late 1959 and submitted to the Majlis. This bill was ill-advised and against the *sharīʿah*, he declared. He strongly implied that the Shah's advisers were culpable of this misdeed, since he noted that the Shah would not have gone off on a trip abroad had he known that the bill would be submitted—a bill that not only contravened the holy law of Islam but the Constitution, as well. The *marjaʿ-i taqlīd* urged Bihbihānī to moot the matter in the Majlis; in response, Bihbihānī sent the Burūjirdī communication to the Speaker of the Majlis, together with a covering letter stating his own objections to the bill.[1]

This adverse reaction by the Burūjirdī-Bihbihānī coalition to the government's land reform bill marked a break in the cooperation between clergy and state in public policy. Yet, although it was the first truly public manifestation of clergy displeasure, signs of dissatisfaction had lain underneath the surface for some two or three years prior to this time. Dissatisfaction with the nature of the relationship probably had to do with *ʿulamā'* anxiety that the state's jurisdiction was growing too extensively. And while it is difficult to pin down exactly what the clergy may have grown to consider harmful to their interests, in general terms it concerned their earlier willingness to allow the state to determine what constituted social justice in exchange for concessions by the state to the clergy on a series of relatively narrow issues.[2] In terming the issues narrow, one cannot deny their importance to the *ʿulamā'*; but in the relative scale of things, the nature of social justice looms more significant since it is a question of the structure of political power in society.[3] The items conceded by the government to the clergy elite are familiar enough: augmenting the scope of religious instruction in the secular schools; closing down places of public entertainment on days of religious observances; reaffirming the Shah's commitment to uphold the faith; assisting in the construction of new mosques; permitting greater numbers of pilgrims to participate in the annual pilgrimmages to Mecca as organized by the Endowments Organization; etc.

In retrospect, the cooperation between ʿulamāʾ and state during the previous era should be seen as a tactical alliance between two groups with fundamentally different perspectives and vested interests. The opposition of the clergy to the land reform bill thus constituted a strategic difference between the way they saw the relationship of authority and society and the manner in which the political leadership viewed these matters. As Ann Lambton noted at the time when clergy opposition initially emerged:[4]

> The opposition of the religious classes [to the land reform bill of December 1959] was probably due not only, or even mainly, to obscurantism and reaction but rather to an instinctive feeling that the whittling away in one field by the temporal Government (which during the occultation of the hidden Imam is in the eyes of the orthodox 'unrighteous') of personal rights guaranteed by the divine law and the Constitution is likely to weaken the position all along the line. The tendency of the religious classes is to acquiesce in the exercise of arbitrary power by the temporal government; very occasionally, they are provoked to make a fleeting protest.

During the late 1950's, neglect of the clergy's needs and interests was reflected in the dearth of coverage of religious issues in the press.[5] The growing distress of the ʿulamāʾ that the regime wished to bypass them was strengthened by the conviction that the government under Manūchihr Iqbāl was cynically permitting high levels of corruption at a time when the trend toward increasing arbitrariness of rule seemed undeniable. Yet, as mentioned above, relations between clergy and state during the greater part of the decade had been relatively cordial. Burūjirdī had maintained contact with high government officials in this period;[6] and he had expressed his admiration for the Shah in warm and friendly terms.[7]

The protest of the high-ranking clergy to the land reform bill of December 1959 may have surprised some members of the government, in view of the background of clergy-state relations up to that point. The bill evidently, however, endangered the vital interests of the Shīʿī institution and the corporate requirements of the ʿulamāʾ elite. This bill did not represent the sole source of clergy opposition, however. It was simply the first issue over which their general dissatisfaction over the course of events was publicly expressed. Nevertheless, the Shah sought to restrict their hostility to the course of public policy to this one issue, important though it was. The Shah at one point disingenuously stated:[8]

I cannot understand Burūjirdī. He has plenty—more than he wants now. He should be above this. If the clergy must make such protests, why don't they complain about corruption? Or drinking? Or breaking the fast at Ramazān. There are many things in the law they never mention.

In inquiring into the clergy's reaction to the land bill of late 1959, care must be taken to differentiate among a variety of positions. The clergy did not react as a monolithic force. Low-ranking *mullās* in the rural areas followed the Burūjirdī lead because of that individual's eminence. But it would be surprising if there were not those among them who sympathized with the principle of land redistribution.[9] Again, no doubt the more distinguished *mujtahids* responded "instinctively" (Lambton) against the bill. But one could discern the makings of a "radical" position on this issue. Perhaps representative of the "radical" point of view among the religious leadership is that adopted by Sayyid Mahmūd Tāliqānī in October 1961.[10] Tāliqānī's assessment amounted to a stinging criticism of past practice with respect to land tenure matters, combined with a suggestion for a way out of the dilemma posed by the land problem. His somewhat complicated solution would have permitted the landowners to maintain their social standing, even while it would have enhanced the life's chances of the poor peasantry.

Tālinqānī attacked the policies of the Minister of Agriculture, Hasan Arsanjānī for merely having raised expectations without any follow through in actual implementation. Arsanjānī had come to his post with a great deal of fanfare, but very shortly after assuming office he was muzzled. Tāliqānī condemned the nation's political leaders for having "plundered" the lands of the *Imām*. The politicians had engaged in a conspiracy with a band of greedy landowners, in collaboration with functionaries in the offices of land registration, deeds and titles and the mayoralties of various cities in Iran. Their purpose has been to accumulate as much land in their hands as possible, Tāliqānī held. Then, this corrupt minority employs the religious tradition: *al-nās musallitūn 'alā amwālihim* (people are sovereign over their own wealth) as a legal shield to defend their actions and exclude others. He maintained that Iran's system of ownership of the means of production, distribution and exchange "is not based on the economic principles of the international schools [of economic thought] or on Islamic principles, but merely on the principle of pillage, plunder and economic chaos."

His solution to the problem of the deprived, landless peasantry focussed on the Islamic legal concept of "dead lands". In Iran at that time the following categories of land existed: *milk* (private property); *khālisah* (state lands); *vaqf* (endowments); *mavāt* and/or *bayirīyah* (dead and/or waste lands). Dead lands, once reclaimed, could, under Islamic law, be claimed as private property by the reclaimant.[11] His point was that the dead lands then held by the landlords comprised the key to the solution of the problem of landless peasantry; for once the peasants were given these dead lands to reclaim, neither could they be subject to landowner oppression nor would they continue to be destitute. Let the landowners keep those lands that they were sowing, ploughing and developing; but let them relinquish the *mavāt* and *bayirīyah* under their control to peasants intending to reclaim them.

As to the government's role, Tālinqānī suggested that it would consist of being a conduit for any contracts made independently by landowners and peasants in regard to the sale of lands, purchase of properties, and so on. Tāliqānī furnished no clue as to how peasants could, in fact, reclaim dead or waste lands on their own. His intent appeared to be to shatter what he held to be the myth about Islamic theory and practice in matters of land tenure. The *arbāb-ra° īyat* (landlord-peasant) relationship has no sanction within the Islamic system of law. The sole point in matters of land tenure that governs man's relationship to the soil within the Islamic framework is that man should develop the land and make it prosper for his use.[12]

The land bill of December 1959, ratified on 17 May 1960, remained inoperative because of numerous internal loopholes and faulty premises. Burūjirdī's opposition to it had also counted for a great deal. However, his death in late March 1961 produced a new situation in the country. Any hesitation the regime may have felt about pressing on with a new effort because of anticipated religious reaction was probably overcome by the disarray in ʿ ulamāʾ ranks with Burūjirdī's departure. The sequence of events that signalled the Shah's determination to press ahead with his program was as follows: on 9 May 1961 he dissolved the Majlis on the grounds that voting irregularities in the 1960 and 1961 elections had necessitated that move. He resolved that strong rule by decree had to replace the ineffectiveness and even corruption that characterized the previous parliamentary government. On 11 November 1961 he promulgated an edict ordering the government to implement the May 1960 land law. On 9 January 1962 the cabinet approved a new version of that law which eliminated most of its defects.

But riots had broken out at Tehran University, and the regime arrested Jaʿfar Bihbihānī and nine others on charges of incitement to riot. The protesters had been denouncing the suspension of parliament against the provisions of the Constitution.[13] The dissidents objected to the dissolution of parliament, maintaining that (1) it was cynical of the Shah to do so because he must have known about, and shared complicity in, the rigging of the elections; (2) in any case it was constitutionally illegal to suspend the Majlis indefinitely without expeditiously moving to hold new elections. The resulting rule by royal decree amounted to autocracy.

The regime's release of Bihbihānī only five days later suggested that the Shah harbored concern that the clergy might react to his arrest in a manner that would be manifestly adverse to his policies. He wished to preempt ʿ ulamāʾ countermaneuvers that might lead to a consolidated landlord-ʿ ulamāʾ alignment. Since certain landowners were also tribal *khān*s (chiefs), the specter of tribal elements participating in such an alignment must have been disturbing to the Shah, given the historical importance of that configuration of forces in previous periods of Iranian history.

Fear of clergy countermeasures must have been fueled by the memory of recent '*ulamā*' agitation against the re-emergent women's rights question. On 9 January 1959, Ja'far Bihbihānī's uncle, Āyatullāh Bihbihānī, had sharply attacked the speech in the Majlis by Hidāyatullāh Matīn Daftarī—the son-in-law of the late Muhammad Musaddiq—on behalf of women's enfranchisement. This set off a chain reaction among the Tehran clergy, and during a mourning service for a recently deceased senator of the Majlis, held at the Sipah Sālār Mosque on 20 January 1959, the popular preacher, Abū al-Qāsim Falsafī, bitterly denounced the emerging public discussions and debate on women's rights.[14] In that same month, Āyatullāh Burūjirdī received Prime Minister Iqbāl in Qumm and effectively vetoed the regime's plans for a woman's day parade in Tehran.[15]

It is not easy to say which of the four issues exercised the '*ulamā*' more: (1) the growing autocracy of the Shah; (2) the corruption of the regime; (3) women's rights; (4) the land law. Probably it is closer to the truth to suggest that the '*ulamā*' elite considered the various discrete issues to be inextricably bound up with one another. As such, each was an individual dimension of one great problem: rule without justice (i.e., *zulm*).

The matter most threatening to the material interests of the clergy was that of the land law. It is not that the land law would have meant the divestiture of private property from wealthy '*ulamā*' that caused the clergy its chief distress—although this may have been a factor in certain particular instances. Rather, the matter had to do with two other problems: (1) the impact of the law upon lands held by the clergy as *waqf*, the revenues of which supported mosques, *mad rasah*s, ceremonials, and clergy/religious student salaries, stipends, emoluments and pensions; (2) the *sharī'ah* stress on the sanctity of private property.[16]

Only a week after dispatching his letter attacking the December 1959 draft law to Ja'far Bihbihānī, Āyatullāh Burūjirdī received the Director-General of the Endowments Department at his home on 20 February 1960. At this meeting, Burūjirdī was reported to have issued instructions on "the maintenance and safeguarding of income from endowments;" the Director-General of the Endowments Department submitted to him a report on the measures taken by the Department in implementing the wishes of those individuals who had made the bequests.[17] In other words, the clergy leadership was trying to secure the *awqāf* from unwarranted seizure by the state, and at this early point in the development of the land question, they were succeeding in obtaining the government's cooperation. The fear was, from their viewpoint, that such cooperation would not last very long.

It may well be asked to what extent the clergy did own or control under the terms of *awqaf* under their administration land throughout the country. Regrettably, it is impossible to answer this question for a number of reasons, not the least of which is the absence of a reliable cadastral survey at the time when the land reform laws of 1960 and 1962 were issued. It is clear that in Safavid times the *'ulamā'* were among the largest landowners in the society. Lambton remarks:[18]

> Originally, they probably held this land as *mutavallīs* of *awqāf*, or by way of hereditary grants or *soyurghals*. In due course much of this land became private property. In certain parts of the country, notably Āzarbāyjān and Isfahān, the religious classes have continued to form an important element in the landowning class.

Although she does not provide details, this point of view is shared by other sources, which also do not furnish any concrete evidence of the extent of property holdings among the clergy.[19] However, the pattern of invasions and conquests, on the one hand, and the operation of the inheritance laws of Islam (which divide property among the heirs, as opposed to inheritance based on primogeniture) prevented the emergence of a hereditary aristocracy among the *'ulamā'*.[20]

In 1946, the Iranian journal, *Mīhan,* provided a rare glimpse into the relative socio-economic standing of the *'ulamā'* as a landholding stratum in relation to the aristocracy, merchants and professionals. If the report is accurate, one may conclude that the clergy comprised at the time of the journal's publication, a very important landowning element, at least in the Isfahān region, which was the area surveyed by the article. The classification of landowners by occupation is shown on the table on page 97.[21]

If this state of affairs prevailed in the Isfahān region at midcentury, it is reasonable to assume that it obtained a decade later when the land reform laws were being proposed and promulgated. The long list of *'ulamā'* families (three times as many clergy as any other social group) suggests how welcome the Burūjirdī and Tāliqānī positions were in central Iran in clergy circles.

The argument for land divestiture and distribution to the poor did have Islamic legitimation in the sense that Islamic law also holds that land belongs to the community. Yet, verses could be cited from the *Qur'ān* to the effect that social stratification had been intended by Allah as part of the terrestrial existence of mankind. The tension between private and community ownership had seen the hegemony of the former through the centuries of social life in Islamic lands. However, in the post-World War II period, the emergence of "radical regimes in the Middle East has been accompanied by commensurate changes in the interpretation of the *sharī'ah* in regard to property. The press in Iran, which of course was operating as an instrument of the Shah's government, was full of analyses arguing that Iran was not the first Muslim nation to begin consideration and implementation of land redistribution. The Shah, for his part, voiced his concern

Important Landholders in Isfahān Province
By Name and Social Category, 1946

Category	Surname
1. Aristocracy	Bāstān
	Vazīrzādah Khān
	Sadrī
	Amīn al-Dawlah
	ʿĀsif al-Dawlah
2. Merchants	Harīrī
	Malikī
	Misqālī
	Karbası
	Runāsī
3. *Ulamā*	Safavīyah
	Khalīfah Sultān
	Imām Jumʿah
	Pā Qalʿahʾī
	Bīdābādī
	Khīyābānī
	Khurāsānī
	Imāmī
	Jinābī
	Kitābī
	Mīr Muhammad Sādiqī
	Gulistānah
	Nawjūmī
	Munʿimī
	Zavārīʾī
4. Writers	Zarrīn Gulām
	ʿAtāʾī
	Shāhshāhānī
	Chāharsūn
	Shīrvānī
5. Physicians	Dubārahʾī
	Ahmadābādī

on numerous occasions about Iran's lagging behind "the caravan of civilization."

The reaction of the *ulamā* against the reforms of the early sixties has sometimes been explained merely as a function of their fear of losing control over their land. Yet, it is worth remembering that the Shah's six-point program of reform which he termed the "White Revolution" included not only the redistribution of land or the enfranchisement of women; it also entailed the creation of a Literacy Corps (Sipāh-i Dānish), the nationalization of the forests, the sharing in business profits by the workers of industrial and other enterprises; the sale of government owned factories to finance the land reform program. Of these additional measures the ʿulamāʾ risked serious loss of their influence in the rural areas of the country by the establishment of the Literacy Corps. The elementary religious schools (maktabs) continued to be the only source of education for many villagers in the remote regions of rural Iran. Although secular education had spread dramatically over the years, most of the growth had been registered in urban centers and areas of population concentration. The Literacy Corps was specifically intended to fill the need for unavailable teachers in the outlying regions: precisely where clergy influence had continued to wax.[22]

Nationalization of the forests came under some suspicion in general (and not specifically on the part of the ʿulamāʾ) in the same context as the overall suspicion directed by nationalists toward what they viewed as a corrupt regime: illegal appropriation and consumption of resources. Even the seemingly benign plan for workers' shares in business profits was perceived in some circles as a device by which to enable the Court to pressure businesses to allow regime officials to "muscle" into their enterprises. According to the logic behind this line of reasoning, the regime could make it known to compliant entrepreneurs that it would not expeditiously implement the profits sharing scheme in their case if a certain portion of the enterprise would be reserved for its officials.

But, of course, the political reasons for the opposition of the clergy were equally fundamental: arbitrary rule; the granting of extraterritoriality and, more generally, foreign control of certain aspects of the economy; the nation's policy in the Arab-Israel conflict, according to which oil was sold to Israel and cooperation between the two countries' intelligence apparatuses took place.

The foreign policy issues seem all the more interesting in view of the fact that even after 1959 the clergy and the state continued to share some common interests on that level. The anti-communist campaign had abated in the latter part of the fifties, but as the regime of ʿAbd al-Karīm Qāsim (ruled 1958–63) in Iraq began to encourage communist party activity in that country during the fall and winter of 1958 and 1959, tensions between Baghdad and the Shīʿī community of the ʿatabāt began to rise. Things reached such a pass that in late winter 1960 one of the leading religious dignitaries in Najaf issued a fatvā execrating communism.[23] Tehran no doubt welcomed this fatvā because of its own continuing concern with the underground Tūdah Party, whose activists might have received encouragement from Qāsim's patronage of the Iraqi Communist Party.

The Shah's government also had an interest in ʿulamāʾ support of its policies toward Egypt. When Iran broke diplomatic relations with the UAR, the clergy demanded, and received, consultations and explanations for this démarche.[24] The government explained its position in terms of Cairo's depiction of the Arabness of the Persian Gulf and of the oil-producing province of Khūzistān, which Egypt termed respectively the Arabian Gulf and Arabistān.

The break in relations with Egypt placed the regime in a nettlesome situation because the clergy found it difficult to accept the trading relationship that Iran had evolved with Israel. The Rector of al-Azhar had already, in 1959, promulgated his *fatvā* recognizing Jafarī Shīism as one of the legitimate Islamic sects and schools of law. This had met with favor among the Iranian *ùlamā*, despite their own long-held feelings of resentment toward the *Sunnī*s for their persecution of the *Shīàh* over the centuries. The Shah had, moreover, encouraged the efforts of one, Muhammad Taqī Qummī, to bring the *Sunnī* and *Shīʿī* peoples together. Qummī had been Secretary-General of a society known as the Dār al-Taqrīb bayna al-Madhāhib al Islāmīyyah (Organization for Rapprochement Among the Islamic Sects) and had met with the Shah a number of times over the years.[25] Burūjirdı's cautious approval of the idea of rapprochement led him to appoint his own emissary (Qummī was too "political" and overly identified with the Court), one Āyatullāh Khalīl Kamarah'ī, to go to al-Azhar for the purpose of dialogue and propagandizing the message of Shīʿism.[26]

Shaykh Shaltūt, Rector of al-Azhar, discomfited the Shah by sending him a telegram questioning Iran's "pro-Israel" policy, as he termed it. Benefits could accrue, were he to push the rapprochement effort with *Sunnī* Islam, in the possible improvement in relations with Egypt and Iraq. The ruler responded with the convenient legalistic argument that Iranian recognition of Israel was only *de facto*, not *de jure*. He also shrewdly reminded Shaltūt that recognition was extended in 1950 and reaffirmed in 1951 "as you know, by the government of Dr. Musaddiq."[27] Yet, attempting to score debating points in this fashion could not detract from the anxiety of the regime over the revival of deep-seated anti-foreign sentiment in religious circles. It had been Āyatullāh Kāshānī who had successfully stoked the fires of anti-British emotions in the late forties and early fifties. Relations with Israel were later to become a powerful source of conflict between the Shah and Āyatullāh Khumaynī after the mid-sixties. But there was deep resentment of it already in the ranks of some of the less political *Shīʿī rūhānī*, such as, for example, Āyatullāh Āl Kāshif al-Ghitā.[28]

DEEPENING CONFLICT BETWEEN CLERGY AND STATE

By late 1961 and early 1962, the Shah had committed himself to his reform program in a manner that suggested he would no longer hesitate in the face of clergy reaction. He had on numerous occasions expressed the belief that his reforms were entirely compatible with, indeed, foreseen by, the "true religion of Islam." His argument was that the Islamic trinity consisted of piety, justice and equality. Admitting the first to be the appropriate sphere of the clergy, he identified his efforts with "justice and equality, which we are trying to establish in this country." His efforts, he alleged, would make it impossible for people any longer to claim that Iran's political economy is a feudalism that is controlled by "one hundred, two hundred, a thousand families."[29]

The leaderless *Shīʿī mujtahids* were unable to respond to the regime's line with a single coordinated effort. Not only had Burūjirdī's death in March 1961 stunned Shīī Islam and caused an outpouring of grief and mourning; but the clergy feared that the regime would interfere in the process of selecting his successor(s). In Iran there was a number of distinguished *mujtahids*, but none could replace him. The tradition had evolved among the *ūlamā* 'elite that periodically a ''renewer'' would emerge to revitalize the faith almost singlehandedly. In the 19th century, these individuals were Shaykh Murtazā al-Ansārī (d. 1864) and Mīrzā Muhammad Hasan al-Shīrāzī (d. 1894). Burūjirdī's name had been mentioned in this tradition. But now, none could convincingly claim *a'lamīyyat* (superior knowledge in matters of law) over his colleagues.

Several senior clergymen survived Burūjirdī. These included the three *mujtahids* of Qumm: Āyatullāh Muhammad Kāzim Sharīʿatmadārī, Āyatullāh Muhammad Rizā Gulpāygānī, Āyatullāh Shihāb al-Dīn al-Marʿashī al-Najafī. In Tehran, the leading candidate was Āyatullāh Ahmad Khvānsārī. In Mashhad, there were two possibilities: Āyatullāh Ahmad Kafāʾī Khurāsānī and Āyatullāh Hādī Mīlānī. And in the shrine towns in Iraq, there were Āyatullāhs Abū al-Qāsim Khūʾī, Hibat al-Dīn Shahrastānī, Muhammad Husayn Āl Kāshif al-Ghitāʾ, and Muhsin Hakīm. Lesser possibilities included Rūhānī and Khumaynī of Qumm and Shāhrūdī of Najaf. The Court sought to enter the lists of the succession to Burūjirdī by pushing the candidacy of the learned Hakīm:[30]

> On the death of Burūjirdī, the Shah sent a telegram of commiseration to Āyatullāh Shaykh Muhsin al-Hakīm . . . thereby intimating the desirability of his succession to Burūjirdī. Doubtless, it was hoped to lessen the importance of Qumm and prevent the emergence of a center of clerical power within Iran. A *mujtahid* resident in Najaf—one moreover of Arab birth—might be thought unlikely to be intimately aware of and concerned with the affairs of Iran.

The Iranian *mujtahids*, had they wished to do so, could have thereupon invited Hakīm to take up residence in Qumm. For there could be no doubt that they desired that city for their ''capital,'' as it were, and could not have wanted the undoing of the work of Hāʾirī and Burūjirdī in elevating Qumm to its current stature. Hakīm stayed in Najaf, therefore, until his death in 1970. The government did not continue its efforts on behalf of any candidates until Hakīm's death, trying steadfastly to ignore the affairs of what it increasingly termed ''reactionary'' clergy.

The pattern of *ʿulamā'* behavior at this time enables one to suggest the existence of a number of factions in their midst. Of the four different groupings, the ''radical'' faction may be treated first. This faction was led by Āyatullāh Rūhullāh Khumaynī, Āyatullāh Mahallātī Shīrāzī, Āyatullāh Sādiq Rūhānī of Qumm and Āyatullāh Mahmūd Tāliqanī of Tehran. Khumaynī's prominence rested on the fact that he was a *marjaʿ-i taqlīd*, although there can be no contesting that at the time of these events he was considered a junior colleague at this rank by his associates. This designation probably rested on the fact that he had not written as much as the others, his major work to that point having been *Kafsh al-Asrār* (Revealing the Secrets), which he had published in the early post-Riżā Shah period. An additional reason for his somewhat lower status may have been that he had taught philosophy,[31] and as such he was one of the few to do so. Philosophy had long since been regarded with misgivings among the basically conservative teachers of the *madrasah*s.

The objective of the "radicals" was to establish Islamic justice, and therefore their position was no different from that of other groups. It was in their strategy and tactics that it is possible to see elements of a radical political line. Thus, this faction vocally advocated the establishment of a genuine parliamentary system in which the masses could make their voices heard in public policy. It advocated strict limitations on one-man rule.[32] The radical quality of this faction's position was also a function of their demands for an end to social exploitation of the poor and corruption in high places. Khumaynī has been especially associated with sympathy for the impoverished masses, whom he tirelessly was describing as *maẓlūm* (oppressed) and *bī gunāh* (innocent). His solution for improving their socio-economic conditions were not specific, but he did condemn what he viewed to be the government's over-commitment to urbanization, industrialization and over-reliance on foreign investment. An unmistakably radical rhetoric strenuously asserted the "plundering of the nation's wealth" by "traitors" in the government allied to "imperialism." At the same time, this faction was not revolutionary in the early 1960's. It did not advocate workers' councils, nationalization of the economy, enfranchisement of women and their right to work in the market. Neither did it seek the violent replacement of the stratification systems of class, status and/or power in Iran.

A second group among the clergy may be identified as social reformers. This element was less openly political in its activities, concentrating more on social and educational problems of the clerical institution. Nevertheless, it was a most consequential factor and had a profound impact on reform thinking among religious studies students and some *ʿulamāʾ* who were impatient with traditional methods of thinking and organization within the religious institution. This faction was led by Ayatullah Murtażā Muṭahharī, who was assassinated by a group called the Furqān in April 1979, some three months after the departure of the Shah from Iran. But in the early sixties, Muṭahharī was a professor at the Faculty of Theology of Tehran University and a respected contributor to symposia and works on the interfaces of Islam and social matters. Some of the other members of this group included Sayyid Muḥammad Bihishtī (who, like Muṭahharī, was to enjoy high position under the revolutionary regime of Khumaynī after January 1979); Muḥammad Ibrāhīm Āyatī, Husayn Mazīnī, Sayyid Murtaza Shabistarī, and, ultimately, Dr. ʿAlī Sharīʿatī. This group had close relations with Āyatullāh Tāliqānī, of the "radical" faction of the *ʿulamāʾ*; in addition, it was on very friendly terms with Engineer Mihdī Bāzargān (Prime Minister of the Provisional Government of the Islamic Republic of Iran after January 1979). Bāzargān and Tāliqānī, moreover, had established a cordial relationship in their joint struggle against the monarchical regime in the mid-fifties; and they had jointly been sent to prison for their "anti-state" activities during the course of that opposition. (for more on this group and its basic positions on the social issues of the time, see Chapter Five, below.)

The "conservative" wing of the ʿulamāʾ was, of course, the legatee of the heritage of the late Āyatullāh Burūjirdī. This was the powerful Qumm establishment, with its lines of authority to the crucial segment of the clergy: the preachers.[33] Practically all of the grand mujtahids discussed above in connection with the succession to Burūjirdī should be placed in this group. Some members filtered in and out of this group and the reformists just mentioned. For instance, Āyatullāh Sharīʿatmadārī was among those arrested by the government in early June 1963—at the height of the worst riots against the regime since the Musaddiq period. But Sharīʿatmadārī was not a "radical," despite his arrest.[34] Perhaps the quintessential conservative marjaʿ-i taqlīd during the 1963 demonstrations was Āyatullāh Mīlānī of Mashhad. He had strongly come out in favor of a restoration of order during the peak of the riots. This is not to say that the other mujtahids opposed a return to tranquility and peace. But Mīlānī, who was joined by the learned ʿAllāmah Muhammad Husayn Tabāʾtabāʾī Qummī, was the only highest-ranking clergyman to do so without qualification.[35]

The conservatism of this faction stemmed from the practice of Āyatullāh Burūjirdī during his 15-year tenure at the head of the Qumm hawzah (1946–61) to stay out of the public policy arena. It also had a good deal to do with Burūjirdī's already discussed cooperation with the state during the 1953–59 period. The grand mujtahids, under his leadership, apparently felt satisfied during this six year interval, that they counted for a great deal in the nation's social life. Burūjirdī could say to himself that perhaps for the first time since 1925 the clergy could hold their heads up high. True, with the exiling of Riza Shah in 1941 clergy fortunes improved substantially. But all in all the 1941–53 time span was too chaotic to satisfy the demands for stability among the mujtahids as the only appropriate context for the propagation of the faith (tarvīj-i dīn). The leftists and anarchists were too active in that period to suit the Burūjirdī faction. For that reason the 1953–1959 era was more of a "golden age" for them. And now, if the government seemed to be commencing a time of unjust rule, then the clergy would stand firm (but without taking any organized action). Burūjirdī's death in the middle of this 1959–63 confrontation shook the Qumm establishment and left an opening for the younger, more radical, Khumaynī to step in. The "conservatives" were in disarray, but the "radicals" were in the minority and did not have the vital support of the ʿulamāʾ establishment. Even though the riots of 1963 were led by Khumaynī, he was at that time an unknown figure to the National Front organization in Tehran, which had continued to operate off and on after the coup that overthrew Dr. Musaddiq.[36] As a consequence, despite the fact that extensive demonstrations took place in dozens of Iranian cities that spring, the Khumaynī faction among the clergy and the National Front failed to coordinate their activities.

Finally, the faction of *ulamā* ' that was willing to cooperate with the Court should be mentioned. The Imām Jum'ah of Tehran somehow had managed to keep out of the limelight of the conflict between the clergy and the regime during these times. In fact, ever since the early 1950's this individual appears to have all but vanished from the social and political scene. Others in this grouping including Āyatullāh Mahdavī, whose picture appeared in the press voting "yes" in the national referendum of 26 January 1963 on the "White Revolution";[37] 'Allāmah Vahīdī, a Senator and *nā'ib al-tawlīyah* of the Sipah Sālār Mosque; Muhammad Taqī Qummī, director of the Dār al-Taqrīb in Cairo; 'Abbās Muhājirānī, a functionary within the Endowments Department; and possibly Hujjat al-Islam Muhammad Riżā Bihbihānī, who led the clergy delegation that congratulated the Shah on the occasion of the Iranian New Year on 21 March 1963.[38]

The range of involvement of the *ulamā* ' in the crisis of 1962–63 included: (a) support for the government; (b) public neutrality, but privately expressed opposition; (c) qualified verbal public opposition; (d) open and clearcut verbal opposition; (e) outright clashes with the military and police. The great mass of the clergy may be placed in categories b, c. Naturally, the regime officials tended to downplay the relative proportion of the *ulamā* ' that participated in the demonstrations and other forms of protest; or else, they implied that the bulk of the clergy was pro-regime.[39]

Movement among categories b, c and d took on significant proportions, one may surmise. Information about the nature of this movement is scarce, but the behavior of Ja'far Bihbihānī may be representative. Impelled to abandon his formerly pro-regime stand (his speech on the Baghdad Pact in the Majlis in October 1955, q.v.) by Burūjirdī's note against the land bill of 1959, he was arrested in January 1962 for instigating anti-regime riots at Tehran University. Some of his followers clashed violently with the police, although Bihbihānī himself contained his behavior to verbal assaults against the government's policies. After a brief detention and interrogation, he was released, and, chastened from his experience, he then abjured further public protest. His release had the makings of a compromise reached with his uncle, Āyatullāh Bihbihānī, who may have vouched for the silence of his nephew in exchange for his freedom. There were signs of further compromises some five months later, in June 1963, when the government released some 27 *ulamā* ' who had been arrested in the course of the last few months.[40] Among those whom the regime arrested, albeit for a very brief time, was the grand *mujtahid* of Qumm, Sharī'at-madārī.[41] Khumaynī, himself, was arrested in the wake of a series of fiery speeches at the

Fayzīyah Madrasah in which he articulated practically all of the grievances of the *ulamā* that have been set forth above. He was seized at his home in the early morning hours of 15 June 1963 in order to avoid the Qumm crowds that surely would have attempted to restrain the authorities from arresting and dispatching him to Tehran. Thence, he was sent to exile in Turkey where he stayed until October 1965, when he took himself to Iraq and resided in Najaf until the early fall of 1978.

The Shah attempted to appeal directly to the masses during the height of these disturbances. His regime underwrote the costs of bringing masses of rural people into the cities for carefully orchestrated pro-regime demonstrations. In public speeches, he deliberately chose phrases invoking the themes of ethics and social justice from the *Qur'ān* and the traditions of the behavior of the prophet and *imāms*. At one of the bitterest moments of the conflict with the *ulamā* the Shah travelled to the bastion of the opposition and personally transfered titles to lands in the Qumm district to peasants. He denounced the clergy as reactionaries who did not want to heed the demands of Islam for equality and asserted: "No one can claim that he is closer to God or to the *imāms* than I am."[42] The Prime Minister, Asadullāh ʿAlam (who had been Minister of the Interior during the Bahāʾī crisis of 1955, q.v.) alleged that a number of landlords had bribed the clergy and offered documents purportedly detailing the collaboration of these two social strata.[43]

Yet, no *fatvā* had ever been issued by a *mujtahid* against the land reform program; and the government pointedly ignored queries demanding that it produce one.[44] Instead of engaging in such blatant forms of protest as the issue of *fatvās* judging land reform as *harām* (forbidden), the *ulamā* response was typically more indirect and subtle. For example, in the Qumm region a number of clergymen from the shrine city are said to have met with the *mutavallī*s of *awqāf* in and near Qumm in order to urge them not to carry on the tilling of the soil or the harvesting of the crops. The *mutavallī*s then directed the supervisors (*mutasaddī*s) of these endowments to cancel plans for sowing 200 *kharvār*s (equal to 50,000 kilograms) of wheat in the Zanbīlābād *vaqf*.[45]   ·

Lack of data concerning the range of clergy behavior during the 1962 and 1963 disturbances prohibits a rigorous analysis. Most of the observations have been stated in the form of generalized allegations. Even the most sustained "analysis" presented by the government of the clergy-state conflict remains at a high level of generality: a series of expository editorials in the pages of the leading Tehran daily, *Ittilāʿāt*. The articles attempted to outline the proper role of the clergy in society; and they also provided some information as to what its actual behavior had been in the last two years. In summary, the argument consisted of injunctions to the *ulamā* to confine themselves to matters of piety and homiletics regarding individual ethical conduct. Nothing was mentioned about *valāyat; al-amr bi al-maʿrūf wa al-nahy ʿan al-munkar;* or even the social role of the *imāms*. It was as though the editors of the paper had never heard of *marjaʿīyat* or *ijtihad*. A highly suspicious clergyman might even see in the *Ittilāʿāt* arguments the seeds of an incipient return to the Akhbārī position that Shīʿism did not really need *mujtahids*; that all that was needed was for the people to obey God and the prophet; and that if the people had to follow "those in authority among you" (*ʿulā al-amr minkum*), then the "those" had better be secular, not religious, leaders. Finally, as to the tone of these articles, it was didactic and assertive. They were more notable for how they were trying to cast the issues in question, rather than the logic with which it was done.

THE REGIME'S VIEW OF THE PROPER CLERGY ROLE IN SOCIETY

Ittilāʿāt declared that it was necessary to investigate the proper role of the clergy in society in view of the recent unrest; its observations were inspired, it stressed, by a series of letters to the editor by "well-meaning" citizens expressing concern about the growing gap between the religious and political spheres.

The first editorial divided the *ʿulamā'* into two groups, just as the letters it had received had bifurcated them into two camps.[46] But *Ittilāʿāt* disagreed with the notion, advanced by these letters, that the numbers of clergymen in the two groups, pro- and anti-regime, were equal. The *ʿulamā'*, it stated, are, after all, the guardians of the *sharīʿah;* and "nothing has been done against the *sharīʿah* in Iran." Every element of the six-point reform program of the Shah had been already implemented in other Islamic countries, it maintained. Therefore, unless Iranians are prepared to argue that Islam is different at home than in Syria, Iraq, Jordan, Algeria, Pakistan and other lands, then the experience of these countries is relevant for Iran.

In fact, it went on, "We Shīʿah are more progressive, even, than other Muslim sects. . . . " It therefore behooves Iranians to be in the vanguard of social reform, rather than in its rearguard. Only some unreconstructed reactionary *ʿulamā'* object to Iran's modernization, it observed. These individuals oppose radios, television, the cinema and similar technological signs of progress; and they are perfectly entitled to their views. Only let them not mix their personal tastes and preferences, *Ittilāʿāt* admonished, with the contents of the *sharīʿah*. For if they do, they will misguide Iranian youth into the warped belief that Islam in their country was appropriate only to the times of Imām Husayn but irrelevant for their own times. In fact, the paper continued, Islam, and all monotheistic faiths, are timeless, and therefore proper for every age in the evolution of human history.

> By this same token, religion is a matter apart from politics. Politics is an everday term, religion an eternal one. Politics says one thing today, something else tomorrow. Religion says the same thing—and none other than it—yesterday, today, tomorrow and always.

The article concluded with an admonition against employing religion to block progress. In the medieval history of Europe, the opposition of the Church to science ultimately failed. But if Muslim leaders succeeded in blocking Iran's technical and scientific achievements, they would have much to answer for to the masses, whose deprivations would then be due to clergy recalcitrance. The learned men of the religious law in Iran ought to realize, the editorial concluded, that Islam and modernization can be mutually supportive. A glance at the fortunes of the Christian Church in the West, where industrialization has developed to the greatest extent in the world, will show that this Church has never been stronger.

To summarize: (1) only some clergymen oppose social reform; (2) these confuse their preferences with the *shari̇‘ah;* (3) the regime's policies accord with the *shari̇‘ah;* (4) the retrograde clergy risk alienating youth from Shī‘ism; (5) religion and politics must be separated because (sic) Islam is timeless; (6) the Western experience shows that religion and science are natural partners.

While the first thesis was undoubtedly correct, the second purposefully missed the point. The *‘ulamā’* objection was not to modernization but to the consumption of resources by this elite as the modernization drive called forth the mobilization of national and political resources in a new way. Yet, the charge carried the seeds of a half-truth, since there probably were some among the clergy who did frown on the concept of modernization. Nevertheless, the bulk of the opponents of the Shah's White Revolution among the clergy appear to have opposed not the *concept* of modernization but the particular manner in which this regime's program was to be implemented. For them, therefore, "the fundamental issue was a feeling, justified or not, that the use of arbitrary power by the government had exceeded all reasonable bounds."[47]

The fourth thesis was a shrewd reversal of the charge levelled by the *‘ulamā’* against the regime: that its corruption would alienate youth against their own national heritage and suborn them with material compensations. That this was a tactical argument may be seen by the fact that if youth had been alienated from Shī‘ism by the attitude and actions of the clergy, the regime would have not been discomfited. The asserted logical connection between the eternal nature of Islam and the consequent need to keep it immune from the quotidian mendacities that are supposedly inevitable in politics as a vocation was a blatant effort to confine the clergy to questions of piety and ritual. Finally, the analogy to Christianity in the flowering of Western material achievements did not seem clearly thought through. Since even if it were the case that Christianity was never so strong as at that time, in what way was this caused by Western industrialization. The existence of a correlation does not prove cause and effect. Furthermore, among the objections of the *‘ulamā’* was precisely the idea that Western materialism had proved a corruptive influence throughout the world. Yet, here was *Ittilā‘āt,* extolling its virtues.

In a second editorial, an especially tendentious argument was presented concerning the growth of Christianity as a great force in the contemporary period. The medieval Christian Church coerced and intimidated its faithful, the argument maintained. As evidence, it pointed to the Spanish Inquisition. In the 20th century, however, the Christian Church rests on the solid bedrock of volunteered belief. Fortunately, the paper continued, the reactionary stand of the Christian priesthood in the Middle Ages has no parallel in Medieval Islam; the *'ulamā'*, in other words, did not experience the corrosion of their ethical values and so escaped the fate of the *curiae* in the Church. But, the essay warned, the foundations of religious belief in Iran had become corrupted, and if things continue in this train, the clergy, too, will become corrupted. The clergy had better respond appropriately to the impiety and disbelief that had set in. The editorial sounded a tocsin for the clergy to man their pulpits and fully involve themselves in matters of ethics and worship (*'ibādāt*). "Since the greatness and power of the *'ulamā'* is fully and totally connected to the degree of public *faith* and *belief,* the more people are believers, the stronger the clergy."[48]

The article again cleverly turned the tables on the clergy by suggesting that unless the *'ulamā'* changed course, they would have to take the blame for the corruption of belief and faith among the masses. (What had the Iranian theologians been arguing for the last five years, if it was not that the regime's policies were contaminating the morals of the Iranian people?) The fallacy was proposed that the Spanish Catholic Church was equivalent to Christianity, ignoring the revolutionary developments under Luther that had spawned Protestantism. The fallacy was compounded by the suggestion that corruption in the "church" of Islam could be adequately combatted by the *'ulamā'* immersing themselves in narrow matters of worship. Luther's revolution attacked not only the corruption of the Catholic Church but what he regarded as the incestuous relationship between the Catholic Church and the secular emperors of the Holy Roman Empire. Thus, if the analogy were to have meaning, then the Iranian clergy would have to revolt against the too cosy relationship that had been developed in the 1950's between clergy and state!

In the last of the three editorials of March 1963 the theme of the increasing tendency by Iranian students to reject their own society was developed. Emigration by Iranian intellectuals, the essay noted, stemmed from the social and economic backwardness they perceived at home. Increasingly, Iran is experiencing a phenomenon of sons rebelling against their fathers. The irreligion of the younger generation can only be faced by a clergy that can summon all the ethical precepts at its command. Activity that detracts from this ingathering of moral integrity in the personal codes of conduct of the clergy will provoke youth to yet more bitter rejection of their society. Ergo: *'ulamā'* could better perform a service for their nation, which they have always tried to succor, by standing as shining examples of individual probity. This is the only appropriate way for them to attract alienated intellectuals back to Islam, which in many ways is the keystone of Iranian culture.[49]

These ruminations yielded, some five months later, to another group of editorials in early August. In the meanwhile, the severest conflicts had occurred and resulted in the triumph of the regime. The annual anniversary of the defeat of Muhammad Musaddiq was fast approaching. The anti-government demonstrations had ceased, but the government feared new outbreaks in conjunction with the commemoration of the overthrow of the Musaddiq regime a decade before. The first August editorial on clergy-state relations was published on the fifth. It may be viewed as the government's effort to lay its side of the story of the demonstrations before the people.[50]

The discussion in this article underscored the need to tell the truth about the open conflicts that had broken out between the *ulamā* and the state: the government is not trying to annihilate the religious institution. No better proof that this is not the case, it suggested, exists than the Shah's piety, zealous defense of Shīʿism, belief in Allah, the prophet and the *imāms*. The Shah, it iterated, is distressed at the weakened foundations of faith in Iran. Belief has been shaken, and people ignore pulpit and mosque. Not so their Shah, whose religious convictions remain firm, it alleged. These are days of adversity for the *Shīʿah*, in contrast to other Muslims in the world. The Shah, *Ittilāʿāt* offered, considers that "in their ethics and their spirituality Iranian *Shīʿah* have fallen far behind the caravan of the world." Happily, the editorial went on, the Shah believes that the principles of *Shīʿism* are dynamic, and this factor makes for its being the most progressive creed in the world, in his view.

The cause of laxity and even turpitude on the part of Iranians in regard to matters of faith, the Shah holds, is the interference of certain *ulamā* in politics. The consequent sacrificing of their own constituencies for their personal ambitions not only besmirches them as incumbent religious leaders; but it sullies the whole religious institution. The actions of these activist clergymen "in no way have to do with the calling of the religious institution," *Ittilāʿāt*, presenting the Shah's views, noted. It is the Shah's opinion, the article went on, that the genuinely pious clergymen must follow the model of Church-state relations in the advanced industrial countries of the West. The separation of Church and state in Europe centuries ago actually led to the strengthening of the religion, not its weakening, the editorial argued. A glance at societies in the West shows "everyone is going to Church, full of faith . . . attending to religious sermons . . . and carrying out [the injunctions of the sermons]."

The Shah has alerted the *ulamā* of the existence of undesirables in their ranks who aspire to material reward. Unless dedicated clergymen police their own membership to eliminate pretenders, the essay continued, everyone will be the loser. In the Shah's opinion the proper role of the clergy, in the words of

Ittilāʿāt, consists in enlightening the masses and strengthening their moral and religious beliefs.[51]

The sycophantic tone of the article seemd to go beyond the earlier essays of March. Beyond that, another thing that was new was the broad implication that, in the event the ʿ*ulamāʾ* failed to recover from their derelictions, the Shah would take matters into his own hands and intervene in religious matters. After all, the Shah's religious convictions have stood the test when those of others had failed them. The argument seemed not far from suggesting that this monarch was as close to God and to the *imāms* as the Safavid shahs, whose claims to descent from Imām Mūsā al-Kāżim had given them exceptional legitimacy in their subjects' minds.

A final element that one may adduce is the paper's apparent reversal of a position it had taken in March concerning the corruption of religion in Iran. In the earlier version, *Ittilāʿāt* appeared to be arguing that the corruption of belief would, unchecked, lead to the corruption of the clergy; but in August, the relationship is reversed. The cause of the problems of Iranian Shīʿism in the later version is the scandalous behavior of some members of the clergy.

The constant harping on the analogy of Christianity is puzzling. To propose such a model for emulation to Shīʿī Muslims defies logic, unless the objective were to defy the religious institution. The latter's adversary relationship to Western culture was certainly not unknown to the regime. Moreover, the grounds for claiming high levels of religiosity in the West were not presented; these high levels were merely asserted.

The concluding essay in the *Ittilāʿāt* series acknowledged, tacitly, what it had been arguing against all along: in Shīʿī history one could not find the tradition of separation of religion and state in the clear-cut fashion of "Render unto God that which is God's and to Caesar that which is Caesar's." The article attempted to differentiate between a "desirable" and undesirable form of clergy involvement in politics.[52] "We cannot ever say absolutely and decisively that the ʿ*ulamāʾ* must not intervene in politics, and we have not said such a thing up to now." Since politics is a part of every person's life, and only those barred by the law from participating in it may be justly excluded, it would be wrong to make a blanket exclusion from it for the clergy. If the law permits illiterate grocers and vendors to vote, how can a similar right be denied to such an enlightened group as the ʿ*ulamāʾ*?

But participating in politics and trafficking in it are two different things. These are days of mob rule, rowdyism and the cowing of officials duly elected and selected to govern. Politics is a gamble, and politicians are gamblers, even in the best of times. One day the politician is able to have his way, the next he is packed off to jail, accompanied by the people's curses. "The politician can lie, and the customary law [ʿ*urf*] of politics guides his deceitfulness."

For these reasons, *Ittilā' āt* claimed, the clergy must not traffic in politics. They are the trustees of the prophet, and their politics are "divine politics, a politics transcending small issues and earthly office." The clergyman's mission is "a heavenly one going beyond the ordinary and legal political theses, promises, lies and deceits." The '*ulamā*' have no right to lie; unlike the politician who gives currency to his own ideas, the '*ulamā*' must give currency to God's. They, "being immune from the contamination that trafficking in politics produces, have a greater ability to preserve their lofty status and dignity, which are above political issues and politicians."

Significantly, this essay began with the proposition that the '*ulamā*' have a right to involve themselves in legitimate politics. But rather than define what this consists of, it focused on what it held to be inappropriate forms of political expression for the clergy: deceit, lies, chicanery. Moreover, the article presumably provided cold comfort to the politicians of the regime, who were depicted in such an unflattering light by the editorial. The article seemed to define out of existence any practical role for the clergy in the political system, apart from the very narrow function of voting. Decision-making, policy-formulation, interest articulation, interest aggregation, mobilization of resources, etc.—all these were in effect made *makrūh* (distasteful and therefore discouraged).[53]

THE BĀZARGĀN LECTURE AND THE VIEW OF THE SOCIALLY ACTIVE '*ULAMĀ*'

These editorials and others like them in the press were the expression of the political leadership to the challenge laid down by the clergy in its social action; but they also may have been an attempt to answer one of the most systematic treatments to that point in time of the relationship between religion and politics by Muhandis Mihdī Bāzargān. His status as a lay colleague of a circle of socially prominent theoligians, most notably Āyatullāh Mahmūd Tāliqānī, has already been noted. The Bāzargān analysis of the interfaces of religion and politics was in the form of a lecture to the Second Congress of Islamic Societies of Iran, presented at the Masjid-i Jāmi' of Nārmak of 12 September 1962.[54] The following paragraphs are a paraphrasing and summary of the major points brought out by the author in the course of his inquiry.

Both religion and politics are primary influences in Iranian society, and there are "always linkages and contradictions [between them]. . . . " There is therefore no escaping the clergy's responsibility to clarify the mutual relationships of religion and politics in society.[55] If they do so in good faith, the learned men of the religious law will divide the facets of religion into two categories: (1) individual customs and rituals, including prayer, *rawzah khvānī*, pilgrimmage, and the like; (2) more general aspects, such as ideology, ethics, education. These broader facets he then subsumes under the rubric of *umūr-i ummat* (matters pertaining to the community), which he further qualifies as "people, the fate of the world, eternity." While it is true that "politics," as it were, has not intruded itself into religion in the sense of the first category, above, it has "in no way left us free" with respect to the second. Quite the contrary, the politicians have historically "deeply and thoroughly interfered in and burdened the whole of our religious life and worldly affairs."[56]

Islam cannot be seen as immune to a number of faults that have appeared over the centuries. The First Congress of Islamic Societies had noted these deficiencies, but in general they may be summarized as the reluctance and/or failure of Muslims to take an active interest in questions of "gain and work, practical functions *in toto,* and the dynamic matters of livelihood—especially administrative and social [matters]." Muslims have historically paid greater attention to surface issues, rhetoric and form than to meaning, action and reality in Iran. The clergy has seemingly held itself above society and left practical matters to "the lower class"—i.e., to others—because they regard these issues as unhonorable and insignificant." The ʿ*ulamāʾ*'s refusal to attend to matters of administration, organization, maintaining security, rule, and the like reflects their aversion to dynamic activity, hard work, acceptance of responsibility, attention to mundane detail.[57]

This renunciation of the everyday world has left the field to men of lesser stature. Whereas Greek philosophers oriented their ideas to household management and economy, civics, social management and administration, Bāzargān suggested, Eastern philosophers have always concerned themselves with utopias. The peoples of the East have accordingly been deprived of the actual leadership of their sages.[58]

The state today influences individuals from the cradle to the grave. Its jurisdiction covers matters ranging from health, commerce, culture, education, ethics, ideology to ideas in their generic sense. This has reached the point that people are losing control over their lives. Without a change in this pattern, politics shall "annihilate" religion.[59]

The clergy need not search far for examples of theologians who have advocated the existence of a close linkage between politics and religion. Among the individuals Bāzargān mentions in this regard are Jamāl al-Dīn al-Afghānī (d. 1897) and Āyatullāh Muhammad Husayn Nāʾīnī (d. 1936). Bāzargān is especially impressed with Nāʾīnī's constitutional treatise of 1909, to which reference has already been made earlier. That document made it a religious duty to establish a constitution and a parliament; and it warned of usurpation of terrestrial power beyond that needed for the state to fullfil certain tasks. Yet, complained Bāzargān, Iran's experience since the constitutional revolution has entailed a withdrawal of the religious leadership from constitutional and parliamentary affairs: from a standing of parity with the political authorities to one of inferiority. While many clergymen sat in the first parliament, by the fourth session of that body only Mudarris, Āshtīyānī, Yaʿqūb and perhaps one or two others were left.[60]

Bāzargān, who had himself been a member of the National Front in the fifties,[61] criticized those clergymen who remained publicly neutral in the growing controversy between the regime and those who believed the guardians of the religious law had a political role to play. But, he noted, there were, at that time, even, a number of "enlightened" ʿulamāʾ who did join the contest on the side of those who held a positive view of the clergy's role in social affairs. By 1962, the clergy had effectively split into two unequal groups: (1) a larger group cleaving to neutrality; (2) a smaller activist group that called for political involvement of themselves and their colleagues.[62]

But it is not enough simply to wish that more of the clergy would place themselves into the second group. The reason is that there are those who would take too extreme a view of their role in politics. In fact, moderation is needed in treading the fine line between religion and politics and creatively interweaving the two together without fully integrating them into a monolithic whole. The problem is that some clergymen would become "too political," as it were. This would be as bad as the far more recognized phenomenon of political authorities using religion instrumentally; i.e., the tendency of the regime to identify itself with Shīʿism, to wrap itself in the mantle of the imāms, in order the better to combat communism; or the predilection of political party leaderships invoking religious themes to advance their own interests.[63]

Religious leaders in Iran ought not to fret over the possibility of playing a political role. The Shīʿah engaged in political matters from the very beginning. The first three imāms clearly tread this path. The fourth through the eleventh imāms may not have been politically active; but it was not for lack of wishing to partake of politics, rather it was due to their being "thrust aside" from it. Yet, even they were not neutrally submissive from their vantage point on the margins of social activity. They disseminated their prayers everywhere, they taught, they struggled.[64]

The imāms met with persecution because they thoroughly resisted constituted authority and pursued khilāfat, saltanat, hukūmat (the caliphate, kingship, government). But, for the sake of argument, let us suppose that indeed there is a marked difference between the political involvement of the first three imāms and the other eight (excluding the infant son of the eleventh imām, of course, who went into occultation): whose partisans are we Iranians? Are Iranians the Shīʿah (partisans) of ʿAlī or of Hasan al-ʿAskarī (the 11th imām)? If Iranian Shīʿah cry out the name of ʿAlī and beat themselves in anguish over the fate of Husayn, what reason can there be for practicing taqīyah (prudent dissimulation of belief, a practice associated with the behavior of the fourth through the eleventh imāms)?[65]

At this point, Bāzargān rejects the notion that anticipation of the Mahdī (return of the hidden Imām), whose re-emergence will mean the overturning of the existing order and inauguration of the golden age of justice, is a passive principle. If Shīʿah resign themselves and sit back to wait for the messiah, this would be an invitation to evil men to usurp authority. If the Shīʿah adopt a passive interpretation of the meaning of the occultation of the Imām, then this means that they do nothing, the Imām will do everything. In that event, no one should pray, no one should teach, no one should exercise ijtihād.[66]

To reiterate, then, the tradition of Shīʿism—unlike Sunnism—is one that has raised grand questions about social reality. This is not a matter of the ordinances of religion, where the similarity to Sunnism may be said to be close. Because for Shīʿah the issues of politics and government cannot be avoided, and the imams behaved accordingly, the Iranian faithful emphatically reject the derogatory remark by Ahmad Kasravī (the secular nationalist thinker who was assassinated in 1945) that since the imāms never acceded to the caliphate, "therefore they opened a store."[67] Not only did the imāms have better things to do than to become shop proprietors, they faced pressing issues of everday social and even political life. And if there are those who would argue that Shīʿī tradition historically located the imams and other leaders of that community in the mosques in prayer, not in the divāns raising revenues? Bāzargān rejoins that prayer would always be followed by shūrā (a council meeting), involving discussion of the social and political issues of the times.[68]

Combatting the rule of the prince who fails to apply ʿismat (the virtue of chastity; here, meaning frugality in the application of power in benefiting the commonweal) is sanctioned by verses from the Qurʾān. These show Allah's hatred of corruption, and such hatred in turn is the premise on which the Shīʿah must confront rule that is bereft of reform. It is a religious duty to struggle against the corruption of valāyat and hukumat by the predatory actions of secular authorities. Moreover, it is insufficient to fight this corruption on an individual basis: what is needed is muqāvimat (struggle), irtibāt (mutual linkages), tashkīl (organizational structure), and tajammuʿ (association).[69] These factors will be held together by the twin elements of shūrā (collegiality) and democracy. In the last analysis, government is government by shūrā and struggle is struggle by the people against arbitrary rule. There is no room for the attitude often to be encountered in Iran, that government is the concern of officials, and the people should look out for their own individual interests in "pulling their own gilīms out of the water."[70]

Urging communal solidarity rather than individual separateness, Bāzargān cited the Qurʾānic verse: kuntum khayru ummatin akhrajtu li al-nās taʾ marūna bi al-maʿrūf wa tanhūna ʿan al-munkar (you are the best community that I have sent out among the people, commanding the good and forbidding the bad). If some Shīʿah have forgotten that verse, perhaps they will not have ignored the fact that of the eight "branches" (*furū*) of Islam, four deal with government and politics: *khums* (a form of Islamic income tax exacted from believers); (2) *jihād;* (3) *al-amr bi al-maʿ rūf;* (4) *al-nahy ʿan al-munkar.*[71]

The political authorities certainly recognize, in their hearts, the potential for political involvement that inheres in Shīʿism as both a faith and as action. "Politics wants something from religion;" it is not something innocuous but rather something of great significance and the reckoning is a "life and death matter." Either politics will prevail—in which case it will mean the destruction of religion—or religion will. In that event, politics will not be "destroyed" but rather will be reformed and resuscitated.[72]

Somewhat paradoxically, however, Bāzargān invokes the theme of moderation on the religious side. The integrity of the boundary between religion and politics must be maintained. The Islamic *anjumans* (societies) must not (sic) engage in daily political activity. If they do this, they will become tainted. Political parties, in their turn, may be Muslim and desirous of hitching Islamic ethics and goals to their programs; but they must not be blindly Islamic or fanatically propagate religious tenets. For this could lead to Islam's becoming the target of criticism for mistakes committed by such fanatics.[73]

In conclusion, Bāzargān appealed for a far-reaching and extensive research effort on Islam and faith and movement. The best means for achieving this is to establish an Islamic Society for the Social Sciences. The work of this institution would differ from the scholarship of *Shīʿ ī* theologians of the past in that it would focus on the social aspects of the faith and deal with these in a systematic fashion.[74]

Mihdī Bāzargān's discussion of the legitimacy of religion as a political force is a significant, if somewhat flawed, presentation of the point of view of the socially active clergy in the late fifties and early sixties. The basic points have already been summarized. The tone of the essay is, of course, exhortatory. It was originally a lecture which he meant as an ideological statement. To repeat the cliché about Islam as a "way of life" is to suggest that the propagators of that faith and interpreters of its law must confront questions of power. Clearly, the lecture does not conceptualize political power and analyze the clergy's role in political interactions in terms of their resources, demands and organizational structure. Instead, it is an effort to get the ʿ*ulamā*ʾ to think of themselves as a political force. And this is where his emphasis on administration, management and political economy enters in. He does not elaborate on these aspects of society but limits himself to an appeal for recognizing them as a substantial component of the religious side of things. The lecture is unusual for the forthrightness with which he advocates a political role for the clergy.

Among the notable elements are two points which anticipated the position of Dr. ʿAlī Sharīʿatī, who at that time was studying in France: (1) the theme that waiting for the return of the hidden *Imām* should not be construed as a passive stand but indeed as an active effort of preparing the way for it; (2) the idea that the enlightened *Shī'ah* ought to establish an institution for the social science study of Islam. In addition to these specifics, the whole approach of this lecture was one that Sharī'atī would later embrace in his numerous presentations and writings in the period of the mid-sixties through the early-seventies.

It is also noteworthy that Bāzargān was careful to "cover himself" by appealing to the sacred sources of the *Qur'ān, hadiths* and *rivāyāt* (traditions) of the *imāms*, as well as to constitutional arguments; to Muhammad and the *imāms*, as well as to the Nā'īnī treatise of 1909 and the Majlis.

But he is less convincing about the putative political role of the fourth through the eleventh *imāms*. To be sure, he acknowledges that the *Sunnī* caliphate prevented them from engaging in political activities. But in his statement that these particular *imāms* prayed, taught and struggled he seems to be trying to magnify what apparently was an extremely marginal involvement in political matters. Perhaps some of the confusion here arises from Bāzargān's failure to define what is meant by "political." One does not have to protest or join the opposition to behave politically. But there must be some conscious effort to contend for the power to advance one's interests—whether these be material or moral. This kind of conscious effort to mobilize the resources necessary to exert such power is very difficult to accomplish for people who are prudently dissimulating their belief in the hopes of escaping official notice. Martyrdom is itself a political act, of course; but Bāzargān is trying to find precedents in the traditions of the *imāms* for such things as administration and management. As though recognizing the problems here, he thereupon suggests that the Iranian people are the *Shī'ah* of 'Alī, Hasan, and Husayn at any rate—not of the others.

The stress on *shūrā* and democracy is Bāzargān's way of attacking the regime's failure to implement Article 2 of the Constitution (q.v.) and ruling by decree in the absence of the dissolved parliament. It was a key argument of the National Front, and its restatement here is a logical component of the author's argument in view of his long-standing membership in that organization. Yet, a problem arises. He holds that Iranians must make the time and effort to assess the political system. It is not easy to detect and then elect suitable nominees for political office: "It is precisely the duty of every Muslim to keep his eye upon, and to act and intervene in, politics. And such intervention must become a general phenomenon on the part of the masses."[75] Yet, then how can he prescribe that Islamic organizations stay out of daily political life? This is especially surprising, since he had not only urged political engagement, but had pleaded for the growth of a spirit of communality, collective effort and mutual association and the triumph of these over the "me-first" attitude that was typical.

Notwithstanding its inconsistencies, Bāzargān's "The Boundary between Religion and Social Affairs" lecture of late 1962 carried much conviction among the opposition in Iran. It was, so to speak, a manifesto of the socially active clergy, as well as the committed laymen in the nationalist movement who protested the regime's centralization of power. Defeat of the opposition enabled the regime in the next fifteen years to pursue its own course. Two notable movements within the religious institution were active in the 1960's and 1970's. The bureaucratization of the regime's power proceeded in the face of these movements, to a consideration of which we will now turn.

CHAPTER FIVE

THE TWO CLERGY REFORM MOVEMENTS AND STATE BUREAUCRATIZATION OF POWER IN THE SIXTIES AND SEVENTIES

THE ARGUMENTS AND OBJECTIVES OF THE FIRST REFORM MOVEMENT

The cardinal issues touched upon during the fertile period of internal debate in the first of two movements of religious reform in Iran (1959–63) included the following: the nature and significance of the imāmate; the concept of delegation of authority and sustaining the practice of Imām ʿAlī in rulership (*valāyat*); the problematic of emulating "the best and the brightest" of society's learned men in the absence of the *Imām (marjaʿīyat);* and the doctrine of creative deduction of points of law from the traditional corpus of jurisprudence to satisfy the exigencies of new situations (*ijtihād).* Reform of the religious education system was also an important component of the discussion.

The fact that this movement to reform Shīʿism in Iran occurred simultaneously with the conflict of the clergy with the government over the latter's own "White Revolution" reforms heightened the sensitivities on both sides. The clash with the government, as noted previously, had its roots in the clergy's perception that the government lacked a legal mandate and could only regain it by abiding by the Constitution. Failing that, the clergy had no option but to protest. Such protest, as reviewed above, took various forms, only one of which was open conflict.

Withal, the first of the reform movements of the 1960's appeared to be mainly an endogenous matter. Āyatullāh Burūjirdī's death had a bearing on the movement, although it was not the precipitating factor. His departure appears to have quickened the need to adapt Shīʿism to the changing circumstances of the modern world.

To be sure, not all the ʿ*ulamāʾ*, nor even a majority, participated in the reform

117

movement. Instead, it was led by a few distinguished scholars, mainly in Tehran, who had ties with the religious establishments in the major cities: Mashhad, Isfahān, Shīrāz and Tabrīz. Nor was the "radical" clergy the dominant force in this movement. Indeed, its most notable exponent, Āyatullāh Khumaynī, played virtually no known role in it. The clerical ally of Mihdī Bāzargān, Āyatullāh Tāliqānī, was an important contributor to the movement; to that extent the "radicals" did take part.

There is little doubt that the thought of these individuals had a profound impact on the ʿulamāʾ of Iran. Their ideas provided a ground for vigorous debate on the part of the religious studies students, too; at the very least, in consequence, even the conservative clergy was touched by the movement. These conservatives were apprehensive at the scope of changes desired by the reformists and probably instinctively resisted their suggestions. The state, for the same reasons, could not have welcomed the advocated changes. One of the leaders of the reformist movement has argued, in fact, that the political authorities could not allow the movement to succeed because its advocates actually desired a change in the structure of the religious institution. Tinkering with modifications at the superficial level would be all right; but structural change was too dangerous as the regime perceived things.[1]

A summary of some of the ideas treated by the reforms has been made available by Lambton.[2] In the main, however, the major principles have been debated and elaborated—and therefore known—only within Iran. Those looking at the social problems of the country from the outside necessarily have encountered difficulty in obtaining accurate data of the reform ideas because they have been summarized by regime reports. In this way, the gist of the reforms has been presented by these hostile "analyses" in oversimplified terms as ideological fanaticism of the clergy against progress. Even if the reformists were not thus misrepresented by those with ties close to the regime, the alternative was to suggest that reforms were not necessary. In this manner, such views joined hands with the views of the more conservative clergy.[3]

If, therefore, the times must be adjusted to the needs of Islam, as the conservative opponents of reform were suggesting, then what practical consequence did this have for such doctrines as imāmate or valāyat; or for the principles of marjaʿīyat or ijtihād? To take the last as an example: if one holds, with the conservative view, Islam to be changeless, then the conclusion seems inescapable that "[N]ominally, the door of ijtihād might be open, but if [the mujtahids'] intellectual horizon was limited by the past, it would, in fact, be closed."[4]

The brief history of the development of the first reform movement began in early fall 1960. In that year a group of ʿulamāʾ in Tehran, led by Professor Murtazā Mutahharī of the Faculty of Theology of Tehran University, began a series of public lectures in the southeastern part of the capital, behind the parliament buildings. The series lasted for almost two and a half years, and three volumes of proceedings were published under the general title: *Guftār-i Māh* (Monthly Lectures). The sponsoring organization of these lectures was the *Anjuman-i Māhhānah-yi Dīnī* (Monthly Religious Society). These lectures excited the minds of a number of clergymen and religious students, but their coincidence with the troubles of the early sixties led the regime to shut down the organization and its lecture series in mid-March 1963.

A second development in this first reform movement came in connection with a volume of essays written shortly after the death of Āyatullāh Burūjirdī in March 1961 by many of the participants of the *Guftār-i Māh* series. Indeed, some of the ideas and whole sections of the essays appeared originally as lectures for the Monthly Religious Society. Immediately after its publication the work quickly ran out of its first printing and additional copies also soon disappeared from the newstands. The government forced the publisher to forego further printings or editions. Some considered the work to have been the most important work to have been published in Iran in the last fifty years, meaning since Nā'īnī's constitutional treatise. It was entitled *An Inquiry into the Principle of Marja'īyat and the Religious Institution,* and was published in a 1961 and a 1962 edition.

Its wide circulation and success among the students, preachers and younger *ulamā'* in various religious centers throughout the country caused the senior conservative clergy to be uneasy. Two reasons for their discomfort may be mentioned. First was the concern that the regime might be provoked against the clergy in general as a result of the volume's contents, rather than against only the contributors to the volume. The fact that there was nothing in the volume in the way of an attack on the government did not really matter, since it was a question of the regime's perception of the work, not its actual content. Secondly, the conservative hegemony over the *madrasahs* and organizational structure of the religious institution came under attack in the book. And this was an unprecedented development. "These papers . . . represent, perhaps, the first attempt by a group of writers in modern times in Persia, to examine and reappraise the different aspects of a fundamental issue of the faith."[5]

A review of the papers presented by the various individuals and published in the works mentioned above reveals emphasis on the following points: (1) the need for an independent financial organization for the clergy; (2) the necessity of a *shūrā-yi fatvā*—i.e., a permanent committee of *mujtahids,* the members of which were to be drawn from the country at large, to issue collective authoritative opinions in matters of law; (3) the idea that no *Shī'ī* society is possible without the delegation of the *Imām*'s authority; (4) an interpretation of Islam as a total way of life, therefore incorporating social, economic and political issues into the religious ones; (5) the need to replace the central importance of *fiq* in the *madrasah* curricula with *akhlāq* (ethics), *'aqā'id* (ideology) and *falsafah* (philosophy); (6) the need for a new concept of leadership of youth based on a correct understanding of responsibility; (7) the development of *ijtihād* as a powerful instrument for the adaptation of Islam to changing circumstances; (8) a revival of the nearly defunct principle of *al-amr bi-maʿrūf wa al-nahy ʿan al-munkar* as a means of expressing a collective and public will; (9) specialization among *mujtahids* and making *taqlīd* (emulation of a *mujtahid*) contingent upon it; (10) the need for mutuality and communal spirit to overcome the individuality and mistrust that pervades Iranian culture.

The realization of these points would have led to the emergence of an autonomous religious institution which might effectively have challenged the state's domination of that institution since the Safavid period. It would have produced two competing centers for the allegiance of the people, each proposing its own formulas for social justice, cultural development, organization of the community, and the like.

The reformists were able to consider specific issues that clergymen had long taken for granted (and thus not clearly grasped their potential) as tools for staking out political positions. This is exemplified by their treatment of *al-amr bi al-maʿrūf wa al-nahy ʿan al-munkar*. On the face of it, this principle appears to be a simple moral axiom: do what is right and avoid what is wrong. Because they have so long regarded it as a cliché, the principle has been forgotten by all but a handful of Iranians as the powerful precept that it ought to be. It is not simply something to be invoked by a small group of ʿulamāʾ out of concern that the people be righteous in the eyes of God. Rather, it must be a principle espoused by the masses. Because it is treated in so many different subject areas of the religious sciences (*fiq, usūl, akhlāq*) by so many distinguished and eminent classic authors (Nasīr al-Dīn Tūsī, ʿAllāmah Hillī, Muhaqqiq Hillī), there can be no doubt that the principle was meant to be "the foundation for the reform of society."[6]

Yet, Iranians appear to have ignored its implications, with adverse consequences for the spirit of cooperation and mutuality:[7]

> *Al-amr bi al-maʿrūf* has become [a] limited [concept] in the view of the people, who pay no attention to that aspect of it that is concerned with improving the social affairs of their lives. This has resulted in situations such as the following: suppose a mayor, for example, wants to take steps to improve the feeding and provisioning [of the citizens] or to take measures to clean up the city, block price gouging, or make good arrangements for automobile traffic. The people do not cooperate. The reason is that they do not feel that this, too, from the religious viewpoint, is a duty.

Or, alternatively, note how these reformers use such an apparently innocuous concept as *taqvā* (piety) to suggest collective and social protest. In this manner, they are employing the concept as a *dynamic*, rather than as a passive and strictly internalized, individualistic outlook on life. Discussing the elections of 1960 and 1961 (both annulled as a result of blatant chicanery and manipulation of the ballots), Mutahharī denies the argument that the obsolete election law was to blame for the problems. Although conceding that no doubt the fifty year law had its defects, and he did not wish to defend it, Mutahharī felt the reason for the rigging of the elections had to do not with the law but people's failure even to observe its provisions. When a candidate is handpicked by the regime to represent a city and is totally an outsider who is unknown to its inhabitants; and when this individual nonetheless declares that for better or for worse he is their man; and when he declares that he will win whether or not they vote for him: when these things happen (as they had in the southeastern town of Rafsanjān for example), this demonstrates the disappearance of piety among the authorities.[8]

These, then, were confident reformers who appealed for a fresh vision. Rescuing Islam in Iran from centuries of stagnation had to happen in time and space. It could not simply be wished, as though somehow it could occur *in vaccuo*. The reformers felt that a "new breed" of Iranian *Shīʿī* had been born. With representatives in the key cities of the land, this element would fullfil the dreams of Āyatullāh Nāʾīnī. It would shake the *ʿulamāʾ* awake from 10 centuries of slumber.[9]

Yet, the reformists did not wish to exaggerate in the use of such metaphors as an entire tradition of thought having gone to sleep many centuries ago. Since the reformist wishes to build on the traditions of the past, these gentlemen desired to recognize the inestimable importance of the classic writers, the traditional interpreters of the law. They were, themselves, after all, inheritors of the traditional methods and scholarship.

The victory of the Usūlī movement over the rival Akhbārī school in the late 17th and early 18th centuries was acknowledged by the reformers as the cornerstone of contemporary *Shīʿī* theology. On its basis, the *Shīʿah* could successfully argue that Shīʿism is more responsive to social reality, more flexible, more "creative", as it were, than Sunnism. The Usūlī school, affirming the need for *mujtahid*s to exercise independent judgment on matters of law, advanced *ʿaql* (reason) as a source for the development of Islamic jurisprudence. In thus keeping open the gates of *ijtihād*, then, the Usūlī efforts have issued in the active participation of men in shaping their existence. Had the Akhbārīs triumphed, Shīʿī jurisprudence would have stagnated in much the manner of Sunnī jurisprudence.

A second signal achievement by the classic thinkers of Shīʿism was related to the methodology of dialectical inquiry associated with the teachings of Shaykh Murtazā al-Ansārī (d. 1864), who had been dubbed al-Mujaddid and Khatam al-Mujtahidīn (renewer of the faith, seal of the *mujtahid*s). In the study of jurisprudence, Ansārī introduced the methodology known as *masʾalah sāzī*, which may be translated somewhat awkwardly as "argumentation through hypothetical construction". As a result of this innovation in methodology, the reformists noted, *Shīʿī* religious studies students have acquired a dazzling brilliance in the art of abstract discursive argumentation in the dialectical manner.

There was, even so, a negative side to this as the method became an end in itself. It is therefore to the credit of Āyatullāh Burūjirdī during his fifteen year tenure in Qumm to admonish against excessive argumentation through hypothetical construction and the kind of synoptic knowledge (ʿilm-i ijmālī) that resulted from such excess. But despite the admonition, some of the most rewarding and richest branches of Islamic learning—tafsīr, tārīkh, maʿrifah al-rijāl, for instance—had shrivelled.[10]

But Burūjirdī, himself, had been too conservative in the view of the reformers. He seemed to have temporized and lacked commitment when it became a question of changing the madrasah curriculum. Curiously, despite his own extensive learning in tafsīr, rijāl, hadīth, tārīkh, he did not allow these subjects to wax in the madrasah. Consequently, fiq continued to be the queen of the sciences of theology. Because fiq concerns subjects which are to be memorized (the ordinances of the religion), the more creative students who would otherwise matriculate in the madrasahs, tended to turn away from religious studies in favor of secular education.[11]

Dissatisfaction with Burūjirdī's role in not sponsoring the growth of the substantive subjects listed above had its counterpart in the reformers' desire for change in marjaʿīyat. As a matter of practice, Iranians had had the choice of following or emulating one marjaʿ-i taqlīd out of several who are active at a given time. But Burūjirdī had earned the title of al-Mujadid and had become the sole marjaʿ-i taqlīd of his era. This gave rise to anxiety on the part of the reformers, who believed that the complexity of their epoch militated against this practice. At any rate, the elitism of the marjaʿīyat-i mutlaq invited comparisons to the role of the Imām in a disturbing manner. Therefore, some of the reformers stressed the need to decentralize religious authority and suggested the creation of a commission of distinguished mujtahids (shūrā-yi fatvā). These individuals would then collectively sit and issue joint opinions on questions of moment for the Shīʿī community.[12] The argument was advanced that a single individual could not hope to have command over the many issues of religion and society, even if it was theoretically possible to designate one mujtahid as aʿlam (most learned). Yet, lurking beneath the surface of this rationalization probably lay another: the desire to prevent the emergence of jealousies among the top-ranking clergymen.

Of the several proposals advanced by the reformers, the shūrā-yi fatvā probably was one of those which greatly alarmed the government. It would have created, at a stroke, a corporate entity of religious leaders with both quasi-executive and quasi-legislative powers. Its creation would have signified the institutionalization of the political authority of the clergy that had eluded the ʿulamāʾ throughout the previous fifty years. It may be argued that a sole marjaʿ-i taqlīd constituted a formidable religious authority in his own right; that the creation of a committee would diffuse the enormous influence that could be wielded by a single individual. But to argue in these terms is to miss the point of the reformers' position: i.e., individualism has led to deviations and detracted from potential gains by Shīʿism; a *shūrā*, secondly, would be a permanent fixture which, once established, could not easily be removed. On the other hand, the sole *marjaʿ* was always subject to the limits of his own mortality; the long search for a replacement would be time-consuming, continuity would be disrupted, and the successor would have to establish his own relations with the other *ʿulamāʾ* in any case. As to the argument that the title of *marjaʿ-yi mutlaq* ought to simply be abolished and the traditional practice of having several *marājiʿ* sustained, without creating the *shūrā*: the reformers would respond that it would mean needlessly foregoing the advantages of organization. However a compromise might be acceptable.

This compromise between diversity of *marājiʿ* and organizational unity consists of permitting individuals to follow different *marājiʿ* on different matters, depending on the expertise of each particular *marjaʿ*. At the same time, the *shūrā-yi fatvā* would exist to rule on the most important matters and, perhaps, to arbitrate conflicts. The notion of Iranians emulating different *marājiʿ* on different matters of law dates back to a proposal made by Shaykh ʿAbd al-Karīm Hāʾirī, and it was supported by Murtazā Mutahharī on grounds that *fiq* has grown too complex to be authoritatively mastered by a single individual in all its facets.[13]

Ultimately, these issues are questions of leadership. Leadership must be exercised in a new way, it was urged. The older generation, which was epitomized by Burūjirdī's sway, had a different conception of the leadership role than that of the younger generation. Of course, the generation gap is to some extent a given factor of social life. But simply invoking the gap by way of explaining why reforms have not been accomplished is puerile. Rigorous inquiry into the matter of leadership reveals that it is a matter of the proper exercise of one's responsibility before one's own group, and guidance of that group towards the best result. Responsibility, itself, may be seen as divided into two aspects: (a) responsibility of doing (*masʾūlīyat-i kār*); (2) responsibility for a result (*masʾūlīyat-i natījah*). In Islam, too, there are the two kinds of responsibility. Prayer, giving alms and other ritualistic matters compose the first kind of responsibility; undertaking holy war exemplifies the second type. Now, it must be understood that every generation in Islam is responsible to the next in both senses of the word. This must not be taken for granted as a hackneyed phrase. Indeed, the religious leadership of today should seek to understand the world of the younger generation. Instead of bemoaning youth's putative disrespect of its elders, the *ʿulamāʾ* elite must accept the youth's tendency toward open mindedness and skepticism. It must not always advise this youth to be "realistic" but rather ought to recognize the deep significance for it of its high ideals and standards.[14]

Because today's younger generation is much better educated than its predecessor, the old propaganda (*bayān va tablīgh*) ought to be discarded. Preachers in the pulpits must not take it amiss if younger members in the audience challenge their ideas. Indeed, they, as well as all members of the senior clergy, must themselves challenge youth by working out an ideology that will attract it away from its alienated state and toward a meaningful religious orientation to social reality. If materialistic philosophy has its appeal among young Iranians, this is an indictment of the lifeless version of Islam being served up by the clergy in the *madrasah*s and mosques. The formula for the materialists' success is over-simplification of complex issues; that of the *'ulamā* 's failure is mindless imita-tion of outworn practices.[15]

The argument of the older generation that youth today is Godless and ignorant of the *Qur'ān* will not wash, either. Of course, the lack of religious knowledge on their part is to be regretted, but in what manner have their elders alleviated these defects? Do they really believe that youth can be attracted back to Islam "by this same *fiq,* by this same sacred law and this *Qur'ān* that exist in the religious schools?" The fault, the reformers were saying, were not in the *tullab* but in the teachers. Consider the *'ulamā* 's behavior concerning the relative importance in the *madrasah* curriculum of *fiq* and *tafsīr.* All the prestige that can accrue to a scholar of the religious sciences derives from mastery of *fiq;* the expert in Qur'ānic commentary has no standing whatsoever. This is the case despite the fact that *tafsīr* is the dynamic and vital science of construing the *Qur'ān,* whereas *fiq* is a dead subject of learning that requires of the student rote memorization of ordinances of religion. If the older leadership does not hold *tafsīr* up as the crown jewel of the Islamic sciences, then it is hypocrisy for it to deride the younger generation for faulty knowledge about the *Qur'ān.* For what else has this leadership done, in its preference for *fiq,* but *avoid (i'rāz)* the holy scripture?[16]

Therefore, the *'ulamā* elite had virtually forefeited the right to leadership of the youth. The concern of that elite was "not of this world", and until it came down to earth to grapple with the day to day problems of society, the new generation would continue to ignore it:[17]

> A religious leader is someone who identifies the way to achieve the lofty religious
> goals *in society:* how to transact trade, win friends, make peace, wage war, to
> whom to be enemies, to whom allies, which lesson to read, what to agree to, what
> to struggle against, etc., in order to reach the final aims of religion *in society.*

If the clergy were truly candid to itself and to others, then it would realize that Shī'ism is a religion of "struggle against corrupt politicians and attentiveness to the interests of the majority."[18]

The strong effort of the reformist literature to show the proper role of the clergy to be both religious *and social* had its counterpart in the recommendation that they seek to establish the financial autonomy of the religious institution. Historically, the sources of revenue of the *'ulamā* had consisted of: (1) income from legal and clerical duties, such as registration of titles, notarization of affidavits, court fees, etc.; (2) annual revenues from endowed properties; (3) contributions by the faithful in the form of religious taxes (*khums*).

Now, the legal reforms by Rizā Shah had eliminated the first source, while the decline in *awqāf* in this century and the trend against the establishment of new endowments after World War II effectively restricted the second source. Some *ʿulamāʾ*, too, had supplemented their role as religious leaders by being tradesmen and earning income independent of their religious duties. Indeed, it was rationalized that since the prophet and his early associates themselves had been merchants and the like, it was appropriate for the clergy to follow their examples in the contemporary period.

But the nub, for the reformists, was not to recommend a supplementary employment for the clergy. It was to become independent from the increasingly unique source of financial support for that stratum: voluntary contributions by the people. Of course, reliance on the people's largesse rendered the Iranian *ʿulamāʾ* independent of the state, a situation that was perhaps unique in the entire Middle East, over most of which the state had coopted the clergy through its subsidization. But because the masses control the *ʿulamāʾ*'s income, attempts at reforming the structure of the religious institution must receive their approval. And, unfortunately for the reformists, the masses have proven to be conservative in regard to social change.[19]

In addition to financial dependence on the population at large, another feature of the financial organization of the Iranian clergy was its extreme decentralization. As the system was then constituted (1962), the various *marājiʿ-i taqlīd* sent their agents out to the provinces to collect the *khums* from the faithful. This *khums*—which itself is divided into two halves, one earmarked for the subsidization of impoverished *sayyid*s, and the other for supporting the clergy's institutions—was therefore obtained in somewhat of an *ad hoc* fashion.

One of Āyatullāh Burūjirdī's contributions to the rationalization of the financial structure had been to order the creation of a registry of agents and the amounts they collected. This helped to overcome some of the abuses of the past: false agents, for example, pretending to represent an individual *marjaʿ;* or, for instance, the inability, even of a *marjaʿ*, to keep track of his own agents in the field, there being no existing record of appointments.[20]

Yet, in itself Burūjirdī's innovation was but a small step in the right direction. In the first place, it still did not address the primary question of rationalization of financial administration, for the maintenance of a registry did not solve the problem of revenue inflows and disbursements: it merely identified the collecting agents and the amounts each had secured. Secondly, who would retain such a register after Burūjirdī's death? The post-1961 period was an era of several *marajiʿ*, and they would probably maintain their own registers.

What the *ʿulamāʾ* consequently really needed was a financial organization (*sāzmān*). Such an institution would have the inestimable advantage of centralization, the budgeting of financial operations, the elaboration of an investment policy, the extension of credit: ultimately, it would mean total financial independence of the clergy. The institutionalization of the financial structure (*sāzmān dādan bi sahm-i imām*)[21] would have made it possible for *mujtahid*s in the *shūrā-yi fatvā* and in their *hawzah*s to constitute a national and provincial and district level religious establishment of great influence and prestige.

These suggestions were particularly alarming to the government, and it is no wonder that the reformists never received an iota of support on the part of the regime.[22] Nevertheless, unless the clergy elite could secure its *sāzmān*, its finance administration, the religious institution was bound to decay, said the reformists. This would hit especially hard the *madrasah* system, which, without the large infusions of revenue that were needed to reform its curriculum, would continue to remain in the backwaters of education for the younger generation.

Some time around 1950 the town of Qumm had witnessed a debate among the *ʿulamāʾ* as to why all the country's *hawzah*s had fallen into such torpor. It was generally agreed, during the discussions, that these *hawzah*s, including Qumm, had lost the prestige that had, in earlier times, marked them as universities (*dānishgāhhā*). The erosion had reached such a pass that the *hawzah*s in the contemporary period could pretend to nothing better than mere colleges or faculties (dānishkadahhā) of *fiq*. One by one, the great substantive subjects had vanished: commentary, philosophy, history, sayings of the prophet, biography, ethics, medicine, mathematics. According to the reformists, these tremendous losses in the curriculum were due to "all these devastations [*tamām-i īn kharābīhā*] that had been wreaked on the *sahm-i imām*."[23]

The criticism by the reformists did not center on the *sahm-i imām*, of course, but on the manner of its uses and abuses. In the hands of retrogressive senior clergymen the *sahm-i imām* had been expended foolishly, with insufficient regard for the transformation of society in an age of social change. It is due to their stewardship that the great religious universities of Iran had become mere arenas for pedantic, legalistic, scholastic debate.[24] The leader of this group of reformists pointed out, some 13 years after they had sounded the tocsin of reform, that things had continued to deteriorate along much the same lines.[25]

The regime, on the other hand, wished to let matters stand as they were. To the appeals by the reformers for its acquiescence to rationalizing the finances of the clergy, the government could answer: you already have financial autonomy; the government does not have leverage over you. But the reformers' response was: yes, we have financial autonomy from the government; but not from the masses. Among the negative consequences of reliance on the people is their impatientce with new ideas. The Egyptian *ʿulamāʾ* do not have to worry about this problem. For if they *are* financially dependent on the state, they at least are not forced to articulate their ideas before the masses in order to get their initial approval. If the Egyptian *ʿulamāʾ* do not have *power*, at least they have "academic freedom" to formulate new ideas. By contrast, the Iranian ʿulamāʾ enjoy power but lack such freedom. The need always to be looking over one's shoulder makes a negative impression on the *progressive* clergymen, at any rate. These individuals then view the Iranian people as an albatross around the necks of the religious institution. The masses' ever viable threat is to withhold the *sahm-i imām,* which would result in the destitution of the ʿulamāʾ as a corporate group. It is for fear of the masses' reaction that the Iranian ʿulamāʾ have so consistently produced only practical treatises and minor tracts. The Iranian progressive ʿulamāʾ have thus been reduced to reading the writings of their Egyptian counterparts *faute de mieux.* If this continues much longer, Iranian Shīʿah will be forced to say that their most recent creative thinker lived a century ago. And the progressive clergymen will have nothing better to do than to sit in their homes or classrooms and complain of "the effects of mass mindlessness" (ʿavām zadigī). Better to be afflicted by "floods, earthquakes, snakes and scorpions" than to be subject to the veto power of the masses over reform.[26]

On balance, the reformers were optimistic that changes of the kind they were recommending would lead to a revival of the religious institution. They felt that conflict between the latter and the state constituted an ineluctable given[27] but that a reaffirmation of *ijtihād* and a dynamic conception of *taqlīd* involving alert and responsible emulation (not blind imitation)[28] would enable religion to prevail. The reformers did not attempt to justify or authorize the existence of temporal government, although it was recognized in passing that temporal governments not beholden to religious requisites had come into being because of the failure of the Shīʿī leadership to apply the principles of the holy law in their true form. It is true that ʿAllāmah Muhammad Husayn Tabāʾtabāʾī did distinguish between the immutable laws of Islam and the decrees and edicts of rulers which were subject to change as circumstances evolved. But Tabāʾtabāʾī "also alleges that integrity in the administration of laws is virtually non-existent in Persia;"[29] more, he insists on an Islamic community in which rulership must follow the *sunnah* of the prophet. The implication seems to be that rule which deviates—even in minor fashion—from Muhammad's model is not legitimate.[30]

In summary, this first clergy reform movement of the 1960's touched on a broad range of issues. It will be noted that no more than some 20 individuals participated in its efforts.[31] By all accounts, their writings did not receive a wide circulation among the population,[32] but no doubt this was due to the somewhat esoteric nature of the arguments and complexity of the issues. They did have, it was often suggested, a great impact on Iranian youth in particular. In order to increase the audience for these contributions, the reformers tried to get the Ministry of Culture and the Endowments Department to take an interest in their efforts with a view to publicizing and publishing the lectures in the form of brochures.[33] In retrospect, it seems that this optimism on their part was unwarranted, given the regime's obvious displeasure with the nature of their work and ultimate decision to close down the Society "for an indefinite and unknown period of time.''[34] It will be recalled, in retrospect, that at the time when the Society was forced to terminate its activities (March 1963), some of the severest clashes were taking place between the military/police and the nationalists, clergy, students.

The discussion followed good scholarly tradition, with the authors consistently seeking to ground their arguments in the sayings, traditions and verses of the prophet, the *imām*s and the *Qur'ān*. Yet, much that was criticized seemed to lack specific and concrete remedies. Thus, if the message urged the people and the *ʿulamā'* to "come down to earth" and cooperate with one another in attending to daily social questions, it was often left implicit as to how this could best be achieved.

Nonetheless, there is no denying that these recommendations, as Mutahharī modestly put it in the beginning, had a "new angle" to them.[35] The writers' references to the mainstream clergy were couched in the following terms: retrogressive; subject to pressure by the political authorities; scholastic; timid; irrelevant for their times, and so on. It is interesting that they were most reluctant to identify the clergy as the repository of power and authority. If anything, most of them argued against the concentration of *marjaʿīyat* and in favor of a collegial body of the most learned. The idea that somehow these highest ranking *mujtahids* had a special relationship to the *imams* was not raised. The recommendation of a council of distinguished *mujtahid*s, each of whom would be most learned in a certain field, places the *mujtahid*s at one remove from the *marjaʿ-yi mutlaq* and two steps removed from the *imams*.

The reformers approach to the clergy was that it constituted a corporate social force in society to be reckoned with. They were best qualified to defend the faith and work to establish as nearly as they could the justice of the *Imām* (something they could not completely do, of course); but they were going about this in the wrong way. Still, the specific recommendations that they offered—a financial organization, a council of mujtahids discussing social questions and issuing authoritative decisions on them, restoration of lapsed subjects in *madrasah* curricula, involvement in the rational calculus of management and administration, forging dynamic linkages with the masses in a manner transcending the *marjaʿ-muqallid* relationship, solid cooperation among themselves—these were meant to achieve one goal: bring the *ʿulamā'* into the real world again where they could be real leaders of real people who badly needed them; rather than, as was then the case, "hovering over the world" and invoking through prayer the succor of God, Muhammad and the *imams* for an abstract community of believers. At its most "political," as it were, the reformers called upon the people to supervise the government, ensure that it carry out the appropriate tasks to implement, as closely as possible, the justice demanded by the *Imām;* and, if it fail, to work to establish a government that would do so.[36] They criticized, by analogy and the use of hypothetical examples, the government's stewardship of the resources of the country, referring to the Qur'anic verse: *lā tu'tū al-sufahā' amwālakum alatī ja'ala Allāh lakum qīyāman* (Do not give your wealth, with which God has caused you to rise up, to those who are foolish).[37] But such attacks were the exception, and most criticism was directed at the clergy leadership. Although the essays stimulated much discussion in the *hawzah*s, they ultimately failed in their purpose owing to the opposition both of the conservative clergy and the regime.

CONTINUING SECULARIZATION AND BUREAUCRATIZATION

In 1965 official government figures showed that there were 100 *mujtahid*s, 10,000 *mullā*s and 20,000 mosques in Iran.[38]* In 1968, data made available to 'Īsā Sadīq and published in the seventh edition of his book *The History of Culture in Iran* (1975) showed that there were only 138 *madrasah*s in the country and some 7,500 *tullāb*.[39] Most of these *madrasah*s had only a handful of students, and some continued to exist as monuments or landmarks more than instructional institutions.

A comparison of the *madrasah*s of Tehran between the years 1960 and 1975 shows that the capital city lost 9 of a total of 32 *madrasah*s over the fifteen year period. In the meanwhile, one new one was built in the village of Chīzar, just outside the city in the northeastern suburbs some 15 kilometers away from the center of town. The list on page 130 shows the names of the *madrasah*s for each of the two years.[40]

Of these theological colleges, the Marvī, Sipah Sālār (Jadīd) and Āghā had the largest number of *tullāb*. According to the then *nā'ib al-tawlīyah* of the Sipah Sālār, 'Allāmah Muhammad 'Alī Vahīdī (executed by the revolutionary regime), his madrasah had 120 students in 1975.[41] Āyatullāh Āshtīyānī claimed in that year that his school (Marvī) had 150 pupils, divided roughly evenly between boarders and non-boarders. In addition, as of the fall of 1975 he was host to some 80 students who had come from Najaf.[42] The same individual stated that the Āghā *madrasah* had about 50–80 tullāb. Among them, then, these three schools had a combined enrollment of regular students of about 250 at all levels of learning. The combined total of all the remaining *madrasah*s in that year likely did not surpass 250, although close estimates were difficult to make.[43]

The *'ulamā'*'s control of the *madrasah*s was gradually declining, and the clergy in general felt that they were slowly losing their influence in one of the only spheres in public life in which the regime had permitted them to continue to be active: religious education. It used to be relatively common for a single

*But in 1975 the Endowments Organization reported only 9,015 mosques throughout the country. See appendices.

Name of *Madrasah*	1960	1975
1. M. Hājj Abū al-Fath	x	x
2. M. Hājj Abū al-Hasan	x	x
3. M. Amīn al-Sultān	x	—
4. M. Mīrzā Abū al-Hasan Īlchī Kabīr	x	x
5. M. Mīrzā Rizā Qulī Khān	x	—
6. M. Mīrzā Khāzan al-Mulk	x	—
7. M. Rizā ʾīyah	x	x
8. M. Hājj Mīrzā Zakī	x	—
9. M. Āghā	x	—
10. M. Sipah Sālār-i Qadīm	x	x
11. M. ʿAlī-yi Sipah Sālār (Jadīd)	x	x
12. M. Shāhzādah Khānum	x	x
13. M. Sadr	x	x
14. M. Shaykh ʿAbd al-Husayn (Āzarbāyjānīhā)	x	x
15. M. ʿAbdullāh Khān	x	x
16. M. Faylsūf al-Dawlah	x	x
17. M. Qanbar ʿAlī Khān	x	x
18. M. Kāzimīyah	x	x
19. M. Muhammadīyah	x	x
20. M. Muʿayyir al-Mamālik	x	x
21. M. Khān Marvī	x	x
22. M. Munīrīyah	x	—
23. M. Mahmūdīyah	x	x
24. M. Āghā Mahmūd	x	x
25. M. Najmābādī	x	x
26. M. Mīrzā ʾĪsā Vazīr	x	x
27. M. Nizām al-Dawlah	x	—
28. M. Yūnis Khān	x	—
29. M. Amīn al-Sultān (Ray)	x	x
30. M. Āyatullāh Burūjirdī	x	—
31. M. Mullā Āghā Rizā	x	x
32. M. Mushīr al-Saltanah	x	x
33. M. Chīzar	—	x

x indicates *madrasah* existed that year; — indicates it did not exist.

mujtahid or other ʿālim simultaneously to be *mutavallī* of a number of *madrasah*s. For example, upon his death in late 1950 Āyatullāh ʿAlī Akbar Isfahānī had been the *mutavallī* of three theological colleges in Tehran: (1) Sipah Sālār (Qadīm); (2) Hājj Abū al-Hasan; (3) ʿAbdullāh Khān.[44] In the sixties and seventies, this pattern increasingly became exceptional. In 1971, for instance, upon the death of Āyatullāh Ahmad Khurāsānī Kafāʾī in Mashhad all three *madrasah*s of which he had been the *mutavallī* came under control of the administration of the Mashhad Department of Endowments.[45] In 1975, Āyatullāh Āshtiyānī, whose family had administered the Marvī *madrasah* ever since the Constitutional Revolution, revealed that he had assented to an arrangement where the Tehran De-

partment of Endowments "has a say" in that school's administration.[46] And
Āshtīyānī's *tawlīyat* of the Madrasah-yi Hājj Abū al-Hasan (which he assumed
upon the death of Āyatullāh ʿAlī Akbar Isfahānī, as noted above) was shaky; the
school had only seven or eight students and was no doubt susceptible to encroachment and takeover by the Endowments Department of the capital. The
Āshtīyānī family's declining influence over the Tehran *madrasah*s in the late
Pahlavī period could also be seen in another instance: Āyatullāh Āshtīyānī's
son-in-law had been the *mutavallī* of the Khāzan al-Mulk *madrasah;* but over
the years, the enrollment dwindled to some five or six students. then, as a result
of the *mutavallī*'s accident, in which he suffered a broken leg, even less attention
could be paid to the administration of this school. The few students thereupon
withdrew to seek other schools, leaving the institution vulnerable to the Endowments Department to take it over and convert it into a historical landmark.[47] In
short, the important *mujtahid*s of such key areas as Mashhad and Tehran could
not guarantee the continued control of their *madrasah*s for members of their own
families. At the same time, the role of the state bureaucracy in the administration
of these schools seemed to be increasing rapidly, if the examples cited are
representative.

Further problems had overtaken the *hawzah*s since the 1963 riots and the
defeat of the clergy. The death in 1975 of Āyatullāh Hādī Mīlānī of Mashhad had
a double significance. As one of the seven *marājiʿ-yi taqlīd* at that time, he had
had a very large following among Iranians. His students were forced to find other
mentors and, perhaps, to move to other *hawzah*s. Furthermore, Mīlānī's death
came only four years after Kafāʾī's, thereby depriving the city of two leading
*mujtahid*s in rapid succession. The transformation of the character of the Mashhad shrine area by a municipal program of rennovations—in which Mīlānī's
school was razed—added impetus to the efflux of *tullāb* to other centers of
religious education (presumably Qumm and Najaf in that order).

The *hawzah* of Najaf had been under severe pressure as a result of Iraqi
intimidation of the *Shīʿī* populations in southern Iraq. The campaign was especially directed at Iranian nationals residing in the ʿatabāt, and these began
emigrating to Iran in numbers. Persecution of the Iranians in Najaf, Karbalāʾ,
Kāzimayn and Sāmarāʿ was intermittent but no less real for its irregularity.
Already in 1969 Āyatullāh Muhsin Hakīm had felt compelled to protest the
Baʿthist regime in Baghdad's treatment of the *Shīʿī* ʿulamāʾ in those shrine cities.
He admonished the Iraqi government for its "degradation of tte religious leaders" there and termed the government officials of Iraq "infidels". About that
same time many resident Iranian clergymen and their followers sent telegrams
objecting to the harrassments mentioned.[48] Tensions remained at a high level
through early 1975. Thus, in late 1974 Āyatullāh Ahmad al-Mūsavī Khvānsārī
(the leader of the Tehran ʿulamāʾ) wrote to the Shah to urge him to protect
Iranian *Shīʿī* residents of Iraq. This request, together with the Shah's reply, was

published in the Iranian press to underscore the importance with which these matters were viewed; and, perhaps, to indicate that coalition-building between regime and ʿulamāʾ was still a possibility.[49] The exchange between Khvānsārī and the Shah may be analyzed in the context of the Shah's telegram to Khvānsārī some four years earlier in which he extended his sympathies on the death of Āyatullāh Hakīm in 1970. That message had been interpreted by many as an attempt by the Shah to intervene in the process by which the high-ranking ʿulamāʾ advanced within their own hierarchy. At that time, Khvānsārī had replied in reserved tones, and the Shah dropped the matter at this point. Yet, here was Khvānsārī in 1974 appealing to the Shah to come to the assistance of the Shīʿī clergy. It was probably a moment which the Shah relished, even if, in fact, there was nothing very much he could do on behalf of the Iranians in Iraq at the time. All the same, one wonders what the contributions of the ʿulamāʾ of Iran were to the entente that the governments of Iran and Iraq reached in March 1975 at the Algiers Summit Conference. It may be conjectured, however, that among the reasons that led the Iranian government to reach an acommodation, one was anxiety lest the inflow of students and ʿulamāʾ from Najaf to Qumm augment Qumm's stature, thereby causing greater problems for the regime in its policies toward the clergy.

In the 1960's and 1970's, then, the clergy increasingly found itself on the defensive. The Pahlavi dynasty's policies had succeeded in converting it into a déclassé stratum. The Endowments Organization (Sāzmān-i Awqāf), which had come into existence after a bureaucratic reform in 1964, released figures of the extent of awqāf properties and their incomes on a national basis in that year. It warned that properties in outlying areas would not be reflected in these figures because of the lack of proper surveys; in addition, it noted that the appropriation of awqāf through illicit means had continued into the contemporary period and so these properties which in fact should be registered as vaqf but in fact had been illegally seized would also fail to be reflected in the figures. The following table gives the reported data on endowed properties and income from these properties.

Granted the defectiveness of the figures as a result of the absence of a reliable cadastral survey, these figures suggest that the total annual income of all types of awqāf as of 1960 was an astoundingly low $3.6 million. Unfortunately, data for either an earlier period or after 1960 does not exist in order that we might compare the trends in awqāf. But certain revelations arising from the revolutionary regime's inquiry into the status of awqāf in the late Pahlavī period suggest that illegal appropriations of endowed properties was common, and that officials of the regime routinely were presented with large tracts of land either as "hush money" or as reward for services or simple extortion.

In this manner, Mr. Manūchihr Āzmūn, Director of the Endowments Organization in the seventies, had made the following grants of land from properties under the jurisdiction of his institution: (1) an undeterminate amount of property

DATA ON *AWQĀF* IN IRAN, 1964

I. Statistics on Vaqf Properties.	
1. Total Agricultural Properties	38,519
2. Total Real Properties	15,881
3. Total Shrines, Mosques, *Madrasahs*	7,015*
4. Total Palm Plantations	417
5. Total Pasturelands	524
6. Total Waterways and Canals	7,609
7. Total Mines	15
8. Miscellaneous Properties and Groves	3,713
9. Total	73,694
II. Income of Properties.	
1. Total Income, Occupied Properties (*Mutasarrifī*) in 1960	34,654,419 rials**
2. Total Income, Unoccupied Properties (*Ghayr-i Mutasarrifī*), 1960	240,803,943 rials
3. Total	275,458,362 rials
III. Religious Schools.	
1. Total Number of *Madrasahs* and Mosques in Which *Tullāb* are Studying	214***
2. Total Number of *Tullāb* and Teachers	13,016
3. Total Stipend Disbursed to *Tullāb* and Teachers Per Annum from the Endowed Properties	11,000,000 rials

*This figure is far below that given by the *Iran Almanac* data on the number of mosques in Iran as of 1965 (fn. 38 q.v.)

**At that time one rial was equal to approximately $0.013

***This figure differs from that arrived at by adding the number of *madrasahs* per province according to the breakdown presented in later pages of the article which is the source of this table. That datum is 236.

SOURCE: "Awqāf," *Kitāb-i Irānshahr,* Vol. II (Tehran: Tehran University Press, in conjunction with UNESCO, 1343 H. Sh./1964), p. 1264–1398

in the exclusive Shimīrān suburbs to the north of Tehran to the singer, Hāyadah; (2) 1,417 square meters of property, also in Shimīrān, to another singer, Gītī; (3) 10,000 square meters to Īraj Gulsurkhī, a musician, in the Karaj district—a town to the west of Tehran; (4) some 5,000 square meters, to as yet unnamed artists; (5) 15,548 square meters of land in the Kāshānak district to the Imperial Court; (6) 81,000 square meters from the endowed property of Mustawfī al-Mamālik (a Qājār statesman) to the private office of Empress Farah; (7) 3,350 square meters to the Lions Club from the properties known as the Mullā Bāqir *vaqf* in Shimīrān; (8) 230 hectares (equivalent to 2.3 million square meters!) of land in Karaj to one Ahmad Dārā'ī; (9) unspecified amount of land known as the Army Commander Khudāyār *vaqf* in Karaj to Īraj and Jahāngīr Sipahbud; (10) 200 hectares (2 million square meters) of land in the Karaj district to General Fardūst [title deed document #10,650 of the Karaj Land Registry No. 3]; (11) 50 hectares (0.2 million square meters) of land, to a certain Sālār Jāf, in the Karaj district; (12) 200 hectares of land in the Karaj district to General Nāzim; (13) 1,000 hectares (10 million square meters) of land in the Qazvīn (a town some 90 miles to the west of Tehran) district to Mrs. Mīhan Hāshimī Nizhād, the wife of General Hāshimī Nizhād; of which 500 hectares had been transferred, according to title deed document #1708 of the Qazvīn Land Registry and dated 27 Āzar 1350 H. Sh./1971, to a certain Hazhbīr Yazdānī; (14) 750 hectares (7.5 million square meters) of land in the Dawlatābād region to a certain Zhīlā Farshchī; (15) 150 hectares (1.5 million square meters) of land in the Qazvīn district to Mrs. Tal'at Banī Ādam; (16) 200 hectares of land in the Dawlatābād region to General Khazā'ī.[50] Much of the grants of land involved properties in Karaj and Qazvīn, and it may be speculated that these tracts were offered with the purpose in mind that the new owners would begin industrial enterprises there. The regime had passed a law forbidding the construction of any new industrial enterprises in the capital city due to the congestion and population the build-up of new industries had created there. Since one of the objectives of the government had been to create an industrialist stratum that would support the Shah's programs, it may be that these grants of land had been intended to aid in the process of creating this stratum.

The usurpation of endowed properties, of course, had been standard practice in Safavid and Qājār times, as well. In the 1960's–70's it had involved appropriations of revenues not only by state officials, as was the case in the example of Āzmūn and the Endowments Organization. It also occurred through the consumption of revenues from awqāf by their mutavallīs. In few cases would this kind of embezzlement create more of a reaction than in Qumm, it may be imagined. Yet, the mutavallī of the shrine in Qumm, Mr. 'Abd al-Wahhāb Iqbāl from 1968 onward had apparently engaged in this kind of activity according to the revelation of the revolutionary regime in 1979. This individual, we are told, together with his son-in-law and one another official, were the "jacks of all trades" of the Āstānah-yi Muqaddas (the shrine in Qumm). Iqbāl, who only came to Qumm once a week, pocketed some 10 percent of the revenues earned by the shrine's endowments, an average monthly "salary" of 1 million rials (about $13,000); his two associates reputedly received equivalent amounts. They also engaged in the practice of parcelling the endowed properties adjacent to the shrine into smaller lots and selling them to their relatives. In order to have a free hand in their activities, they offered some of these properties to government officials, including the officials of SAVAK in Qumm. These individuals would then sell the lands for exorbitant prices and use the proceeds to buy properties elsewhere. The Deputy Director of SAVAK in Qumm is alleged to have used his profits from the sale of such real estate and land to buy a large park and hunting area in the Lāhījān region on the Caspian Sea littoral.[51]

In the administrative reform that had rendered the old Endowments Department of the Ministry of Culture into an independent Endowments Organization, efforts were undertaken to whittle down the influence of the clergy in ways beyond the appropriation of revenues, properties and *madrasahs*. Direct confrontation between the opposition among the clergy and the rest of the people of Iran became a policy commitment of the Endowments Organization in the early 1970's.

In a memorandum sent by the Director of the Endowments Organization to the Prime Minister, Amīr ʿAbbās Huvaydā, dated 6 Murdād 1351 H. Sh./1972, a plan of action to destroy the influence of Āyatullāh Rūhullāh al-Mūsavī Khumaynī was mooted. The individuals who assumed responsibility for this were the Director of the Endowments Organization and the Governors of Tehran and Khurāsān provinces. One objective was to try to link Khumaynī with the Baʿthist regime in Iraq, with which the Iranian government at that time was experiencing very tense relations over the questions of the frontier, the Kurdish rebellion, and the issue of Iranian *Shīʿah* in southern Iraq. The memorandum stated that the fabrication of documents showing the collaboration between Khumaynī and the Iraqi government could be facilitated through the resources of several ministries: Foreign Affairs, Information and SAVAK.

It called for contacting the clergy, "especially the *marājiʿ-yi taqlīd* throughout the country and in particular in the *hawzah*s of Mashhad, Qumm and Tehran to charge Khumaynī with error . . ." The memorandum, which was signed simply as "The Methods and Policy Committee", noted that the clergy had to be persuaded that Āyatullāh Khumaynī was not only wrong in his comportment as a member of the clergy stratum because he was besmirching the reputation of the *ʿulamāʾ*; but it also advocated firmly tying the Āyatullāh's efforts to the interests of foreigners who wish harm to the interests of Iran. (This, of course, was an ironic twist to the charges consistently levelled by Khumaynī since 1963 that the Shah's policies had no other aim but to serve foreign interests.) The memorandum articulated the need for the regime to present the *marājiʿ-yi taqlīd* with the urgency of taking a stand against Khumaynī's behavior. Their neutrality would not be sufficient:

> The religious institution, which is face to face with all the gifts of this country, its freedoms, stability and national security under the aegis of the Iranian Revolution, must undertake its duties to strengthen the foundations of these great national advances with sincerity and conviction; and they must not give permission to traitors wearing clerical robes to trade against the interests of the country.

The memorandum did note, however, that Khumaynī had of late sharply attacked the Iraqi government for its treatment of Iranian *Shīʿah* in the *ʿatabāt*, and that he had become so distressed that he had wanted to leave his place of exile in Iraq for Lebanon but had been prevented from doing so by the Baʿthist regime. The memorandum also noted that the Āyatullāh's adherents in Iran, including a

number of preachers, had disseminated this information to the masses. Therefore, the job of linking the Āyatullāh to a conspiracy with the Iraqi government
against Iranian interests was going to require some preparatory laying of the
groundwork by the Iranian propaganda machinery.

Furthermore, the memorandum continued, it would be necessary to get the
governors of the provinces of Khurāsān and Tehran (where Qumm was located),
as well as the governors of all other provinces and all the cities of the country to
meet with the *marāji'-yi taqlīd* of the *hawzah*s in their areas. The objective of
such meetings would be to importune the *marāji'* to direct criticisms of Āyatullāh
Khumaynī in their classes.

Additionally, it was recommended that the *'ulamā'* be apprised of how much
they had benefitted from the existing state of affairs, from the policies of the
monarchy, and from the stability and tranquility that prevailed throughout the
land. It should be expected, the document continued, that not all *'ulamā'* would
go along with the proposed plan of action, and some might even react violently
against it. Therefore, the government would do well to study what its reactions
might be to such opposition. It recommended harsh measures of reprisal in the
event and combined it with a policy of suborning the *marāji'*, the preachers and
the religious sciences students in the *madrasah*s. It warned that a great deal of
time and patience would be required to implement the plan to bribe the clergy.

Anticipating that the regime might prefer the harsh reprisals path in the face of
resistance to its plan of action, the memorandum outlined a three-phase action:
(1) a warning stage, in which the *marāji'* would be sternly reminded that no
social force, including the clergy, would be permitted to try to alter the policy of
the regime; (2) a preliminary stage of suppression, in which the *marāji'* choosing
to resist the plan of action would be told that the benefits of the monarchical
regime's policies would be withheld from them until they were to experience a
change of heart; (3) a stage of sharp suppression, involving the arrest of resisting
marāji', and the regime's treatment of them under the terms of a state of seige.
This stage would require a propaganda effort to gain the support of the masses. It
would be particularly important to deny the arrested clergymen the opportunity to
build up a social base of support among the masses at this point.

The memorandum thereupon pressed for the immediate implementation of
measures to realize the Committee's objectives. It directed that all preachers in
all mosques would be ordered to attack Āyatullāh Khumaynī's ideas indirectly
and without mentioning his name specifically. All rural and village *mullā*s were
to be given prepared statements in an effort to coordinate their criticism of
Khumaynī's thought and behavior to the villagers of Iran. The press would have
to drum up a public debate over the harm to the nation's unity that Khumaynī's
efforts had already engendered and, if not halted, would gravely damage. In
doing so, it would be particularly useful to seize upon the arguments of the
Persian language broadcasts of Radio Baghdad, implicating Khumaynī in conse-

quence. But the public debate must be guided not only by the press but also through the use of informers and others loyal to the regime. These could, indeed, should use rumormongering tactics to supplement their more "legitimate" anti-Khumaynī propaganda. The regime must also, it went on, create obstacles for the resistant marājiʿ-yi taqlīd to make it more difficult for them to carry out their functions. This must not be done directly, however, and ought to come by way of popular action. (Presumably, the masses might be encouraged by the regime to threaten a shift in allegiances to other, more "cooperative", marājiʿ in matters of religious emulation.) Iraq's actions must be attacked by the teachers of classes in the madrasahs. Preachers at funerals and commemorations of that sort must also be instructed to condemn the Baʿthist government of Iraq. Even the Boy Scouts organization of Iran must engage in anti-Khumaynī efforts, stated the memo, as must all political parties. In conclusion, it said that the plan of action as outlined would be successful to the extent that coordination and centralization of efforts to communicate and propagandize marked the whole endeavor to destroy the credibility of Āyatullāh Khumaynī.[52]

Much of the significance of this memorandum to clergy-state relations is self-evident. Its date—late July 1972—suggests that the regime was increasingly seeking ways of orchestrating its efforts against the clergy. It was about this time that it had brought into being a Religion Corps and shut down the Husaynīyah Irshād (about which events see below). This was also shortly after the commemoration of the 2500th year of monarchy in Iran (1971), as well as the year when Āyatullāh Khumaynī's book of lectures in Najaf, Islamic Government, was published. These developments no doubt hastened the effort at coordinated efforts in the 1960's to penetrate the religious institution by the instruments available to the bureaucratic state. In such efforts, the Endowments Organization was supposed to play a key role. In the mid-sixties, the Organization began the publication of a journal which attempted to glorify the cultural and mystical aspects of Islam. The image it wished to convey was of Islam as a state religion. In its first two numbers it contained a section entitled "News of the Activities of the Sāzmān-i Awqāf." Although discontinued after the second issue, one can gain an impression of the method by which the Organization intended to penetrate the religious institution by reading its brief paragraphs.

It committed the Organization to repair two of Tehran's madrasahs annually, with particular attention to students' quarters, kitchens, bath houses and medical facilities. Although such measures seemed salutory from the viewpoint of clergy interests, it is worth noting that in the past such assistance had been tied to acceptance by the mutavallis of the schools affected of a greater influence by the Sāzmān-i Awqāf, as had occurred with the Marvī madrasah, for example. Moreover, the journal indicated that the Organization would conduct internal reviews of such areas of madrasah activity as curriculum, study and instructional methods, and student morality. Internal reviews of this kind had been mandated by statutes and administrative decrees in the Rizā Shah period, to be sure; but they had quietly been allowed to lapse in the forties and fifties. Finally, the Organization would train its officials in "the American method of double-entry bookkeeping" in view of the disarray it alleged to exist in the accounts. Again, this kind of rationalization of the financial structure may be viewed as an attempt to establish greater efficiency and effectiveness of control over endowments. It is possible, of course, that improved rationalization could redound to the interests of the clergy; but in view of developments reviewed so far, there is reason to suggest objectives adverse to ʿulamāʾ interests, as well as supportive of them.[53]

A final note in regard to the contents of Maʿārif-i Islāmī, the journal of the Endowments Organization. It refused to carry the kinds of material that the progressives in the first reform movement of the 1960's (q.v.) had asked the Sāzmān-i Awqāf officials to publish. The articles had nothing to do with the sociology of religion and lacked any connection with the organization of the religious institution in Iran. In every issue appeared a two or three page biography of an individual who had contributed to the growth of Islam in the country. But with the exception of Āghā Buzurg-i Tihrānī (himself a biographer of contemporary ʿulamāʾ), the sketches were of classic writers of past eras. The theosophic and gnostic aspects of Islam were covered through contributions by such authors as ʿAllāmah Tabāʾtabāʾī and Seyyed Hossein Nasr. Correspondence of pre-20th century figures became the subject of analysis by historians. Excerpts from the writings of Western orientalists, such as Anne Marie Schimmel, and the texts of ancient endowment documents (vaqfnāmahs) were reproduced.

The only alternative that the regime permitted to these kinds of subjects was the material that appeared in Qumm's two periodicals, Darshaʾī az Maktab-i Islam and al-Hādī. But, of course, those journals refused to publish the reformist material as well. Instead, as might be expected, their contents were characterized by efforts to prove the existence of God, homilies on the anticipated return of the Imām, exhortations to prayer, parables and allegories on ethical conduct, contributions by Muslims to world civilization in historical periods, and contemporary developments in other Islamic lands.

The Endowments Organization could easily afford Qumm's complaints about the need for greater Arabic instruction in the national educational system and a commensurate reduction in western languages. This kind of specific and narrow demand had been the staple of ʿulamāʾ circles over the long term in this century. The regime could answer, as it did in the mid-1950's, in the affirmative; or it could ignore the whole thing, as it was then doing. But the Organization had evidently been charged by the Shah with more substantive anti-clerical activity directed at those members of the ʿulamāʾ stratum who insisted on giving religion a political and social "aspect" (janbah).

In keeping with the basic structure of policy, an imperial edict commanded the creation of the Religion Corps in August 1971, some seven months after this had been intimated by the Shah in a press conference. The reason for the creation of this Sipāh-i Dīn, as it was called, was implied in the edict to be the need to propagate the ordinances of Islam and place spirituality at an equal level with desires for material progress under the banner of the "White Revolution". The corpsmen were to be chosen from among those young graduates of the Islamic sciences who were eligible for military service (i.e., not *tullāb* but bachelors of humanities and social science from Tehran and Mashhad Universities' Faculties of Theology.) The administration of the affairs of the Sipāh-i Dīn was centered in the Sāzmān-i Awqāf, which created a General Department for the Religion Corps and Religious Affairs to handle its management.[54] The first class of corpsmen consisted not only of bachelors of divinity at Tehran and Mashhad Universities. Indeed, the 39 members of this class had specialized in diverse fields at undergraduate college: (1) political science; (2) geography; (3) theology; (4) Arabic literature; (5) philosophy; (6) social science; (7) archaeology. The first class was

Distribution of First Class of Sipāh-i Dīn (1972)
by *Shahrastān (N=39)*

   I. Tehran (10)
       a. General Department of the Religion Corps (2)
       b. Bureau of Construction and Development (1)
       c. General Department of Financial Affairs (2)
       d. Bureau of Statistics and Surveys (4)
       e. General Department of Administrative Affairs (1)
   II. Shimīrān (2)
  III. Karaj (1)
  IV. Tabrīz (3)
   V. Iṣfahān (8)
  VI. Marāghah (2)
 VII. Hamadān (1)
VIII. Shīrāz (2)
  IX. Sanandaj (2)
   X. Ahvāz (1)
  XI. Riżāʾīyah (1)
 XII. Kāshān (1)
XIII. Simnān (1)
XIV. Gurgān (1)
 XV. Zanjān (1)
VXI. Bābul (1)
XVII. Mashhad (1)

Source: Dawlat-i Shāh-in-Shāhī-yi Iran. Sāzmān-i Awqāf. Daftar-i Āmār va Muhandisī -yi Raqabāt. "Guzārish-i Pīshrafthā va Faʿʿālīyathā-yi Sāzmān-i Awqāf, 1352 H. Sh./1973." Tehran: Sāzmān-i Awqāf, 1353 H. Sh./1974. Mimeo/Internal Report, p. 52 ff.

matriculated in October–November 1972, and their employment—both regionally and functionally—furnishes some clues as to the areas of concentration and need of the Endowments Organization.

The second class of Religion Corpsmen began their employment for the Endowments Organization in late January 1974. This class of 41 had studied the following fields at the bachelor of arts level: (1) theology; (2) Arabic literature; (3) Persian literature; (4) philosophy; (5) social sciences. These individuals were employed in many of the same *shahrastans* (cities) as the first class, but by far the largest proportion secured positions in Tehran (some 40%). The following geographical distribution characterized the second class:

Distribution of Second Class of Sipāh-i Dīn (1974)
by *Shahrastān* (N=41)

     I. Tehran (16)
    II. Shimīrān (3)
   III. Isfahān (3)
   IV. Rizāʾīyah (2)
    V. Tabrīz (3)
   VI. Mashhad (4)
  VII. Kirmānshāh (1)
 VIII. Qumm (1)
   IX. Arāk (1)
    X. Bābul (1)
   XI. Kirmān (1)
  XII. Zanjān (1)
 XIII. Ahvāz (1)
 XIV. Sārī (1)
  XV. Gurgān (1)
 XVI. Khurramābād (1)
Source: Same as for First Class of Sipāh-i Dīn (1972)

Evidently feeling the need to supplement the activities of the Religion Corps, with its jurisdiction basically in the state bureaucracy, the regime also created within the Endowments Organization a Department for Religious Propaganda. This Department was to be responsible for the training of Religious Propagandists, whose main tasks were to involve work in the country's rural areas. As of late February 1974 some 480 Religious Propagandists had been dispatched to engage in the areas of activity listed on page 141.

One may see from this list that the Religious Propagandists were meant to be generalists in social affairs. The overlap with the activities of the clergy in both religious and social solidary work is clear. The Religion Corps and the Religious Propagandists evidently constituted the regime's vanguard of loyalists of whom the Āzmūn memorandum to Prime Minister Huvaydā of July 1972 had spoken.

Activities of the Religious Propagandists
(Muravvijīn i Dīn)

I. Religious and Educational Activities
   1. Sermons.
   2. Leading the prayer.
   3. Instruction (in collaboration with the Literacy Corps).
      a. *Fiq.*
      b. *Shar'īyyāt.*
      c. *Qur'ān.*
II. Health and Development Activities (in cooperation with the Literacy Corps)
   1. Caring for the sick.
   2. Building water heaters.
   3. Constructing and repairing mosques.
   4. Paving roads.
   5. Constructing baths.
   6. Building schools.
   7. Building bridges.
   8. Building water towers and reservoirs.
   9. Vaccinating livestock.
III. Social and Patriotic Activities.
   1. Speaking on national policies in some 500 rural areas of the country.
   2. Activities related to cooperatives, the nationalization of forests, oil.
IV. Administrative Duties.
   1. Dissemination of pamphlets on numerous social issues.

Source: Same as previous table, pp. 56–60.

Together with their associates in the Literacy Corps, they were meant to be the "*mullā*s of modernization."

Sāzmān-i Awqāf financial assistance to teachers and students of the *madrasah*s is detailed in the appendices for the years 1972 and 1973. The striking things about these figures are: (1) the Endowments Organization in 1973 was helping 3100 *tullāb*, enrolled in 111 *madrasah*s, with financial assistance. Using figures for total number of *tullāb* and *madrasah*s in the country as of 1968 (latest year for which figures are available), this indicates the state was subsidizing about 41 percent of all *tullāb* in about 80 percent of all *madrasah*s. In 1973, the average monthly stipend to students from the state was 228 rials. [A decade earlier (1963), the monthly student stipend in Qumm had been between 300–400 rials on average (and in some cases as high as 1,000 rials), as distributed by the clergy from the *sahm-i imām*. In 1975, funds distributed by six *marāji'-yi taqlīd* to Qumm students from the *sahm-i imām* averaged 1467 rials.][55]

Additional data of interest from the statistics include the fact of a marked drop in average monthly stipends allocated by the Sāzmān-i Awqāf between the two years 1972 and 1973 of from 331 rials to 228 rials. Was this in keeping with the points of the Āzmūn memorandum to put pressure on the religious studies students and ʿulamāʾ unwilling to go along with the state's plan of action? The suspicion that this may have been so is increased by the drop, over the same two year period, in Awqāf subsidization of teachers in the madrasahs. The decline was from 1967 rials per month to 1115 on the average—a drop of 43 percent. The geographic variations in the state's subsidization of religious studies students nation-wide indicate the following: (a) exceptionally high levels in Kirmānshāh (a province with a high (Sunnī) Kurdish population), Simnān Governorate (to the northeast of Tehran Province) and Hamadān (in western Iran); (b) Lower than average levels in all other provinces, with outstandingly low amounts, in view of their importance for the clergy, of Khurāsān, Isfahān and Tehran provinces.[56]

With such limited time-spans, it is impossible to generalize in terms of regime-clergy relations. The ideal situation for the state would be for the Endowments Organization increasingly to take over madrasah administration while tightening its allocations to students and teachers there in the hopes that dwindling clergy revenues from awqāf and khums (although the latter was beyond direct regime control) would stimulate the exodus of tullāb from madrasah to vocational and/or other educational training. Increasing dependence on the Sāzmān-i Awqāf plus rapid reduction of financial assistance by it could not immediately, nor perhaps even in the medium run, have adverse consequences for Qumm. But a region such as Isfahān, with its historical importance as a center of ʿulamāʾ influence might be vulnerable. Figures for 1960 reveal that the city of Isfahān had some 30 madrasahs; in 1967, 28 were still alleged to exist. But by 1975 the Isfahān hawzah could not have had more than 1,000 tullāb.[57] With a low student enrollment, very low Awqāf levels of student financial aid, the city's fate seemed to be moving in the direction if its madrasahs being preserved as historical landmarks. It has already been shown that extensive appropriations of awqāf by their mutavallīs had occured in Iran throughout the 19th and 20th centuries. The effect of such appropriations, of course, was to remove sources of revenue for student stipends, inter alia. By 1973, the Endowments Organization was supporting only 72 tullāb in all of Isfahān province. simultaneously, the state's modernization efforts had caused a number of industrialization programs to be initiated in the Isfahān region, including the great steel mill complex. Given the labor shortage, the thought must have occurred to the regime that constriction in the financial condition of the madrasahs would encourage their students to make themselves available for the badly undermanned labor market. With variations, this scenario likely had been drawn for other regions of the country.

The Endowments Organization had also provided financial support to students in the dabistāns (primary schools), dabīristāns (secondary schools) and dānishgāhs (universities). These secular schools did include certain programs of religious education in which some candidates could specialize. This was especially the case for the higher levels of learning. According to the information provided in the internal report of the Endowments Organization for 1973, it was assisting some 35 university students and some 300 primary schools plus 352 secondary schools.[58] The nature of the obligations contracted by such students is not clear, but at minimum the Endowments Organization probably expected that they would constitute a manpower pool for employment in various sectors over which that institution had jurisdiction.

THE SECOND REFORM MOVEMENT: THE HUSAYNĪYAH IRSHĀD INTERLUDE

As a protest movement of reform, the activities of the Husaynīyah Irshād, under the leadership of Dr. ʿAlī Sharīʿatī, differed from the first reform effort of the early 1960's. During the time when he was active in the Husaynīyah Irshād (1967–1973), he protested against what he conceived to be the backwardness of the clergy; but he combined this criticism with attacks on the bureaucratization of power. To be sure, he did this in allegorical terms and through analogy only. But the vehemence of his language and emotional tone of his lectures provided his audiences with the tool to cut through the implicit, aesopian formulas to the essence of his message: *Shīʿah* lived under oppression in Iran and must actively strive to change their condition. Sharīʿatī's writings were eagerly read by Iranian youth, including many in the traditional religious schools. The clergy took offense at his rhetoric and denigrated his learning, since Sharīʿatī had not formally studied the higher cycle of religious education in a *madrasah* and had never obtained a diploma of *ijtihād*. No doubt the state hoped that Sharīʿatī's activities would sow discord within the religious institution. To that extent, it was willing to allow him to present his point of view. It also perhaps wished to compensate for its harsh suppression of the 1962–1963 protests, which had involved the incarceration of many ʿulamāʾ and the termination of the activities of the Monthly Religious Society, q.v. If so, then its motivations were purely tactical.

The founder of the Husaynīyah Irshād was a philanthropist by the name of Muhammad Humāyūn who had been inspired by the Monthly Religious Society lectures. He initially volunteered funds to buy 1,000 square meters of land to build the institution upon; but the plans kept changing and calling for more space. Eventually, a property of 4,000 square meters was purchased in Qulhak, on the way to the Shimīrān suburbs to the north of Tehran. Humāyūn had to purchase such a large tract because its owner did not wish to parcel it up. He therefore bought the entire lot with the view in mind of himself selling 2,000 square meters afterwards. Ordinarily, such details would not be very interesting, but in this particular case, Humāyūn decided to keep the additional land because the phenomenal success of the Husaynīyah Irshād in drawing attendance required him to build a larger structure. It began its operations in 1965, and Iranians outside the capital deluged its directors for assistance in establishing similar *husaynīyah*s (literally, a place where mourning for the martyrdom of Imām Husayn takes place) elsewhere.[59]

The Husaynīyah Irshād had a nation-wide impact that the deliberations and lectures of the antecedent Monthly Religious Society never enjoyed. The very choice of name indicated that its members and audiences would adopt the role model of martyrdom for the sake of the cause of social justice. Writing about the goals of the organization, which he himself had a hand in establishing in the first place, Āyatullāh Mutahharī wrote in 1968:[60]

> In recent years our educated youth, after passing through a period of being astonished, even repulsed [by religion] are paying an attention and concern for it that defies description . . . The Husaynīyah Irshād, a new institution, in existence for less than three years, knows its task to be to answer, to the extent that it can, these needs [of youth today] and to introduce Islamic ideology [to them] such as it is. This institution deems it sufficient to unveil the beautiful face of the beloved martyr of Islam [Imām Husayn] in order to transform the true seekers into restless lovers [of Shīʿism].

Among the original members of the managing board of the Husaynīyah Irshād were Āyatullāh Mutahharī, Seyyed Hossein Nasr (then Dean of the Faculty of Literature of Tehran University), [ʿIzatullāh?] Sahābī, Husayn Mazīnī, and Sharīʿatī. By the time that the regime closed down the institution in the summer of 1973, Sharīʿatī was said to have been the only remaining founding board member. The departure of these gentlemen stemmed from the regime's constant harrassment, making it harder and harder for it to stay within the bounds of what was permitted. Also, the group was internally divided into those who felt that the Husaynīyah Irshād had overstepped its initial objectives. This group of early departers included Nasr. A second group left later on, but before the Husaynīyah Irshād was shut down by military units of the government. This group apparently considered that Sharīʿatī's willingness to bring the institution's activities to the brink of political protest was compromising its reformist message. As Mutahharī put it, *pāhishrā rūyah janbah-yi sīyāsī fishār mīdād* (Dr. Sharīʿatī brought pressure to bear on the political aspect [of the Husaynīyah's activities]).[61]

Not much is known about Sharīʿatī's early years. His father, Muhammad Taqī Sharīʿatī, was a well-known specialist in *tafsīr* in Mashhad. He, himself, was born in 1933 in a village near the town of Sabzivār. The family apparently were partisans of Prime Minister Muhammad Musaddiq, since we are told that between 1953 and 1960 they were active in the National Front. In 1957, the pair were imprisoned as part of a general purge that took place at that time; it seems they were released in 1960, and in that year he is said to have gone to France. There, Sharīʿatī studied sociology and religion at the Sorbonne, earning his doctorate in sociology. In 1964, he returned to Iran and, after a short imprisonment was again freed. From there, he had a brief stint of teaching at the Firdawsī University in Mashhad but evidently was compelled to leave. It was at that time that he joined the Husaynīyah Irshād group, where he was its most prolific contributor. The regime arrested Sharīʿatī in the summer of 1973 and imprisoned him for a year and a half. When he was released in the early winter of 1975, he was kept under police surveillance in exile in Mazīnān, near the town of Sabzivār in Khurāsān province. He remained there for more than two years, apparently languishing from lack of contact with visitors and generally feeling the need to break out of his isolation. In June 1977, he was permitted to travel to Europe. His dead body was found in the home of his brother in southern England on 19 June 1977. His sudden death in mysterious circumstances there has been interpreted virtually by all observers to have been the work of SAVAK agents operating abroad.[62]

Sharīʿatī's writings sought to clarify his own thinking about the Islamic response to modernism and to develop sources for the instructional program of the Husaynīyah Irshād. If one reads his monographs closely, one must conclude that he did not reach the point that the sociologist of religion must of divorcing his analytical rigor from his passionate attachment to Shīʿī Islam. This conclusion will not be accepted by his committed followers, for whom he stands as the foremost enlightened thinker of Iran in the contemporary period. They see his genius in his capacity as a pioneer of a new methodology for the study of Islam; in terms of his trenchant criticism of the "hidebound clergy" (ʿulamāʾ-yi qishrī); in regard to his unremitting courage in the face of regime repression. This line of thinking, therefore, considers that he never sought to reconcile sociological analysis and the exigencies of Shīʿī Islam: monotheism, belief in the prophecy of Muhammad, belief in the imāmate and the valāyat of ʿAlī. If such, indeed, had not been his aim, then the point must be conceded. But if Sharīʿatī seriously meant to apply sociological rigor in his analysis of Iranian society, then we must follow him as sociologists ourselves, ready to concede the point only at the end of the inquiry if it is possible to show his logical consistency; or to critique in a constructive manner in the event the logic does not hold at certain points.

Sharīʿatī's message was that the Husaynīyah Irshād ought to be a model for the hawzahs of Iran. He seemingly had in mind a free university, in which the students and teachers would play a co-equal role in devising their own programs, contributing to the content of the curriculum, making their own recommendations about methods.[63] Such egalitarianism provoked the traditionalists among the ʿulamāʾ. For despite the "democracy" that characterized the learning process in the madrasahs, in the sense of mutuality of respect between teacher and student, the ʿulamāʾ did consider themselves as aʿlam (most knowledgeable) vis-à-vis their students. This fundamental change would not be acceptable to them.

Sharīʿatī's hostility to the traditionalists among the ʿulamāʾ was sharply etched into nearly all of his lectures, sermons and writings. To him, they were "the timeless ones"—*bī zamān*, as he called them. He saw them operating, as it were, in a vacuum, oblivious to social reality in any meaningfully temporal sense. In a simile he frequently employed, he likened these unreconstructed *ʿulamāʾ* to zombies mindlessly regurgitating *fiq* lessons.[64] His heroes and role models for Iranian religionaries were Jamāl al-Dīn al-Afghānī (d. 1897), the vehement adversary of Western imperialism; Muhammad ʿAbdūh (d. 1905), the force behind the Egyptian religious reform movement in the early 20th century; and Muhammad Iqbāl (d. 1938), the great Muslim reformer of India who stood for activism and creative self-realization, as against what he saw to be the typical passivity and acceptance of Muslim man in modern times.[65] Much of the rhetorical argumentation to be found in Sharīʿatī's writings center on the theme of anti-imperialism. Like al-Afghānī, his attacks against the West were inspired by zeal to defend Islam; but unlike the former, Sharīʿatī's efforts were firmly impressed by the imprimatur of nationalism and his experiences in Iran in the 1950's. Like ʿAbdūh, Sharīʿatī meant to revitalize Islam and effect a reconciliation between its premises and logic with that of natural and social science. But he went beyond ʿAbdūh in the latter's criticisms of the traditional *ʿulamāʾ*. For Sharīʿatī sought to link the traditionalists' stubbornness with the defections that he perceived from Islam to Western culture: imperialism is triumphant because the conservative clergymen are driving Iranian youth into the arms of the West.[66]

These stinging rebukes provided the traditionalist *ʿulamāʾ* with the excuse of censoring him in the *madrasah*s and debunking his level of erudition. To be sure, anti-imperialism has long struck a responsive chord in clergy circles in Iran. But here was a layman, educated in Europe, having studied Marxist thought with Jean-Paul Sartre, who was laying the blame for the success of imperialism at the feet of the clergy! His western education made him unfit to be a spokesman for religious interests. How can Imām ʿAlī, Imām Husayn, Abū Zarr, Hazrat ʿAbbās, and the rest of the *Shīʿī* saints be mentioned in the same breath as Sartre, Frantz Fanon, Emile Durkheim, Max Weber and Alexis Karl? Here was a young man who defended Islamic democracy by citing the *Sunnī* precedent of *shūrā* in the election of the caliph of Islam! Yet, to modernists the choice of Afghānī, ʿAbdūh and Iqbāl made sense. These vigorous defenders of Islam were themselves modernists in the sense that they positively confronted the challenges of social reality of modern times. By contrast, the famous Iranian *ʿulamāʾ* from Muhammad Bāqir (Vahīd) Bihbihānī (d. 1803) to Āyatullāh Muhammad Husayn Burūjirdī (d. 1961) had made doctrinal and theoretical contributions; but they had on the whole lacked the social commitment that would have carried them beyond the construction of mosques and development of *madrasah*s to the leadership of a nation's people. This is what Sharīʿatī wanted above all else.

For him, to be a leader in Iran means to partake of the third world revolution against foreign hegemony. His citations of Afghānī and Fanon are, of course, entirely consistent with this line. Iqbāl appears somewhat more difficult to explain to the extent that a good deal of his writing seemed mystical and a-rational; and his epistomological basis was not grounded in praxis, as with Fanon, but instead in theosophical premises in which direct intuition plays the major role. Here, the sociologist in Sharīʿatī becomes somewhat blurred; however, if it is considered that Sharīʿatī's sociology went hand-in-hand with his own intuitional epistemology, then the importance to him of Iqbāl becomes clearer. This, plus the fact that exhortation to reform, to be active, was the other part of the tandem in Iqbāl. Such urgings, complementing that philosopher's emphasis on knowing through the self's interaction with God, elucidates for us Iqbāl's place in Sharīʿatī's own development.

Things become considerably murkier, however, when Sharīʿatī begins to use such concepts as class, dialectic, contradictions, development, history. It is almost as if the mere mention of these categories of philosophical and sociological analysis is sufficient to then proceed to the claims of Islam as progressive, Shīʿism as the best varient of Islam, and so on. Yet, it is precisely the introduction of those social variables into the study of religion for which Sharīʿatī had expended so much of his energies. It is here, then, that the tightness of the logic is wanting.

Nonetheless, it must be remembered that Sharīʿatī was operating in extremely difficult circumstances. The regime had repeatedly warned him to understate the sociology and stress the ʿaqāʾid (ideology of Shīʿī belief). Moreover, he did not see his own role as an ʿAbdūh to the Iranian people. Because he was himself an *activist,* much of what he had to say perforce was in the form of pamphleteering. He wrote to spread a message. He operated under the constraints of a hurried schedule, appointments, lectures, classes, meetings. The urgent quality of his thinking is reflected in the titles of his works; *What Is To Be Done?*[67] *Whence Shall We Begin?*[68] *Martyrdom. Waiting for the Religion of Protest.* These, along with his *Community and Imamate, ʿAlīʾs Shīʿism and Safavid Shīʿism, The Methodology of Understanding Islam* comprise his most well-known works.[69] He was, in a word, a partisan who rejected bourgeois sociology in its positivist and functionalist forms, and borrowed from Marxism what he believed helped in the analysis of Iranian society. The following words by an anonymous friend of Sharīʿatī suggest his position concisely: "Shariʿati always placed his finger on the realities and avoided abstract thought. He was a realistic and committed sociologist. . . ."[70]

At one point he presents himself as a sociologist of religion interested in applying this discipline to Islam. However, it becomes clear that his purpose is not to apply sociological analysis to interpret Islam. Instead, he notes that he has used the *Qurʾān* to deduce many principles of history and sociology from a thorough exegesis of it. He appears to be saying, in other words, that Islam furnishes him with a philosophy of history; equipped with this, he turns to the disciplines of sociology and history as they are known in the West; and studying sociology and history, he finds verification of issues lying at the heart of Islam.

As an example of Islam's contribution to sociology (which is, it must be repeated, the way he wants to put it, *not* sociology's contribution to the study of Islam), he cites the emigration of the prophet from Mecca to Medina in 622 A.D. Muslims have typically regarded this event (*hijrah*) as a discrete happenstance in this history; it took place once and supposedly has no further significance. But, says Sharīʿatī, to leave it at that would be to deprive Islam of a very rich contribution to comparative history. He asserts that in his study of Islam the *Qurʾān* has led him to conclude that *hijrah* is a profound philosophical and sociological element in human civilization. *Hijrah* is the only constant that he, the comparative historian, has found in "all 27 civilizations in human history" that he was able to identify.[71] Yet, it is not clear where he wants to go with this factor. For, if it were in fact the case that emigration is the unique constant in all the cases he cites, is this discovery deriveable from a reading of the *Qurʾān* alone? Or can the researcher make this discovery without benefit of knowledge of its contents? Perhaps Sharīʿatī's point is to demonstrate not that the *Qurʾān* holds the key to the study of comparative civilization but that the alert Muslim will find concepts that at least implicitly hold out the promise of greater understanding of other cultures. If this is the case, will he also accept the idea of an autonomous comparative historical sociology as a discipline for which Islam then becomes a laboratory for inquiry and research? For instance, the disciplinarian (whose subject matter is broad ranging, indeed and encompasses such diverse issues as land tenure relations, urbanization patterns, the political economy of the market, etc.) may choose emigration in general for research; Islamic society(ies) might then become the specific context in which a particular structure of emigration is analyzed.

Sharīʿatī is probably willing to accept this is as appropriate research strategy for the scholar. But it does not interest him except as a passing contribution to the edification of the minds of Iranian intellectuals. His central effort is still to promote Shīʿism. All well and good, but the emigration of Muhammad appears to Sharʿatī itself to be an independent variable in the study of history—a sort of yardstick against which other emigration patterns are to be assessed. This *hijrah* then becomes "an endless new element, full of splendor." *Shīʿah* will recognize the validity of this conceptualization of *hijrah* as axiomatic. But what exactly are the structural relationships between this *hijrah* and other manifestations of emigration in recorded history? What hypotheses and propositions might one generate concerning it? Is the Islamic *hijrah* an independent, dependent, intervening variable in the theoretical statements to be made about emigration as a structural component of human civilization and social change? These concerns of the sociologist are peripheral to Sharīʿatī's own investigations for reasons already delineated.

Elsewhere, Sharīʿatī appears to be grappling with the central issues of his discipline more than endeavoring to show how Islam has influenced history. Here, he seeks to apply broad concepts to Islamic institutions and processes in the manner of the "social engineer" who seeks to change people's estimations of themselves, their roles and their participation in their societies for the better. This is the Sharīʿatī for whom "the social and class contradictions which exist at the foundations of society" are crucial for an explanation of social reality. His objective is to analyze these and bring the fruits of his inquiry to the social consciousness of the Iranian people. Here, the influence of Sartre and French radical sociology appears to prevail.

But how is this to be done? He answers his own question:[72]

> By writing, talking and other possible [means] at one's disposal . . . by casting the flame of one's social awareness and highly refined, life-giving prophetic knowledge onto the night and winter of the people, the same divine fire that Prometheus gave to man.

Sharīʿatī is convinced that people's awareness of class contradictions will not be stimulated as long as the intellectual vanguard in Iran continues to manifest gnostic orientations (the urbanized intellectual elite, presumably), or purvey the ordinances of religion (the ʿulamāʾ). Writing and talking are traditional means of intellectual and scholarly discourse, of course; but "other [means] at one's disposal" broadly hints at political activism. The symbolism of Prometheus rings strangely in a Shīʿī context given its importance for Marxists in "unmasking" religion. But for Sharīʿatī, reconciling Divine revelation and the Promethean challenge to the divinity was the essence of the activist's role and behavior.

For the most part, Sharīʿatī's emphasis is on exhorting his audience to be aware Muslims. He wants to restore the supremacy of ʿAlī's practice. Safavid Shīʿism (read the Pahlavī brand of Shīʿism) has as its objective the advancement of raison d'état. For this reason, "Safavid" Shīʿism saw the elevation of the imāms and the ʿulamāʾ to an abstracted pinnacle. They thus became "out of this world." This then freed the state, according to Sharīʿatī, from responsible rule. If imāms and ʿulamāʾ regulate extra-terrestrial matters, then the state can proceed in matters of social justice through the interpretations of its officials. Whatever responsibility is exercised by the Shah, his vazīrs (ministers), and even the clergy appointed to administrative positions has nothing to do with the justice of the Imām. This is another way of saying that for the Iranian state, one must render to the Imām what is the Imām's, but only in the next world! In the meanwhile, says Sharīʿatī, state officials will carry out their responsibility in their own, base way. Such arguments are to be found in different places in his writings, but it is thrown into sharp relief in his book, ʿAlī's Shīʿism and Safavid Shīʿism.[73] The acceptance of Safavid Shīʿism is tantamount to submission not to

Allah but to the whimsy of secular power. To this, ʿAlī's Shīʿism "says no!" True *Shīʿī* faith is a faith of protest.

It might be considered that Sharīʿatī's message of protest would have rendered him a logical ally of Āyatullāh Khumaynī, but there is a difference between the two. Whereas the latter had been explicit in his opposition to the government and its political formulas, Sharīʿatī could not emulate the Āyatullāh's open attacks. It is true that his writings see in *Shīʿī* thought and practice revolutionary action. But he always had to link his discussion of the revolutionary quality of the faith with the practice of Muhammad, ʿAlī and Husayn. His remonstrations against tyranny had to be couched in the form of dramaturgical symbols.[74] Sharīʿatī never called upon the Iranian army, for example, "to make this government fall,"[75] as Āyatullāh Khumaynī had done. Further, Sharīʿatī's lower level of erudition in the transmitted and intellectual sciences of Shīʿism, and his numerous theological errors early in his sermonizing created an individious distinction in the minds of Iranian clergymen between the two individuals. Finally, the target of ʿAlī Sharīʿatī's attacks in the *madrasah*s were clergymen with traditional education and interests. Even though Āyatullāh Khumaynī had acted in a manner which Sharīʿatī had been urging, he seems to have regarded Sharīʿatī as something of a newcomer. There is little evidence that the two individuals met, corresponded, read each others' works, exchanged critiques. What information does exist seems to indicate that Sharīʿatī acknowledged the Āyatullāh as a great leader; but Khumaynī seems mainly to have ignored Sharīʿatī.

Nonetheless, similarities exist, as well, in their mutual treatment of certain basic themes (for Khumaynī's analysis, see below). There is a subtlety in Sharīʿatī that emerges from time to time. It is a subtlety that takes into account the complexity of social and human reality, and his orientation to these bespeaks his exposure to two cultures: the Iranian and the European. The subtlety surfaces in his view of religion as symbol, as against religion as *a priori* truth. When he wants to push his message of political activism, he sees Islam in terms of symbolic forms. Thus, to quietists who say one must wait for the *Imām* his answer is not that the *Imām* is himself symbolic (a heresy), but rather that the *imām*s had meant that men should live responsibly in the world; their waiting for the Sāhib-i Zamān (Ruler of the Age) symbolized their determination to be ready for him when he comes; the *Imām* would naturally love those best who were faithful to ʿAlī's way: and this way had taught men to be committed, to do, to be, to say no.

This is one side of Sharīʿatī. Another side features his more didactic and polemical aspect, in which Islam, being timeless, maintains eternally its currency. Thus, he holds that the hidden Imām has not, like Christ, gone to live in another world. The *Mahdī* (messiah) indeed lives in the real world, and he has his "feet on the ground." It is only that people cannot recognize him, even if they look him right in the face. So, he is "hidden" in the sense of being unrecognizeable, disguised; but he is certainly encounterable, and who knows if he is not this bazaar merchant or that farmer?![76]

Then, too, there is the Sharīʿatī who is the pragmatist and utilitarian. Acknowledging that the study of Islam is possible through different methodological applications (he lists natural science, inductive methods, those associated with theology, others attributed to philosophy, and still others common to mysticism) he asks: who is right? His response is whichever method "has a positive, creative and progressive influence" on the lives of Muslims.[77]

Above all, Sharīʿatī stressed the politicization of Shīʿism. In a remarkable passage discussing his notion that Islam may be seen as two component factors: ideology and culture, he clearly states his preference for interpreting it as ideology. Or at least he wishes to rectify an imbalance that he discerns has thrown chief emphasis to Islam as culture over the years. Accordingly, he develops this dichotomy:

Islam as Ideology	Islam as Culture
1. Abū Zarr [a political activist and an early partisan of ʿAlī] constructs it.	1. Ibn Sīnā constructs it.
2. One undertaking *jihād* constructs it.	2. A *mujtahid* constructs it.
3. Means belief, and an enlightened person [*rawshan-fikr*] constructs it.	3. An ʿalim constructs it.

To Sharīʿatī it is commitment and engagement that count. For that reason, an uneducated person might understand Islam better and think and live more fully within the Islamic framework than an educated person, a *faqīh*, a *faylsūf* or an *ʿārif*. Responsibility and choice become almost code words with Sharīʿatī, who castigates the bookish passivity of the guardians of the Islamic sciences. A person who reads treatises and the *Makāsib* (by Shaykh Murtazā Ansārī) cannot transcend comprehension of Islamic regulations, ordinances, and law; but one who has read the life (*sīrah*) of Muhammad will have grasped the real meaning of Islam.[78] It is no wonder, then, that the ʿulamāʾ responded with such antipathy to his views, these learned men whom he charged in the following passage with nothing less than the denaturing of Islam:[79]

> And they have brought all of this forward with a policy which took the prayer book from the graveyard to the city and took the *Qurʾān* from life and city to the graveyard and made an offering to the spirits of the dead; they established in the *hawzah*s of religious education the principles of jurisprudence before the students of the Islamic sciences and took the *Qurʾān* away from them, placing it on the shelf of their cells. It is clear that when the *Qurʾān* leaves the life of the Muslim people and Islam is taken out of the life of the Muslim ʿulamāʾ, in their absence one can do anything, just as they *have* done everything [to harm the Muslim people].

Sharīʿatī insisted upon an Islamic humanism. In this context, he saw man not as an abject worshipper of a forbidding God but as the embodiment of the spirit of life which God breathed into him at the creation of the world and mankind. The literalists have extracted the dynamic, the vital elements of the faith. They fight tooth and nail against any effort at symbolic expression in which consists the richness of Shīʿī belief, he holds.[80]

Having made the case for an Islam which renders man responsible for his actions, a creator of his destiny, Sharīʿatī believes that man acts in history. He is a historical individual; therefore, he would do well to examine the traditional concepts of his faith with attention to its evolution in time and space: "from the social, historical and class points of view."[81] In doing so, he accepts not Aristotelian epistemological premises (A = A, A ≠ non-A) but dialectical foundations of truth. A thing or being contains within itself contradictory tendencies which, in opposition to one another, produce a further version of itself which is closer to truth but yet is still evolving. In an intriguing attempt to make the principles of waiting for the return of the *Mahdī* over into a positive prescription for action, he places it within the process whereby a synthesis emerges from "the ruling, false reality" of post-Safavid Shīʿism and the "commanded, salvational truth" of the true religion.[82] The growth, maturation and ultimate perfection of human civilization is therefore, for him, not a linear process of development but, at bottom, dialectical. In a passage which elucidates this orientation, he argues:[83]

> The enlightened thinkers of today generally believe that when a dialectical con-
> tradiction exists in the structure [*matn*] of society, this factor of contradiction and
> struggle between thesis and antithesis impels society to movement and draws it to
> revolution and moves it forward, frees it and, ultimately, enters it into a new stage.

But what is the motor force of historical development? Sharīʿatī says that there can be no doubt that it constitutes "the biggest difficulty of history and sociology . . . to find the basic factor of social change and development." Islam in general, and Shīʿism, in particular, rejects the notion that either great personalities, happenstance or immutable and unchangeable laws constitute the engine of historical development. Instead, it is the people. Sharīʿatī feels that the *Qurʾān*'s repeated references to the people—*al-nās*—suggest that they play an autonomous role in the world. As we have already seen, it is this basic stress on *homo faber* that underlies his essentially humanistic interpretation of Shīʿism.[84]

Sharīʿatī claims that this position differs from that of Marxism, since the central tenet of Marxism is, he believes, that "history itself like a living society, is independent of individuals."[85] In thus arguing, Sharīʿatī has apparently accepted the Engels, Lenin, Stalin and other vulgarizations of Marx's original conception about dialectics and historical development. The central underpinning concept of Marx's epistemology is, in fact, praxis; it features, as does Sharīʿatī's own epistemology, *homo faber:* man, the doer. It was then Engels who vulgarized the Marxian idea of a conjuncture of "mind and matter," "man and thing" in a complex scheme of social evolution. Sharīʿatī could have more effectively critiqued Marx not for positing a putative "mind vs. matter" dichotomy in which matter was primary (Engels); but rather Marx's failure to specify how individuals act as a class. It seems that this is fertile ground for debate between the Islamic humanist and Marx's theory of knowledge and philosophy of history.

For Sharīʿatī, Shīʿism envisages the movement of history toward the harmonious society, a society free of conflict. And why is it that a *Shīʿī* society, above all others, characteristically evolves toward social justice, piety and chastity; toward a community devoid of antagonistic contradictions? Because of the operation of the mechanism of *intiẓār* (waiting for the messiah). The masses's view of *intiẓār* must be a positive, action-oriented, voluntaristic one. It must not be passive, inert and fatalistic. The contradictions contained, he argues, between *intiẓār-i musbat* (Positive *intiẓār*) and *intiẓār-i manfi* (negative *intiẓār*) will force the ultimate emergence of truth and justice in a historically determinative way. He then grandly sums up:[86]

> My philosophy can explain the course of human history and the continuity of events within a logical, scientific and ongoing conjunction. He who is mentally and practically/materially waiting for the return of the Imām is a person who is ready . . . . In our own villages, up to a while ago, our clergy and *imām jumʿahs* . . . would take our youth to drill practice and taught horseback riding; and with sheathed sword and arms, they would participate in Friday prayer. . . . Thus, we see that one who is waiting for the return of the Imām is one who is prepared; so that at any moment it is possible for the trumpet to sound, and he will see himself responsible in participating in this divine law; and he is automatically ready, both engaging himself and equipped, every *Shīʿī* steps forward with the hope of hearing the call of the *Imām*.

It is at such points in the argument that the logic becomes unclear. Is there some dialectical relationship involved in man's relationship to his God? Yes, answers Sharīʿatī, for God, man and nature derive from the same source: "All have the same direction, the same will, the same spirit, the same motion, and the same life." Monotheism means, for Sharīʿatī, the unity of God, man and nature precisely because they derive from the same source.[87] But if, as he acknowledges, God, man and nature "do not have each a separate and independent direction,"[88] does this mean that man's action will have a regulating effect on God's? Ultimately, the monotheist must draw the line between the essentially humanist position that Sharīʿatī the sociologist of comparative history has adopted and the demands of a religious commitment to monotheism and revelation. If the humanist establishes an analytical view of history that focuses on man in society, the monotheist believer in the revelation accepts unquestionaly the

Qur'ānic admonition: "God knows and you do not know." But the relationship is dialectical, Sharʿatī would rejoin. It is Aristotelean linear logic that insists on a contradiction between a sociological humanism and belief in a transcendent faith requiring *a priori* acceptance of certain truths. The bridge Sharīʿatī wishes to build between God and man (they are, after all not unified "in essence and quiddity" is responsibility and acceptance of God's Trust (the creation).

Yet, confusion still lurks in the argument. God has created the universe; He has offered it to any of His creatures as a Trust, but only man accepts. Man, created by God, is *ipso facto* contingent upon His will. Yet, God has also breathed life into the lump of clay that was man as corpse. Now alive and vital, man takes, in Sharīʿatī's view, upon himself some aspect of God, for the two are in dialectical relationship to one another. Yet, dialectical development does not proceed along the linear lines of A colliding with B to produce C. Rather, it proceeds through the overcoming (*Aufhebung*) of internal contradictions within A which lead to B, which itself yields a synthetic overcoming of the contradictions inherent in it; and so on. In this dialectic, it is not clear in the Sharīʿatī scheme, where God is and where man is. He appears to say they are merged, yet not congruent, proximate, yet not identical, unified yet not monolithic. As if convinced that the problem at this level is intractable, he advises his listeners to "not permit these philosophical and theological terms to tire your brain; simply expel them from your mind."[89]

In addition, why should class analysis not apply to *Shīʿī* society? Because *Shīʿī* society is that under the rule of ʿAlī and the *imām*s, and man should obey their rule because they were superior in piety, knowledge and justice. How did this happen? Muhammad invested ʿAlī and his progeny with the necessary qualities of leadership, and the mysteries of the Divine were transferred to those individuals for purposes of rule over men in God's name. Then, does the sociologist of comparative history refuse to apply class analysis to the Islamic community under ʿAlī's rule? Yes he does. For what reason must he do so? Because contradictions could not exist under ʿAlī's government. But was it not man in general who accepted God's creation in Trust. Yes, but without the leadership of those who know best, are most virtuous, chaste, honorable and just, man can still deviate. Then why must man not expect the generations after ʿAli and the *imām*s increasingly to become more pious, virtuous, just, in the dialectical evolution of history? Why, that is, must the dialectical process somehow stop at 661 A.D.? Or at 680, 874?

Sharīʿatī would perhaps say that it does not stop at those times but proceeds into the future until the return of the *Imām*? Why must one accept that this is so? Because of the widespread conviction that Muhammad was the seal of the prophets. But why should not the dialectic proceed after Muhammad's prophecy. Because one must accept the premises of the *Qur'ān*. Is it possible to explain the emergence of Muhammad in terms of class or structural analysis? Not unless his action is explained in terms of God's knowledge and will.

Finally, the dialogue with Sharīʿatī might well address the revolutionary return of the hidden Imam: when the trumpet shall sound and the Mahdī shall have returned, you have said the *Shīʿah* will responsibly be participating; yet it will be "deterministic divine law" that shall be the regulatory mechanism of the Imam's reappearance. What organizational means for the unity of the *Shīʿah* will there be in place so that as the time for the reappearance of the *Imām* approaches, the *Shīʿah* will be able to act responsibly? In short, what will the dialectical relationship between God and man have wrought up to that time, given the oppression that has afflicted the *Shīʿī* community since the death of ʿAlī. Here, we are dealing with social phenomena which are subject to sociological analysis: cadres; party structures; recruitment patterns; distribution of power; patron-client networks. Can the sociologist of comparative history continue to make his analyses of *Shīʿī* social and religious institutions, *up to, and including,* the reappearance of the Mahdī? Can he investigate power structures in order to correlate these with historical development? Or is a *Shīʿī* community somehow immune from these investigations?

These considerations of Sharīʿatī's theoretical positions raise issues which he no doubt faced from time to time. Given his extensive scholarship and deep interest in them, it would be surprising to learn that he considered them unimportant. More than likely, had his life not been so quickly ended at the age of 44, he would have pursued these matters in his writings and speeches.

Apart from the theoretical orientation and his criticism of the traditionalist *ʿulamāʾ*, ʿAlī Sharīʿatī offered recommendations of reform for the educational system of the *madrasah*s. If these recommendations had not been combined with his political activism, he may have been given an opportunity to attempt curriculum change. But his politics provoked the fear of the regime. They ultimately amounted to a call for a change in the social order. Consider the final passages of his book, *Intiẓār-i Maẕhab-i Iʿtirāz:*[90]

> Therefore, *intiẓār* is a religion of protest and absolute denial of the status quo in whatever form. *Intiẓār* not only does not negate man's responsibility, but indeed it makes his responsibility for his own course, the course of truth, the course of mankind, heavy, immediate, logical and vital.
>
> The religion of *intiẓār*, which is a 'positive philosophy of history,' a 'historical determinism'... is ultimately a philosophy of protest against the *status quo*....

Sometimes, his references came within a hair's breadth of being specific, as in his prayer at the end of his book, *Martyrdom,* when he calls out: "Friends, we are [living] in a bad period;" and a bit later: "O, God! We want freedom, awareness, justice and glory from you. Forgive us that we are in dire need,

[being] more painfully than at any other time . . . sacrificed to captivity, ignorance and abjectness.''[91] More generally, his constant allegorical style and allusions piled up a series of judgments which, if individually not that serious, in
their accumulation proved intolerable to the regime.

In his book *What Is To Be Done?* Sharīʿatī appends an exhaustive outline of
the academic and other programs of the Husaynīyah Irshād. By training Iranians
in these subjects and methodologies, he hoped to overcome the domination of the
traditionalist ʿulamāʾ in the *hawzah*s. The program of study and activities involved four broad areas: research, teaching, propagation of Shīʿism and agencies
activities. The overwhelming emphasis in the proposed curriculum consisted in
research (some 78 out of about 85-90 pages in all):

Program of the Husaynīyah Irshād (Projected)*
I.   Research Division.
     A. Six research groups.
        1. Sociology of Islam (*Islāmshināsī*).
        2. History.
        3. Islamic culture and science.
        4. Social sciences.
        5. Islamic countries.
        6. Literature and the arts.
II. Teaching Division.
     A. Five teaching groups.
        1. Sociology of Islam.
        2. Sociology of the *Qurʾān (Qurʾānshināsī)*
        3. Missionary training.
        4. Literature and the arts.
        5. Arabic and English languages and literatures.
III. Propaganda Division.
     A. Religious preaching and sermonizing.
     B. Scientific conferences.
     C. Scientific congresses, seminars, interviews.
IV. Agencies.
     A. Publications: *Nashrīyāt* [i.e., journals, pamphlets, mimeos, etc.]
     B. Printing press.
     C. Translation.
     D. Pilgrimmage to Mecca, rites and observances.
     E. Book center and center for documents and statistics.
     F. Publications: *Matbūʿāt* [i.e., books, monographs, etc.]
*Source: *Chih Bāyad Kard?* pp. 59-60.

The program called for significant departures from the curricula of the
theological seminaries. Inclusion of attention to art, if it involved the depiction of
graven images or music, would have been innovations. Among the orientations
to the sociology of Islam were inquiries using the methodologies of biological,

psychological and philosophical sciences as known in the West and associated with such thinkers as Carl Jung, Max Planck, Albert Einstein, Charles Darwin and others; cross cultural studies of deism and monotheism; survey of the evolution of non-theistic belief systems, including monism, dualism, humanism, positivism and utilitarianism.

Sharī'atī's program, too, involved an idiomatic translation of the *Qur'ān* into Persian—again an unusual difference from the pedagogy of the traditional *madrasahs*. The program also envisaged the translation into Persian of all research which Middle Eastern and Western orientalists had produced on Islam. This would have been a truly vast undertaking but, from Sharī'atī's point of view, a necessary corrective to the dearth of analytical scholarship on the Islamic sciences. Other areas of substantial emphasis included social biographies of the prophet and his companions, and histories of the codification of *hadiths*, not excluding the efforts of pariah groups such as the Mu'tazilites and Akhbārīs. Another departure was Sharī'atī's conviction that it was necessary to construct sound *hadīths de novo*, utilizing "the most advanced scientific methods" (left unspecified). Such an effort obviously antagonized the clergy, for whom the *hadīth* literature had long since been perfected.

Beyond these subjects, there was to be a rigorous analysis of the history of the prophet's family. Here, again, social science disciplines such as anthropology, sociology and history were to form the grid through which Muhammad, 'Alī and the *imāms* were to be studied. The city in Islamic history was to receive its share of attention. Here, it was to be a matter of the political economy and urban sociology of the towns of Mecca and Medina, as well as other towns. Jewish-Arab and Christian-Arab relations were to form part of this inquiry into urban development, as were the social and political functions of the mosque and other institutions associated integrally with the growth of cities.

Sharī'atī had much to add to the history segment of the research program, including many of the categories traditionally covered in survey courses of the Middle East taught in Western universities and also encountered in the traditional *madrasahs*: the development of the caliphate; the growth of the schools of law and their significance for questions of authority and order in the Islamic *ummah;* political movements, ideologies, Islamic revolts and heresies; the growth of philosophy, mysticism. It must be said that these subjects *were* taught in the *madrasahs* but Sharī'atī's contribution would have been to study them from an analytical, rather than the ideological and idiographic, perspectives of *Shī'ī* chroniclers.

Perhaps the most disappointing section, from the point of view of the political sociologist, consisted of the social sciences part of the Research Division. Seven items comprised this category:

1. Political theory and governmental systems in Islam in various periods of history.

2. Social and political institutions in Islamic societies; the caliphate, *dīvān*s; jurisprudence; non-litigous jurisprudence [*hisbah*]; the military; the treasury; finances.

3. Municipal agencies.

4. Waqf ownership; *maftūh al -ʿanwa* (conquered by force); *tuyūl* (fiefs); *iqtāʿāt* (tax farms).

5. Commerce; municipal and industrial output; bazaar; money.

6. Social and economic classes, groups; the *sayyid*s; justice; jurisprudence affecting professionals, artisans.

7. The system of production; economic geography; conversion of the agricultural output infrastructure into a municipal one.

The items in themselves are inherently of great interest; the disappointment lies in the very brief attention accorded to them in the program. It is possible, however, that the methodological innovations he had mentioned in connection with other aspects of the program were meant to apply to this section.

In conclusion one might say that the lengthy program presented by ʿAlī Sharīʿatī for the Husaynīyah Irshād represented both an exceptionally ambitious undertaking and an unprecedented break with the past. The clergy opposed Sharīʿatī's *madrasah* curriculum reform because its implementation would have made their learning dysfunctional. If they had been willing to meet the reformer half-way, perhaps the Husaynīyah Irshād might have made a greater impact on the *hawzah*s. Āyatullāh Sharīʿatmadārī's Dār al-Tablīgh in Qumm might have gone beyond the limited changes in the traditional curriculum that it introduced (such as teaching foreign languages, using blackboards, and the like). But Sharīʿatī's rhetoric—he accused the traditionalists of having managed to "stand Islam on its head"[92] and called them the "supporters of Yazid"[93] (the *Sunnī* caliph who had ordered the murder of Imām Husayn)—made a rapprochement difficult. Having thus offended both the government and the conservative ʿulamāʾ, he was not able to see his program for Islamic education through to fruition. As a consequence of his having antagonized both regime and the clergy power structure, he found himself isolated and without allies at the time of his arrest in the summer of 1973.[94] His supporters will look with considerable interest at future attempts to reform the *madrasah*s in the light of his own pioneering efforts in the late sixties and early seventies.

CHAPTER SIX

THE 'ULAMĀ', ISLAMIC GOVERNMENT, AND THE COLLAPSE OF THE BUREAUCRATIC STATE

THE CLERGY'S POLITICS IN THE MID-SIXTIES TO LATE SEVENTIES

The power of the government's repression against the opposition in the early 1960's forced the 'ulamā' into quietism. With the exile of Āyatullah Khumaynī and incarceration of Ayatullāh Tāliqānī the religious leadership inside Iran was reduced to a passive acquiescence of the status quo. The penetration of their ranks by SAVAK and those in the employ of the Endowments Organization reduced the chances for open protest in any case. After the coronation of the Shah in 1967, and the celebration of the 2500th anniversary of monarchy in 1971, the room for criticism of existing lines of policy became so limited that any public complaint was known to produce military trials, quick convictions and long prison terms.

The regime had established, in the 1950's, the principle that the nation's press and publishing houses would censor themselves. Sometime in the middle of 1966 this previous practice of not requiring advance censorship by the regime was changed. Henceforth, all publishers were to submit prepublication copies of their books to the Ministry of Culture's Department for Writing (Idārah-yi Nigārish). Protests arose on the part of a number of eminent writers. These descended upon Prime Minister Huvaydā to complain of the new official policy, which, they reminded him, was forbidden under the Constitution. They also, in early 1968, moved to establish the Writer's Syndicate. However, the regime refused to license the new organization, and it proved stillborn. Nevertheless, under the hue and cry against official censorship, the Minister of Culture submitted a bill to the Majlis, which, after a number of amendments were added, enacted it into law. Publishers no longer were bound to submit copies of their works to the Ministry. And, in response to objections that the copyright to works were being indiscriminately violated, the law mandated the issue of two copies of every book to the National Library. The latter would be responsible for certifying the copyright to protect the interests of authors. However, this procedure merely led to the National Library becoming a conduit of works which it would, upon receipt, then send an extra copy to the very same Ministry of Culture for its preview and approval/disapproval. In consequence of the very long time lapses between submission of works and information by the National Library as to whether the copyright had actually been granted, a number of writers publically stated that they would not avail themselves of the benefits of the copyright. The regime then apparently retaliated by ordering officials into the book stores and demanding that the managers remove all copies of works lacking the copyright seal of the National Library.

In the meanwhile, writers were being arrested for the publication of works deemed provocative by the government. Thus, in early 1970 the writer Firaydūn Tunukābunī, was seized for having written *Memories of a City in Tumult*. When his arrest became the subject of protest by a number of other writers, some of these in turn were taken into custody as well. In that particular case the charge under which the regime arrested the protestors was "incitement of armed rebellion against the national government." It was later explained, when an explanation was sought, that the word "armed" need not be interpreted literally, in terms of actual weapons being employed in the incitement; the word included the use of ideas as weapons against the government's line.

Under the pressure of further remonstrations by writers against the harshness of the regime's behavior, Prime Minister Huvaydā, in the summer of 1976, revealed the continuation of censorship despite the contents of the 1968 Publications Law prohibiting it. At a "Book Seminar," which was attended by a number of authors and officials from the Ministry of Culture, the Ministry of Information and Tourism and SAVAK, Huvaydā declared angrily: "Yes, we censor books and have no need to disguise the fact. The interests of the country and the monarchical system are above everything."[1]

The clergy, it may be thought, had reasons to be optimistic, since, according to regime statistics, half of the books published in Iran dealt with religious subjects. However, because of the censorship policies that went into effect after 1966, a general decline in volume of published works in non-religious subjects occurred. Because of this decline, the relative proportion of religious books increased over time. This is not a matter of a determined decision by the government to increase the output of works dealing with religion. In addition to this caveat, as we have seen with the examples of the symposium on *Marja'iyat* and the Religious Institution (*Bahs̱ī dar Bārah-yi Marja'īyat va Rūhānīyat*), the *Guftār-i Māh* series, and the writings of 'Alī Sharī'atī, not all kinds of works on religion were permitted to be published. Most were characterized as either practical guide books written by *marājī'-yi taqlīd* to instruct the faithful on rituals of worship; or else they were in the form of pamphlets urging Muslim unity, attacking the decay in the morality of youth, or scholarly inquiries into mysticism or theosophy. Periodical searches ("at least twice a month", in the words of an opposition publication)[2] used to be conducted of all mosque libraries to ensure that banned works were not on the shelves.

The story is told of how even the Qumm-based monthly, *Darshā'ī az Maktab-i Islam,* published by Āyatullāh Sharī'atmadārī's Dār al-Tablīgh, and enjoying a circulation estimated by its editors at 200,000 (probably an inflated figure, but cf. *Ittila'āt*'s reported circulation of 150,000) was shut down. The paper refused to publish the newly mandated calendar date of 2535 (dating back to the Achaemenid Empire) in its masthead. At least this was the version, much disbelieved, given by the regime investigating group, which was headed by General Fardūst (apparently the very individual to whom the Endowments Organization had reportedly given some 2 million meters of land in the Karaj district). The regime version of the incident was that the journal was following instructions from Āyatullāh Khumaynī, who had issued an opinion that forbade acceptance of the date. But the opposition believes that Āyatullāh Sharī'atmadārī's establishment would emulate him, not another *marja'*. Apart from that, it is conjectured that *Maktab-i Islam* was shut down because of its increasing circulation and carping against the negative impact of the modernization efforts of the government upon public morality, religious vigilance and duty, etc.

The political activities of the *'ulamā'* in the late sixties and into the seventies centered around the growing emphasis the regime was giving to the place of monarchy in the culture of society in Iran. Although the regime did not, of course, attack Islam, the politically active clergy claimed that eulogies of the imperial tradition naturally invoked pre-Islamic themes and thus served to deni grate the faith. Such feelings did not uniquely regulate the protests of the clergy against government policies, however. The growing American presence in the form of personnel, joint business ventures, multinational corporation activities the inflation brought about by heavy spending programs and the presence of Americans in Iran, and such symbolic manifestations as music, dress, etc.—all these played their role in the occasional criticism emanating from the religious leadership.

A good deal of this criticism occurred around 1970–1972. In 1970, in a notorious case, the *mujtahid,* Āyatullāh Muhammad Rizā Sa'īdī of Tehran, was arrested and tortured to death for having objected to a conference exploring further possibilities of American investment in Iran.[3] Such treatment evinced the regime's extreme sensitivity to charges which Āyatullāh Khumaynī had made since the early 1960's about the regime's selling out of Iran's national interests to foreigners. The government in particular attempted to curb the pilgrimmage traffic between Iran and the Iraqi shrine cities. Typically during this time, ʿulamāʾ were arrested crossing the border into Iran on charges of having collaborated with Āyatullāh Khumaynī's efforts.[4]

As a result of disturbances in the late fall of 1970 at some universities in Tehran and elsewhere, a number of students in Qumm called for a one-day sympathy strike and boycotted classes. It was reported that the protest was successful, by and large; however, the adversaries of Āyatullāh Sharīʿatmadārī noted that he had refused to call off his own classes that day "and in this manner demonstrated the anti-nationalist and anti-religious [sic] essence of himself. . . ."[5]

In the late spring of 1971 a number of ʿulamāʾ in Qumm sought to commemorate the death of Āyatullāh Saʿīdī at the Fātimīyah Mosque and at the Fayzīyah Madrasah—the town's most important. Security forces surrounded the mosque and prohibited ingress and egress for 48 hours. They attacked the Fayzīyah and during the course of a sweep of arrests, seized Āyatullāh Muntazirī and promptly exiled him to Najafābād.[6]

Manifestos in the form of wall posters, "poly-copies" and other forms of Iranian "samizdat" appeared at this time signed simply "Hawzah-yi ʿIlmīyah-yi Qumm" (The Qumm Hawzah) denouncing paratroop attacks against workers' demonstrations and student protests throughout the country. Such criticisms noted that vast sums were being readied for expenditure on the 2500 anniversary celebrations at a time of famine and starvation in Balūchistān, Saystān and Fārs provinces. It was argued that the only thing that the celebrations might produce would be a revitalization of Zoroastrianism—i.e., a further debilitation of the true religion of Islam.[7]

It was in this time period, too, that a new organization came into existence: the Mujāhidin-i Khalq. This organization resembled the suppressed Fidāʾīyān-i Islam organization of the 1940's and 1950's, but its adherents utilized commando and guerrilla tactics in their urban-based opposition to the government. In early 1972 the regime arrested, tried and executed five individuals with ties to this group. However, their arrest had led to an outpouring of appeals for clemency for these particular individuals on the part of respected ʿulamāʾ. In Shīrāz the town's leading clergymen appealed for support for the five to Āyatullāh Sayyid Hādī Mīlānī, chief mujtahid in Mashhad. It was reported that a number of marājiʿ-yi taqlīd in Qumm, Mashhad and Ahvāz had sent appeals to the regime; allegedly, they were joined by numerous students of the hawzahs in Qumm, Tehran and Tabrīz. One source of optimism for the clergy was the fact that the five individuals in question had been bona fide students of the religious sciences who had been studying tafsīr with Āyatullāh Tāliqānī. It was therefore hoped that the government would not deal as severely with them as it would with guerrillas under standard procedures. However, the executions took place, and Āyatullāh Tāliqānī was once again sent into internal exile.[8]

Around the middle of 1972, another manifesto from Qumm (actually written in Najaf and secreted into the country) wrote that the regime had finally decided to "annihilate" the Qumm religious establishment and cited the figure of some 300 individuals who had already been arrested in connection with the recent events. Presumably, the manifesto meant opposition to the 2500 anniversary celebrations, which were formally inaugurated in October 1971. The heroes of the politically active clergy and their students at this time included Khumaynī, Rabānī Shīrāzī, Mahallātī, Tāliqānī, Muntaẓirī, the late Saʿīdī and Muhammad Hasan Tabāʾ-tabāʾī Qummī (not to be confused with ʿAllāmah Sayyid Muhammad Husayn Tabāʾtabāʾī Qummī). Āyatullāh Hasan Tabāʾtabāʾī excoriated the government's policy in a dramatically worded broadside in the late spring of 1972. In that proclamation, he particularly lashed out against the muzzling of preachers and the dispatch of the Sipāh-i Dīn and Muravvijīn (q.v.) to wreak havoc on the rural population's conception of the *'ulamāʾ* role in society. He summarized the efforts of the Sipah-i Dīn and the Muravvijīn as attempts to spread "evil propaganda" and stressed that five years of exile would not succeed in silencing him about the course of events.[9] It will be recalled, in connection with this manifesto and the other activities summarized above, that this was approximately the time of the Āzmun memorandum to Prime Minister Huvaydā regarding an "appropriate" plan of action against the senior clergy.

ĀYATULLĀH KHUMAYNĪ AND THE CONCEPT OF AN ISLAMIC REPUBLIC

Āyatullāh Khumaynī's early book, *Revealing of the Secrets,* did not, as might have been expected, consist of a firm denunciation of monarchy. Instead, it constituted a stinging attack against secularism and against Rizā Shah's autocratic rule. In it, Khumaynī undertook a mild defense of the monarchical system. Thus, on the one hand he could condemn Rizā Shah's policy and, on the other, say it is better to have an ineffective, even harmful government than none at all. He called for cancellation of legislation passed between 1925-1941 because it had violated the will of God; yet he reminded his readers that distinguished clergymen in previous Islamic eras had lent their support to monarchs.[10]

By spring, 1971 his position had evolved to the point of declaring forthrightly: "Islam is fundamentally opposed to the pillar of monarchy...."[11] It was at this time that SAVAK privately revealed that it had uncovered an Iraqi plot to assassinate Khumaynī. This announcement led to outcries and telegrams to the President of Iraq demanding punishment for the conspirators in the plot.[12] Iraqi harsh treatment of Iranian *Shīʿah* had given the Iranian government an opportunity to be viewed as the defender of the faith, but Khumaynī's supporters rejected that image.

Khumaynī would not be deterred and, in the early spring of 1972, issued a *fatvā* requiring that financial assistance be extended to the families of political prisoners. In so mandating this, he argued on the basis of two *furū* of the faith: *jihād*, and *al-amr bi al-maʿrūf*.[13] These two principles, he argued, had provided the justification that "from the beginning of mankind prophets and the clergy were charged . . . with rebelling against despotic governments. . . ."[14]

Such views are forcefully argued in his book, *Islamic Government* (1971), actually his class presentations at Najaf, whence he had been directing his campaign against the government in Iran for several years.[15] In that work he boldly attacks both monarchy and dynastic succession as alien to Islam (p. 12). As we have already seen, Āyatullāh Khumaynī strongly cleaves to the position that Islam does possess a political dimension and attacks as deceit the contrary view. (p. 21). He offers that *taqīyāh* cannot be an excuse for clergymen to renounce political involvement, given the principles of *valāyat, jihād, amr bi al-maʿrūf* and *nahy ʿan al-munkar*. It had never been the intention of the prophet to call the faithful to Islam and then leave matters of social organization to take care of themselves. The *ʿulamāʾ* must not confine themselves to the routine churning out of regulations for the faith. Having an obligation to tend to political issues, they consequently commit themselves to oust corrupt officials and overthrow tyrannical regimes. (p. 39) On the positive side, ordinances in the Islamic law pertaining to finances, national defense, administration of justice (*ihqāq-i huqūq*) and the like are conclusive, he suggests: "The essence and characteristics of these laws lead to the conclusion that they were legislated for the purpose of creating a state and for the political, economic and cultural administering of society." (p. 32)

Islamic government will differ from representative and/or constitutional monarchies because of the elimination of the separation of powers that Islamic government will implement. The latter refuses to consider the need for new legislation because all necessary law has already been promulgated and revealed by the prophet and the *imam*s. There will be a parliament, to be sure, but it will not engage in enactment of laws (*qānūn guzārī*); instead, it will be an "agenda-setting" (*barnāmah rīzī*) institution to clarify for the ministries the best means for administering social services throughout the land. (p. 53) Furthermore, sovereignty shall repose in God, alone. There is no question of royal rule in Islamic government, much less a government that is based on kingship or empire. (pp. 55–56).

Khumaynī, after describing the necessary qualities of the leader of an Islamic government, and establishing that no Islamic government exists, demands its creation. Reason dictates that in the absence of such a government, Islam itself will disappear. Countless learned men of the Islamic law exist today; it is only a matter of uniting them "in order to create a government of universal justice in the world." Such a government would be *valāyat-i faqīh*.[16] (p. 63 ff.)

Khumaynī does concede the possibility that there may be a theoretical/ doctrinal justification for Muslims not to create an Islamic government in the absence of the *Imām*. This complex issue is raised in the context of a sound *hadith* attributed to Imām 'Alī, who is said to have related about the prophet's supplication to God to bless those coming after him: "The prophet of God (blessings and peace be upon him) said: 'O, God, bless those who will come after me (he repeated this three times).' The prophet was asked who will be your successors? And he answered: 'Those who come after me who transmit my sayings and traditions and teach them to the people in my absence.'" Now, the problem for Khumaynī arises in that the *hadith* is contained in the authoritative codex of Ibn Bābūyah (d. 991) in different places. In those places where the chain of names is unbroken (i.e., the *hadīth* is sounder), the last part of the *hadīth* does not appear—i.e., *fa yu'allimūnahā al-nās min ba'dī* (and teach them to the people in my absence). On the other hand, where the *hadīth* is cited with the inclusion of the last part, the chain is broken.

Khumaynī argues that the phrase must have been dropped mistakenly in the process of compilation of the hadīth by ibn Bābūyah. To support this supposition, he cites Muhammad ibn Hasan Shaykh Hurr-i 'Āmilī (d. in the 17th century), *Wasā'il al-Shī'ah ilā Ahkām al-Sharī'ah*. In this work, Book *Qadā'*, in the chapters "Characteristics of Judges", section 8, *hadīth* # 50, and also in section 11, *hadīth* # 7, the controversial *hadith* is cited fully and the chain is not broken (*bi tawr-i irsāl āvurdah ast*). Shaykh Hurr-i 'Āmilī has in turn based himself on previous work by ibn Bābūyah's student, Shaykh Mufīd Abū 'Abdullāh Muhammad ibn al-Nu'mān (d. 1022). This is important because the transmission of the *hadīth* by Āmilī (through Mufīd) rests on the independent transmission of three individuals unknown to each other and living as far away from one another as Marv, Nayshāpūr and Balkh.

This kind of scholarly debate is important to Khumaynī, because he wishes to make the point that there is legal and doctrinal justification for an active role on the part of the *'ulamā'* in bringing about an Islamic government under the principle of *valāyat-i faqīh*. If it can be shown that Muhammad thought his successors would not only transmit his sayings and traditions but also that they would teach them to the people, then obviously this suggests a dynamic role for the learned men, not a passive one of waiting for the return of the hidden *Imām*. The only problem is one of sources: Ibn Bābūyah is one of the most authoritative of *Shī'ī* scholars of *fiq*. Shaykh Hurr-i 'Āmilī is not of equal authority, but Khumaynī seeks to compensate by suggesting that the independent transmission of the *hadīth* by three individuals living so far away from one another is compelling. And it must mean that ibn Bābūyah for some reason had left the critical phrase out in those parts of his *Man La Yahduruhu al-Faqīh* containing sound (unbroken) *hadīths*. (see pp. 74 ff for this fascinating exercise in argument)

Khumaynī also suggests that the *'ulamā'* themselves are partially to blame for the fact that foreign laws have been imported in the constitutions and statutes of Islamic societies. As long as the clergy adhere to the notion that they are "word experts", they will continue to abdicate their responsibility as social leaders. (p. 96) Time and again he invokes traditions to suggest that they were meant for more than memorization and transmission. The community of Islam is a real community *in this world*. Matters requiring arbitration, distribution, education and the like necessarily arise. They must be addressed *in practice*. The *'ulamā'* must teach matters relating to worship. "But the important things are the political, economic and legal questions of Islam." (p. 173)

Later, he urges the *tullāb* of Qumm, Mashhad, Najaf to create contemporary versions of the tragedy of Imām Husayn. The *madrasah* students should "instigate and stimulate the masses" toward this end. (p. 183) This time, however, such a confrontation will not end in the unhappy defeat of the true *Shī'ah* as happened in 680 A. D. At this point, he turns to the practice of *taqīyah* (prudent dissimulation of belief), to which the *Shī'ah* were reduced after the martyrdom of Imām Husayn. This practice is only to be allowed in the contemporary period if it permits its practitioner to infiltrate into the ranks of despotic government and thereby permits him to overthrow it. Otherwise, the clergy must act in the open, and their students must do the same. Prudent dissimulation of belief may be permitted the rank and file but certainly not the *tullāb* or the *'ulamā'*. (pp. 200-201). Then, in a populist vein, he urges the religious studies students in the *madrasah*s to "go to the people" and spread the faith of Islam. But, as though realizing that such political activism could redound against the interests of scholarship, he qualifies his advice:

> I do not say abandon your studies... You must study, must become a *faqīh* [learned man of Islamic law] ... do not permit these theological centers of learning to discard *faqāhat* [Islamic jurisprudence]. As long as you do not become a *faqīh*, you cannot serve Islam. But during your study, keep it in mind to teach Islam to the people ... (pp. 203-04)

Khumaynī seems to be saying in this book that the *'ulamā'* should not abjure political power and political office. Indoctrination, stimulating the political consciousness of the people, clarifying issues and exercising a general oversight over public policy do not, alone, seem to satisfy the requirements of *valāyat-i faqīh*. Yet, some six years later he equivocated on this issue and appeared to argue that clergymen should not accept ministerial positions. The day to day running of the government ought to be the function of others, while the task of the clergy would consist in demanding an extensive purge of the state apparatus (in pre-1979 Iran, that is), calling for an end to all "unproductive" expenditures (i.e., military procurements), returning the nation's wealth to the masses and ousting foreigners and ending foreign control of the country.[17]

One could say that the point at which both the monarchy as an institution and the Pahlavī Dynasty as the royal house of Iran became totally unacceptable to Khumaynī occurred in early 1978. From 1963–77 during his long exile he had stingingly rebuked the regime and the Shah for having failed to defend Islam, for having promoted despotism, trampeled on democracy, insulted the clergy and permitted foreigners to exercise control over the country's resources. But he seemed always to stop short of calling for the overthrow of the Shah and of monarchy. In his vehement reactions to the Shah's panegyrics concerning Iran's imperial traditions, the most he was willing to say was that Islam opposed the system of monarchy.

However, in his proclamation of January 1978, he declared: "... Muhammad Rizā Khān [Shah] is a traitor and rebel whose overthrow is ordained by law. ..."[18] And some ten months later, in November 1978, in calling for the establishment of an Islamic republic in Iran, he asserted: "Our Islamic objective is the toppling of the monarchical regime and the overthrow of the Pahlavī Dynasty. ..."[19] This is not only his position, he argued, but the Iranian people have "voted with their feet" in favor of it by their year long demonstrations against the policies of the regime.

At this time, Khumaynī referred to the principle of "those who are not for us are against us." (This is a position that was to be a source of conflict between him and Āyatullāh Sharīʿatmadārī after the departure of the Shah on 16 January 1979.) In his remarks, Khumaynī suggested the tactics by which he intended to engineer the establishment of an Islamic republic. These included continuation of the vast demonstrations within the context of the general strike; recompensing striking workers, peasants, functionaries, artisans and others for lost wages during their strike action; desertion by members of the armed forces and fraternization with civilians. Failure to act against the Shah and the political system he considered "suicidal."[20]

As to the structure of the political system, configurations of power, circulation of elites, policy-making processes, political economy, agricultural policy, etc., in the new Islamic republic, Khumaynī avoided specifics during numerous interviews while in exile. The equivocation between wishing to have as "the only frame of reference for us ... the time of the prophet and Imām ʿAlī"[21] and not intending to forego the advantages produced by more than 1300 years of science[22] seemed unimportant to him in the face of the overriding struggle to overthrow the regime.

During the year-long general strikes and demonstrations, which were marked by the regime's release of political prisoners, change of Prime Minister, imposition of martial law and statements of contrition about past mistakes by the Shah, Āyatullāh Khumaynī himself left Najaf for France. During his brief three and a half month exile there, he was able to demonstrate extraordinary political leadership in terms of maintaining organizational control of his supporters in Iran. Throughout 1978, inevitably comparisons emerged between the position adopted by Āyatullāh Khumaynī and that of other senior *mujtahids*, especially Āyatullāh Kāżim Sharīʿatmadārī. The latter is leader of some 14 million Iranians living in Āzarbāyjān or residing elsewhere whose provenience was the Turkish-Āzarī speaking regions of Āzarbāyjān, Gīlān and Zanjān. It became clear that Sharīʿat̄madārī held views that differed from his colleague. Part of this difference must be attributed to the fact that Sharīʿatmadārī was in Iran and had necessarily to be cautious in his statements for fear of retribution. However, he had on a number of occasions in the 1960's and 1970's acted or failed to act in such manner as to evince real divergence in vision and tactics with Āyatullāh Khumaynī. Nevertheless, he had been cautious to put on notice foreign journalists descending upon Qumm in the second half of 1978 to interview him that Khumaynī "represents the will of the people."[23]

The burden of Sharīʿatmadārī's position was that the ʿ*ulamāʾ* oppose dictatorial rule, not the modernization of the country—as the government had been charging all along.[24] Stressing his deep desire to restore the Constitution, Sharīʿatmadārī had acknowledged that he was not concerned with whether or not the Shah were to remain as a titular monarch, a much debated issue in certain circles at that time.[25] Still, it could be rejoined that since the Shah had publicly declared his opposition to the implementation of Article Two (concerning the establishment of a five-member clergy committee to oversee legislation),[26] Sharīʿatmadārī's greater moderation on this score would make no difference. Free elections leading to the creation of a vigorous parliament to replace the existing moribund legislature was an indispensible feature of the new order for Sharīʿatmadārī. In taking this position, he appeared to be aligning himself with the constitutionalist views of Āyatullāh Muhammad Husayn Nāʾīnī. The difference in vision for the role of the Majlis with that of Khumaynī is evident, since, as we have already seen, for him the legislature merely sets an agenda.

During the course of the year Sharīʿatmadārī felt it necessary to deny rumors that he had secretly negotiated with the Court and that such contacts had led to a rift within clergy ranks.[27] Yet, his detractors pointed to certain actions on his part that could have lent credence to his "splitting" tactics: (1) his order to the townsmen of Qumm to stay indoors during the *arbaʿīn* (fortieth day commemoration) scheduled for 19 June;[28] (2) the fact that he urged members of the illicit, though regime-tolerated, Workers' Party (composed mainly of theology students) to engage in *passive* resistance to the regime.[29] Despite that, it was he who had argued that "the state has from the very beginning [of the Pahlavī dynasty] violated the Constitution which it claims to have been upholding;" and thus, it had "forefeited . . . any claim to probable rightness of conduct."[30]

Sharīʿatmadārī did not associate himself with Khumaynī's call for "rivers of blood" to flow on the 10th of Muharram (ʿĀshūrā), or the 11th of December 1978, in order to topple the monarchy.[31] Instead, he threatened to call for a *jihād* unless the government were to declare the illegitimacy of the existing Majlis and call for new, genuinely free elections.[32] Execrating the martial law government imposed on 7 November 1978, Sharīʿatmadārī declared: "We have not made any decision on armed struggle, but if they [the regime] close all the other channels, we will have to go that route."[33] He inveighed against "the tyrannical state apparatus" and sought the "dismantling of the despotic imperialist system." Success in doing so would lead, in his view, to "the establishment of social justice, a restitution of the Islamic order, and the application of the regulations of the Qurʾān."[34]

In late September, after rumors of 'ulamā'-Court contacts became intensified once again, Sharīʿatmadārī stated that the clergy "have nothing to say to the Shah or the government. Our demands are clear. We want a government of the people and for the people." He additionally attempted to dampen speculation of a rift between Khumaynī and himself by stating that he had no conflict with his colleague; rather, he was in "full agreement with him."[35] One ought not take this assertion at face value, however, even while recognizing that tremendous pressures were—and continue to be—exerted on Sharīʿatmadārī not to take positions at variance with Khumaynī's and thereby weaken the clergy's unity.

Sharīʿatmadārī could not have argued with a fourteen point manifesto issued by Āyatullāh Abū al-Hasan Shīrāzī in Mashhad in late summer 1978 and which could be construed as a document of clergy demands. By contrast, although Khumaynī probably agreed with its contents, in all probability he felt that it did not go far enough. Crucially, the Shīrāzī broadside did not address the question of monarchy at all. The following items appeared in that statement:

1. The abolition of laws contrary to Islam.

2. Freedom of expression for the clergy and other social forces.

3. Cancellation of the prohibition against clergy involvement in politics.

4. Amnesty for prisoners jailed in the defense of Islam.

5. Invitation to exiles—especially Āyatullāh Khumaynī—to return to Iran.

6. Prohibition of wasteful spending of natural resources and the national income.

7. Punishment of those responsible for the deaths of demonstrators throughout the 1978 period.

8. Elimination of casinos, gambling clubs, cinemas, etc.

9. Reconciliation of Iranian culture with the traditions of Islam, prescriptions of the Qurʾān and ordinances of the imāms.

10. Replacing "secular universal history" (sic) with Islamic history.

11. 'Ulamā' and lay supervision of parliamentary elections.

12. Requiring cabinet ministers to be of the Jaʿfarī Shīʿī faith.

13. Elimination of Bahāʾīs and Bahāʾism from official positions.

14. Nullification of all parliamentary legislation conflicting with the tenets of Jaʿfarī Shīʿism.[36]

While the application of any one of several of these provisions would necessitate a restructuring of power and influence in local and national politics, the last point would be particularly difficult to confine in impact. For example, it may be that the Majlis law that granted extraterritorial rights to American citizens in Iran was one of the targets of that point. But, depending on its interpretation, point #14 could lead to the abrogation of the Education Law of 1911 and the restitution of the *madrasah* system as the unique educational institution in the country. It could alter the Constitution's provisions on freedom of speech, association, press, and so on, because the model upon which it was based was the Belgian Constitution. Moreover, it would presumably call into question statutory law, such as the civil, criminal and commercial codes. Again, the influence brought to bear by the French, Italian and Swiss codes respectively on the Iranian codes could be cited as sufficient reason.

This document obviously, then, had revolutionary implications, even though it did not appeal for a united front to *make* revolution. It may be considered a minimal statement of the clergy's demands and cannot offer insight into the factions, such as they were, that existed among them. The clergy alignments, we see in retrospect, included men supporting Khumaynī's unremitting position of a totally Islamic system (Mahallatī, Rabānī, Muntaẓirī, for example); those preferring the clergy to play the role of guardians of the political order (Sharīʿatmadārī, Gulpāygānī), those who sought a middle ground between the two (Tāliqānī, Bihishtī, Mutahharī), and those who preferred to have nothing to do with politics but preferred to teach fiq (Khūʾī, for instance). It should come as no surprise that the individuals who had played a role in the reform movements of the 1960's would become important coalition partners in the ever on-going process of interaction among the ʿulamāʾ from mid-1978 onward. It will also be noted that some shifting of position took place—notably involving Āyatullāh Mahmūd Tāliqānī's move away from a vigorous advocacy of ʿulamāʾ political activity to the view, in spring 1979, that the place of the clergy is in the mosques, not the political arena (see below). Moreover, it is even more difficult to sort out where the allegiances of the *tullāb* lie. According to Āyatullāh Khumaynī there were some 5,000 of them in Qumm in late 1971–early 1972.[37] Figures compiled by Fischer in 1975 suggested the student enrollment to be "over 6,500."[38] And by November 1978 the (probably exaggerated) figure cited in the press was 13,000.[39] How many of these might be put into the Khumaynī group? How many may be called "constitutionalists"? Or do these political affiliations not matter, and it is simply a matter of the *hawzah*'s disproportionately large Āzarī component (probably about nineteen percent[40]) supporting Sharīʿatmadārī, who is from Āzarbāyjān himself; and similar considerations applying for other important *mujtahid*s? How many signers of the telegram to Āyatullāh Khumaynī, who had just fled to France, in October 1978 by 33 clergymen from Tehran ought to be considered pro-Khumaynī or pro-Sharīʿatmadārī? Or how many of those who did not sign were latent supporters of each *marjaʿ*?[41] It is not possible to resolve these questions from the data. Nor would the clergy themselves think them relevant, given their view that in serving Islam they are united.

INTER-*'ULAMĀ'* RELATIONS IN 1979

The *'ulamā'* did not, by themselves, make the revolution of 1978-1979. The collapse of the political system, culminating in the departure of the Shah (16 January 1979), the resignation of the caretaker government of Shāhpūr Bakhtīyār (11 Feburary 1979) and the referendum in favor of the Islamic Republic (30 March 1979) was nevertheless directed by the clergy. Their participation, given the centuries of *'ulamā'* quietism and aversion to overthrowing regimes, was an unprecedented action in Iranian history.

The numerous causes of the Iranian revolution cannot be sought here, since the task at hand is an analysis of clergy-state relations. Certainly, it may be said that clergy rationalizations, ideological statements, organizational activity and mobilization of resources proved absolutely critical in the unfolding developments. The issues to which the *'ulamā'* had been responding were issues which also affected other social forces in society. The intellectuals had long been sharply attacking censorship and the unidimensional "official culture" that the regime had been attempting to universalize in Iran. The regime's vast modernization expenditures from the enormous revenues obtained through its petroleum industry had fed inflation and spawned widespread corruption. This had bred a cynicism among bureaucrats in the state administration to an extent not seen before—and this despite the fact that cynicism was a far from unknown quality in the bureaucracy. The entrepreneurs and industrialists who had entered into big business from their former positions as landowners faced a deteriorating credit and cash-flow problem in the years 1976-78 as the country found itself borrowing on the international financial markets. Agriculturalists suffered from the highly irrational and chaotic agrarian policies of the regime. The breakneck pace of industrialization had entirely destroyed the balance between the industrial and agricultural sectors. Peasants were becoming alienated because of the endemic weaknesses in the cooperative institutions in the rural areas; moreover, the peasants increasingly found themselves caught in the middle of a serious "scissors crisis" as prices for materials that they required for working their land continued to go up while the amounts their produce could fetch in the market either declined, remained stagnant or failed to keep pace with costs. Laborers, who ought otherwise to have been in a better position because of the shortage of workers in the labor market, complained about the regime's on again, off again programs to induce divestiture of shares in favor of the workers. All these sectors had complaints about the phenomenal rise in the cost of living produced by weapons purchases, the growth of a substantial middle-man stratum (that drained a great deal of wealth from potential savings and investments) and the purchase of high technologies in the West.

Under such circumstances, because the religious institution had remained the only element in society that the regime had failed to co-opt, it became the central force of revolutionary activity. The entire process was set in motion by a miscalculated attempt to sully the reputation of Āyatullāh Khumaynī when an editorial appeared in the nation's newspapers on the 7th of January 1978. The article attacked his alleged links with communist elements and calumniated him as a virtual troubador of verse.[42]

The clerical leadership, of course, skillfully publicized the forthright role that the ʿulamāʾ had played in 1891-92, 1905-21 and 1948-53. In the end, a clergyman, Sayyid Jalāl al-Dīn Tihrānī,[43] seemed to compromise the ʿulamāʾ ranks by accepting appointment to the Regency Council that was to reign on behalf of the Shah during what was at the time described as a long vacation abroad. But this individual rapidly had a change of heart and offered his resignation to Āyatullāh Khumaynī, himself at his Neuphlé-le-Château exile near Paris. In this way ended the regime's last effort to split the ranks of the mujtahids who had led the demonstrations against the government throughout the last year.

Nevertheless, after the collapse of the Bakhtīyār government, which had lasted only from 3 January to 11 February 1979), divisions within the ranks of the clergy surfaced once again. The major cleavages included those pitting Āyatullāh Khumaynī's backers against those who rallied to the side of both Āyatullāh Sharīʿatmadārī and Tāliqānī. It is very evident that neither of the latter two mujtahids wished to be classified as opposing some of the lines of Āyatullāh Khumaynī's policies. A careful inspection of their statements, nonetheless, reveals fairly clear discrepancies in position. In addition, a faction that attacked the professional clergy in general has articulated positions reminiscent in some respects of the orientation of ʿAlī Sharīʿatī. This group, the Furqān, has received very little support among the teachers and students of the madrasahs as far as can be determined. But it has forced the clergy to respond to it and assassinated one of the leading reformers of the last two decades, Ayatullah Murtazā Mutahharī. To that extent, its position bears examination.

In his statement of 12 January 1979 Āyatullāh Khumaynī declared:[44]

> In accordance with the rights conferred by the law of Islam and on the basis of the vote of confidence given to me by the overwhelming majority of the Iranian people . . . a temporary council has been appointed, to be known as the Council of the Islamic Revolution. Composed of competent, committed and trustworthy Muslims, it will soon begin functioning. The composition of this council will be disclosed at the first appropriate occasion. Well-defined and specific tasks have been assigned to this council. It has been entrusted with the task of examining and studying conditions for the establishment of a transitional government and making all necessary preliminary arrangements. The composition of the transitional government will also be disclosed at the first opportune and appropriate moment.

A number of points merit attention about this proclamation. First, Āyatullāh Khumaynī's conviction that he had the authority to appoint the members of the Council, based on the year-long demonstrations in Iran that had invoked his name above all others. Secondly, any government would be subordinate to the activities of the Council. Thirdly, he was careful to preserve the secrecy of identity of the members of both organs, and this for two reasons: (1) secrecy of identity would preserve an element of control over the process and prevent a sudden diffusion of power; (b) disclosure of identities at that point would have risked the arrest of the individuals concerned.

Not long after the 12 January 1979 proclamation, Āyatullāh Sharī'atmadārī was invited to comment on Āyatullāh Khumaynī's decision to appoint Muhandis Mihdī Bāzargān as the new Prime Minister in a provisional government. Did Sharī'atmadārī believe that the unilateral designation by Khumaynī of Bāzargān as Prime Minister was legal? To this the theologian gave an equivocal answer: if by legal is meant is it legal according to Islamic law, then the answer is in the affirmative; but if the question is whether or not the action is legal according to international law (*bi mūjib-i qavānīn-i bayn al-milalī*), then it must be asked of someone else. The point is that Sharī'atmadārī was willing to go out of his way to indicate that two possible interpretations of this action could exist. And while he averted commiting himself by suggesting that an expert in international law had better be consulted, he left the door open to the possibility that it was a questionable action.

Not only was Sharī'atmadārī expressing caution over the technical issue of designation of the head of the provisional government but the very issue of an Islamic Republic seemed problematical for him.* During the course of this interview he was reminded that he had on previous occasions expressed anxiety at the establishment of an Islamic Republic in Iran in the context of uncertainty as to whether such a system would be acceptable to the army and even the people of Iran, as well as the world community of nations. Given this, did Āyatullāh Khumaynī have the right to act unilaterally on the issues of the Islamic Republic and provisional government or should he have consulted the other *marājiʿ-yi taqlīd?* To this Sharī'atmadārī in effect engaged in a sort of self-criticism. A provisional government is announced only in times of emergency. At such junctures, those who oppose the establishment of that regime must remain silent.

Āyatullāh Sharī'atmadārī iterated his concern about a potential military coup d'etat in reaction to too doctrinaire an implementation of Islamic rule under the new order. However, his spokesmen, noted the reporter conducting the interview, had issued clarifications of the theologian's position, stating that he would not raise his voice in opposition to Khumaynī's undertakings even if he disagreed with them.

*He later strongly endorsed the concept of an Islamic republic and voted for it in the national referendum in late March 1979.

And finally, Sharīʿatmadārī was queried about Āyatullāh Khymaynī's uncompromising attitude that opposition to the provisional government appointed by him was tantamount to apostasy and anathema against Islam. Sharīʿatmadārī ventured that he intended to raise this issue with his colleague but that in his own view peacefully expressed criticism and opposition should not be punished. The interviewer noted that on this particular issue Āyatullāh Khumaynī had received a good deal of negative comments in the pages of some of the Tehran newspapers.[45]

But, apart from a courtesy call shortly after his arrival in Qumm, Khumaynī was not to meet with Sharīʿatmadārī for serious substantive discussions until mid-June 1979. And even this meeting lasted for only an hour, having been convened at the house of Āyatullāh Muhammad Rizā Gulpāygānī and in the company of the fourth of Iran's living *marājiʿ-yi taqlīd*, Āyatullāh Shihāb al-Dīn al-Marʿashī al-Najafī.[46] The meeting reportedly ended with the four senior *mujtahids* appealing for unity and declaring that this had been achieved among them.

Yet, to that point, at least potentially significant differences between Āyatullāh Sharīʿatmadārī and Āyatullāh Khumaynī continued to surface between February and June 1979. Thus, in May Sharīʿatmadārī stated that "In Islam there is no provision that the clergy must absolutely intervene in matters [of state]."[47] Such a statement is in evident contradiction to the position adopted by Khumaynī over the years. Indeed, in a subsequent declaration he, together with Āyatullāh Tāliqānī, suggested that *ʿulamāʾ* political activity be reserved for exceptional circumstances and appealed to the clergy to return to the mosques in view of the chaos that the revolutionary committees had wreaked on Iranian society. Tāliqānī declared, in contrast to earlier assertion, that acceptance of political office by clergymen would "increase existing problems." And Sharīʿatmadārī proclaimed, in light of excesses by the Revolutionary Court under its self-proclaimed leader, Sādiq Khalkhālī, that if arbitrary proceedings and property expropriations were to continue, he would leave Qumm for Tabrīz.[48] Such a move would effectively have created the conditions for a civil war, given the antecedent rebellions in the Turkomen regions (Gurgān), Kurdistān, Khūzistān (with a large ethnic Arab population), and Balūchistān (in southeast Iran). In Sharīʿatmadārī's view *ʿulamāʾ* political activity could be justified only in extraordinary circumstances: (a) if parliament were about to enact legislation inimical to Islam; (2) no leader was available to establish order in society.[49]

Still later, when pressed for clarification on this issue and reminded of an alleged statement he had issued that *marājiʿ-yi taqlīd* should avoid politics (although it was permissible for second and third ranking clergymen to participate) he issued a disclaimer. At this point he declared that no legal obstacle exists to a clergyman's assuming political office if he wanted to do so. On the other hand, he did feel that the eminence enjoyed by a *marjaʿ-i taqlīd* would be demeaned were he to become a political official.[50]

Āyatullāh Sharī'atmadārī's cautionary orientation and his more liberal opin- ions (liberal in the context of issues relating to peaceful dissent) may be additionally seen in the following: (1) Prior to the late March referendum on the future political system of the country, he suggested that the formulation of the question on the ballot was too narrow. Instead of asking the masses whether they favor an Islamic republic or a monarchy—an evident case of forcing a preferred decision—the question ought to be the open-ended ''what kind of political sys- tem would you prefer?''[51]

(2) Sharī'atmadārī's supporters, presumably with his blessing, created a politi- cal party under his leadership which they called the Iranian Muslims' Islamic Republic People's Party (IMIRPP). Since Khumaynī was himself the leader of the Islamic Republic Party (IRP), this effort came to be seen as establishing a rival organization. While Sharī'atmadārī has rejected such conclusions, his sup- porters pointedly have declared that in a democarcy there ought to be a multi- party system. These individuals, Hujjat al-Islam Sadr Balāghī and Hujjat al- Islam Muhammad Gulsurkhī, argued that ''it is best to open all the doors for the people.'' When asked what the difference between IMIRPP (''which is by no means an imitation'') and the IRP was, Balāghī responded with the *non sequitur* that Āyatullāh Sharī'atmadarı was ''more moderate'' than Āyatullāh Khumaynī. The main thing is not the establishment of an Islamic republic, they argued, for that will come to pass in any event. The principal thing is how to achieve this on the basis of freedom, democracy, Islamic government and Islamic laws.'' Then, in an apparent contradiction, Balāghī stated that Iranians should have more of a choice than that given to them between an Islamic republic and a monarchy.[52]

(3) Āyatullāh Sharī'atmadārī's unmistakable use of terms in the political lexi- con of democrats is a subtle but significant divergence of orientation from that of Āyatullāh Khumaynī. On numerous occasions he has declared that an Islamic government and republic would secure government of the people for the people. Even when pressed to explain why the term ''democratic'' ought not to be interposed between the words ''Islamic republic,'' he suggested that no cause for worry existed for liberals because the essence of rule under such a system would be government of the people for the people. Consequently, the cherished objec- tive of democrats would be achieved.[53] But Khumaynī has often attacked the National Democratic Front, headed by Hidāyatullāh Matīn Daftarī, the son-in- law of the late Muhammad Musaddiq; his argument is that the liberal democrats who belonged to that organization seek a non-Islamic form of government and have been irrevocably corrupted in their political views by Western influence. In consequence, he urges his followers to exercise vigilance against such influential individuals. In response to his urgings, Hujjat al-Islam Sayyid 'Alī Khāmanah launched a campaign to urge the masses to adhere to the IRP, which, in his view, alone represented the interests of the Iranian nation. And the ever-available Hujjat al-Islam Abū al-Qāsim Falsafī bitterly attacked the adherents of Prime

Minister Musaddiq in ceremonies commemorating the deaths of Āyatullāh Muhammad Rizā Saʿīdī and Āyatullāh Murtazā Mutahharī at the Madrasah-yi Fayzīyah in Qumm in early June.[54] In sum, the two senior religious leaders hold markedly different positions on the scope of activity to be permitted to those whose *primary* concern is for the right to dissent and not so much an Islamic order.

(4) Āyatullāh Sharīʿatmadārī had urged the convening of a Constituent Assembly to deliberate over the crucial economic and political questions of the new order, in particular the draft Constitution. Now, Āyatullāh Khumaynī had early on come out in favor of the convening of a Constituent Assembly, as an examination of his edict of appointment of Midhī Bāzargān as Prime Minister of the provisional government will show. In that edict, Khumaynī had written:[55]

> Your Excellency [Bāzargān] is charged with forming a provisional government, without regard to your relations with parties or affiliation with any special group, in order that you may arrange for administering the affairs of the country; in particular with respect to the holding of a referendum seeking the opinions of the nation in regard to changing the political system of the country to an Islamic republic, establishing a Constituent Assembly, to be composed of the elected deputies of the people, which will direct itself to approving the constitution of the new order and electing the Majlis in accordance with the new constitution.

Yet, he eventually changed his mind on this issue and began to insist upon a Consultative Committee of 45 individuals whom he would appoint to take the place of the Constituent Assembly. Presumably, he took this decision when it became clear to him that his supporters would not necessarily be able to determine the outcome. This then led Āyatullāh Sharīʿatmadārī, who had all along been insisting on the need to convene a Constitutent Assembly, to declare that he would not participate in the referendum that was to determine the acceptability of the draft. The new constitution contained too many fine and subtle points not to be discussed by a representative assembly of the nation's experts and legal specialists. Submitting the draft directly to the people did not meet the requirements that informed delibration necessitates. Because of his extreme concern over any violence that might grow out of his opposition to the Khumaynī plan, Sharīʿatmadārī announced that he did not intend to allow his dissatisfaction to extend to any active opposition.[56] The debate that the press carried over the two plans—Khumaynī's advisory committee and Sharīʿatmadārī's constituent assembly—indicates that Āyatullāh Khumaynī's overwhelming prestige did not automatically translate into unanimous acceptance of his position. In his support were most of the country's preachers and a good many, perhaps the majority, of the second rank *āyatullāhs,* such as Sayyid Muhammad Bihishtī, Muhammad Rabānī Shīrāzī, Husayn ʿAlī Muntazirī, Sādiq Rūhānī, Bahāʾ al-Dīn Mahallātī, Shīrāzī, Nāsir Makārim Shīrāzī, Hādī Khusrūshāhī, Lāhūtī Rūdsarī.[57] With Sharī atmadārī were Āyatullāh Mahmūd Tāliqānī (whose name consistently appeared in the announcements of a very broad spectrum of organizations as the unique nominee for the post of president of the republic); Āyatullāh Hājj Sayyid Abū al-Fazl al-Mūsavī Zanjānī (a close supporter of Dr. Musaddiq); and Ayatullah Kāzim Dīnūrī of Tabriz. Arrayed with Sharīʿatmadārī were the National Democratic Front, the Mujāhidīn-i Khalq, the Fidāʾīyān-i Khalq, the Revolutionary Movement of the Muslim People of Iran. Among the organizations in support of Āyatullāh Khumaynī was the newly resuscitated Fidāʾīyān-i Islam, whose leader now had become the dismissed self-appointed head of the Revolutionary Court, Āyatullah Sādiq Khalkhālī.[58]

Evidently, a compromise was eventually negotiated between Khumaynī and Sharīʿatmadārī on this issue, with members of the provisional government possibly exercising an intermediation role. According to its terms, a Constituent Assembly of 75 individuals was to be elected (cf. the 270 that Sharīʿatmadārī originally had hoped for). This body would receive the draft constitution that Khumaynī's Council of the Islamic Revolution had drawn up after a month-long national debate on its contents. The draft that was issued had been sent to Sharʿatmadārī for his comments already in early March, and he had added amendments to several articles. The seventy five member Constituent Assembly would thereupon deliberate on the original draft, the amendments proposed to it by all those who had submitted changes, and promulgate a final copy that would then be presented for approval in a national referendum.[59]

(5) Āyatullāh Sharīʿatmadārī adopted a liberal position with respect to the freedom of the press to publish material about the clergy. This became particularly consequential in the context of the *Āyandigān* (an important Tehran daily) exposition of the activities of the clandestine Furqān. Little is known of the origins or membership of this faction, although Āyatullāh Hādī Khusrūshāhī, Chairman of the District #9 Revolutionary Committee of Tehran, has revealed that it was established in 1963 and had a tiny membership of 50 individuals, which by 1979 had declined to about 30.[60]

Furqān apparently rejects the infallibility, esoteric knowledge and purity of the *imam*s, believing merely that they were inspired leaders of their time. Press speculation suggested that their own political activities were nourished by the writings of Dr. ʿAlī Sharīʿatī, given the Furqān's militant attacks upon what they termed "ākhūndism." The word, *ākhūnd*,* has acquired a pejorative connotation—although some of the most eminent *Shīʿī* theologians (such as Ākhūnd Mullā Muhammad Kāzim Khurāsānī) have been called by that name. At the time of the assassination of Āyatullāh Murtazā Mutahharī, the large circulation daily newspaper, *Āyandigān*, wrote a feature article in the form of an exposition of Furqān's ideology. Although the paper itself did not adopt an

---

*A derogatory word meaning low-level clergyman, one not having knowledge.

editorial stand on the group's behavior and political orientation, Āyatullāh Khu-maynī directed a withering criticism at it for being an "anti-Islamic" newspaper. His hostility to it led to its inability to sell its issues on the newsstands and ugly incidents involving physical attacks upon its employees by adherents of the Āyatullāh.

The episode is an interesting one because Āyatullāh Khumaynī had blamed the assassination of Mutahharī on American intelligence operatives. Yet, *Āyandi-gān*'s exposition revealed that *religiously*-based opposition to the role of the clergy in social affairs—not to mention direct involvement in politics—existed in Iran. The revelation of this fact by the newspaper was the source of Khumaynī's anger, not any supposed support on the part of the newspaper for it. Furqān, it will be noted, based itself on *Qur'ān* and the mission of the prophet. Therefore, it could not easily be dismissed as "anti-Islamic." During the course of its long feature article on the group, the reporters of *Āyandigān* revealed publicly how bitter was the enmity that Dr. ʿAlī Sharīʿatī specifically had harbored toward the late *marjaʿ-i taqlīd,* Āyatullāh Sayyid Hādī Mīlānī of Mashhad (d. 1975). Fur-qān's hostility to Mīlānī is shown by *Āyandigān* as deriving from Sharīʿatī's comment that Georges Gurevich, the French Marxist sociologist who had com-batted both fascism and Stalinism and supported the Algerian Revolution, was closer to Shīʿism than Mīlānī! Whatever *fatvā*s Mīlānī had issued in his lifetime, Sharīʿatī had argued, they served to divide Muslims from one another, rather than to unite them. But Furqān's orientation to Mīlānī, observed *Āyandigān,* could also be deduced from that organization's assassination of Major General Muhammad Valī Qaranah'ī in April 1979. This figure, the first Chief of Staff of the revolutionary regime's army, had reportedly had close ties with Āyatullāh Mīlānī and received substantial "spiritual and material" assistance from him. *Āyandigān* therefore deduced that Qaranah'ī's participation in the American-Iranian arrangement to settle the Kurdish question in March 1975 inevitably implicated Mīlānī. That arrangement, it will be recalled, had been managed by Secretary of State Henry Kissinger in negotiations with the Kurds and the Iranian government. Subsequently, as the Kurds fell victim to the regime's harsh policies, it was widely believed that Kissinger had betrayed the Kurds. Qaranah'ī's role in this context, alleged the Furqān, consisted in facilitating the destruction of a large segment of the Kurdish population at the hands of both the Iraqi and Iranian governments.[61]

Such commentary aroused the wrath of numerous ʿ*ulamāʾ*, responding, as might be expected, to Āyatullāh Khumaynī's own furious condemnation of the newspaper. Typical of the clergy response was an open letter to the Iranian people signed by some 98 theologians from Tehran protesting *Āyandigān*'s al-leged description of the *ākhūnd*s of Iran as being "worse than the unbelievers." That *Āyandigān* was not in fact subscribing to that description but only attributing it to the Furqān did not seem to matter to the ʿulamāʾ, who, in their emotional statement, concluded by urging their followers to boycott the newspaper.[62]

Āyatullāh Sharīʿatmadārī's response to this affair depicted him in the light of a civil libertarian—as misleading as that description might be to a certain extent. The press bears a very heavy responsibility and should not publish material "against the principles of Islam." It should avert procoative statements and "completely observe Islamic standards." It must cultivate the unity of the people. Such sentiments on Sharīʿatmadārī's part reveal him to be a conservative defender of the faith. But his attitude was tempered by the notion that people should choose their own fare and can decide not to read material with which they disagree. He also has chosen to couple the terms "Islamic and humanist" in a. way Āyatullāh Khumaynī has not done when referring to the mission of the press. Moreover, he has urged a self-censorship on writers to avoid provocations that could lead to open conflicts, but warned sharply against direct intervention on the part of the masses in the direction and spirit of forcing journalists to adopt a certain line.[63] If one places in juxtaposition the comments by Āyatullāhs Khumaynī and Sharīʿatmadārī on the press, it becomes clear that the latter's appeals for care, precision, reasonableness stand out against the former's urging of militant vigilance and proscription.

Such observations about the differences between Āyatullāh Khumaynī and Āyatullāh Sharīʿatmadārī are ultimately overly simplistic and do not permit us to draw firm conclusions about the structure of intraclergy relations. Clergymen in Iran continue to disburse funds, aggregate followers on specific issues, articulate needs, wield the symbols of the culture, administer shrines, manage and own lands. An inquiry into the strategic and tactical differences between the two marājiʿ-yi ʿuẓẓām regretably shed practically no light on these issues. What such an exercise does allow, however, is to depict the broad outlines of cooperation and contention. And it does this on two levels: that of the past, since to a certain extent positions articulated in the current period can clarify obscurities of previously held orientations; and that of the future, to the extent that statements uttered in the present may offer clues to future patterns of behavior. Of course, the incumbents in this "grand debate," as it were, that has been highlighted here are acutely aware of these considerations. Thus, when Āyatullāh Sharīʿatmadārī faces the potentially embarrassing question as to whether his words have not provoked disunity in clergy ranks, his response is an instinctively firm "No!" Thus, in the aftermath of the meeting between the four senior āyatullāhs on 19 June 1979 at the home of Muhammad Riżā Gulpāygānī, Sharīʿatmadārī declared: "I disclaim the idea that any kind of difference in point of view exists concerning the constitution." And later: "Only unanimity will strengthen the foundations of Islam." Yet, in the very same statement belying conflict between himself and Khumaynī, he hints that differences had surfaced: "To the extent that I give my opinion, it is in the interests of the nation.'[64] Therefore, it is well to be attentive to nuances in the respective positions of the grand *āyatullāh*s for the purpose of better understanding the nature of their political interactions. To this degree, then, their own positions provide insights into lines of affiliation involving their supporters in the clergy ranks as well.

CHAPTER SEVEN

CONCLUSIONS

The existence or absence of doctrinal justifications for political involvement by the clergy appear to have become academic for a political system in which theologians exercise such great power as they currently do in Iran. Fascination with the clergy's political power should not obscure for us the fact that we still know very little with respect to the sociology of the Iranian religious institution. Perhaps, data collection and problems of access to information will become less severe to the social scientist in future. Certainly the task of clarifying the degree of the clergy's resources and, to that extent, the nature of influence networks among them, as well as between them and other forces in the society, as experienced in the Pahlavī period will be facilitated by: the release of certain archival material regarding the activities of state agencies regulating religious matters, especially SAVAK and the Endowments Organization; the greater readiness on the part of politically active or interested clergymen to write their memoirs; and the possibility of a revitalized interest in reforming the religious institution along the lines advocated by the reform movements of the 1960's and early 1970's. Of the features to be hoped for by the scholar of Iranian society under the new regime is an interest in generating and making available data on the structures and processes of the great social and economic institutions of society. Previous scholarship has labored under certain difficulties in showing specific trends, relationships and configurations as a result of weaknesses in the data. The present study has encountered these problems in equal, if not greater, proportion. If research on Islam and social change was problematical in the past because of the oppositional currents to the regime that centered in the religious institution, it will possibly encounter resistance in the future to the extent it is perceived as calculated to damage the unity of that institution by Western-trained intellectuals with no stake in Islam. Nevertheless, the clergy's enhanced confidence under the present circumstances should lead one to be more optimistic. The function of the current study has consisted in providing some of the basic documentation that is essential if we are to gain a greater understanding of the role of religion in society in Iran. Future efforts will build on these preliminary efforts to explain clergy-state relations in the contemporary period.

Social change involves developments affecting the economy, society and polity of human communities. In regard to the economy, modernizers seeking to effect social change address the issues of gross national product, net national income, energy production, industrial output, growth in infrastructure, savings and investment trends, etc. On this dimension, modernizers believe positive social change occurs as the indicators for these concepts can be shown to be increasing.

At the social level, social change involves transformations affecting the family, religion and education above all. It also refers to developments influencing employment, health and services (typically provided by the state). Modernizers view beneficial social change as taking place on this dimension when the institutions represented here, and the *culture* that evolves from them, experience consolidation, maturation, differentiation and growth. However, many modernizers adduce measures of consolidation, maturation, etc., which are closely tied to their own parochial vision of success. In this respect, then, the stress they place on maintaining the upward trend of the economic indicators often creates serious dislocations in the social sector.

Social change theory counts the political dimension as a critical one in the social change process. Modernizers, on the other hand, tend to ignore or suppress development on this level because, in their view, it conflicts with attempts on the previous two dimensions of economy and society. The widening of the scope of actual individual choice in policy generation and implementation underpins the notion of political development. Thus, if policy is the marshalling of resources by those in authority for the achievement of certain ends,[1] then social change on the political dimension means increasing opportunities to share in this process; here, the idea is not only to achieve the collective ends of the community but the particular objectives of one's own group, family or person.

Now, "Islam," as it were, has had to face the process of social change in Iran from the perspective of its own previous orientation. The present study has sought to outline what these were both in the theoretical and the practical sense. "Islam," too, has responded to social change in a variety of ways. This variety, as well, has been the subject of inquiry in this book. It is worth stating some conclusions at this point concerning social change within the broad context of clergy-state relations in the Pahlavī period in the form of the following propositions:

(1) Modernization attempts by secular rulers ignored the traditional sectors of society at a cost to their own efforts. Alternatively, they deliberately provoked them in a tactical effort to demonstrate to the people the clergy's ineluctable opposition to "progress." This conclusion is easy to state with the advantage of hindsight, but its outlines ought to have been clear to informed observers in various periods of rule by the Pahlavī Shahs. The crises of modernization

suggested by theorists of social and political change are so complex to resolve that they can not be addressed by the well-known pattern in Iranian history of bureaucratization of power. Although Iranians faced the pressures of social change in this century with a relatively strong concept of their own identity, the policies adopted by the various regimes to overcome the crises of participation, distribution, legitimacy and capacity created in fact an overwhelming identity crisis. The process of declassing the religious stratum led inexorably to attempts to appropriate the clergy's last resource: the cultural symbols which in the past have been so vital in inculcating among Iranians a sense of self, an explanation of the cosmos and of social reality. In short, bureaucratization of power led to the seizure of the clergy's jobs, lands, revenues, *madrasah*s and administration of shrines. In an *ad hoc* and *post facto* manner it may be ventured that if the regime had not gone beyond this to the attempt to monopolize cultural symbols, the revolution may not have occured. The relation between clergy and state from the 1963 disturbances until January 1979 must be seen largely in terms of the regime's belief that a technocratic value system ought to undergird its modernization efforts; and the clergy's ultimately fatal objection to such an effort.

(2) The clergy seriously miscalculated the meaning for its own institution of social change in the twentieth century. To say as much is not to suggest that the *'ulamā'* had contented themselves with inactivity and ritualistic repetition of outworn methods. Such generalities do not serve the purpose of analysis. What strikes attention is the strong streak of defensiveness on the part of the clergy with respect to social change. Defensiveness as a reaction to macro-scale, long-term secular changes which have their roots in the Western impact upon Iran is understandable, given the dual role of the *'ulamā'*: (a) guardians of the traditions of the prophet and the *imām*s; (b) protectors of the resources of the community against non-believer exploitation of this wealth. Now, the clergy's guardianship involved their efforts to preserve the meaning of the divine grace bestowed by God upon man in the Islamic community. And although, of course, it is the *imām*s who incarnate such grace, the *'ulamā'* strive to defend it in this world. Against the admonitions of their reformist colleagues the majority of the clergy seemingly feared that attempts to reform the religious institution would make them vulnerable to the charge that they were seeking to create a separate political sphere for their own activity. The creation of such an autonomous realm, so goes the argument, would of necessity require them to give up their guardianship of the sacral and salvational underpinnings of Islam. Yet, the reformist response to this is that despite the quietistic tradition that forms such a salient aspect of *Shī'ī* development, the *social* (cf. purely internally spiritual and soteriological) aspect of the ethical injunctions of *amr bi al-ma'rūf wa nahy 'an al-munkar* are undeniable. Even in the depths of the most quietistic periods of *Shī'ī* history the obligations of commanding the good and forbidding the bad have political impli-

cations in the sense that a literal abandonment of the field to evil-doing temporal rulers would not only not hasten the return of the *Imām* but would, in fact, render *Shī'ah* unprepared to receive him.

(3) The weaker the state has been, the more confidently has the religious institution's leadership conducted their social activities in society. The twenty year interval between 1905-1925, the decade between 1948-1958, and the most recent period of the last two years demonstrate the inverse relationship that has existed in this century between clergy authority and influence and state power in matters of social and political import.

(4) No categorical statement can be made that *Shī'ī* doctrine holds temporal rule to be illegitimate. Clearly such a conclusion has no doctrinal justification in the *Shī'ī* sources.[2] But the doctrine does uphold the right of the *'ulamā'* to protest injustice (*żulm*), without, however, requiring the clergy to rule. Thus, to speak of a "divorce" or "disjunction" between the theocratic and political sphere is an overdrawn depiction. Āyatullāh Sharī'atmadārī's recent statements in mid-1979 that in *Shī'ī* Islam there is no provision requiring the clergy to intervene in politics by seizing power is consonant with doctrine. But it would be misleading to hold, therefore, that doctrine ignores the problematic of *'ulamā'* (i.e., the *'ulā al-amr*) oversight of temporal behavior. In this manner, then, the political role of the clergy may be likened to that of advising and consenting. In implementing such an advise and consent role, they involve themselves in politics, if by that term is meant the process whereby individuals engage in social action to influence and shape the patterns by which resources are mobilized and employed to achieve certain objectives. Yet, withal the clergy do not have the doctrinal justification to establish their rule and thus create the circumstances for their exercise of executive power.

Presumably, clergy and state activity under the Islamic republic will be to a certain extent coextensive, as *'ulamā'* enter into employment in the state administration and stand for election to the Majlis. The draft of the constitution issued in June 1979 contains seven entire articles devoted to a Committee to Protect the Constitution. These provisions establish legal precedent for a judicial review process in which the *'ulamā'*, acting in that Committee, will obviously find themselves in the interstices of processes and functions appertaining to the state apparatus. Āyatullāh Khumaynī's insistence on a *purely* Islamic constitution is not reflected in the June draft, which features two thoroughly Western-influenced characteristics: soveriegnty resides in the people (cf. sovereignty devolving as a contingent factor through acquisition [*iktisāb*] from Allah); and separation of powers into legislative, judicial and executive branches of government.

And, in place of the famous Article Two of the Supplementary Fundamental Laws of the first Iranian constitution, the 1979 Constitution, as stated, contains seven articles devoted to a Committee to Protect the Constitution (*shūrā-yi nigahbān-i qānūn-i asāsī*) Somewhat surprisingly, the composition of this

Committee—the task of which is to determine the compatibility of statutory acts of the Majlis with the fundamental law of the land—is not dominated by the clergy. The membership includes five *mujtahids*, three professors of law and three members of the state Supreme Court. The particular mix constitutes a compromise between Āyatullāh Khumaynī's Council for the Islamic Revolution and the nonclergy nationalist leadership (e.g., Mihdī Bāzargān, ʿAlī Shāygān, Matīn Daftarī, Dariūsh Farūhar, Yadullāh Sahābī, Muhsin Pizishkpūr, ʿAlī Asghar Hājj Sayyid Javādī, Hasan Nazīh, Karīm Sanjābī, Ahmad Banī Ahmad and ʿAbd al-Karīm Lāhījī). Tensions between the clergy and the lay nationalists suggest certain parallels between those in 1953 between Āyatullāh Kāshānī and his supporters on the one hand, and Dr. Musaddiq and the National Front on the other.[3] Whether or not the Islamic republic which the Iranian people agreed by referendum to accept as their political system will be a theocratic order or an uneasy synthesis of religious and secular principles will in large measure depend on the extent to which the clerical leadership maintains its solidarity with Āyatullāh Khumaynī's vision of the new order. The dramatic exercise of power by the *ulamāʾ* in the Iranian revolution may suggest that the religious institution is a monolithic force. But as has been repeatedly shown here, the clerical leaders have inevitably acted in the social realm. On that account, they have expressed thoughts, needs and interests which have differed considerably, even while they have all operated within the broad consensus provided by the Muslim's vision of social and religious reality.

APPENDIXES

Table I. Comparative Data, *Madrasah*s and *Tullab*
in Iran, Various Years Since 1302 H. Sh./1923

Years	*Madrasah*s	*Tullāb*
1302–03/1923–24	240	4979
1303–04/1924–25	282	5984
1305–06/1926–27	279	4948
1306–07/1927–28	310	8514
1307–08/1928–29	303	5532
1308–09/1929–30	315	4598
1310–11/1931–32	328	3991
1311–12/1932–33	334	4404
1312–13/1933–34	372	4110
1313–14/1934–35	389	4004
1314–15/1935–36	353	2935
1315–16/1936–37	311	2981
1316–17/1937–38	298	1301[b]
1317–18/1938–39	298	2373[c]
1318–19/1939–40	238	1341[b]
1319–20/1940–41	250	784[b]
1320–21/1941–42	226	1010[b]
1321–22/1942–43	189	890[b]
1322–23/1943–44	196	1299[b]
1323–24/1944–45	173	2907[b]
1324–25/1945–46	172	3057[b]
1325–26/1946–47	242	5829[c]
1326–27/1947–48	217	6531[c]
1338–39/1959–60	252[a]	14419[d]
1339–40/1960–61	236	13016[e]
1341–42/1962–63	229	13800[d]
1346–47/1967–68	138	7482[d]

[a]Figure cited is 522 but must be a typographical error in which the first and second digits were transposed
[b]Figure excludes *tullāb* in the *'atabāt;* cf. earlier years when they were included.
[c]Figure includes *tullāb* in the *'atabāt.*
[d]Not known if figure includes *tullāb* in the *'atabāt.*
[e]Figure includes *mudarrisīn;* not known if figure includes *'atabāt.*
NB: the very low figures between 1941–45 for both *madrasah*s and *tullāb* can partially be explained by

187

the fact that information for key areas, such as Khurāsān, Māzandarān, Āzarbāyjān provinces was unavailable. Such areas on the whole coincided with zones of Soviet occupation during the war.

SOURCES: The data in Table I were obtained from the various annuals published under a variety of titles by the Ministry of Education in Tehran between 1297/1918 and 1327/1948. Data for 1338–39/1959–60 is from ʿĪsā Sadīq, *Tārīkh-i Farhang-i Iran.* 2nd ed. (Tehran: Tehran University Press, 1338 H. Sh./1959), p. 478. Data for 1339–40/1960–61 is from the article, "Awqāf," *Kitāb-i Īrānshahr.* Vol. II (Tehran: Tehran University Press, in conjunction with UNESCO, 1343 H. Sh./1964), pp. 1264–1398. Data for 1341–42/1962–63 is from Sadīq, *op. cit.,* 3rd ed. (Tehran: Tehran University Press, 1343 H. Sh./1964), p. 498. Data for 1346–47/1967–68 is from Sadīq, *op. cit.,* 7th ed. (Tehran: Tehran University Press, 1354 H. Sh./1975), p. 480.

For the year 1339/1960 there is conflicting opinion on the number of *madrasah*s, although not the number of *tullāb.* The figures cited by *Sadīq* and the encyclopaedia article, "Awqāf," are 252 and 236 for the successive years 1338–39 and 1339–40/1959–60 and 1960–61. In the Persian edition of his memoirs the Shah stated that there were in 1959 "two hundred religious schools in Iran . . . still in operation." Muhammad Rizā Shah Pahlavī, *Maʾmūrīyat barā-yi Vatanam* (Tehran: Chāpkhānah-yi Sāzmān-i Samʿī va Basrī-yi Hunarhā-yi Zībā-yi Kishvar, n. d.), p. 494. In the English language edition, he declared that "more than two hundred Moslem religious schools and colleges still survived in 1959." *Mission for My Country* (London: Hutchinson & Co., Ltd., 1961), p. 244. In general, his figures are in line with those cited in the table. But for a higher figure, see M. S. Ivanov, *Iran Segodnia* (Moscow: Izdatelstvo "Nauka", 1969), p. 161, where he claims that in 1960 there were 315 *madrasah*s. He repeated this figure a year later in his article, "Izmeneniia v Kulture i Byte Sovremennogo Irana," *Vestnik Moskovskogo Universiteta: Vostokovedenie,* No. 2 (1970), p. 41. His figures seem too high in view of the data produced in the Persian sources; moreover, these data are more in line with the 1967–68 figures, which are in the opposite direction from those given by Ivanov. Also suspicious is Ivanov's failure to specify his sources. A final anomaly pertains to the information provided in the "Awqāf" article. On p. 1277 the figure of 214 *madrasah*s is cited; but pp. 1344–98, containing a listing of *madrasah*s by *shahrastān*s (cities), yield a cumulative figure of 236. The higher figure has been accepted because it is based on the sum of all theological colleges listed by name under each *shahrastān;* whereas the lower figure is simply stated as such.

Table II.   Percentage Change in Number of *Madrasah*s and *Tullāb*
in Iran, Various Years Since 1302 H. Sh./1923

Years	% Change *Madrasah*s	% Change *Tullāb*
1302/03–1303/04 (1923/24–1924/25)	+ 17.5	+ 20.2
1303/04–1305/06 (1924/25–1926/27)	− 1.1	− 17.3
1305/06–1306/07 (1926/27–1927/28)	+ 11.1	+ 72.1
1306/07–1307/08 (1927/28–1928/29)	− 2.3	− 35.0
1307/08–1308/09 (1928/29–1929/30)	+ 4.0	− 16.9
1308/09–1310/11 (1929/30–1931/32)	+ 4.1	− 13.2
1310/11–1311/12 (1931/32–1932/33)	+ 1.8	+ 10.3
1311/12–1312/13 (1932/33–1933/34)	+ 11.1	− 6.7
1312/13–1313/14 (1933/34–1934/35)	+ 5.1	− 2.6
1313/14–1314/15 (1934/35–1935/36)	− 9.5	− 26.7
1314/15–1315/16 (1935/36–1936/37)	− 11.9	+ 1.6
1315/16–1316/17 (1936/37–1937/38)	− 4.1	− 56.4
1316/17–1317/18 (1937/38–1338/39)	0	+ 82.4
1317/18–1318/19 (1938/39–1939/40)	− 20.1	− 41.5
1318/19–1319/20 (1939/40–1940/41)	+ 5.0	+ 28.8
1319/20–1320/21 (1940/41–1941/42)	− 9.6	− 11.9
1320/21–1321/22 (1941/42–1942/43)	− 16.4	− 11.9
1321/22–1322/23 (1942/43–1943/44)	+ 3.7	+ 46.0
1322/23–1323/24 (1943/44–1944/45)	− 11.7	+ 123.8
1323/24–1324/25 (1944/45–1945/46)	− 0.6	+ 5.6
1324/25–1325/26 (1945/46–1946/47)	+ 40.7	+ 90.7
1325/26–1326/27 (1946/47–1947/48)	− 14.5	+ 12.0
1326/27–1338/39 (1947/48–1959/60)	+ 16.1	+ 120.8
1338/39–1339/40 (1959/60–1960/61)	− 6.3	− 9.7
1339/40–1341/42 (1960/61–1962/63)	− 3.0	+ 6.0*
1341/42–1346/47 (1962/63–1967/68)	− 40.0	− 45.8

*It will be recalled that the figure listed for number of *tullāb* in 1339/40 (1960/61) included teachers,
and therefore the six percent increase that shows up needs modification.

Table III. Comparative Data on Madrasahs by Geographic Area

Locality	1922–23	1923–24	1924–25	1926–27	1927–28	1928–29	1929–30	1931–32	1932–33	1933–34	1934–35	1935–36
1. East Āzarbāyjān*		16	19	—	9	6	14	10	6	7	12	12
2. West Āzarbāyjān*		7	7	6	14	15	14	14	23	46	43	55
3. Astarābād (Gurgān)		15	13	14	18	18	20	20	23	19	16	9
4. Isfahān		—	5	3	—	—	—	4	20	33	33	33
5. Southern Ports			3	1					6	5	4	2
6. Tunukāban												
7. Tuysirkān*		2	1	1	1	1	3	3	3	2	3	
8. Malāyir*	40											—
9. Tehran		46	46	46	46	46	46	58	35	20	37	20
10. Khurāsān		34	26	42	57	60	55	52	51	55	47	44
11. Khūzistān		1	7	7	13	13	11	14	13	18	18	14
12. Zanjān (Khamsah)		11	11	11	10	8	12	11	11	11	11	11
13. Simnān*				1	1	1	1	1		—	3	1
14. Dāmghān*		4	4	3	3	3	3	3	5	5	5	4
15. Shāhrūd*				3	3	4	4	4	4	4	4	4
16. Bastām*		3	4	1								
17. Arāk		3	3	3	3	3	3	3	3	4	3	3
18. Fārs		21	19	19	21	22	23	24	27	32	31	31
19. Qā'ināt		5	5	5								
20. Qazvīn		8	8	8	8	8	13	13	13	13	13	13
21. Qumm*		7	6	6	8	8	7	8	8	8	8	8
22. Mahallāt*				—								
23. Kāshān		5	5	5	5	5	5	5	5	5	5	5
24. Kurdistān		17	28	25	32	26	23	27	23	23	28	28
25. Kirmān		6	7	8	6	6	5	4	4	7	6	7
26. Kirmānshāhān		2	4	4	4	5	3	3	3	3	4	4
27. Gulpāygān**							.2	2				
28. Kamarah**		3	3		3	3			4	4	4	4
29. Khvānsār**				1								
30. Gilān		7	7	8	7	7	7	7	7	7	7	6
31. Luristān***		1	2	2	2	1	4	3	3	4	4	—

Locality	1936-37	1937-38	1938-39	1939-40	1940-41	1941-42	1942-43	1943-44	1944-45	1945-46	1946-47	1947-48	1960-61
1. East Āẕarbāyjān	8	11	10	9	9	9	10	10	5	—	—	—	8
2. West Āẕarbāyjān	55	55	76	74	74	—	—	—	—	—	15	12	2
3. Gurgān	9	9	6	9	9	6	—	—	—	—	5	—	7
4. Isfahān	32	32	32	28	28	27	29	29	28	28	19	23	30
5. Southern Ports	—	—	—	—	—	—	—	—	—	—	—	—	—
6. Tunukābān	—	—	—	—	—	—	—	—	—	—	—	—	—
7. Tūyirskān*	—	—	—	—	—	—	—	—	—	—	—	—	—
8. Malāyir*	3	—	—	—	—	—	—	—	—	—	—	—	2
9. Tehran	22	19	18	9	14	11	10	15	20	13	26	17	32
10. Khurāsān	41	42	42	—	—	43	43	38	23	36	37	29	37
11. Khūzistān	1	1	—	—	1	1	1	1	—	—	—	—	10
12. Zanjān	12	12	12	12	12	12	12	12	14	14	14	5	3
13. Simnān	3	3	3	3	14	—	—	—	—	—	—	—	3
14. Dāmghān	—	—	—	—	—	—	—	—	—	—	—	—	3
15. Shāhrūd	4	4	4	4	4	4	4	4	4	2	—	—	—
16. Bastām	—	—	—	—	—	—	—	—	—	—	—	—	—
17. Arāk	3	3	3	3	3	3	3	3	3	3	3	3	3
18. Fārs	31	31	27	28	28	28	28	28	28	30	67	67	19
19. Qā'ināt	—	—	—	—	—	—	—	—	—	—	—	—	—
20. Qazvīn	13	13	13	13	13	13	13	13	13	13	13	13	7
21. Qumm	8	8	8	8	8	8	8	7	7	7	8	8	12
22. Mahallāt	—	—	—	—	—	—	—	—	—	—	—	—	—
23. Kāshān	5	5	5	5	5	5	5	5	5	5	5	5	5
24. Kurdistān	—	—	—	—	—	—	—	—	—	—	—	—	9
25. Kirmān	7	7	7	7	7	7	7	7	7	1	5	6	5
32. Māzandarān	7	7	26	21	24	17	25	23	23	23	26	23	15
33. Nahāvand	1	1	1	1	1	—	—	—	—	—	—	—	2
34. Hamadān	3	3	3	3	4	4	4	4	4	3	3	2	7
35. Yazd	5	5	9	4	8	10	7	7	7	7	7	13	4
36. Sāvah	—	—	—	—	—	—	—	—	—	—	—	—	1
37. Khurramābād	—	—	—	—	—	—	—	—	—	—	—	1	1
38. Makrān	—	—	—	—	—	—	—	—	—	—	—	—	2

26. Kirmānshāhān	4	4	—	—	—	—	—	—	—	—	—	2	1	—
27. Gulpāygān	3	3	—	—	—	—	—	—	—	—	—	—	1	1	2
28. Kamarah	—	—	—	—	—	—	—	—	—	—	—	—	—	—
29. Khvānsār	6	5	5	4	—	—	—	2	3	3	3	—	5
30. Gīlān	—	—	—	—	—	—	—	—	—	3	3	3	5
31. Luristān***	21	21	15	14	5	14	10	2	13	8	12	6
32. Māzandarān	—	—	—	—	—	—	—	2	13	2	3	5
33. Nahāvand	2	—	—	—	1	1	1	—	—	2	3
34. Hamadān	7	7	7	8	8	8	8	1	1	3	5
35. Yazd	—	—	—	—	—	—	1	1	1
36. Sāvah	1	—	1	—	—	1	—	1
37. Khurramābād*	2	—	1	1	1	2	1	1	—	1
38. Burūjird*	4	4	4	4	4	1	—	3	4
39. Sabzivār	4	—	—	—	—	—	—	—
40. Makrān	4	—	—	—	—	—	—	—
41. Bīrjand	—	—	—	—	8	8	1	1	1	8
42. 'Atabāt	—	—	—	—	—	—	—	—
43. Ābādān & Khurramshahr	—	—	—	—	—	—	3	3
44. Karaj	—	—	—	—	—	—	—	—	—	3
45. Shahr-i Kurd	—	—	—	—	—	—	—	2

*The areas with one asterisk were sometimes reported in pairs and sometimes discretely

**The towns with two asterisks were reported together for most of the period between 1922–1936.

***In 1931–32, Luristān was replaced by Burūjird, the major town of that province.

NB. It is difficult to interpret the wide variations in the number of *madrasahs* reported from a single year to the next. Either this is a question of failure to report accurately or city or province districts have been redrawn in the interim to include or exclude areas that previously had been excluded or included. The large number of entries reported by the symbol, —, may mean either that the data were not available or *madrasahs* did not exist. Finally, a certain duplication may have entered into these figures, inasmuch as the regions of Sabzivār and Birjand, for instance, are areas of Khurāsān province and yet are reported separately for the 1936 period onward.

SOURCES: The data in Table III is from the annuals published by the Ministry of Education in Tehran under various titles over the period 1301/1922–1327/48; and from the "Awqaf" article mentioned in the note to Table I.

Table IV. Comparative Data on *Tullāb* by Geographic Area

Locality	1922-23	1923-24	1924-25	1926-27	1927-28	1928-29	1929-30	1931-32	1932-33	1933-34	1934-35	1935-36
1. East Āẕarbāyjān*	—	308	291	214	1042	153	325	158	117	84	136	44
2. West Āẕarbāyjān*	—	—	105	219	93	283	280	90	78	224	216	168
3. Gurgān	—	96	330	259	430	353	283	198	209	68	40	12
4. Isfahān	—	357	180	50	93	—	—	131	170	138	214	116
5. Southern Ports	—	—	62	36	—	—	—	—	88	73	25	20
6. Tunukābān	—	—	—	—	—	—	—	—	—	—	—	—
7. Tūysirkān*	—	—	—	—	—	—	—	4	—	—	—	—
8. Malāyir*	—	48	43	45	56	14	22	6	28	15	—	37
9. Tehran	626	560	579	563	1825	425	425	280	360	235	319	239
10. Khurāsān	—	1349	1340	1894	1068	2041	1379	1080	871	921	967	412
11. Khūzistān	—	61	52	106	254	273	152	134	107	123	27	20
12. Zanjān	—	150	187	187	92	116	123	109	88	109	105	65
13. Simnān*	—	102	97	22	82	10	12	7	—	—	—	—
14. Dāmghān*	—	—	—	58	16	9	7	13	13	16	12	3
15. Shāhrūd*	—	—	—	—	—	—	—	9	11	7	3	—
16. Bastām*	—	82	—	31	52	34	16	—	—	—	—	—
17. Arāk	—	98	135	146	132	75	55	60	41	13	80	20
18. Fārs	—	122	178	194	474	194	103	166	174	162	166	135
19. Qā'ināt	—	175	167	175	—	—	—	—	—	—	—	—
20. Qazvīn	—	160	158	154	166	90	92	59	44	47	47	28
21. Qumm	—	548	769	519	167	869	812	764	745	543	390	489
22. Mahallāt	—	—	—	—	—	—	—	—	—	—	—	—
23. Kāshān	—	39	32	24	85	18	20	20	21	17	18	—
24. Kurdistān	—	66	130	99	132	71	54	62	37	26	22	19
25. Kirmān	—	70	88	95	307	84	44	60	22	20	11	14
26. Kirmānshāhān	—	20	41	44	214	33	10	—	2	2	6	—
27. Gulpāygān**	—	—	—	—	—	—	—	14	—	—	—	—
28. Kamarah**	—	—	3	—	—	—	—	—	—	—	—	—
29. Khvānsār**	—	—	—	20	38	16	16	—	10	6	13	5

193

Locality	1936–37	1937–38	1938–39	1939–40	1940–41	1941–42	1942–43	1943–44	1944–45	1945–46	1946–47	1947–48
1. East Āzarbāyjān	75	72	92	60	73	94	309	290	422	—	—	—
2. West Āzarbāyjān	174	28	95	348	—	—	—	—	—	—	444	590
3. Gurgān	—	—	4	—	—	—	—	—	—	—	20	—
4. Isfāhān	149	109	128	109	—	109	131	131	314	600	759	842
5. Southern Ports	—	—	—	—	—	—	—	—	—	—	—	—
6. Tunukāban	—	—	—	—	—	—	—	—	—	—	—	—
7. Tūysirkān	—	—	—	—	—	—	—	—	—	—	—	—
8. Malāyir	320	118	83	170	62	109	52	158	319	194	179	126
9. Tehran	329	599	12	—	—	—	—	—	251	538	788	1127
10. Khurāsān	13	—	—	—	—	—	—	—	—	—	—	—
11. Khūzistān	50	25	—	—	—	—	—	118	179	—	161	198
12. Zanjān	—	—	—	—	—	—	—	—	—	—	—	—
13. Simnān	—	—	—	—	—	—	—	—	—	—	—	—
14. Dāmghān	—	—	—	—	—	—	—	—	—	—	—	—
15. Shāhrūd	—	—	—	—	—	—	—	—	—	—	—	—
16. Bastām	16	16	16	13	12	—	—	—	—	48	154	70
17. Arāk	119	15	11	38	38	40	—	92	147	64	210	236
18. Fārs	—	—	—	—	—	—	—	—	—	—	—	—
19. Qā'ināt	—	—	—	—	—	—	—	—	—	—	—	—
30. Gilān	115	118	90	672	60	66	37	47	40	35	24	
31. Luristān***	120	40	90	137	117	75	85	47	19	17	38	
32. Māzandarān	127	494	653	366	32	83	38	30	36	55	3	
33. Nahāvand	2	3	—	—	—	—	10	—	—	—	—	
34. Hamadān	99	129	96	213	62	59	43	57	70	61	37	
35. Yazd	95	111	72	188	193	64	20	23	17	21	14	
36. Sāvah	10	10	—	—	17	21	6	3	—	—	—	
37. Khurramābād	—	—	—	—	—	—	—	3	2	5	—	
38. 'Atabāt	—	—	—	—	—	—	328	—	1077	992	974	
Grand Totals		4979	5884	6155	8394	5642	4598	3991	3446	4110	4003	2936

194

	C1	C2	C3	C4	C5	C6	C7	C8	C9	C10	C11	C12
20. Qazvín	25	19	15	18	14	14	14	37	12	44	42	95
21. Qumm	273	320	585	585	585	585	374	380	1200	1200	1650	1800
22. Mahallát	—	—	—	—	—	—	—	—	—	—	—	—
23. Káshán	—	—	—	—	—	—	—	—	—	—	—	15
24. Kurdistán	—	—	—	—	—	—	—	—	—	—	—	—
25. Kirmán	—	—	—	—	—	—	—	—	34	35	35	45
26. Kirmánsháhán	—	—	—	—	—	—	—	—	—	25	28	22
27. Gulpáygán	5	5	—	—	—	—	—	—	—	5	—	10
28. Kamarah	—	—	—	—	—	—	—	—	—	—	—	—
29. Khvánsár	—	—	—	—	—	—	—	—	—	—	—	—
30. Gílán	11	—	—	—	—	—	—	—	—	33	49	40
31. Luristán***	—	—	—	—	—	—	—	—	—	—	—	—
32. Mázandarán	3	—	—	—	—	—	—	38	29	180	105	20
33. Nahávand	—	—	—	—	—	—	—	—	—	—	—	—
34. Hamadán	29	—	—	—	—	59	—	—	—	—	24	122
35. Yazd	11	—	—	—	—	—	—	—	—	—	—	32
36. Sávah	—	—	—	—	—	—	—	—	—	51	51	51
37. Khurramábád*	—	—	—	—	—	—	10	—	—	—	—	—
38. Burújird*	—	—	—	—	—	—	—	—	—	—	—	—
39. Sabzivár	40	41	—	—	—	—	—	50	—	—	80	160
40. Makrán	13	—	—	—	—	—	—	—	—	—	—	40
41. Birjand	—	—	—	—	—	—	—	—	—	40	40	40
42. 'Atabát	1304	—	1332	—	—	—	—	—	—	—	—	—
Grand Totals	2959	1367	2373	1341	784	1010	890	1294	2907	3057	4819	5641

*The areas with one asterisk were sometimes reported in pairs and sometimes discretely.

**The towns with two asterisks were reported together for most of the period between 1922–1936.

***In 1931–32 Luristán was replaced by Burújird, the major town of that province.

SOURCES: The data in Table IV is from the annuals published by the Ministry of Education in Tehran under various titles over the period 1301/1922–1327/1948. The numerous blanks in the table may be attributable to the problems of data gathering in outlying areas, the disruptions caused by the war, poor census efforts, deliberate regime policies of harrassing the religious sciences students and, perhaps, the tendency of students to move from one hawzah to another for a variety of reasons.

195

Table V. *Tullāb* in Qumm, Grouped in Shahrastāns According to Province, 1953 (Column I); and Qumm Graduates in Shahrastāns, According to Province, 1953 (Column II). Adapted from Muhammad Rāzī, *Āsār al-Hujjah*, II (Qumm: Hikmat, 1332 H. Sh./1953), pp. 203–392

	I	II		I	II
I. Markazī (Tehran)			IV. Gīlān (*cont.*)		
1. Tehran	150	59	3. Rūdsar	60	3
2. Qazvīn	140	8	4. Lāhījān	40	6
3. Qumm	250	—	5. Arāk	50	4
4. Damāvand	"several"	1	6. Zanjān	200	2
5. Sāvah	20	2	7. Ābhar	45	1
6. Varāmīn	8	1	Totals	575	42
7. Shahr-i Ray	25	9	%	18.1	13.2
8. Khumayn	12	—			
9. Mahallāt	20	3	V. MāzandarānGurgān		
10. Mazlaqān &	80	—	1. Gurgān	20	2
Khārqān			2. Sārī	45	—
11. Tāliqān	40	—	3. Bābul	45	2
Totals	745	83	4. Āmul	10	—
%	23.3	26.2	5. Bihshahr	25	—
			6. Chālūs	25	1
II. East Āzarbāyjan			7. Shāhī	10	1
1. Tabrīz	200	7	8. Fīrūzkūh	8	—
2. Ardabīl	140	2	9. Bandar-i Gaz	—	1
3. Sarāb	30	—	10. Dāmghān	—	1
4. Mishkīn	"several"	—	11. Kāshān	40	4
5. Marāghah &	100	1	12. Simnān	10	—
Hashtrūd			13. Shāhrūd	10	—
6. Marand	50	—	Totals	248	12
7. Miyānah &	200	—	%	7.8	3.8
Garmrūd					
8. Mīlān	—	1	VI. Khurāsān		
9. Khalkhāl	20	—	1. Mashhad	70	1
Totals	740	11	2. Nayshāpūr	30	4
%	23.3	3.5	Totals	100	5
			%	3.2	1.6
III. West Āzarbāyjān					
1. Rizā'īyah	30	1	VII. Khūzistān-Luristān		
2. Khūy	25	4	1. Ābādān	4	—
3. Bastām	"several"	1	2. Dizfūl	12	2
4. Mīyān-i Dū	—	1	3. Bihbihān	6	"several"
Āb			4. Ahvāz	—	1
Totals	55	7	5. Shūshtar	—	1
%	1.7	2.2	6. Masjid-i Sulaymān	—	1
			7. Gulpāygān	50	—
			8. Burūjird	20	1
IV. Gīlān			9. Khurramābād	14	7
1. Rasht	100	9	Totals	106	13
2. Langarūd	80	15	%	3.3	4.1

VIII.	Kirmān	'	'		XI.	Fars-Gulf Ports		
	1. Kirmān	30	2			1. Shīrāz	40	2
	2. Rafsanjān	10	1			2. Ābādah	—	1
	3. Zarand	14	—			Totals	40	3
	4. Shahrīyār	—	1			%	1.3	0.95
	Totals	54	4		XII.	ʿAtabāt		
	%	1.7	1.3			1. Najaf	—	110
IX.	Isfahān-Yazd					Totals	—	110
	1. Bafrū	10	1			%	0	34.7
	2. Yazd	70	2					
	3. Isfahān	200	—		XIII.	Other		
	4. Khvānsār	20	2			1. Madīnah	—	2
	5. Najafābād	60	2			(Saudi Arabia)		
	Totals	360	7			Totals	—	2
	%	11.3	2.2			%	—	0.63
X.	Kirmānshāhān					Grand Totals (N=)	3168	317
	1. Hamadān	100	11					
	2. Muhājirān	5	1					
	3. Tūysirkān	5	1					
	4. Malāyir	15	2					
	5. Nahāvand	10	2					
	6. Kirmān-shāhān	10	2					
	7. Īlām	—	1					
	Totals	145	20					
	%	4.6	6.3					

B: the information provided in Table V should be treated with even greater caution than those in the previous tables since it is based on a single individual's canvassing effort and is to that extent subject to internal and external validity challenges. Nevertheless, the general trend is suggestive, especially the 43% of the total figures reported by Rāzī as comprising the enrollment of Qumm in 1953 which were of Turkish-Āzarī background .e., their provenience was Āzarbāyjān, Zanjān or Gīlān.) The grouping by province follows the administrative divisions of the country as of 1953. The enrollment figure in 1953 may be compared to that in early 1956, which was cited by the Tehran daily, *Kayhān*, 22 Urdībihisht 1335 H. Sh./1956, at an estimated 5,000.

Table VI.   Urban-Rural Characteristics, Professors, Instructors
and Graduates of Qumm as of 1332 H. Sh./1953

	N	%
I. Professors		
Urban	37	80.4
Rural	9	19.6
Totals	46	100.0
II. Instructors		
Urban	83	79.0
Rural	22	21.0
Totals	105	100.0
III. Graduates (1920–53)		
Urban	132	84.6
Rural	24	15.4
Totals	156	100.0

SOURCE: Razi, Āṣār al-Hujjah, passim. It should be understood that the term "urban" refers to towns with a population of 5,000 or more and therefore must be conceived in terms of the specifically Iranian context. Individuals were classified as having urban origins if Rāzī stated that they hailed from one of the country's shahrastāns; they were classified as having rural origins if the author declared that they hailed from the environs (hūmah) of one of the shahrastāns or else from a qal'ah or qasabah or dih.

Table VII.   *Madrasah*s of Mashhad, Various Years, Number of *Tullāb* and Annual Income, in Rials

Name of *Madrasah*	1926-1927 No. *Tullāb*	Annual Inc.	1953-1954 No. *Tullāb*	Annual Inc.	1971-1973 No. *Tullāb*	Annual Inc.
1. Fāzilkhān	190	23,840	*	*	*	*
2. Nuvvāb	130	40,070	150	n.a.	125/150	832,259
3. Bāqirīyah	120	46,660	100	n.a.	50	369,360
4. Mīrzā Ja'far	130	11,360	200	60,000	300/150	178,260
5. Khayrāt Khān	100	30,000	n.a.	n.a.	195	103,200
6. Pāyin Pā	60	11,400	*	*	*	*
7. Bālā Sar	35	6,600	n.a.	n.a.	70/30	15,840
8. Dū Dar	75	12,600	n.a.	n.a.	140/80	60,000
9. Rizvān	5	10,800	n.a.	n.a.	15	n.a.
10. Mustashār	16	3,000	*	*	*	*
11. 'Abbās Qulī Khān	132	11,040	150	204,000	250/200	244,072
12. Sulaymān Khān	18	2,700	n.a.	n.a.	40	n.a.
13. Parīzād	16	14,400	n.a.	n.a.	0/20	92,880
14. Hājj Hasan	60	8,400	n.a.	n.a.	80	60,000
15. Hājj Sālih	40	5,500	*	*	*	*
16. Ibdāl Khān	60	15,000	n.a.	117,000	30	n.a.
17. Hājj Āghā Khān	6	1,440	*	*	*	*
18. Sabzivārīhā	n.a.	n.a.	*	*	*	*
19. Ja'farīyah	*	*	*	*	40	n.a.
20. Mīlānī	*	*	*	*	20	n.a.

*Denotes *madrasah* either non-existent at the time or destroyed.

SOURCES: Data for 1926-1927 is adapted from Dawlat-i 'Alīyah-yi Iran, Vizārat-i Ma'ārif va Awqāf va Sanāyi'yi Mustazrafah. *Qavānīn va Niẓāmnāmahhā, Ihsā 'īyah-yi Madāris va Makātib, Ihsā 'īyah-yi A 'zā' va Mustakhdimīn* [1305-1306 H. Sh./1926-1927] (Tehran: Chāpkhānah yi Firdawsī, n.d., pp. 56-188. The incomplete and sketchy information for 1953-54 is from Elena Alekseevich Doroshenko, *Shiitskoe Dukhovenstvo v Sovremennom Irane* (Moscow: Izdatelstvo "Nauka," 1975), p. 49. Data for the 1971-73 period is from two different sources, one a series of article published throughout 1971-72; and the second from a book published in 1974. The relevant sources are: Mahmūd Fāzil, "Madāris-i Qadīm-i Mashhad," *Vahīd* Vol. IX, nos. 10-12 (Āzar-Isfand 1350 H. Sh./1971-72), pp. 1450-1453, 1661-68, 1773-78; Vol. X, nos. 1-3, 6, 7, 10 (Farvardīn-Khurdād, Shahrīvar, Mihr, Day 1351 H. Sh./1972-1973), pp. 40-44, 207-213, 283-88, 675-79, 1128-32; Vol. XI, no. 1 (Farvardīn 1352 H. Sh./1973), pp. 75-78. Also, Muhammad Khujastah Mubashshirī, *Tārīkh-i Mashhad* (Mashhad: Chāpkhānah-yi Khurāsān, 1353 H. Sh./1974), pp. 311-29. The two figures given for student enrollment in certain cases reflect each author's respective sources and conclusions.

The overall student population of these schools was:	1926-27	1193
	1953-54	953*
	1971-73	1295/1100
The total number of *madrasah*s each of these years was	1926-27	18
	1953-54	12
	1971-73	14

*Doroshenko cites an overall figure of 953 for Mashhad but only gives specific breakdowns for the four schools indicated in the table.

Table VIII.   Comparative Data on Gainfully Employed in Religious
Occupations In Iran, 1956 and 1966

	1956	1966
Total Gainful Employment In Religious Occupations	14,855	12,455
Total Urban Employment In Religious Occupations	7,640	7,606
Total Rural Employment in Religious Occupations	7,215	4,849
% Change, Total Gainful Employment in Religious Occupations, 1956-1966	-16.2%	
% Change, Urban Employment in Religious Occupations, 1956-1966	- 0.4%	
% Change, Rural Employment in Religious Occupations, 1956-1966	-32.8%	

SOURCES: Government of Iran. Ministry of the Interior. *National and Province Statistics of the First Census of Iran: November 1956*. Vol. II. (Tehran: n. p. 1961), pp. 311-12; Imperial Government of Iran. Plan Organization. *National Census, 1966*. Vol. 168 (Tehran: n. p. 1969), *passim*.

Table IX.   Provinces in Iran Ranked According to Number and Proportion
of Gainfully Employed in Religious Occupations In 1966

Province	N	%
1. Markazī (Tehran)	3054	24.5
2. Khurāsān	1960	15.7
3. East Āzarbāyjān	1467	11.8
4. Isfahān	1239	9.9
5. West Āzarbāyjān	776	6.2
6. Māzandarān	506	4.1
7. Gīlān	495	4.0
8. Kurdistān	493	4.0
9. Balūchistān and Saystān	373	3.0
10. Hamadān	336	2.7
11. Kirmān	217	1.7
12. Gulf of 'Uman Ports and Islands	168	1.3
13. Luristān	163	1.3
14. Kirmānshāhān	132	1.0
15. Simnān	121	1.0
16. Persian Gulf Ports and Islands	68	0.5
17. Chahār Mahāll	15	0.1
18. Būyir Ahmad and Kuhkilūyah	11	0.1
19. Īlām	1	0.01
Totals	11,595	92.91

Data unavailable for Khūzistan; Zanjān included under Gīlān; Yazd included under Isfahān.
SOURCE: Imperial Government of Iran. Plan Organization. *National Census* (Tehran: n.p., 1969).

Table X. First Ten Cities in Iran Ranked According to Number And Proportion of Gainfully Employed in Religious Occupations, 1966

City	N	%
1. Tehran	1753	14.1
2. Mashhad	1048	8.4
3. Tabrīz	700	5.6
4. Isfahān	650	5.2
5. Qumm	521	4.2
6. Yazd	316	2.5
7. Hamadān	270	2.2
8. Mahābād	196	1.6
9. Shīrāz	195	1.6
10. Rizā'īyah	153	1.2
Totals	5802	46.6

SOURCE: Imperial Government of Iran. Plan Organization. *National Census* (Tehran: n.p., 1969).

Table XI. Occupational Categories of Tehran in the Secondary Sector of the Economy in 1962

	N Gov't Posts	N Private Posts	Total
I. Group 1			
1. Physical Sciences	29	13	42
2. Biological Sciences	132	41	173
3. Medical Sciences	3719	2028	5747
4. Education	7274*	2014	9288
5. Statistical Economics	9	8	17
6. Social Relations	9	1524	1533
7. Artists, Writers	68	1027	1095
8. Various Other	1723	1652	3375
Totals	12963	9675	22638
II. Group 2			
1. Administrative Cadres**	42135	9816	51951
2. Clergy	2280	1855	4135
Totals	44415	11671	56896
III. Group 3			
1. Retail Stores	379	57245	57624
2. Bazaar Shops	89	9844	9933
3. Wholesale Stores	12	6059	6071
Totals	480	73148	75628

*Figure actually cited in source is 756, an obvious error, given the overall totals of this category of 12,963. The number 7,274 was reached by subtracting the sum of all other categories from the figure 12,963.

**Figures given for administrative cadres and clergy were originally cited in reverse order from that cited above; this would mean the 'ulamā' in 1966 were about 1750 times as numerous as the bureaucracy in the capital city—a patent absurdity. The given numbers for the two categories were therefore switched.

SOURCE: Fredy Bemont, *Les Villes de l'Iran* (Paris: n. p., 1969), p. 121.

Table XII.   Occupational Breakdown of Qumm, 1957

Occupational Category	N
1. Doctors, teachers, lawyers, artists, scientists, technicians	840
2. Administrative cadres and clergy	1150
3. Commerce	3900
4. Agricultural labor, hunting, fishing	2830
5. Mining, quarrying	710
6. Transport	1400
7. Industry and handicrafts	12960
8. Functionaries	3700
9. Military and unidentified	490
Totals	27980

SOURCE: Bemont, *Les Villes*, p. 181.

Table XIII.   Occupational Breakdown of Mashhad, 1962

Occupational Category	Males	Females	Total
1. Technicians (i.e., researchers, biologists, physicists, agronomists, doctors, hygenists, teachers, lawyers, artists, writers, *mutavallīs*)	2300	600	2900*
2. Administrative cadres and clergy	4800	200	5000
3. Commerce	11900	100	1200
4. Agricultural labor, hunting, fishing	700	100	800
5. Mining, quarrying	4800	0	4800
6. Transport	4000	0	4000
7. Handicrafts and industry	27000	3000	30000
8. Functionaries	7300	3700	11000**
9. Military and unidentified	7000	0	7000
Totals	70500	7500	78000

*of which 800 were engaged in the organization and administration of *awqāf*.
**of which 6000 were *'ulamā'*, according to the records of the mayoralty of the city but which were not shown in the census data of 1956. Also, out of the 5000 in the second category above, an unknown number were also *'ulamā'*. A conservative estimate would therefore be that the city had about 7000 individuals gainfully employed in religious occupations as of 1962. Cf. census data for the city for 1966 as shown in Table X, above!
SOURCE: *Ibid.*, p. 169.

Table XIV. Madrasahs in Mashhad Under Endowments Organization
Administration, 1970-1971

1. Parīzād	4. Khayrāt Khān	7. Hājj Hasan
2. Dū Dar	5. ʿAbbās Qulī Khān	
3. Navvāb	6. Bāqirīyah	

SOURCE: Fāzil, "Madāris-i Qadīm-i Mashhad," *passim*. Since Mashhad
had fourteen schools, the percentage of *madrasahs* under the direct administration of the Endowments Organization in the early seventies was very
high. Three of the seven *madrasahs* abovementioned (i.e., Dū Dar,
Nuvvāb and Hājj Hasan) were taken over in August-September 1971, when
the *mutavallī*, Āyatullāh Hājj Mīrzā Ahmad Kafāʾī, died.

Table XV. *Madrasahs* in Three *Shahrastāns* of Khurāsān Province, According to Number of
Tullāb, Annual Income And Administrator in 1973

Shahrastān	Madrasah	No. Tullāb	Annual Income	Administrator
1. Tabas	Dū Minār	6	15,000	Dr. Bīrjandī
	Vakīlī	6	19,000	Mr. Shaybānī
	Maydān	n.a.	3,000	Mr. Muhsinī
	Hājj Rafīʿ	3	8,600	Dept. Endowments, Tabas
2. Firdaws	ʿUlyā	10	22,500	Sayyid Mahmūd Najafī
	Habībīyah	25	57,550	Husayn Majd
	Sarāyān	10	14,110	Dept. Endowments, Firdaws
	Shaykh	10	27,000	Muhammad Kīyānī
	Hubbīyah	n.a.	150,750	Shaykh Ghulām Rizā Sakhnūr
3. Bīrjand	Maʿsūmīyah	40	47,158	Amīr Asadullāh ʿAlam*
	Gazīk	10	3,645	Mr. Fāzilī
	Dar Mīyān	10	2,858	n.a. (*majhūl al-twalīyah?*)
	Jaʿfarīyah	30	185,809	Shaykh Ghulām Husayn Tawlīyat
	Zahān	n.a.	61,200	Dept. Endowments, Bīrjand

*Incumbent Minister of Court.
SOURCE: Mahmūd Fāzil, "Madāris-i Qadīm-i Khurāsān," *Vahīd*, Vol. XI, nos. 6, 7 (Shahrīvar,
Mihr 1352 H. Sh./1973), pp. 609-10, 787-88; Vol. XII, no. 2 (Urdībihisht 1353 H. Sh./1974),
p. 135.

Table XVI. Expenditures on *Madrasahs*, *Tullāb* and *Mudarrisīn* (in Rials),
by the Endowments Organization in 1972

			Tullāb		Mudarrisīn		
No.	Month	No. *Madrasahs*	No.	Am't. Spent	No.	Am't. Spent	Total
1.	Farvardīn	—	—	—	—	—	—
2.	Urdībihisht	—	—	—	—	—	—
3.	Khurdād	50	1934	593,656	18	114,435	708,09
4.	Tīr	37	1662	354,927	68	102,105	457,03:
5.	Murdād	48	1899	433,381	92	143,705	577,08(
6.	Shahrīvar	33	1562	353,828	54	86,159	439,98
7.	Mihr	33	880	208,161	71	89,066	297,22'
8.	Ābān	25	1267	262,218	31	85,709	347,92'
9.	Āzar	19	183	118,554	39	119,118	237,67:
10.	Day	27	413	194,676	41	120,184	314,86(
11.	Bahman	22	244	107,668	33	72,659	180,32'
12.	Isfand	37	591	335,027	55	178,909	513,93(
	Totals (*Mutasarrafī*)	—	—	2,962,096	—	1,112,049	4,074,14:
1.	Farvardīn	—	—	—	—	—	—
2.	Urdībihisht	—	—	—	—	—	—
3.	Khurdād	—	—	—	—	—	—
4.	Tīr	11	214	82,995	28	23,070	106,06:
5.	Murdād	7	105	31,850	14	26,200	58,05(
6.	Shahrīvar	28	665	234,824	69	87,186	322,01(
7.	Mihr	30	2702	512,517	93	65,409	577,92(
8.	Ābān	30	694	221,385	69	55,666	277,05
9.	Āzar	27	513	212,490	61	115,820	328,31(
10.	Day	15	225	88,164	25	44,296	132,46(
11.	Bahman	13	174	65,754	31	55,986	121,74(
12.	Isfand	17	337	116,309	41	78,366	194,67:
	Totals (Non-*Mutasarrafī*)	—	—	1,566,288	—	551,999	2,118,28'

SOURCE: Dawlat-i Shāh-in-Shāhī-yi Iran. Sāzmān-i Awqāf. Daftar-i Āmār va Muhandisī-yi Raqabāt. *Guzārish-Pīshrafthā va Fa ʿ ʿālīyathā-yi Sāzmān-i Awqāf.* Internal Report, Mimeo. Tehran, 1351 H. Sh./1972. p. 75.

Table XVII. Expenditures on *Madrasah*s, *Tullāb and Mudarrisīn* (In Rials),
According to Province, by the Endowments Organization in 1973

			Tullāb		Mudarrisīn		
No.	Province	Number Schools	No.	Am't. Spent	No.	Am't Spent	Total Spent
1.	Tehran	5	104	216,080	6	199,080	415,160
2.	Māzandarān	6	105	15,500	59	29,400	44,900
3.	Isfahān	5	46	11,864	6	3,700	15,564
4.	Khurāsān	16	1095	540,650	27	46,400	587,050
5.	Yazd	2	11	21,800	2	14,500	36,300
6.	Simnān	4	57	779,965	10	97,960	877,925
7.	W. Āẕarbāyjān	5	29	84,600	7	46,000	130,600
8.	Zanjān	7	148	16,320	8	2,300	18,620
9.	Luristān	1	12	7,280	1	2,800	10,080
10.	Kirmānshāhān	1	7	89,600	2	27,000	116,600
11.	Hamadān	1	27	79,200	1	79,200	158,400
	Total (*Mutasarrafī*)	53	1641	1,862,859	129	548,340	2,411,199
1.	Khurāsān	16	591	414,550	50	117,000	531,550
2.	Tehran	17	120	76,735	16	15,940	92,675
3.	Māzandarān	3	74	1,200	3	—	1,200
4.	Isfahān	2	26	28,400	3	7,450	35,850
5.	Khūzistān	1	26	8,300	4	8,300	16,600
6.	Kirmān	2	30	—	3	—	—
7.	Hamadān	3	12	72,000	3	9,000	81,000
8.	W. Āẕarbāyjān	2	39	7,053	5	310,300	317,353
9.	Simnān	4	192	69,792	18	24,588	94,380
10.	Zanjān	2	52	46,800	3	5,700	52,500
11.	Gīlān	5	115	162,150	16	82,950	245,100
12.	Fārs	1	122	57,442	5	1,575	59,017
	Total (Non *Mutasarrafī*)	58	1459	944,422	129	582,803	1,527,225
	Grand Totals	111	3100	—	258	—	3,938,424

SOURCE: Same as Table XVI, 1352 H. Sh./1973, pp. 106–107.

Table XVIII. Average Annual and Monthly Stipends (In Rials) Offered to *Tullāb* by the Endowments Organization, According to Province, 1973

Province	Average Monthly Stipend	Average Yearly Stipend
I. *Mutasarrafī*		
1. Tehran	208	2078
2. Māzandarān	15	148
3. Isfahān	26	258
4. Khurāsān	49	494
5. Yazd	198	1981
6. Simnān	1368	13684
7. W. Āzarbāyjān	292	2917
8. Zanjān	11	110
9. Luristān	61	607
10. Kirmānshāhān	1280	12800
11. Hamadān	293	2933
Average Total	346	3455
II. Non-*Mutasarrafī*		
1. Khurāsān	70	701
2. Tehran	64	640
3. Māzandarān	2	16
4. Isfahān	109	1092
5. Khūzistān	32	319
6. Kirmān	n.a.	n.a.
7. Hamadān	600	6000
8. W. Āzarbāyjān	18	181
9. Simnān	36	364
10. Zanjān	90	900
11. Gīlān	141	1410
12. Fārs	47	471
Average Total	110	1099
III. *Mutasarrafī* and Non-*Mutasarrafī* Combined		
1. Tehran	136	1359
2. Māzandarān	8	82
3. Isfahān	68	675
4. Khurāsān	60	598
5. Yazd	198	1981
6. Simnān	702	7024
7. W. Āzarbāyjān	155	1614
8. Zanjān	51	505
9. Luristān	61	607
10. Kirmānshāhān	1280	12800
11. Hamadān	447	4467
12. Khūzistān	32	319
13. Gīlān	141	1410
14. Fārs	47	471
Average Total	228	2277

SOURCE: Adapted from the same source as Table XVII. Figures have been rounded off to the nearest whole number.

Table XIX. Average Annual and Monthly Stipends (In Rials) Offered to
Mudarrisīn by the Endowments Organization, According to Province, 1973

Province	Average Monthly Stipend	Average Yearly Stipend
I. *Mutasarrafī*		
1. Tehran	3318	33180
2. Māzandarān	50	498
3. Isfahān	62	617
4. Khurāsān	172	1719
5. Yazd	725	7250
6. Simnān	980	9796
7. W. Āẕarbāyjān	657	6571
8. Zanjān	29	288
9. Luristān	280	2800
10. Kirmānshāhān	1350	13500
11. Hamadān	7920	79200
Average Total	1413	14129
II. Non-*Mutasarrafī*		
1. Khurāsān	234	2340
2. Tehran	100	996
3. Māzandarān	—	—
4. Isfahān	248	2483
5. Khūzistān	208	2075
6. Kirmān	—	—
7. W. Āẕarbāyjān	6206	62060
8. Simnān	137	1366
9. Zanjān	190	1900
10. Gīlān	518	5184
11. Fārs	32	315
12. Hamadān	300	3000
Average Total	817	8172
III. *Mutasarrafī* and Non-*Mutasarrafī* Combined		
1. Tehran	1709	17760
2. Māzandarān	50	498
3. Isfahān	155	1550
4. Khurāsān	203	2029
5. Yazd	725	7250
6. Simnān	558	5581
7. W. Āẕarbāyjān	3432	34316
8. Zanjān	109	1094
9. Luristān	280	2800
10. Kirmānshāhān	1350	13500
11. Hamadān	4110	41100
12. Khūzistān	208	2075
13. Gīlān	518	5184
14. Fārs	32	315
Average Total	1115	11151

SOURCE: Adapted from the same source as Table XVIII. Figures have been rounded off to the nearest whole number.

Table XX. Number of Mosques in Iran According to Province, 1975

Province	Number of Mosques
1. Tehran	1843
2. Khurāsān	587
3. Isfahān	689
4. East Āzarbāyjān	1051
5. Khūzistān	259
6. Māzandarān	288
7. Fārs	690
8. Gīlān	138
9. East Āzarbāyjān	582
10. Kirmān	198
11. Kirmānshāhān	153
12. Bulūchistān and Saystān	418
13. Kurdistān	1399
14. Hamadān	99
15. Luristān	80
16. Simnān	117
17. Īlām	6
18. Zanjān	56
19. Yazd	189
20. Būshihr	58
21. Chahār Mahāl va Bakhtīyārī	16
22. Sāhilī	99
Totals	9015

SOURCE: Dawlat-i Shāh-in-Shāhī-yi Iran. Sāzmān-i Awqāf. Daftar-i Kull-i Āmār va Muhandisī-yi Raqabāt. "Āmār-i Masājid va Amākin-i Mutabarrakah-yi Ustānhā." Tehran: Sāzmān-i Awqāf mimeo internal report, 1354 H. Sh./1975.

NOTES

Notes to the Preface

[1]Clifford Geertz, Islam Observed (New Haven: Yale University Press, 1968), p. 1.

[2]Edward Shils, "Center and Periphery," in The Logic of Personal Knowledge (Glencoe, Ill.: The Free Press, 1961), pp. 117-30. These problems include vast distances, tribalism, tendency toward the development of satrapies, autonomy of the landed magnates, very strong ʿulamāʾ influence among the peasantry and urban lower strata, and the like.

Notes to Chapter One

[1]On the antithetical relationship between charisma and bureaucracy and administration, see Max Weber, "The Sociology of Charismatic Authority," in From Max Weber, ed. H. H. Gerth and C. Wright Mills (New York: Oxford University Press, 1958), p. 246.

[2]Hamilton A. R. Gibb, Mohammedanism (New York: Oxford University Press, 1961), p. 27.

[3]According to the widely cited hadith, the prophet asserted that "My community shall never agree upon error." This is understood to be the source of the idea that the community is infallible, even though the lawgiver of Islam never specified how the will of the community was to be made known in practice.

[4]Julius Welhausen, The Arab Kingdom and Its Fall (Beirut: Khayat, 1964). Based on the chronicle of al-Tabari, this classic work cuts through the integument of biased historical inquiry and underscores the dynastic principles that were at play during the crucial Umāyyad period, 661-750 A.D.

[5]Gustave von Grunebaum, Classical Islam (Chicago: Aldine, 1970), p. 62. It is ironic that the Shīʿah, who were charged with the accusation that they wanted to establish the principle of dynasty in the caliphate, witnessed the assumption of power by those who themselves instituted the principle. Even more ironical is the fact that whereas the Shīʿah could find very little support anywhere in "Arab tradition" for the argument that the caliphate should be available only to the lineal descendants of Muhammad, the Umāyyads' passing the caliphate from father to son, brother to brother, or cousin to collateral cousin, was accepted.

[6]Hamilton A. R. Gibb, "The Evolution of Government in Early Islam," in Studies on the Civilization of Islam, by H. A. R. Gibb, ed. Stanford J. Shaw (London: Routledge & Kegan Paul, Ltd., 1962), p. 34.

[7]The Cambridge History of Islam, Vol. 2B, ed. P. M. Holt, Ann K. S. Lambton and Bernard Lewis (Cambridge, England: Cambridge University Press, 1970), p. 543.

[8]W. Montgomery Watt, Islamic Philosophy and Theology (Edinburgh: Edinburgh University Press, 1962), p. 52.

[9]Even the Kūfans—the partisans in Iraq of the caliph, ʿAlī, who rallied to the banner of Imām Husayn in the battle of Karbalāʾ—were a very small group.

[10]Gibb, "Structure of Religious Thought in Islam," in Studies in the Civilization of Islam, p. 199.

[11]Marshall G. S. Hodgson, *The Venture of Islam: Conscience and History in a World Civilization,* Vol. I (Chicago: University of Chicago Press, 1974), p. 238.

[12]Fazlur Rahman, *Islam* (Garden City, N.Y.: Anchor Books, 1968), p. xx.

[13]W. Montgomery Watt, *The Formative Period of Islamic Thought* (Edinburgh: Edinburgh University Press, 1973), p. 167.

[14]Watt, *Islamic Philosophy and Theology,* p. 52.

[15]Wilfred Madelung, "Imama," *Encyclopaedia of Islam,* New Edition Vol. III (Leiden: E. J. Brill, 19), p. 116.

[16]Watt, *Formative Period,* p. 275.

[17]For the view, however, that the power of Allah was in no sense regarded as political but referred instead to lordship over the universe, see Said Amir Arjomand, "Religion, Political Action and Legitimate Domination in *Shīʿī* Iran: 14th to 18th Centuries, A.D." typescript, University of Chicago, 1976), p. 12.

[18]Cf. von Grunebaum, *Classic Islam,* p. 82. "In Islam, too, the lack of a church organization means that the representation of specifically religious interests is left to the consensus of the Community, though in fact to respected theologians. The Community as religious association is thus never forced to face reality, so that the fulfillment of the ethical obligation of faith can be seen in the debate of abstract principles, and at the same time peace can be concluded with whatever state order is in force."

[19]Ann K. S. Lambton, "Quis Custodiet Custodes?" I, *Studia Islamica,* V (1956), p. 137.

[20]*Ibid.,* p. 138.

[21]Lambton, "Quis Custodiet Custodes?" II, *Studia Islamica,* VI (1956), p. 129. Emphasis supplied.

[22]Hamid Algar, *Religion and State in Iran, 1785-1906: The Role of the ʿUlamāʾ in the Qājār Period* (Berkeley: University of California Press, 1969), p. 6.

[23]*Idem.*

[24]*Mihdī Bāzargān,* "Intiẓārāt-i Mardum az Marājiʿ," in *Bahthī Dar Bārah-yi Marjaʿīyat va Rūhānīyat* (Tehran: Intishār, 1341 H. Sh./1962 A.D.), p. 63.

[25]Joseph Eliash, "Some Misconceptions Concerning *Shīʿī* Political Theory," *International Journal of Middle East Studies,* Vol. IX, no. 1 (Feb. 1979), pp. 9-25.

[26]Eliash, "The *Ithnāʿasharī-Shīʿī* Juristic Theory of Political and Legal Authority," *Studia Islamica,* XXIX (1969), p. 17. Elsewhere, pp. 18-19, he writes: "one is constantly astounded by the vehement polemic centered on the subject of the legitimate and just governance ... Later *Ithnāʿasharī* divines ... expressed basically the same views in respect to the doctrine of the Imāmate as those exposed in al-Kāfī." This and the next two paragraphs are based on *ibid., passim.*

[27]Lambton, "Quis Custodiet Custodes?" II, p. 133.

[28]*Ibid.,* p. 143.

[29]In his recent inquiry into the interface between political and religious authority in Shīʿism Arjomand claims the existence of a disjunction between the two. He argues that Allah does not wield political authority; rather, lordship over the universe. In his view, Allah is "not directly involved in mundane political events ... nor is he the explicit source of political authority." Yet, the references to Allah's mastery and lordship are couched in the concept *rabb,* denoting master-slave relationships then current in Arabia and clearly conveying ties of a political nature. Also, the doctrine of *kasb,* or acquisition, of responsibility and authority by mortals is an established one in Islamic thought. This leads to the notion of sovereignty as exercised by human beings as being contingent upon the sovereignty of Allah. On this issue, see Malcolm H. Kerr, *Islamic Reform* (Berkeley: University of California Press, 1966), pp. 3 ff.

Arjomand attacks what he calls the prevalent thesis that the *Imām* wields political authority simultaneously with religious authority. He sees the *ʿulamāʾ,* in their turn, as essentially religious figures excluded from practical matters of legitimate political authority. Yet, his argument is based on indirect reasoning and is not entirely convincing. His view that the principles of *amr bi al-maʿrūf wa al-nahy min al-munkar* and of *jihād* (holy war) do not confer broad political authority on the leaders of the community because Islamic rewards for ethical uprightness are "other-worldly" is not wholly persuasive, either. The prophet and *imāms* wielded political as well as religious authority because Islam is a "this worldly" religion. Even the quietism of most of the *imāms* does not in itself lend credence to Arjomand's position, given the fusion of sacred and temporal rule in the charismatic practice of Muhammad, ʿAlī and Husayn. The treatment of oppression (*żulm*) in *Shīʿī* juristic theory is evidently within the context of the social and political justice of the rule of the *Imām*. It is difficult to sustain the putative disjunction between religion and politics in Shīʿism if these considerations hold. See also, W. Madelung, "Imama," p. 1166: "Although the *Imām* was entitled to political leadership as much as to religious authority, his imamate did not depend on his actual rule . . ." This implies the *Imām*'s political authority was a central feature of the doctrine of the imāmate.

³⁰Thanks to Mr. Arjomand for calling this work to my attention.

³¹Ervand Abrahamian, "Oriental Despotism in the Middle East: the Case of Qājār Iran," *International Journal of Middle East Studies*, Vol. V, no. 1 (January 1974), *passim*.

³²Rauf Alievich Seidov, *Iranskaia Burzhuaziia v. Kontse XIX-Nachale XXV*. (Moscow: Izdatelstvo "Nauka", 1974), pp. 136, 159. Of the 134 leading creditors of the Tehran branch of the Discount Loan Bank with assets of 50,000 rials or more between the years 1900 and 1905 were "one or two ʿulamāʾ. This is hardly a staggeringly high statistic; and in none of the other ten branches in other cities were ʿulamāʾ listed independently, although they may have been encompassed by the catch-all "other" category. Seidov also cites Malcolm Khān's "Ādamīyat" Society, with its "bourgeois objectives," as needing the support of the clergy in view of the latter's influence over the masses. See also, in relationship to clergy-bourgois linkages, Nikki Keddie, *Religion and Rebellion in Iran: The Tobacco Protest of 1891-1892* (London: Frank Cass, Ltd., 1966), p. 18. There, the closest of relations is alleged between Hājj Amīn al-Zarb, one of the wealthiest merchants of the time with wide international connections, and Sayyid Jamāl al-Dīn al-Afghānī.

³³Examples in Qājār times are plentiful. Hamid Algar, in *Religion and State*, p. 57, cites the example of Mullā Ahmad Narāqī:

> who had studied at Najaf under Sayyid Mihdī Bahr al-ʿUlūm, generally accounted the most learned of the ʿulamāʾ at the ʿatabāt [Shīʿī shrine towns in Iraq] after the death of Sayyid Muhammad Bāqir Bihbihānī. He had returned to Iran and taken up residence in Kāshān. Here he found a tyrannical governor oppressing the populace, and he took it upon himself to expel him from the town   FathʿAlī Shah [the ruling monarch] summoned Mullā Ahmad Narāqī to Tehran and angrily reproached him for what he had done. The *mullā*, far from showing repentence, lifted his hands up and tearfully exclaimed: "O, God! This unjust king appointed an unjust governor over the people. I put an end to his oppression; and now this oppressor is angry with me." FathʿAlī Shah, afraid of being further condemned, requested his pardon and appointed a new governor for Kāshān in accordance with the *mullā*'s wishes.

³⁴Donald Eugene Smith, *Religion and Political Development* (Boston: Little, Brown & Co., 1970), p. 15.

³⁵Bernard Lewis, *The Emergence of Modern Turkey* (London: Oxford University Press, 1961), pp. 253-54, 260.

³⁶*Ibid.*, p. 398.

³⁷Bernard Lewis, "The Islamic Guilds," *Economic History Review*, 8 (1937), pp. 35-36; Gabriel Baer, "The Administrative, Economic and Social Functions of Turkish Guilds," International Journal of Middle *East Studies*, Vol. I, no. 1 (January 1970), pp. 28-50; Baer, *Egyptian Guilds in Modern Times* (Jerusalem: Hebrew Universities Press, 1964).

³⁸Lewis, *Emergence of Modern Turkey*, p. 405.

³⁹*Ibid.*, p. 407.

⁴⁰Nur Yalman, "Some Observations on Secularism in Islam: The Cultural Revolution in Turkey," *Daedalus*, Vol. 102, no. 1 (Winter, 1973), esp. 154 *et. seq.*

[41] Morroe Berger, *Islam in Egypt Today* (Cambridge: Cambridge University Press, 1970), p. 9.

[42] *Ibid.*, p. 61.

[43] E. I. J. Rosenthal, *Islam in the Modern National State* (Cambridge: Cambridge University Press, 1965), p. 104. The Mixed Courts inaugurated a period in Egyptian history wherein the religious (*sharʿ*) tribunals slowly gave ground to judicial institutions dispensing secularly grounded law.

[44] Daniel Crecelius, "Non-Ideological Responses of the Egyptian *ʿUlamā'* to Modernization," in *Scholars, Saints and Sufis: Muslim Religious Institutions Since 1500*, ed. Nikki R. Keddie (Berkeley: University of California Press, 1971), esp. 195–209.

[45] See Crecelius, "Al-Azhar in the Revolution," *Middle East Journal*, Vol. XX, no. 1 (Winter 1966), pp. 31–49 for debates on the role of Islam at the time of the reorganization of al-Azhar in 1961, and the clergy's solicitude about maintaining high levels of religious commitment. One should also mention the emergence in the Sadat period around 1975 of certain religious tendencies and revival in urban areas. This last has featured the increasing popularity of sermonizers building up local bases of support in particular quarters or wards of Egyptian cities.

Notes to Chapter Two

[1] Cited in Hamid Algar, "The Oppositional Role of the *ʿUlamā'* in Twentieth Century Iran," in *Scholars, Saints and Sufis*, ed. Nikki Keddie (Berkeley: University of California Press, 1971), pp. 252–53.

[2] Muhandis Mihdī Bāzargān, "Marz Mīyān-i Dīn va Sīyāsat," in *Mazhab dar Urūpā* (Tehran: Bungāh-i Matbūʿātī-yi Īrān, 1344/1965), pp. 113–46.

[3] Sayyid Hādī Khusrūshāhī, *Du Mazhab* (Qumm: n.p. 1343/1964), pp. 82–83, cited in A. E. Doroshenko, "O Nekotorykh Kontseptsiakh Sovremennogo Iranskogo Dukhoventsva po Voprosu Religii i Gosudarstva," in *Iran: Sbornik Statei* (Moscow: Izdatelstvo "Nauka'', 1971), p. 121.

[4] Mahmūd Tāliqānī, "Introduction," *Tanbīh al-Ummah wa Tanzīh al-Millah*, 2nd ed. (Tehran: n.p. 1374 H. Q./1954), p. 9.

[5] Murtazā Jazāyirī, "Luzūm-i Sarāhat dar Rahbarīhā-yi Dīnī va Ijtimāʿī," in *Guftār-i Māh*, Vol. III (Tehran: Kitābfurūshī-yi Saddūq," pp. 82–100, esp. 97 ff.

[6] This leaves out of consideration the service in government of pro-Shah clergymen, such as Hasan Imāmī (for many years the Imām Jumʿah of Tehran); ʿAbbas Muhājirānī (Director of the Bureau of Religious Affairs of the Endowments Organization in the 1970's); Ghulām Husayn Dāneshī, Majlis Deputy from Ābādān and the sole clergyman in the parliament at the time of the revolution against the monarchy; and the like.

[7] Āyatallāh Sayyid Rūhallāh al-Mūsavī Khumaynī begins his book on Islamic Government with a chapter entitled "*valāyat-i faqīh*," by which he means [political] rule exercised by the legal scholar/clergyman in the absence of the *Imām*. On p. 64, he makes the point forcefully:

> The fancy that the governmental power and authority [*ikhtīyārāt*] of the prophet are greater than those of ʿAlī and that the governmental power and authority of ʿAlī are greater than those of the Muslim scholar of jurisprudence is faulty and erroneous. Of course, the virtues of the prophet were greater than those of ʿAlī; and those of ʿAlī greater than those of all others. But the abundance of spiritual virtues does not increase governmental power and authority. God has arranged that the actual government [on earth] have that same power, authority and rule that the prophet and the *imām*s possessed in terms of provisioning and mobilizing troops, appointing governors, collecting revenues, and expending them in the interests of the Muslims. But [the only difference is that] there is no specific person [who has such power, authority and rule]; instead [these are wielded by] 'a just clergyman'. [*ʿālim-i ʿādil*]
>
> When I say that the Muslim scholar of jurisprudence who is just possesses that rule [*valāyat*] possessed by the prophet and the *imām*s, no one should imagine that the standing of the Muslim scholars of jurisprudence is the same as that of the *imām*s and the prophet. For we are not here speaking of standing, but of duty. *Valāyat* means governing and administering

the country and implementing the sacred laws of the *sharīʿah*, a heavy and important duty; it is not a question of its bringing forth for someone an extraordinary rank or position such as to elevate him above the common man . . .

It must be stated that *valāyat* means sanctity, holiness, spiritual initiation by the *Imām* of his adepts—the "friends" (*Awlīyā*) of God—into the divine mysteries. It is, then a concept transcending mere rule, just as the prophecy (*nubūwwah*) of Muhammad went beyond the notion of community leadership. But Khumaynī, and others who share his view that Shīʿism is a social and political religion, refer to the famous verse in the Qurʾan: Yā ayyuhā aladhīn āmanū, utīʿū Allāh wa utīʿū al-rasūl wa ʾūlā al-amr minkum . . . ("O, ye who believe, obey Allah, obey the prophet and those in authority among you"). Khumaynī says that the phrase "*ʾūlā al-amr*" refers to the *imāms*, who are charged with a number of duties which can be subsumed under two categories: the description/ explanation of the beliefs, ordinances and systems of Islam; the *implementation* of the ordinances and the *establishment* of Islamic systems throughout the world. After the *imāms*, i.e., after 874 A.D., the "just men of Islamic jurisprudence" (*fuqahā-yi ʿādil*) are entrusted with the twin tasks. The second set of tasks Khumaynī sees as distinctly of a social/political nature. (see. pp. 27-28 of his book, *Hukūmat-i Islāmī*).

Khumaynī also cites a tradition attributed to the Eighth Imām, Ridā (765-817), concerning the reason God commanded the faithful to "obey those in authority among you", citing the Shīʿī codex, *Sharāyiʿ* of Muhaqqiq Hillī (d. 1277), Vol. I, p. 183, *hadīth* #9: the Imām answered the question posed to him concerning the reason Allah decreed that the believers obey "those in authority" (*ʾūlā al-amr*) by stating: (1) the people will err in the absence of a specific person or force to keep them on the right path, for either they will become corrupt in the pursuit of their own pleasures or they will transgress on the rights of others; (2) a leaderless community of believers will not be able to maintain itself as a social collectivity in the real world, where it is a question—on a daily, weekly, monthly, yearly basis—of fighting one's enemies, dividing the community's annual income equitably among the members, participating in the Friday and other prayers, and in general struggling against those who would oppress the innocent through depriving them of their rights; (3) the religion will lose its vitality, become stagnant and ultimately suffer the disintegration of the ordinances and precepts of the faith—a phenomenon that will leave the field open to heretics to add blasphemous accretions to Islam in such a way as entirely to denature it. (pp. 45-48)

Āyatallāh Khumaynī naturally would wish to interpret the doctrine of *valāyat* in this manner. But one can as easily refer to the exegesis of a "non-political" clergyman, ʿAllāmah Sayyid Muhammad Husayn Tabāʾ-tabāʾī, for supporting arguments. In his important essay, "Valāyat va Ziʿāmat dar Islam," Tabāʾtabāʾī stresses that *valāyat* is one of the laws of nature. The delegation of authority is an unavoidable phenomenon in all societies, but since the time of the prophet and the death of ʿAlī ibn Abī Tālib Islamic governments have sinned. Tabāʾtabāʾī argues that 20th century Iran has not proven an exception to this pattern of sinfulness. The office of *valāyat*, however, is such that the incumbent must imitate the traditions set by the prophet. Since temporal governors are inherently incapable of such emulation, the task falls of necessity upon those who have shown outstanding achievement as to piety, justice, administration. The implication is clear that this can only be the *mujtahids*—the *ʾūlā al-amr*. For this essay, see *Bahthī dar Bārah-yi Marjaʿīyyat va Rūhānīyat*. Regrettably, I have not been able to obtain a copy of ʿAllāmah Tabāʾtabāʾī's *Risālah Dar Hukumat-i Islāmī* (Treatise on Islamic Government), cited by Sayyid Hossein Nasr in his compilation of the author's works in the book *Shīʿite Islam* (the original in Persian: *Shīʿah Dar Islam*), ed. and tr. by Nasr (Albany: SUNY Press, 1975), p. 239.

[8]Peter Avery, *Modern Iran* (New York: Praeger, 1967), p. 167.

[9]*Ibid.*, pp. 130-31. If apparel may be used as an index of *ulamāʾ* presence and influence, then, judging from a picture of the first Majlis members (7 October 1906-23 June 1908), sixty deputies are seen to be wearing turbans; forty six are wearing the fez-type headgear. This perhaps trivial piece of "evidence" is nonetheless indicative of the extent of the *ulamāʾ*'s role in the constitutional

revolution. See Edward G. Browne, *The Persian Revolution of 1905–1909* (Cambridge, England: Cambridge University Press, 1910), opp. p. 124.

[10] According to Sayyid Hossein Nasr, Hāʾirī was invited by the government in Tehran to establish a center of *Shīʿī* learning in Qumm in order to diminish the monopoly position of the *ʿatabāt* (shrines in Iraq). This would enable him to administer a centrally located religious establishment, as opposed to the far-flung position of Mashhad in the northeastern part of the country. Personal interview, 11 February 1975. This account conflicts with that provided by Hāʾirī's biographers, such as Āghā Buzurg-i Tihrānī, *Tabaqāt Aʿlām al-Shīʿah*, Vol. III (Najaf, Iraq: Matbaʿah al-Ādāb, 1381 H. Q./1962), pp. 1158–67. Their contention is that local merchants and clergymen in Qumm, as well as in the capital, petitioned Hāʾirī to leave his residence in the town of Arāk and install himself in Qumm.

[11] Conflicting evidence exists on Hāʾirī's formal behavior toward Isfahānī and Nāʾinī. Some report that he was warm and friendly, as for example, Tihrānī, *Tabaqāt Aʿlām al-Shīʿah*, pp. 1160–61. By contrast, another source has stated that Hāʾirī "did not attach much importance" to this incident and minimized his dealings with the *marājiʿ-yi taqlīd*. For this view, consult Yahyā Dawlatābādī, *Tārīkh-i Muʿāsir, Yā Hayāt-i Yahyā*, Vol. IV (Tehran: Kitābfurūshī-yi Ibn Sīnā, 1331 H. Sh./1952), p. 290.

[12] Cited in ʿAbdullāh Mustawfī, *Sharh-i Zindigānī-yi Man, Yā Tārīkh-i Ijtimāʿī va Idārī-yi Dawrah-yi Qājārīyah*. Vol. III, 2nd. ed. (Tehran: Kitābfurūshī-yi Zaddār, 1343 H. Sh./1964), p. 601.

[13] *Idem.*

[14] Abdul-Hadi Hairi, *Shiʿism and Constitutionalism: A Study of the Life and Views of Mirza Muhammad Husayn Naʾini, A Shiʿi Mujtahid of Iran,* unpublished Ph.D. dissertation, Institute of Islamic Studies, McGill University, Montreal, Canada, 1973, Vol. I, pp. 268–70. Much of the manifesto, if not most of it, was probably forged. Yet, Nāʾinī's support for Rizā Khān had already become well-known. Even if forged, and notwithstanding the inaccuracy of the attributions and references, it is interesting that the Prime Minister's supporters felt confident enough of Nāʾinī's benevolence toward their cause that they would risk *takzīb* (belying) by one of Shiʿism's greatest contemporary leaders. I would like to thank Mr. Said Amir Arjomand for calling my attention to this dissertation, which has subsequently been published by Leiden: E. J. Brill, 1975. The author is the second son of Shaykh ʿAbd al-Karīm.

[15] Leonard Binder, *Iran: Political Development in a Changing Society* (Berkeley and Los Angeles: University of California Press, 1961), p. 105.

[16] Amin Banani, *The Modernization of Iran, 1921–1941* (Stanford: Stanford University Press, 1961), p. 89.

[17] Dawlat-i Shāh-in-Shāhī-yi Īrān. Vizārat-i Farhang. Idārah-yi Mutālaʿāt va Āmār. *Sālnāmah va Āmār*, 1322–1327 H. Sh./1943–1948 (Tehran: Tābān, n.d.), p. 5.

[18] Browne, *Persian Revolution*, pp. 407, 418.

[19] Shafīʿ Javādī, *Tabrīz va Pīrāmūn* (Tabrīz: Bunyād-i Farhangī-yi Rizā Pahlavī, 1350 H. Sh./1971), p. 173.

[20] ʿĪsā Sadīq (Aʿlam), *Tārīkh-i Farhang-i Īrān az Āghāz tā Zamān-i Hāzir*, 7th ed. (Tehran: Chāpp-i Zībā, 1354 H. Sh./1975), pp. 364–65.

[21] Dawlatābādī, *Tārīkh-i Muʿāsir*, II, pp. 110–111; ʿĪsā Sadīq, *Yād-i Gār-i ʿUmr*, Vol. I (Tehran: Shirkat-i Sahhāmī-yi Tabʿ-i Kutub, 1340 H. Sh./1961), pp. 14–16.

[22] Sadīq, *Yād-i Gār*, I, pp. 8, 13–14, 17.

[23] Dawlatābādī, II, p. 110.

[24] Dawlatābādī, III, p. 3, cited in Algar, *Religion and State*, p. 241.

[25] Cited in Browne, *Persian Revolution*, p. 375.

[26] Cited in Reza Arasteh, *Education and Social Awakening In Iran, 1850–1968*, 2nd rev. and enl. ed. (Leiden: E. J. Bill, 1969), p. 230. The various agencies that have had jurisdiction over education

in Iran have been many, and it may be helpful to list them and their dates at this point: (1) Vizārat-i ʿUlūm (The Ministry of Science), 1860-1906; (2) Vizārat-i ʿUlūm va Maʿārif (The Ministry of Science and Education), 1906-1910; (3) Vizārat-i Maʿārif va Awqāf va Sanāyiʿ-yi Mustazrafah (The Ministry of Education, Endowments and Fine Arts), 1910-1939; (4) Vizārat-i Farhang va Awqāf (The Ministry of Culture and Endowments), 1939-1964; (5) Vizārat-i Āmūzish va Parvarish (The Ministry of Education), 1969-, which is in charge of elementary and secondary education; (6) Vizārat-i ʿUlūm va Āmūzish-i ʿĀlī (The Ministry of Science and Higher Education), 1967-; Vizārat-i Farhang va Hunar (The Ministry of Culture and Arts), 1964-. As for the administration of religious endowments, an office of *awqāf* existed under the Safavids and Qājārs. In 1918, endowments became the jurisdiction of the Ministry of Education, Endowments and Fine Arts. In 1949, the administration of the *awqāf* was separated from the Ministry of Education, and a new organization, the General Department of Religious Endowments (Idārah-yi Kull-i Awqāf) was established under the general bureaucratic reform of that year. Then, in 1964, this agency was upgraded under the general reform of that year. Thenceforth known as the Endowments Organization (Sāzmān-i Awqāf), its Superintendent (sarparast) became a Deputy Prime Minister in the cabinet. The Endowments Organization under the revolutionary regime has been reorganized and a Board of Trustees created under the leadership of two clergymen, 10 merchants and one official of the Ministry of Justice. On this reorganization, see *Kayhān*, 23 Isfand 1357 H. Sh./1979.

[27]Dawlat-i ʿAlīyah-yi Īrān. Vizārat-i Maʿārif va Āwqāf va Sanāyiʿyi Mustazrafah. *Ihsāʾiyah-yi Maʿarif va Madāris, 1307-08* H. Sh./1938-39 (Tehran: Matbaʿah Rawshanāʾī, n.d.), p. 19.

[28]Arasteh, *Education and Social Awakening*, pp. 227-28; Sadīq, *Tārīkh*, p. 370. Only one of the ten members of this Council of Higher Education was a religious figure. In 1951 six new members were added to the Council, none of whom was an *ʿālim*. Further, it seems that the subcommittee envisaged by article 14 of the 1921 Law did not come into existence. In 1943 an attempt was made to establish this Committee on Religious Affairs, regarding which see below. For the 1951 changes, see *Ittilāʿāt*, 20 Day 1331 H. Sh./1953.

[29]Browne, *Persian Revolution*, pp. 374-78.

[30]Banani, *Modernization of Iran*, p. 90, ʿIssa Sadiq, *Modern Persia and her Educational System* (New York: Teacher's College, Columbia University, 1931), p. 34. Sadiq writes: "Now the Qurʾān is taught in its entirety in all elementary schools, in the original, of course, that is, in Arabic, which is not understood by the Persian children. The number of hours per week assigned to it is as follows:

Grades	II	III	IV	V	VI
Hours per Week	6	6	4	2	1

The catechism is also taught in elementary schools and in the First Cycle of high schools, from one to two hours a week. It goes without saying that the afternoon prayers must be performed in elementary schools, soon after the pupils have returned from their lunch."

[31]*Ihsāʿiyah-yi Maʿārif va Madāris, 1307-1308*, p. 21.

[32]Algar, *Religion and State*, p. 11.

[33]Banani, *Modernization of Iran*, p. 68.

[34]*Ibid.*, p. 71.

[35]*Ibid.*, p. 72.

[36]*Ibid.*, p. 73.

[37]*Ibid.*, pp. 78-79.

[38]Muhammad Rāzī, *Āṣār-i Hujjah*, Vol. 1 (Qumm: Hikmat, 1332 H. Sh./1953), pp. 35-36; but cf. Tihrānī, *Tabaqāt Aʿlām al-Shīʿah*, I, p. 249.

[39]Dawlatābādī, IV, pp. 294-97.

[40]Hairi, *Shīʿism and Constitutionalism*, I, pp. 215-16. But Cf. Tihrānī, *Tabaqāt Aʿlām al-Shīʿah*,

I, 198-99, who does not mention the uprising in his brief biographical sketch of Bāqir.
[41]*Rāzī*, I, pp. 35-36.
[42]Avery, *Modern Iran*, p. 288; he gives no source, however.
[43]*Ihsāʿīyah-yi Maʿārif va Madāris, 1307-1308*, pp. 70-71.
[44]*Ibid.*, p. 114. The emphasis on continuing study and teaching is notable.
[45]*Rāzī*, I, pp. 48-51.
[46]*Ihsāʿīyah-yi Maʿārif va Madāris, 1307-1308*, p. 38.
[47]Tihrānī, *Tabaqāt Aʿlām al-Shīʿah*, III, p. 1162.
[48]For data on these aspects, see below.
[49]*Ihsāʿīyah-yi Maʿārif va Madāris, 1307-1308*, pp. 119-20.119-20.
[50]Dawlat-i Shāh-in-Shāhī-yi Īrān. Vizārat-i Maʿārif va Awqāf va Sanāyiʿ-yi Mustażrafah. Idārah-yi Intibāʿāt, Dāʾirah-yi Ihsāʿīyah. *Sālnāmah-yi 1310-1311* H. Sh./1931-1932 (Tehran: Matbaʿah-yi Rawshanāʾī, n.d., Part II, pp. 54-57.
[51]Muhammad Parvīn Gunābādī, "Madāris-i Qadīm-i Mashhad va Shīvah-yi Tadrīs-i Ānhā," *Sukhan*, Vol. XXIV, no. 2 (Bahman 1353 H. Sh./1975), pp. 155-66. As a historical footnote, the Madrasah-yi Fāzilīyah was destroyed as part of a renewal project in the vicinity of the Shrine of Imām Rizā in 1931.
[52]*Ibid.*, p. 160.
[53]This treatise was published in 1975 by Iraj Afshār, *Farhang-i Īrān Zamīn*, Vol. XX (1353 H. Sh./1975), pp. 39-82; cited in Seyyid Hossein Nasr, "The Traditional Texts Used in the Persian *Madrasahs*," *Islamic Quarterly*, Vol. XIX, nos. 3-4 (July-December 1975), p. 172.
[54]Tihrānī, *Tabaqāt Aʿlām al-Shīʿah*, III, p. 945.
[55]Ann K. S. Lambton, *Landlord and Peasant in Persia* (London: Oxford University Press, 1969), p. 236. She mentions that *awqāf* created for the purpose of supporting *rawzah khvānī* became *mutaʿazzir al-masraf* (meaning their revenue could not be used for their original purpose).
[56]ʿAlī Akbar Sahābī, *Tārīkhchah-yi Vaqf dar Islam* (Tehran: Tehran University Press, 1343 H. Sh./1964), p. 10. The author was Director-General of the Endowments Department at the time.
[57]V. V. Minorsky, ed. and tr. *Tadhkirah al-Muluk*. E. J. W. Gibb Memorial Publications, N. S. Vol. 16 (London: Luzac, 1943), pp. 42, 78-79, 111, 146-47.
[58]Lambton, *Landlord and Peasant*, pp. 131-32, 147, 155.
[59]Algar, *Religion and State*, pp. 40 ff.
[60]Browne, *Persian Revolution*, p. 417.
[61]A. I. Demin, *Selskoe Khoziastvo Sovremenogo Irana* (Moscow: Izdatelstvo "Nauka", 1967), p. 22.
[62]Dawlat-i Shāh-in-Shāhī-yi Īrān. Vizārat-i Maʿārif va Awqāf va Sanāyiʿ-yi Mustażrafah. Idarah-yi Kull-i Intibāʿāt. Dāʾirah-yi Ihsāʿīyah. *Sālnāmah va Ihsāʿīyah, 1312/13-1313/14 H. Sh./1933/34-1934/35* (Tehran: Shirkat-i Sahhāmī-yi Chāp, n. d.), Part I, pp. 6-7, 23-32.
[63]"Hāyidah va Gītī az Mushtarīyān-i Awqāf," *Iran Times* (Washington, D.C.), 20 April 1979, pp. 7, 8.
[64]Elena Alekseevich Doroshenko, *Shiitskoe Dukhovenstvo v Sovremennom Irane* (Moscow: Izdatelstvo "Nauka," 1975), p. 73. A further instance of his relenting towards the religious leadership involved the Law of 18 March 1931 on monetary and currency reform. The Shīrāz *mujtahid*, Sayyid Nūr al-Dīn Shīrāzī protested this law and in the election supported Majlis candidates who backed his position. After his arrest, the bazaar of the city struck and commerce came to a halt. Shīrāzī allegedly had marital ties to a number of Iran's aristocracy of "1000 families", and these connections led to the Shah's magnanimity toward him in ordering his release. Norman Jacobs, *The Sociology of Development: Iran in an Asian Case* (New York: Praeger, 1966), p. 220, cited in *ibid.*, pp. 72-73.
[65]Dawlatābādī, IV, pp. 431-32.
[66]Tihrānī, *Tabaqāt Aʿlām al-Shīʿah*, III, p. 1166.
[67]Mohammad Hassan Faghfoory, *The Role of the Ulama in Twentieth Century Iran With Particu-*

lar Reference to Ayatullah Haj Sayyid Abul-Qasim Kashani. Unpublished Ph.D. dissertation in the Department of History at the University of Wisconsin (Madison), 1978, p. 82, citing Donald Wilber, *Reza Shah: The Resurrection and Reconstruction of Iran* (New York, 1975), p. 263.

[68]In his conversations with the Shah E. A. Bayne received the impression that the former had been pleased with the way the role of the rural clergy was being undermined by the activities of the Literacy Corps, to the members of which he referred as the "mullas of modernization", and declaring: "The peasants in the reformed villages are rejecting the old mullas and looking toward the Literacy Corps for their guidance." Bayne, *Persian Kingship in Transition* (New York: American Universities Field Staff, 1968), pp. 51–52.

Notes to Chapter Three

[1]Doroshenko, *Shiitskoe Dukhovenstvo,* pp. 76–77.

[2]Abū Qāsim Sahāb, Tārīkh-i Madrasah-yi ʿAlī-yi Sipah Sālār (Tehran: n. p., 1329 H. Sh./1950), p. 122.

[3]Dawlat-i Shāh-in-Shāhī-yi Īrān. *Sūrat-i Mashrūh-i Muẕakkarāt-i Majlis-i Shawrā-yi Millī.* Jalasah-yi 13, 29 Ābān 1322 H. Sh. (Tehran: Chāpkhanah-yi Majlis, 1322 H. Sh./1943), p. 51. This amendment had been preceded by a constitution and curriculum for a newly to be formed state administered Religious Studies High School (Dabīristān-i Maʿqūl va Manqūl) on 17 Khurdād 1322/8 June 1943. The location of this high school was not specified, although it was declared to be a preparatory institution for the Faculty of Theology of Tehran University. As already indicated, one must not confuse the Faculty of Theology with the Madrasah-yi ʿAlī-yi Sipah Sālār. The former was meant to be essentially a research-oriented college; the latter, a theological seminary of the old type (albeit under more explicit regime control). The problem of distinguishing the two is compounded due to the original housing of the Faculty on the grounds of the Sipah Sālār Mosque. The high school seemed to be the first state experiment with the creation of a religious secondary institution within the *dabīristān* (secular high school) track. Its curriculum was identical to that of the other state-administered *dabīristāns* for the first five of the seven years. For the sixth and seventh years, the curriculum was as follows:

SIXTH
1. Persian language: works of writers from the Sāmānids (819–1025) to the present.
2. History of Persian literature: pre-Islamic literature (1 hour).
3. Persian grammar (1 hour).
4. Arabic (2 hours).
5. Morphology: *Sharh-i Niẓām* (2 hours).
6. Syntax: Suyūṭī (2 hours).
7. *Fiq: Sharāyiʿ* (2 hours).
8. *Usul: Maʿālim*—excerpts: (2 hours).
9. French or English: (6 hours).
10. Philosophy and Logic: *Hāshīyah Mullā ʿAbdullāh:* (2 hours).
11. Ancient philosophy (2 hours).
12. Modern philosophy (1 hour).
13. Psychology (1 hour).
14. History (3 hours).
15. Geography (3 hours).
SEVENTH
1. History of post-Islamic Persian literature (3 hours).
2. Persian language (1 hour).
3. Morphology: *Sharh-i Niẓām* (2 hours).
4. Syntax: *Jāmī* (2 hours).
5. Arabic poetry—optional (1 hour).
6. Rhetoric: *Talkhīs* [i-Miftāh] (2 hours).
7. *Fiq: Sharāyiʿ* (2 hours).

8. *Usul: Maʿālim*—excerpts (2 hours).
9. French or English (4 hours).
10. Philosophy and logic: *Shamsīyah* (2 hours).
11. Ancient philosophy (2 hours).
12. Modern philosophy (2 hours).
13. Psychology (1 hour).
14. Ethics (1 hour).
15. History of Islam (2 hours).
16. Geography of the Islamic countries (2 hours).

For this curriculum and the constitution of the Religious Studies High School, consult Dawlat-i Shāh-in-Shāhi-yi Īrān. Vizārat-i Farhang. Idārah-yi Āmār. *Sālnāmah va Āmār az 1322 tā 1327* H. Sh./1943–1948 (Tehran: Tābān, n.d., Part II, pp. 244–47.

As for the reason for its establishment, it is not improbable that it represented a concession to the religious leadership as part of its campaign to restore Shīʿism to what it viewed as its rightful place. Yet, the government's interests would also be served since from among the graduates of this institution would be recruited the students for the Dānishgāh-i Rūhānī-yi Īrān. For although the latter was in fact inaugurated only in 1949, the 1943 amendment to Article 14 of the Education Law of 1911 shows that the government clearly foresaw the need for it that early.

[4]Doroshenko, *Shiitskoe Dukhovenstvo*, p. 78.

[5]*Ittilāʿāt*, 15 Day 1331 H. Sh./1953.

[6]Doroshenko, *Shiitskoe Dukhovenstvo*, p. 88; *Ittilāʿāt*, 2 Isfand 1328 H. Sh./1950.

[7]*Ittilāʿāt*, 24 Bahman 1329 H. Sh./1951.

[8]*Ibid.*, 5, 12 Khurdād 1331 H. Sh./1952.

[9]*Ibid.*, 15, 17, 23, 24, 27 Day 1331 H. Sh./1953; Razi, *Āsār-i Hujjah*, II, pp. 31–35.

[10]Hājj Mullā ʿAlī Vāʿiz Khīyābānī al-Tabrīzī, *Kitāb-i ʿUlamāʾ-yi Muʿāsirīn* (Tabrīz: Shirkat-i Sahhāmī-yi Chāp-i Kitāb, 1366 H. Q./1946), pp. 288–89.

[11]*Ittilāʿāt*, 2 Ābān 1329 H. Sh./1950. A construction of the geneological ties among the Sadrs, Āshtīyānīs and Bihbihānīs should not obscure the fact that Sadr al-Din's daughter was also married to Murtazā Hāʾirī Yazdī, the older son of Shaykh ʿAbd al-Karīm Hāʾirī Yazdī, the founder of Qumm's modern religious education system. Indeed, in a remarkable inquiry, Michael M. J. Fischer shows that all of the leading *marājiʿ-yi taqlīd* of the last two generations can be placed on a single geneological chart. These individuals include Āyatullāhs Hāʾirī, Burūjirdī, Khumaynī, (Muhammad Kāzim) Sharīʿatmadārī, (Muhammad Rizā) Gulpāygānī, (Shihāb al-Dīn) al-Marʿashī al-Najafī, Khvānsārī, Hujjat Kūhkamarī, (Abū al-Qāsim) Khūʾī, and (Hādī)Mīlānī. Michael M. J. Fischer, *Islam and Social Change: Iran: The Qumm Report.* Typescript, 1976, p. 37; this study is forthcoming under a different title and is to be published by Harvard University Press.

[12]Tihrānī, *Tabaqāt Aʿlām al-Shīʿah*, I, pp. 75–76.

[13]Faghfoory, *Role of the Ulama*, pp. 137–38.

[14]*Ibid.*, p. 191.

[15]Joseph Cottam, *Nationalism in Iran* (Pittsburgh: University of Pittsburgh Press, 1964), p. 154.

[16]*Ibid.*, p. 155. An example of Kāshānī's relative isolation from the "mainstream" ʿulamāʾ leadership in Iran which adds to the impression that the Burūjirdī-Bihbihānī majority did not count him as one of their own appeared on the occasion of the death of Āyatullāh Muhammad Taqī Khvānsārī in early August 1952. Kāshānī naturally attended the fortieth day observances (*arbaʿīn*) of this clergyman's death in late September in Qumm. Although he paid his respects to Burūjirdī, Kāshānī had only brief contact with him; and he took up accommodations not at the house of the *marjaʿ-yi mutlaq-i taqlīd* or any of the other clergymen, but at the residence of the governor of the city of Qumm. This would normally seem strange, in light of the standard canons of hospitality extended by the ʿulamāʾ to their colleagues; in this particular case, however, it is less surprising and is indicative of a need felt by both individuals for a certain distancing between one another. On the episode, see *Ittilāʿāt*, 1 Mihr 1331 H. Sh./1952.

[17]*Ittilāʿāt*, 15–17, 21–22 Ābān 1331 H. Sh./1952.

[18]*Ibid.*, 16 Āẕar 1331 H. Sh./1952. Mindful of the tardiness of Mr. Mishkvāt's departure for Qumm, the Minister of Culture denied, however, that the three week delay was due to political considerations. The excuse was advanced that the newly appointed *mutavallī* had had to attend to various personal duties and commitments, which forced him to push back the date of departure.

[19]*Ittilāʿāt*, 22 Tīr 1333 H. Sh./1954 carried an article on the construction of a new mosque in the courtyard of the shrine in Qumm (later to be called the Burūjirdī Mosque). Āyatullāh Burūjirdī informed the press that Mr. Tawlīyat—i.e., not Mishkvāt—would oversee the construction of the new mosque. This obligation clearly rests with the administrator of the shrine. Therefore, the implication is that Tawlīyat had survived the dispute and continued in his post.

[20]*Ittilāʿāt*, 22, 23 Day 1331 H. Sh./1952.

[21]For the 1952 figures, see appendices on student enrollment in Qumm, broken down by province of origin. For 1956, see *Kayhān*, 22 Urdībibihisht 1335 H. Sh./1956, cited in Fredy Bemont, *Les Villes de l'Iran* (Paris: n. p., 1969), p. 179. These figures may be contrasted with the estimate given by Āghā Buzurg-i Tihrānī that in the early days of Shaykh ʿAbd al-Karīm Hāʾirī's stewardship (ca 1925) the student population in the shrine city was approximately 1,000. See *Tabaqāt Aʿlām al-Shīʿah*, III, p. 1159. To place these figures in perspective, it is worth noting that the number of students taking *usūl* from Ākhūnd Mullā Muhammad Kāẓim Khurāsānī in Najaf when the latter became that *hawzah*'s leader after the death of Mīrzā Muhammad Hasan al-Shīrāzī (d. 1894) was some 2,000 *tullāb*. See Āghā Buzurg-i Tihrānī, *Hadīyah al-Rādī* (Najaf: Ashraf, 1387 H. Q./1967), p. 140.

[22]Reflecting the rejection of many aspects of this model of modernization was a perhaps unduly pessimistic statement by the Minister of Culture concerning the putative absence of purpose in Iranian culture in the mid-twentieth century as this culture was purveyed in the schools. He declared that in his view the schools of 30 years ago (i.e., in 1920) had done a better job of training great minds than the current educational system of 1950. See *Ittilāʿāt*, 29 Shahrīvar 1329 H. Sh./1950.

[23]Mahmūd Fāzil, "Rijāl-i Khurāsān: Āyatullāh Kafāʾī Khurāsānī," *Vahīd*, Vol X, no. 11 (Bahman 1351 H. Sh./1972). The reference to Āẕarbāyjān is to the separatist movement in that northwestern province which, with support from the Soviet Union and its Red Army, nearly seceded from Iran during the troubled period between 1945–1947.

[24]Muhammad Muqaddaszādah, *Rijāl-i Qumm* (Qumm?: Chapkhanah-yi Mihr-i Iran, 1335 H. Sh./1956), p. 105.

[25]Doroshenko, *Shiitskoe Dukhovenstvo*, pp. 86–87.

[26]On Kāshānī's abortive protests to the mentioned appointments, see *ibid.*, pp. 81–84.

[27]*Ibid.*, p. 100.

[28]*Ittilāʿāt*, 22, 27 Farvardīn 1332 H. Sh./1953. There were suggestions, too, that Āyatullāh Bihbihānī had received bribes from the Court at the height of the Musaddiq-Shah conflict. Such rumors had also spread concerning the behavior of his father, Sayyid Muhammad Bihbihānī, at the time of the Constitutional Revolution earlier in the century. For these suggestions, see Cottam, *Nationalism in Iran*, p. 155; and Algar, *Religion and State*, pp. 213, 248–49.

[29]*Ittilāʿāt*, 6 Mihr 1332 H. Sh./1953. In the most extensive elaboration of his views concerning the relationship between religion and politics, Āyatullāh Bihbihānī had earlier declared: "In order for social affairs to advance centralization [*markazīyat*] is necessary. Otherwise, ideas and actions would be diffused and dispersed. Ignorant policies resting merely on feeling will cause the corruption and failure of social and political movements." However, it is not clear whether this centralization was supposed to be under the aegis of the *ʿulamāʾ* or not. For when asked whether it was up to the clergy to rectify the chaos and poverty besetting the country, he answered that the *ʿulamāʾ* especially must do their part to end the state of anarchy and backwardness. "But action is strictly the right of the government in power. Without the advice and assistance of the *ʿulamāʾ* no action can progress; but unfortunately, the political authorities have not given the *ʿulamāʾ* the attention that is their due . . ."

These contradictory words indicate that Bihbihānī saw the need to tread the fine line between an exclusively religious and political orientation. His support of nationalization of the AIOC in private meetings with Musaddiq came out in this interview, as did his view that social reformers in the country would do well to "give full attention to the true religion of Islam . . ." At the same time, he thanked the Shah for his words in opening the 17th session of the Majlis in which he committed himself to strengthening the foundations of the faith and propagating its principles. See *Ittilāʿāt*, 17 Khurdād 1331/1952 for this significant expression of views.

30 *Ittilāʿāt*, 11, 13 Mihr 1332 H. Sh./1953.

31 *Ibid.*, 18 Mihr 1332 H. Sh./1953.

32 Khīyābānī, *Kitāb-i ʿUlamāʾ-yi Muʿāsir*, pp. 201–211.

33 *Ittilāʿāt*, 11, 14 Mihr 1332 H. Sh./1952.

34 *Ibid.*, 21 Bahman 1334/1956.

35 ". . . it was the *ʿulamāʾ* who throughout encouraged the state to suppress the movement, and their resistance to it was more consistent than that of [state officials] . . . in this struggle the role of the state appeared to [the clergy], at best, as lacking in enthusiasm and, at worst, as ambiguous." Algar, *Religion and State*, p. 147.

36 Avery, *Modern Iran*, p. 469.

37 For Prime Minister Husayn ʿAlāʾ's very gloomy review of the state of the economy, see *Cahiers de l'Orient Contemporaine*, 12ᵉᵐᵉ Année (Fascicule XXXI), 2ᵉᵐᵉ Semestre, 1955, p. 253.

38 *Ittilāʿāt*, 18 Urdībihisht 1334 H. Sh./1955.

39 *Ibid.* The Bahāʾīs charge that the attack on the old woman and her children did indeed occur, but they note that she was a Bahāʾī, and her attackers Shīʿī Muslims!

40 *Ittilāʿāt*, 19 Urdībihisht 1334 H. Sh./1955.

41 *Ibid.*, 20 Urdībihisht 1334 H. Sh./1955.

42 *Ibid.*

43 *Ibid.*, 24 Urdībihisht 1334 H. Sh./1955.

44 *Cahiers de l'Orient Contemporaine*, 12ᵉᵐᵉ Année, Fasicule XXXII (2ᵉᵐᵉ semestre, 1955), pp. 251–52.

45 On the closed and open sessions of the Majlis and the texts of the Shāhkār amendment and the decree of the Minister of Interior, see *Ittilāʿāt*, 26 Urdībihisht 1334 H. Sh./1955.

46 *Ibid.*, 28 Urdībihisht 1334 H. Sh./1955.

47 *Ibid.*, 21 Khurdād 1334 H. Sh./1955.

48 *Ibid.*, 26 Khurdād 1334 H. Sh./1955.

49 *Ibid.*, 18 Tīr 1334 H. Sh./1955.

50 *Ibid.*, 22 Tīr 1334 H. Sh./1955.

51 The Soviets claim that the government had an interest in putting a lid on the anti-Bahāʾī campaign because Bahāʾīs collectively withdrew from their Bank-i Millī accounts 1.5 billion rials and deposited this money (equivalent to roughly $20 million) in the Russo-Persian Bank. See Doroshenko, *Shiitskoe Dukhovenstvo*, p. 103.

52 Some, like Arsalān Khalʿatbarī, one of the country's leading landholders, claimed that these individuals had taken part in their capacity as private citizens, not officials of the state. *Ittilāʿāt*, 22 Khurdād 1334 H. Sh./1955. But few believed such tendentious statements.

53 *Ibid.*, 5 Tīr 1334 H. Sh./1955.

54 *Ibid.*, 18, 25, 26, 27 Tīr 1334 H. Sh./1955.

55 *Ibid.*, 2 Khurdād 1334 H. Sh./1955.

56 *Ibid.*, 29 Khurdād 1334 H. Sh./1955. It will be recalled that a curriculum and constitution for such a Religious Studies High School had been issued in June 1943. Apparently, due to war time conditions and preoccupation with other, more pressing, matters in the late forties and early fifties, this project had never materialized. The creation of a religious studies high school in the context of clergy reassertion may be considered a victory for the *ʿulamāʾ* in their attempts to get the state to

recognize their influence in contemporary society. But, equally, its establishment in the mid-thirties, at the height of Riżā Shāh's anti-clerical policies, could reasonably be interpreted as a method of weakening the religious institution through the setting up of a school which the regime could easily control and whose graduates would have been socialized to go on themselves, as teachers, to propagate modernist values.

[57] *Ittilāʿāt,* 23 Khurdād 1334 H. Sh./1955.

[58] *Ibid.,* 29 Khurdād 1334 H.Sh./1955. The next day, it was reported in the press that Fīrūzābādī had been granted a royal audience. On the matter of peremptory, formal meetings between Shah and clergy, such audiences were typically very brief. An example is provided by the ceremonial audience granted to the ʿulamāʾ (as well as to the cabinet, Senate, Majlis, etc.) on the day of ʿĪd-i Ghadīr (marking the anniversary celebration of the prophet's appointment of Imām ʿAlī to succeed him). The session lasted a scant 15 minutes. See *Ittilāʿāt,* 14 Murdād 1334 H. Sh./1955. There is, too, the practice of *ad hoc* meetings between members of the Court and leading clergymen. Until the late 1950's the Shah would meet from time to time with Āyatullāh Burūjirdī in Qumm. The Prime Minister, as well, would have such *tête-à-tête* sessions, as for example ʿAlāʾ's appointment with Zahīr al-Islam—the nāʾib altawlīyah of the Sipah Sālār mosque, as reported in *Ittilāʿāt,* 27 Tīr 1334 H. Sh./1955; and during which the administrator of the Sipah Sālār introduced certain members of the Tehran clergy to the Prime Minister; and they discussed the teaching of religion in the schools, righting irreligion, and preventing attacks on Islam in the media. It goes without saying that, from the ʿulamāʾ point of view, institutionalization of meetings with the Shah in such a manner that they could deal with him as a corporate group would be a far better means of presenting their demands and securing concessions.

[59] *Ittilāʿāt,* 3, 4 Shahrīvar 1334 H. Sh./1955. Bihbihānī and other clergymen then followed suit with their own *fatvās.*

[60] *Ibid.,* 24 Murdād 1334 H. Sh./1955.

[61] For Jaʿfar Bihbihānī's Majlis speech on the Baghdad Pact, see *Ittilāʿāt,* 27 Mihr 1334 H. Sh./1955.

Notes to Chapter Four

[1] Gianroberto Scarcia, "Governo, Riformo Agraria e Opposizione in Persia," *Oriente Moderno,* Vol. XLII, nos. 10–11 (Ottobre–Novembre 1962), p. 787, fn. 2.

[2] In a public lecture in late 1961, Sayyid Muhammad Bihishtī—who was to become a central personality of the regime that overthrew Muhammad Riżā Shāh in January 1979—mentioned two fundamental issues related to social justice which he declared to be problematical in Iran: "enormous class disparities"; and differences of opinion which prevent solidarity of views and action. Citing the *Kāfī fī ʿIlm al-Dīn* by al-Kulaynī, the "Furūʿ", Vol. V, the Chapter entitled, "Al Amr bi al-Maʿrūf wa al-Nahyʿan al-Munkar," *hadīth* #2: "Enjoin the good and forbid the bad, otherwise evildoers will be installed over you, and your calls for the best among you [to rule] will go unheeded." When this line of argument by Bihishtī is combined with the author's condemnation that no one is aware of the meaning of communitity interests (*masālih-i ijtimāʿī*) and his appeals for Islamic solidarity, we can perceive the lines of a political critique. What he seems to be saying is that evildoing rulers have, in fact, come to prevail in Iran because Iranians, ever out for their own personal or family interests and totally oblivious to Islam's stress on the community's interests, have not abided by the injunction: enjoin the good and prohibit the bad. In his peroration, he challenges the members of his audience, in particular the youth in attendance, to revert to the Islamic praxis. For this important statement of the ʿulamāʾ's position on Islam and social relations in Iran in the late fifties and early sixties, see Bihishtī, "Islam va Payvandhā-yi Ijtimāʿī," *Guftār-i Māh ·dar Namāyāndan-i Rāh-i Rāst-i Dīn,* Vol. II (Tehran: Kitābkhānah-yi Sadūq, 1341 H. Sh./1961), pp. 78, 83 and *passim.*

[3]That questions of social justice are addressed within the frame work of the configurations and levels of power should be clear, given the fact that arrangements for the resolution of questions of social justice (such as class conflict, for example, as cited by Bihishtī as noted in fn. 2 *supra*) are formed by those possessing such power.

[4]Ann K. S. Lambton, "Persia Today," in *The World Today*, Vol. XVII, no. 2 (February 1961), p. 82.

[5]Elena Alekseevich Doroshenko, "O Nekotorykh Religioznykh Institutakh i Deiatelnosti Shiitskogo Dukhovenstva v Sovremenom Irane," in *Religiia i Obshchestvennaia Mysl Narodov Vostoka*, ed. B. G. Gafurov (Moscow: Izdatelstvo "Nauka", 1971), p. 181.

[6]*Idem;* Binder, *Iran*, p. 251; Bayne, *Persian Kingship*, p. 48.

[7]"I pray day and night for the person of the Shah-in-Shah, for whom I entertain sincere regard," Burūjirdī was quoted in 1960. See *Kayhān*, 2 August 1960, cited in Doroshenko, "O Nekotorykh Religioznykh Institutakh," p. 181.

[8]Bayne, *Persian Kingship*, p. 48. The comment is disingenuous because it suggests that Burūjirdī's grievances were only material in nature; it also implies that the clergy had not denounced such matters as corruption, alcoholic consumption and violations of the Ramazān fast. Indeed, specific issues of this sort were precisely those concerning which the state had made concessions to the religious elite in the post-1953 period.

[9]No less an eminent religious leader than Āyatullāh Sayyid Kāẓim Sharīʿatmadārī of Qumm, one of the country's *marājiʿ-yi taqlīd*, was alleged to be "favorably disposed to a distribution of *vaqf* lands to the peasants." *The Times* (London), 24 June 1970.

[10]For Tāliqānī's analysis, see his "Naẓar-i Islam dar Bārah-yi Mālikīyat," *Guftār-i Māh dar Namāyāndan-i Rāh-i Rāst-i Dīn*, Vol. III (Tehran: Kitābkhānah-yi Sadūq, 1341 H. Sh./1962), pp. 46–68; esp. 66 ff.

[11]Tāliqānī's lecture was given in late 1961, after the passage of the unworkable 1959 bill by the Majlis but before the Shah's commitment to a new version of this law in November 1961. For a more favorable image of Arsanjānī, see Lambton, *The Perisan Land Reform* (London: Oxford University Press, 1969), pp. 61–63. According to her, the cabinet signed the bill amending the 1959 bill on 9 January 1962 (in response to the Shah's *farmān* [decree] of 11 November 1961) only because of Arsanjānī's importunities. The cabinet would have preferred to let matters rest and only signed the bill (the Majlis had been prorogued on 9 May 1961 amidst charges of rigged elections) because they "supposed that the measure, once on the statute book, would be forgotten, like so many other measures before it." p. 63.

[12]Tāliqānī, Naẓar-i Islam," p. 46 begins with a verse from the *Qurʾān:* "Thanks be to God, Master of the worlds, Creator of all creatures, Who made the earth a carpet and the heavens a roof from which He sent down the rains and provided us the fruits of livelihood and brought the earth into being for all of us."

[13]*Ittilāʿāt*, 3 Bahman 1340 H. Sh./1962.

[14]Doroshenko, Shiitskoe Dukhovenstvo, p. 105. This was reminiscent of the *ʿulamāʾ*'s agitation against the election bill of the Musaddiq government in early 1953, which contained provisions on female suffrage. For the reaction of the Qumm *marājiʿ-i taqlīd* (Sadr al-Dīn Sadr, Muhammad Hujjat Kāhkamarahʾī, and Muhammad Husayn Burūjirdī) to that bill, see *Ittilāʿāt*, 15 Day 1331 H. Sh./1953.

[15]Leonard Binder, *Iran*, p. 195.

[16]Tāliqānī, "Naẓar-i Islam," *passim;* Maxime Rodinson, *Islam and Capitalism* (Austin, Texas: University of Texas Press, 1979) argues that the principle of private property ownership is protected under Islamic law.

[17]*Ittilāʿāt*, 1 Isfand 1338 H. Sh./1960.

[18]Lambton, Landlord and Peasant in Persia, 2nd ed. (London: Oxford University Press, 1969), pp. 126–27; also p. 261.

[19]Doroshenko, "O Nekotorykh Religiozynkh Institutakh," p. 182, writes that the *ʿulamā*' "monopoly" on *awqāf* and the great revenues from these "enabled the strengthening of the social, political and property situation of the *ʿulamā*' and *mujtahids*.

"It is thus not fortuitous that many leading *āyatullāh*s and *mujtahids* even today are linked to the great families by bonds [of marriage?] with famous Iranian aristocrats, feudalists, representatives of the grand bourgeoisie . . ."

[20]Lambton, "Rural Development and Land Reform in Iran," *Symposium on Rural Development* (Central Treaty Organization, 1963), cited in Charles Issawi, ed. *The Economic History of Iran, 1800-1914* (Chicago: University of Chicago Press, 1971), p. 54.

[21]Scarcia, "Governo, Riformo Agraria e Opposizione in Persia," pp. 748-49. After the Safavid dynasty collapsed, apparently the clergy lost much of its land, so that "In the region of Isfahān in the beginning of the 19th century there were not any especially great landowners. Afterwards, Governor Sadr and his son, Amīn al-Dawlah, seized great estates. Many estates in this region were appropriated by the *mullās* of the Friday Mosque, the *Imāms Jumʿah;* and at the end of the 19th century the brother of Nasir al-Dīn Shah—Żill-i Sultān—had seized many great properties . . . [Dmitri] Beliaev has written: Żill-i Sultān and the *mujtahids* are the biggest landowners of the Isfahān region . . . Almost all the villages belong to Zill-i Sultān or to the *Āghā*s, that is, to the *mujtahids*.' In Isfahān Żill-i Sultān and the leading *mujtahids* . . . had seized the majority of the properties of the small holders in the upriver area of the Zāyandah Rūd River." G. N. Iľinskii, Agrarnye Otnosheniia v Irane v Kontse XIX-Nachale XX Veka," in *Uchenye Zapiski Instituta Vostokovedeniia: Iranskii Sbornik*, VIII Akademiia Nauk SSSR (Moscow: Izdatelstvo Adakemii Nauk SSSR, 1953), p. 125.

[22]The Shah's view that the *Sipāh-i Dīn* would replace rural clergymen in the process of educating peasantry and tribal elements has already been noted.

[23]*Ittilāʿāt*, 16 Isfand 1338 H. Sh./1960. This was Āyatullāh Muhammad Husayn Āl Kāshif al-Ghiṭāʾ, a *marjaʿ-i taqlīd* with firm ties to the Iranian clergy. He had been invited by his Iranian colleagues a decade earlier to attend the ceremonies inaugurating the Madrasah-yi Sipah Sālār as a Theological University (Dānishgāh-i Rūhānī) in 1950.

[24]*Kayhān*, 2, 6, 26 August 1960, as cited in Doroshenko, "O Nekotorykh Religioznykh Institutakh," p. 181.

[25]*Ittilāʿāt*, 30 Shahrīvar 1330 H. Sh./1951; and 29 Khurdād 1334 H. Sh./1955.

[26]*Ibid.*, 26 Murdād 1334 H. Sh./1955; 8 Isfand 1338 H. Sh./1960. On the latter occasion, upon his return to Iran Kamarah'ī suggested that military science be taught in the *madrasah*s of Qumm, noting that it was offered in the curriculum at al-Azhar. His argument was that since the students of the religious sciences would be the vanguard of an army embarked on *jihād*, such instruction would be valuable. Islamic unity, said Kamarah'ī required the formation of an Islamic army. Though he said he was going to broach the question of military instruction in Qumm's *madrasah*s with Āyatullāh Burūjirdī, nothing seems ever to have come of it. The regime could not be expected to have supported the notion at any rate, since the main reason for a call to *jihād* at that time would have been the Arab-Israel conflict. It would have meant a fundamental change in Iran's policy toward that conflict, which for obvious reasons, the government was not willing to undertake. Neither could the Shah's regime have looked with favor upon a program of military training and, presumably, provisioning, of elements over which it would not have independent control.

[27]*Ittilāʿāt*, 12 Murdād 1339 H. Sh./1960.

[28]Kāshif al-Ghiṭāʾ had gone on record as early as 1950 in a strong effort to achieve Islamic solidarity with the *Sunnī* Muslims. See *Ittilāʿāt*, 24 Murdād 1329 H. Sh./1950 for a translation of an article that he had originally written for the Arabic language journal of the Dār al-Taqrīb: *Risālah al-Islam*, Vol. II, no. 3. He was only one among a good many *Shīʿī ʿulamā*' who considered the government's policy toward the Arab-Israel dispute to be completely wrong.

[29]The Shah deliberately used religious occasions to deliver such statements, as on the ʿĪd-i Mabhaṣ, celebrating the anniversary of Muhammad's call to prophecy. See *Ittilāʿāt*, 6 Bahman 1338. This was

but a variation of the repeatedly stated theme that "our social reforms are completely in accord with the principles of the faith and with the true religion of Islam." *Ibid.*, 11 Shahrīvar 1331 H. Sh./1952.

[30]Algar, "The Oppositional Role of the *'Ulamā'* in Twentieth Century Iran," in *Scholars, Saints and Sufis*, ed. Nikki Keddie (Berkeley: University of California Press, 1971), p. 244; also Doroshenko, "O Nekotorykh Religioznykh Institutakh," p. 193.

[31]Muqaddaszādah, *Rijāl-i Qumm*, p. 117.

[32]In his 1943 book, *Kashf al-Asrār*, Khumaynī, while highly critical of Rizā Shah did not advocate overthrow of the Shah or monarchy.

[33]Some of the leading preachers of the day, of course, joined the "radical" wing and were also arrested for their activities. Among these was the omnipresent Abū al-Qāsim Falsafī.

[34]Nor did Sharī'atmadārī experience a radicalization of his views with his arrest. Algar cites the "effusively loyalistic tone" of his note responding to the Shah's telegram commiserating on the death of Āyatullāh Hakīm in 1970. This action "earned him widespread disapproval." Algar, "Oppositional Role," p. 252.

[35]*Ittilā'āt*, 15 Khurdād 1342 H. Sh./1963. 'Allāmah Tabā'tabā'ī is not a *mujtahid* in the traditional sense of an expert in the "transmitted sciences" of *fiq* and *usūl*. Instead, he has attained eminence in the "intellectual sciences", including *tafsīr* (commentary on the *Qur'ān*), of which he is the acknowledged peerless master of the current period. His additional interest in theosophy (gnosis) [*'irfān*] places him on the periphery of the traditional calling of *mujtahid*s as learned men of the basic foundations and principles of Islamic jurisprudence.

[36]Cottam, *Nationalism in Iran*, p. 308.

[37]*Ittilā'āt*, 6 Bahman 1341 H. Sh./1963. Mahdavī was not further identified by the newspaper, which quoted him as having said an affirmative vote in favor of the White Revolution did not contravene Islam.

[38]*Ibid.*, 6 Farvardīn 1342 H. Sh./1963. This clergy delegation thanked the Shah for upholding public order and tranquility. Unlike previous years, no reference was made to the Shah's defense and propagation of the laws of *Shī'ī* Islam. Therefore, the delegation may have been implicitly criticizing the Shah, rather than supporting him. The relationship of this Bihbihānī to the Ayatullah Bihbihānī of Tehran is not clear.

[39]Thus, Hasan Pākravān, Director of the notorious SAVAK (secret police) claimed the number of clergymen opposed to the "White Revolution" was diminutive. Indeed, he claimed that in his discussions with members of the clergy in the course of several months, he discovered that most supported female emancipation; the handful against it based their position on their personal assessment that Iranian women were not ready to be emancipated, rather than on any Islamic arguments. *Ittilā'āt*, 15 Khurdād 1342 H. Sh./1963. Alternatively, it was alleged that many pro-regime clergymen were behind appeals for order and tranquility: when "an outstanding religious leader of Qumm asked the government to establish peace in the city, and the government immediately complied." *Ibid.*, 4 Bahman 1341 H. Sh./1963. Such egregious statements do not stand up under scrutiny, needless to say.

[40]*Ittilā'at*, 19 Khurdād 1342 H. Sh./1963.

[41]Doroshenko, *Shiitskoe Dukhovenstvo*, p. 108. Sharī'atmadārī's statement that he was not averse to the redistribution of *awqāf* to poor peasantry did not save him from arrest over his remarks of anger over the killings that had taken place. It was said that even the quietist Mīlānī of Mashhad had objected to the methods of the police and military forces. For this, see Marvin Zonis, *The Political Elite of Iran* (Princeton: Princeton University Press, 1971), p. 45, fn. 12.

[42]*Ittilā'āt*, 4 Bahman 1341 H. Sh./1963.

[43]*Ibid.*

[44]Nikki Keddie, "The Roots of the *'Ulamā'*'s Power in Modern Iran," *Studia Islamica*, Vol. XXIX (1966), p. 62.

[45]*Nahīd*, 18 January 1962, cited in A. I. Demin, *Selskoe Khoziastvo Sovremennogo Irana*

(Moscow: Izdatelstvo "Nauka", 1967), p. 209. In effect this was meant to sabotage the land reform law by making the *vaqf* appear unproductive, and therefore not subject to the provisions of the law, which did not really apply to unproductive areas; instead, the law was meant to cover productive land, since this type was considered the one that would be beneficial to the peasantry.

46 "Mazhab va Masā'il-i Rūz," *Ittilāʿāt*, 15 Isfand 1341 H. Sh./1963.

47 Lambton, *The Persian Land Reform*, p. 112.

48 "Nigāhī bi Tārīkh," *Ittilāʿāt*, 16 Isfand 1341 H. Sh./1963. Emphasis added.

49 "Lāhūt va Nāsūt," *ibid.*, 18 Isfand 1341 H. Sh./1963.

50 "Sīyāsat va Dīyānat," *ibid.*, 13 Murdād 1342 H. Sh./1963.

51 And who were the "truly pious" clergymen? A contingent of *ʿulamāʾ* in the *ʿatabāt* who were working on behalf of Muhammad Taqī Qummī's Dār al-Taqrīb, some of whom have already been mentioned, such as Āyatullāh Hibat al-Dīn Shahrastānī; Āyatullāh Abū al-Qāsim Khūʾī; Āyatullāh Muhammad Husayn Āl Kāshif al-Ghitāʾ; and Muhammad Sālih Hāʾirī Māzandarānī. See the contributions of these four to Qummī's volume, *Hambastagī-yi Mazāhib-i Islami* (Tehran: Amīr Kabīr/Sipihr, 1350 H. Sh./1971), pp. 91–98, 195–200, 217–23, 248–54. Of these essays, that of Kāshif al-Ghitāʾ sought to deny the importance of the *Shīʿī* insistence on the doctrine of the imamate as a source of cleavage in the Islamic community; that of Khūʾī attempted to refute the common charge by *Sunnī*s that the *Shīʿah* had tampered with the *Qurʾān*; and that of Shahrastānī a homiletic statement about the unifying effects of the observances of Ramazān. The essay by Hāʾirī Māzandarānī, on the other hand, reflected a theme closer to the thrust of the *Ittilāʿāt* essays. It argued that the imamate and caliphate are separate institutions, each with its own proper jurisdiction. The caliphate is the temporal power and "the best path of peace is for us *Shīʿah* to recognize the caliph [read the Shah] as the trustee and guardian of the treasures of the world, and the *Imām* as the trustee and guardian of divine knowledge and the knowledge of the prophet." (p. 217).

These individuals are given as examples of those whom the Shah believed were true to their religion. In so presenting them, it is not intended to classify them in the same category as the "pro-Court" faction of the *ʿulamāʾ*: Mahdavī, Vahīdī, Imāmī, Qummī and Muhājirānī.

52 "Farq Mīyān-i Sīyāsat va Ālūdagī-yi Sīyāsī," *Ittilāʿāt*, 15 Murdād 1342 H. Sh./1963.

53 In its own way, this last editorial may represent the point of view of a small group in the regime who advocated a less than massive regime response to the clergy's role in politics in 1963. This group is identified by Zonis, *Political Elite of Iran*, pp. 63–66 as former Prime Minister ʿAlāʾ, the Speaker of the Majlis, Hikmat, ʿAbdullāh Intizām (the Director of the NIOC) and General Murtazā Yazdānpanāh (the senior military leader). The hardliners would probably not have conceded any grounds for political involvement for the clergy and have ruled participation in decision-making, policy-formulation, interest articulation, etc. not as *makrūh* but as *harām* (prohibited).

54 "Marz Mīyān-i Dīn va Umūr-i Ijtimāʿī," published in a volume containing a number of Bāzargān's essays and entitled *Mazhab dar Urūpā* (Tehran: Kitābkhānah-yi Bungāh-i Matbūʿātī-yi Iran, 1344 H. Sh./1965), pp. 113–46.

55 *Ibid.*, p. 114.

56 *Ibid.*, pp. 115–16.

57 *Ibid.*, p. 116. These qualities which Bāzargān holds the clergy possesses in short supply are precisely those which the regime—through *Ittilāʿāt*—warned had led to the contamination of the religious leaders' piety.

58 *Ibid.*, pp. 116–17.

59 *Ibid.*, pp. 117–19. The word "annihilate" (*muzmahil*) was used by *Ittilāʿāt* in its 13 Murdād 1342 H. Sh./1963 editorial; but the paper used it in the opposite sense: the government is *not* trying to annihilate religion, contrary to what some of the clergy thinks.

60 *Ibid.*, pp. 120–21. Bāzargān expresses his belief that twentieth century Iran exhibits a one-sided domination by politics over religion over the years.

61 When he was Dean of the Faculty of the Tehran Polytechnic, he was arrested on charges of

treason and anti-state activity. Five other prominent public figures were arrested along with him who also were members of the Front. See *Ittilāʿāt*, 30 Urdībihisht 1334 H. Sh./1955.

62 "Marz Mīyān-i Dīn va Umūr-i Ijtimāʿī," pp. 122–23.

63 *Ibid.*, pp. 124–25.

64 Citing the speeches by Āyatullāh Tāliqānī and Āyatullāh Mutahharī at the 1959 proceedings of the Islamic Society of Engineers during the ʿĀshūrā observances of that year. Ibid., pp. 125–26.

65 *Ibid.*, pp. 126–27.

66 *Ibid.*, p. 127.

67 *Ibid.*, p. 128.

68 *Ibid.*, pp. 132–33.

69 *Ibid.*, pp. 134–35.

70 *Ibid.*, p. 136. A *gilīm* is a short-napped carpet. The expression *gilīm-i Khūdrā az āb dar āvurdan* (to pull one's own *gilīm* out of the water) means to succeed against odds.

71 *Ibid.*, pp. 136–37. The other "branches" are: (1) prayer; (2) *rawzah* (narratives of the lives of the *imām*s); (3) pilgrimmage; (4) alms. The verse cited is from *Qurʾān, sūrah* Āl ʿUmrān, v. 110.

72 *Ibid.*, pp. 137–38.

73 *Ibid.*, p. 145.

74 *Ibid.*, pp. 145–46. Bāzargān's position is similar to that of Sayyid Hādī Khusrūshāhī, *Du Mazhab* (Qumm, 1342 H. Sh./1963), cited in Doroshenko, "O Nekotorykh Kontseptsiakh," p. 122. Citing Khusrūshāhī: "Islam consists of a divine program for a social system, for the good ordering of the affairs of society, and a political program for the administration of society."

75 *Ibid.*, p. 141.

Notes to Chapter Five

1 Āyatullāh Murtazā Mutahharī, personal interview at his home in Tehran, 16 October 1975. Mutahharī noted that every time meaningful reform proposals have been advanced by the clergy for its own institution, the government has suppressed these proposals.

2 A. K. S. Lambton, "A Reconsideration of the Position of *Marjaʿ al-Taqlid* and the Religious Institution," *Studia Islamica*, XX (1964), pp. 115–35.

3 Thus, Seyyed Hossein Nasr, then Director of the Imperial Academy of Philosophy, answered in the following manner to a question which suggested that Islam had become more and more irrelevant over time because of its failure to adapt to the modern era: Islam had no need to adapt itself to the times. It had not come into existence for this purpose, after all. Instead, it is Islam which "must regulate circumstances and create conditions." It is an error to consider that time must regulate man's life and his destiny. For if one were to concede that point, one would have to accept that dialectical materialism be the philosophy of life. Yet, for Muslims, free man, responding to the requirements of the *shariʿah*, upon which he is dependent for his existence, is the regulating force of the world. "Hiwār maʿa al-Duktūr Sayyid Husayn Nasr hawla al-Dīn wa al-Falsafah wa al-Hayāt," *al-Fikr al-Islāmī* (Tehran), Vol. I, no. 6 (Rabīʿ al-Thani, 1393 H. Q./1974), pp. 5–6.

4 Lambton, "A Reconsideration," p. 122.

5 *Ibid.*, pp. 134–35.

6 Muhammad Ibrāhīm Āyatī, "Amr bi Maʿrūf va Nahy az Munkar," *Guftār-i Māh*, Vol. I (Tehran: Saduq, 1340 H. Sh./1961), p. 49–52; citation is at p. 52.

7 Murtazā Mutahharī, "Amr bi Maʿrūf va Nahy az Munkar," *Ibid.*, p. 87. Weaving like a red thread throughout the discussions of both Āyatī and Mutahharī is the idea of work, deed, action, doing, as opposed to listening, talking, thinking.

8 Mutahharī, "Taqvā az Nazar-i Islam," *ibid.*, p. 21. As noted in the text, such shenanigans were illustrated in the specific case of Rafsanjān, although many protests were lodged concerning other

cases and some published in the press at that time. The townspeople protested the candidacy of a hand-picked outsider who was a member of the government supported Millīyūn Party. The citizens' protest was in the form of a telegram to the Imām Jum'ah of Tehran from the city of Yazd, which lies some 300 kilometers to the northwest of Rafsanjān! The governor of Kirmān province, they complained, had encircled Rafsanjān with troops and sealed off the town in a fashion unprecedented since the Constitutional Revolution. They objected that he had violated the Shah's own order that the elections would be free and instead openly had proclaimed the contrary: the elections would not be free and he "will throw out the vote of any one we please." The citizens criticized the governor for assuming that just because he was the borther of the Prime Minister (Manūchihr Iqbāl), he could do as he pleased. For this episode, see *Ittilā'āt*, 11 Murdād 1339 l. Sh./1960.

[9]Sayyid Muhammad Bihishtī, "Qishr-i Jadīd dar Jāmi'-yi Mā," *Guftār-i Māh*, I, p. 264.

[10]Murtaza Mutahharī, "Mazāyā va Khadamāt-i Marhūm Āyatullāh Burūjirdī," in *Bahsī dar Bārah-yi Marja'īyat va Rūhānīyat* (Tehran: N. p. 1342 H. Sh./1962), pp. 151-53.

[11]Interview with Mutahharī, Tehran, 16 October 1975. Mutahharī noted that in the 13 years since he had written the essay on Burūjirdī's achievements, he had become further confirmed in his belief that the domination of *fiq* in the *hawzah*s was producing negative results.

[12]Mahmūd Tāliqānī, "Tamarkuz yā 'Adam-i Tamarkuz-i Marja'īyat va Fatvā," in *Bahsī dar Bārah*, pp. 131-35; and Murtazā Jazā'irī, "Taqlīd-i A'lam yā Shūrā-yi Fatvā?" in *ibid.*, pp. 136-47.

[13]Murtaza Mutahharī, "Asl-i Ijtihād dar Islam," in *Guftār-i Mah*, I, p. 218. This essay also appeared in the volume, *Bahsī dar Bārah-yi Marja'īyat va Rūhānīyat*.

[14]Murtazā Mutahharī, "Rahbarī-yi Nasl-i Javān," *Guftār-i Māh*, III (Tehran: Sadūq, 1342 H. Sh./1963), pp. 32-33; 46.

[15]*Ibid.*, pp. 46-48.

[16]*Ibid.*, pp. 49-51. Mutahharī tells the story of a colleague of his who went to Najaf in August of 1962, where he encountered Marja'-i Taqlīd Abū al-Qāsim Khū'ī. The colleague noticed that Āyatullāh Khū'ī had abandoned the teaching of *tafsīr* in his classes. When he asked about this of the Āyatullāh he was told that *tafsīr* had been dropped in 1954, and frankly the reason had been that *tafsīr* was just too complex and involved many difficulties. When Khū'ī was reminded that 'Allamāh Muhammad Husayn Tabā'tabā'ī continued to teach *tafsīr* in Qumm, Khū'ī remarked that the 'Allāmah had "martyred himself." (*Khūdish rā qurbānī kardand*).

[17]Murtazā Jazā'irī, "Luzūm-i Sarahat dar Rahbarīhā-yi Dīnī va Ijtimā'ī," in *ibid.*, p. 87. Emphasis supplied.

[18]*Ibid.*, p. 97. Ironically, Jazā'irī warned that '*ulamā*' lack of candor had been so pervasive over time that it had become, as it were, one of the principles of the faith (*usūl-i dīn*)! He went on: ". . . error has substituted for truth to the point that if, today, under the influence of the pressures of circumstances, the [religious] leaders want to be more candid and speak the truth, they will be above all afraid of their own disciples. For they have spent a whole lifetime juggling words around [*mujāmalah*] to the effect that religion has nothing to do with social questions." *Ibid.*, p. 98. This is by now a familiar theme. We have seen that Bāzargān and Mutahharī, too, have ridiculed the idea that Islam stands apart from social and political issues. For similar views by yet another of these reformers, see Muhammad Bihishtī, "Islam va Payvandhā-yi Ijtimī'ī," *Guftār-i Māh*, II (Tehran: Sadūq, 1341 H. Sh./1962), pp. 76 ff.

[19]Murtazā Mutahharī, "Mushkil-i Asāsī dar Sāzmān-i Rūhānīyat," in *Bahsī dar Bārah*, pp. 118 ff.

[20]Mutahharī, "Mazāyā va Khadamāt," p. 159.

[21]Mutahharī, "Mushkil-i Asāsī," *passim.*

[22]*Ibid.*, p. 115. Mutahharī remarks that the '*ulamā*' have many times discussed the idea of an autonomous financial arrangement for the clergy with government officials; somewhat disingenuously, he complained: ". . . but for reasons which remain unknown to us [these discussions] have produced no results." It would have been remarkable had they done so!

[23]*Ibid.*, p. 107.

[24]The *madrasah* system had much to commend it, the reformists acknowledged. The motivation of the students was excellent. Their learning was generated by enthusiasm (although this enthusiasm, which carries them through their formal cycles of study, becomes rapidly jaded after they receive the *ijāzah-yi ijtihād* and consequently [sic] become reactionaries). Students in the *madrasah*s have enormous admiration for their instructors, who themselves return such feelings of respect to the students. The instruction is based on dialectical exchange at the more advanced levels, and the students are free to challenge their teacher. It is the system of instruction itself that encourages this free flow of ideas. Students, moreover, may choose not only their own instructors but their own pace of education. All these points stand in marked contrast to the arrangements to be found in the secular education system. There, the students are after grades and diplomas, are assigned courses and professors by the administration, are packed into anonymous lecture halls and have virtually no contact with their professors. Often, an adversary relationship appears to exist in the secular classrooms between teacher and student; accordingly, students become cynical and teachers punitive.

Yet, the catalogue of woes in the *madrasah*s is comprehensive and discouraging for the reformists. There is no collegiality or sharing of ideas in the *madrasah*. There is too much dead wood, apathy, listlessness, going along, and "not sticking one's feet out from under one's robes." A shortage of books and research materials exists. Teachers assign obsolete materials that often are meaningless for the social environment of the 20th century. A significant problem exists in regard to a tendency toward posturing, surface mannerism, "trafficking in honorifics and titles." Reformers who arrive at any position of responsibility are somehow socialized into conservative positions in their new roles and permit themselves to be coopted by their new peers. These individuals then lose whatever zest they had to conduct reforms within the institution. Unqualified students are admitted in the absence of a screening mechanism to eliminate incompetent applicants. The absence of any uniform examination system results in overestimation of one's abilities through ambition and consequently leads to frustration in not making the envisaged progress in courses that turn out to be far too difficult. The exceptional concentration of the students in *fiq* and *usūl* makes for overspecialization at very early ages and one-dimensional clergymen. Instruction in Arabic is hopelessly inadequate. The learning process at the higher levels is dominated by the sterility of abstract argumentation based on hypothetical construction.

The *madrasah* system, in short, can take no comfort from the poor conditions in the secular university and secondary systems; it has its own serious problems. For these points, see *ibid.*, pp. 107, 112–13.

[25]Personal interview with Mutahharī in Tehran, 16 October 1975.

[26]Mutahharī, "Mushkil-i Asāsī," pp. 118 ff. As evidence of the reactionary tendencies of the masses he cites two stories. In the days of Shaykh ʿAbd al-Karīm Hāʾirī the venerable Āyatullāh resolved to teach the students of the *hawzah* in Qumm foreign languages and certain nonreligious subjects so that they could go out and proselytize more effectively in the name of Islam. However, no sooner did he decide on this course of action than a delegation of bazaar merchants and artisans descended from Tehran and threatened to withhold the *khums* if he did not retract. The reason they did this was that they feared the students, their children, would be contaminated by foreign habits and viewpoints.

The second story is told of Āyatullāh Abū al-Hasan Isfahānī (d. 1945) in Najaf. As the senior *Shīʿī mujtahid* he presided over the largest *madrasah* system in the *Shīʿī* community. A meeting took place there, in his absence, in which it was proposed to review the curriculum with an eye to its revamping. Apparently, the proposals included supplementing the traditional *fiq* courses with a number of others that had been allowed to atrophy over the years. However, when Isfahānī returned and was apprised of the recommendations, he ordered a "hands-off" policy and instructed that nothing should be changed in the curriculum "as long as I am alive."

Such discouraging precedents, stated Mutahharī, cannot easily be ignored by the progressives. "It is clear that his [Isfahānī's] action was an educational lesson for those gentlemen who are currently

[1962] the leaders of the *hawzah-yi 'ilmīyah-yi Najaf." Ibid.*, pp. 122–23.
[27]Especially Mihdi Bāzargān, "Intizārāt-i Mardum az Marājiʿ," in *Bahsī dar Bārah*, pp. 71–72; but also Tāliqānī, "Tamarkuz," in *ibid.*, p. 133.
[28]Mutahharī, "Asl-i Ijtihād dar Islam," *Guftār-i Māh*, I, p. 215. He calls such blind obedience "taqlīd-i mīt" (dead imitation).
[29]Lambton, "A Reconsideration," p. 128.
[30]Tabāʾtabāʾī, "Valāyat," pp. 1–12.
[31]The following 16 individuals contributed to the Monthly Religious Society lectures, published in *Guftār-i Māh*, and to the volume, *Bahsī dar Bārah-yi Marjaʿīyat va Rūhānīyat:* Murtazā Mutahharī; Muhammad Ibrāhīm Āyatī; Hājj Mīrzā Khalīl Kamarahʾī; Sayyid Murtazā Shabistarī; ʿAlī Ghafūrī; Sayyid Muhammad Bihishtī; Sayyid Murtazā Jazāʾirī; Sayyid Muhammad Bāqir Sahzivārī; Sayyid Mūsā Sadr; Sayyid Mahmūd Tāliqānī; Husayn Mazīnī; Mīrzā Muhammad Taqī Jaʿfarī, Sayyid Muhammad Farzān; ʿAllāmah Muhammad Husayn Tabāʾtabāʾī; Abū al-Fazl Zanjānī; Mihdī Bāzargān.
[32]Sayyid Muhammad Farzān, "Bāzdīd az 24 Sukhanrānī-yi Guzashtah," *Guftar-i Mah*, II, p. 311, urged that thousands of pamphlets containing the abridged text of individual lectures of the Society be printed and distributed among the masses.
[33]*Idem*. He mentioned Dr. ʿAlī Akbar Shihābī, Director-General of the Endowments Department, and Dr. Rīyāzī, who was Director of the Publications (*Nigārish*) Section of the Ministry of Culture. Financial assistance was requested of these individuals so that the proceedings could be made available to the secondary schools of the country.
[34]Cf. the publisher's statement of surprise and expression of hope that the closing down of the proceedings of the society would soon be reversed in *Guftār-i Māh*, III, frontpiece.
[35]Mutahharī, foreward to *Guftār-i Māh*, I, no pagination indicated.
[36]Sayyid Muhammad Bihishtī, "Rūhānīyat dar Islam va dar Mīyān-i Muslimīn," in *Bahsī dar Bārah*, pp. 102 ff. This prescription comes very close to advocating that the people engage in agitation to overturn an unjust regime.
[37]ʿAlī Ghafūrī, "Anfāl, Yā Sarvathā-yi ʿUmūmī," *Guftar-i Mah*, II, p. 261; on p. 265 he comes within a hair of accusing the existing regime of having despoiled the resources of the people for their own "traitorous" greed and as agents of outsiders.
[38]*Iran Almanac* (Tehran: Echo of Iran, 1965), p. 516.
[39]See appendices.
[40]Data for 1960 from "Awqāf," in *Kitāb-i Irānshahr*, Vol. II (Tehran: Tehran University Press, in conjunction with UNESCO, 1343 H. Sh./1964), pp. 1264–1398. Data for 1975 based on interviews with Ayatullah Murtazā Mutahharī, Jaʿfar Bihbihānī, Āyatullāh Muhammad Bāqir Āshtīyānī (who is *mutavallī* of Tehran's most important *madrasah*, the Marvī), and Āghā-yi Iftikhār (then Director of the Properties Office of the Madrasah-yi ʿĀlī-yi Sipah Sālār, and his associates.
[41]Personal interview, 2 July 1975.
[42]Personal interview, 21 October 1975.
[43]For a comparison of attendance figures given in the early Rizā Shah period—1927—the Sipah Sālār was listed as having exactly the same enrollment; but the Marvī was listed with only seven, and the Āghā with merely eight. See Dawlat-i ʿAlīyah-yi Iran. Vizārat-i Maʿārif, Awqāf va Sanāyiʿ-yi Mustazrafah. *Qavānīn va Nizāmnāmahhā: Ihsāʾīyah-yi Madāris va Makātib, Ihsāʾīyah-yi Aʿzāʾ va Mustakhdimīn*, 1305–1306 H. Sh./1926–1927 (Tehran: Firdawsī, n.d.), pp. 110–11.
[44]*Ittilāʿāt*, 18 Āzar 1329 H. Sh./1950.
[45]See Appendices.
[46]As some gentlemen in Āshtīyānī's circle put it, "*dast-i Awqāf bihish kishīdah shudah ast*," (the Endowment Department of Tehran has a hand in it). Personal interview, 21 October 1975.
[47]*Ibid*.
[48]*Iran Almanac* (Tehran: Echo of Iran, 1970), p. 493.

[49]*Ittilāʿāt,* 10 Āẕar 1353 H. Sh./1974.

[50]"Hāyadah va Gītī az Mushtarīyān-i Awqāf," *Iran Times* (Washington, D.C.), 21 Farvardīn 1358 H. Sh./1979.

[51]"SAVAK Maʾmūr-i Ījād-i Ikhtilāf Mīyān-i Mardum va Rūhānīyat Būd," *Kayhān,* 12 Farvardīn 1358 H. Sh./1979.

[52]"Awqāf ʿalayh-i Maẕhab Tajhīz Shudah Būd," *Kayhān,* 27 Isfand 1357 H. Sh./1979.

[53]*Maʿārif-i Islāmī* (Tehran), Vol. I, nos. 1 and 2 (Shahrīvar and Isfand 1345 H. Sh./1966), pp. 70 and 104–105 respectively. The two *madrasah*s selected in 1966 for repair were the Madrasah-yi Shaykh ʿAbd al-Husayn (Āẕarbāyjānīhā) and Madrasah-yi Sadr. Both are in the Tehran Bazaar and are probably, after the Marvī, Sipah Sālār (Jadīd) and Āghā, the schools with the most students.

[54]For the text of the edict, see *Ittilāʿāt,* 25 Murdād 1350 H. Sh./1971.

[55]On the 1963 data, see the speech by Āyatullāh Khumaynī of 4 June 1963, taped but never published in text form until 1979. The text may be found in the *Iran Times,* 9 February 1979, in Persian. He also claimed that the monthly expenses of the Qumm *hawzah* was 6 million rials. For 1975 information, see Michael M. J. Fischer, *The Qum Report,* p. 20.

[56]For details on stipends by the Sāzmān-i Awqāf to both students and teachers, see the appendices. The calculation of average monthly stipend for teachers and students was achieved by dividing the amount spent by the number of students/teachers (as the case may be), summing these averages, dividing by two (to get an average between *mutasarrifī* and non-*mutassarifī* allocations), dividing the resultant figures by the number of provinces and again dividing that number by 10 months. The decline between 1972 and 1973 in Endowments Organization support to students seems to fit the general trend initiated earlier. Thus, data for 1969–70 show total assistance to students and teachers in the *madrasah*s nation-wide to have been 9,925,955 rials. See *Iran Almanac* (Tehran: Echo of Iran, 1971), p. 593. The appendices figures show, for 1973, a total of 3,938, 424 rials. This represented a loss of some 60%.

[57]For 1960, see "Awqāf," *Kitāb-i Irānshahr,* II, pp. 1264–1398, as given in the appendices; for 1967, see ʿAbd al-Husayn Sipantā, *Tārikhchah-yi Awqāf-i Isfahān* (Isfahān: Muhammadī, 1346 H. Sh./1967), pp. 432–33. The figures of 1,000 students in Isfahān is cited by Michael M. J. Fischer, "The Qum Report," p. 16, which he in turn states is based on a sheer guess by one of the city's *madrasah* instructors. It is likely an overestimate.

[58]Dawlat-i Shāh-in-Shāhī-yi Iran. Sāzmān-i Awqāf. Daftar-i Āmār va Muhandisī-yi Raqabāt. "Guzārish-i Pīshrafthā va Faʿʿālīyathā-yi Sāzmān-i Awqāf, 1352 H. Sh./1973." (Tehran: Sāzmān-i Awqāf, 1353 H. Sh./1974), mimeo/internal report, p. 103.

[59]Personal interview with Āyatullāh Murtazā Mutahharī, 16 October 1975.

[60]From the introduction ot the first volume published by the Husaynīyah Irshād, entitled *Muhammad, Khātam-i Payāmbarān* (Tehran: Shirkat-i Intishār, 1347 H. Sh./1968), pp. xix–xx.

[61]Personal interview with Āyatullāh Mutahharī, 16 October 1975; also, the pamphlet, *Yādnāmah-yi Mujāhid-i Shahīd Dr. ʿAlī Sharīʿatī,* a special issue of the journal, *Fajr,* published by the Anjuman-i Islāmī-yi Dānishjūyān-i Hawzah-yi Oklahoma, Vol. II, no. 5 (Shahrīvar 1356 H. Sh./1977), p. 32.

[62]This summary biographical sketch is drawn from *ibid.,* pp. 84 ff.; and also from *Hijrat va Shahādāt-i Abū Ẕarr-i Zamān: Mujāhid Dr. ʿAlī Sharīʿatī,* a 32 page pamphlet issued by one of the Iranian Islamic Societies of University Students in the United States, n.d.; also, the "Translator's Foreword," by Hamid Algar to his translations of Sharīʿatī's excerpted writings entitled *On the Sociology of Islam* (Berkeley: Mizan Press, 1979), pp. 5–7; also the anonymous sketch in *ibid.,* pp. 33.

[63]ʿAli Sharīʿatī, *Chih Bāyad Kard?* (Tehran: Husaynīyah Irshād, n.d.), pp. 56–57. cf. p. 144, calling the Husaynīyah Irshād "the first vanguard to establish a ʿfree Islamic university...' "

[64]*Ibid.,* p. 15.

[65]*Ibid.,* pp. 32–42.

[66]*Ibid.*, pp. 1-8.

[67]A title which, in Iran, was significant no so much because of Lenin's pamphlet of 1903 as because of the essay by Ahmad Kasravī, written at a time of national crisis in August 1941, entitled *Imrūz Chih Bāyad Kard?* 4th ed. (Tehran: Chāpak, 1336 H. Sh./1957). This was a call for the restoration of the Constitution and social, economic and political reforms.

[68]Recalling to mind the work of the Egyptian conservative thinker, ʿAbbās al-ʿAqqād, *Min Aynā Nabdaʾu?* (Whence Shall We Begin), and the rejoinder by the liberal reformist, Khālid Muhammad Khālid, some years later: *Min Hunā Nabdaʾu* (We Begin From Here).

[69]For a select bibliography of ʿAlī Sharīʿatī's prodigious output, see *On the Sociology of Islam,* tr. Algar, pp. 35-38.

[70]Gh. A. T., "Introduction," in *ibid.,* p. 31.

[71]ʿAlī Sharīʿatī, *Ravish-i Shinākht-i Islam* (Tehran: Husaynīyah Irshād, 1347, H. Sh./1968), pp. 6-8.

[72]Sharīʿatī, *Az Kujā Āghāz Kunīm?* (Tehran: Husaynīyah Irshād, n.d.), p. 55.

[73]Sharīʿatī, *Tashayyuʿ-yi ʿAluvī vu Tushayyuʿ-yi Safavī* (Tehran: Husaynīyah Irshad, 1350 H. Sh./1971), esp. pp. 320-26. On these pages he constructs a balance sheet of the two kinds of Shīʿism and considers their treatment of the following concepts: *visāyat* (appointment as trustee); *imāmat; ʿismat* (chastity, to the point of immunity from sin); *valāyat; shafāʿat* (mediation); *ijtihād; taqlīd; ʿadl* (justice); *duāh* (prayer); *intizār* (waiting for the *Imām); ghaybat* (the Imām's occultation).

	ʿAlī's Shīʿism	Safavid Shīʿism
Visayat	The prophet's appointing, by God's command, the most suitable and right people in his family, on the basis of knowledge, to leadership	The principle of government by designation, based on dynastic inheritance founded on descent and kinship alone.
Imāmat	Pure, revolutionary leadership for guiding the people and the true construction of society, leading to the latter's awareness, growth, independence of judgment by human beings who incarnate the religion.	Belief in 12 pure, sacred and preternatural souls, superhuman beings who are the only means of approaching and having recourse to God; of mediation; 12 angels to worship, hidden creatures, akin to deities.
ʿIsmat	Belief in the *imams'* piety, purity of ideas and social leadership; the *imams* as leaders responsible in their faith, knowledge and rule over the people; i.e., a rejection of traitorous government, of following an impure man of learning, of a deceiving clergyman who is connected to the apparatus of the caliphate.	A special and exceptional feature of hidden creatures, who are not made in man's image, who cannot err; belief that those 14 pure souls [i.e., Muhammad, Fātimah and the 12 *imām*s] have such infallibility; i.e., proof of the naturalness of a traitorous government; acceptance of an impure world; of a wrongdoing clergyman with ties to tyranny.

Valāyat	Friendship for, and leadership and government by, ʿAlī, alone, because he is the supreme example of servitude to Allah. His leadership because he is a bright light of right guidance and sincere scout for the caravan of mankind; his government because man's history has yearned for the justice freedom and equality of his five years of government, which the nations need.	Just loving ʿAlī and therefore being exempt from any responsibility; guaranteeing heaven and not falling into the fires of hell; belief that *valāyat* is irrelevant in the creation and administration of society, since it helps Allah; whereas in the world nature is at work.
Shafā ʾat	A factor for securing the boon of salvation.	A means of unworthy salvation.
Ijtihād	A factor for the movement of religion through time; the companion of history, permanent revolution and integrative revolution in the outlook of religion; a legal perfection and reconciling in changes and development of the system.	A factor of stultification and ossification; a block to progress, change and transformation; a means of blasphemy and perfidy; an absolute censure of any new act on the path of religion, system, life, thought, knowledge, society, everything.
Taqlīd	A logical, scientific, natural and necessary link between a layman or non-specialist with an *ʿālim* of religion on practical and legal questions that have a technical or expertise aspect to them.	Blind obedience to a clergyman; absolute subordination, with no questions asked, to the mind, opinion or decision of a clergyman; or, in the words of the *Qurʾān:* worship of a religious man of the spirit.
ʿAdl	A belief in an attribute of God, that He is just, that the world is based on justice; that the system of society and life must also be based on it; that tyranny and inequality are an unnatural and anti-God system; it is one of the two pillars of religion, the objective of prophethood.	A controversy over the attributes of God that is relevant for the after-life; anticipation or assignation of duty for God in the sense of what judgment will He render at the resurrection. On this side of death it is irrelevant, since prior to death the discussion of justice is related to Shah ʿAbbās; give to Caesar what is his and to God what is God's. The world is the domain of Shah ʿAbbās's reign; the hereafter that of God.
Duʿāh	A text that teaches, makes aware, inculcates good and beauty; an act that uplifts	An incantation mechanically uttered that makes one secure, narcotizes, provides vain hopes,

	the spirit and brings one nearer to God.	brings rewards that have nothing to do with one's circumstances, substitutes for heavy responsibilities.
Intiẓār	Spiritual, ideational and practical preparedness for reform, revolution, changing the world situation, decisive belief in the elimination of tyranny, victory of justice, and the coming into its own of the deprived class, the masses' inheritance of the earth, in tandem with true, self-made men for the world revolution.	Being at spiritual, ideational and practical ease in submitting to the *status quo;* explaining away corruption; fatalism about everything; rejecting responsibility; despair about reform; prior surrender before taking any step.
Ghaybat	The people having responsibility in charting their course; belief; one's own leadership and social and spiritual existence; appointing leaders among the people who are aware, responsible, pure—who can substitute for the *Imām.*	Negation of everyone's responsibility; suspending all the social ordinances of Islam; inutility of any act; viewing the acceptance of any social responsibility to be illegitimate on the pretext that only the *Imām* can lead, one can only follow the *Imām;* one can be responsible before the *Imām,* but since he is in occultation, there is nothing one can do about anything.

---

[74]This theme percolates throughout his *Shahādat* (Tehran: Husayniyah Irshād, 1350 H. Sh./1971), eg. p. 13 following p. 78 in text: "... in the ever present battle of history, time and place ... all stages are Karbalā', all months are Muharram, all days are ʿĀshūrā ..."

[75]Algar, "Opposition Role," p. 247.

[76]Sharīʿatī, *Intiẓār-i Mazhab-i Iʿtirāz* (Tehran: Husaynīyah Irshad, 1350 H. Sh./1971), pp. 10–11. He is clearly uncomfortable with this position, however. Later, he says a student asked him about longevity and the Imām. If scientists have not been able to set any definite limits to human mortality, does Sharīʿatī take this to mean that the hidden Imām can live for many hundreds and even thousands of years? His response was that rather than try to answer that question they should inquire into the meaning of the messianic principle.
Characteristic of the didactic side of Sharīʿatī is his assertion in *Chih Bāyad Kard?,* p. 16, that: "Islam has always been of life, movement, responsibility, holy war, earth, life, mankind." And on p. 21, where he views it as a religion "overflowing with civilization, culture, power, intellectual, scientific, artistic, creativity; glory, victory, power, riches and freedom ..."

[77]Sharīʿatī, *Intiẓār-i Mazhab-i Iʿtirāz,* p. 18.

[78]*Ibid.,* p. 21.

[79]Sharīʿatī, *Hajj* (Tehran: Husaynīyah Irshād, 1350 H. Sh./1971), p. 6. Even such activist clergymen as Āyatullāhs Muntaẓirī, Saʿīdī and Ghaffārī, not to mention Tāliqānī appear not to have responded to Sharīʿatī with manifestations of support.

[80]He argues that religion has to express itself in the language of the common folk to be understood at the time of its emergence as faith. But a religion which lacked symbolic expression would not endure. "It was therefore necessary that religion [Shī'ism] should speak in images and symbols that would become comprehensible with the development of human thought and science." See Sharī'atī, "Man and Islam," in *On the Sociology of Islam*, tr. Algar, p. 72.

[81]Sharī'atī, *Intiẓār-i Maẓhab-i Iʿtirāz*, p. 25.

[82]*Ibid.*, pp. 38–39.

[83]Sharī'atī, *Az Kujā Āghāz Kunīm?* p. 38.

[84]Sharī'atī, *Ravish-i Shinākht-i Islam*, pp. 8–9, 14.

[85]Sharī'atī, *Intiẓār-i Maẓhab-i Iʿtirāz*, p. 42.

[86]*Ibid.*, pp. 44–45.

[87]Sharī'atī, "Islāmshināsī," lesson 21, reprinted and translated as "The World-View of Tauhid," in *On the Sociology of Islam*, p. 83. He immediately disclaims the possibility that God, man and nature share a "substantial" unity but that they are mutually compatible, proximate to one another and "no boundary exists among them."

[88]*Idem.*

[89]*Idem*, fn. 2.

[90]Sharī'atī, *Intiẓār-i Maẓhab-i Iʿtirāz*, p. 52.

[91]Sharī'atī, *Shahādat*, pp. 69–70.

[92]*Sharī'atī, Hajj*, p. 4.

[93]Sharī'atī, *Shahādat*, pp. ii–iii, following p. 78.

[94]The *'ulamā'* appear to have appreciated him only posthumously. Āyatullāh Muhammad Ja'far Tāhirī of Shīrāz held a *majlis-i tarhīm* (mourning ceremony) for him after his death; Āyatullāh Mūsā Sadr, the chief Shī'ī *mujtahid* in Lebanon and a son of Sadr al-Dīn Sadr (q.v.) officiated at his burial in Damascus; and Āyatullāh Khumaynī issued a statement on the occasion of Sharī'atī's death in response to telegrams of condolences sent to him. He exhorted Iranian youth to lead the people out of the wilderness of autocracy, corruption and foreign domination. See *Yādnāmah-yi Mujāhid-i Shahīd, Dr. 'Alī Sharī'atī*, p. 97.

Even the regime paid its respects to Sharī'atī after his death. In *Kayhān*, 2 Tīr 1356 H. Sh./1977, Sharī'atī was described in the following terms: "[Sharī'atī] had not been a simple teacher and instructor. Research, inquiry, writing, discussion, the holding of seminars to study Islamic and social issues had placed his work, which was limited to teaching, under the rays of brilliance. He used to raise profound and precise issues about Islam and the sociology of Islam in his classes and elsewhere." The article tried to convert Sharī'atī into an anti-Marxist nationalist laboring in the service of his country. Also, the administration of Mashhad University, where Sharī'atī had briefly taught, publicized that it would sponsor a *majlis-i tarhīm* at the Imām Husayn Mosque. For these details, see *Hijrat va Shahādat-i Abū Ẓarr-i Zamān*, pp. 21, 23.

Notes to Chapter Six

[1]"Khafaqān-i Sīyāsī dar Iran va Mubārazah 'alayh-i Ān," *Payām-i Dānishjū*, Shumārah-yi Makhsūs (Shahrīvar 1356–1977), p. 63. The previous three paragraphs are based on pp. 59–64 of this publication.

[2]*Ibid.*, p. 65; the present and succeeding paragraphs are based on this source, pp. 64–66.

[3]Algar, "Oppositional Role," pp. 250–52.

[4]*Iran-i Āzād*, No. 74 (Mihr/Ābān 1349 H. Sh./1970), the organ of the National Front of Iran (in exile), listed the names of five Hujjat al-Islams, one preacher and three *tullāb* who had been sentenced to prison terms ranging from 10 months to three years to the districts of Zābul (in Saystān) and Irānshahr (in extreme Western Iran). One of these individuals, Hujjat al-Islam Marvārīd, had only some two months earlier "spoke[n] at the mosque of Hajj 'Azizullah concerning the qualifications of Khumaynī as *marja'* . . ." (Cf. Algar, "Oppositional Role, " p. 252.)

[5]*Iran-i Āzād*, No. 76 (Day/Bahman 1349 H. Sh./1970/1971).

[6]*Khabarnāmah-yi Jabhah-yi Millī-yi Iran*, Murdād 1350 H. Sh./1971.

[7]*Ibid.*

[8]*Mujāhid*, I, 1 (Khurdād 1351 H. Sh./1972) and I, 2 (Tīr 1351 H. Sh./1972). The leaders of the Shīrāz *'ulamā'* were Āyatullāh Bahā' al-Dīn Mahallātī (who had been very active in the 1963 disturbances with Āyatullāh Khumaynī) and Āyatullāh Muhammad Ja'far Tāhirī. *Mujāhid* was apparently the organ of the Mujāhidīn-i Khalq. (Tāliqānī was exiled not only because he had taught Qur'ānic commentary to these five but also for his Ramazān speech that year calling for struggle and *jihād*. *Khabarnāmah*, Bahman 1350-1972.

[9]*Mujāhid*, Tīr 1351 H. Sh./1972.

[10]Ruhullāh al-Mūsavī Khumaynī, *Kashf al-Asrār* (Tehran?: n. p. 1363 H. Q. 1943/44).

[11]Khumaynī's statement of 28 Rabī' al-Thānī 1391 H. Q./1971. He adds: "Anyone who looks at the biography of the prophet in regard to [the matter of] government will see that Islam has come to destroy all these palaces of monarchical oppression ..." The statement is reprinted in *Iran-i Āzād*, No. 80 (Tīr/Murdād 1350 H. Sh./1971. It is, in essence, a disquisition on reasons for opposition to the projected 2500 anniversary celebrations.

[12]See the accounts in *Khabarnāmah*, Murdād 1350 H. Sh./1971, and *Iran-i Āzād*, No. 79 Urdībihisht/Khurdād 1350 H. Sh./1971. According to the latter, the chief of SAVAK in Qumm contacted Khumaynī's son in that city and warned him of the plot against his father, saying that the Iraqis wanted to make it seem as though the Iranian government had been responsible for murdering Khumaynī. The Iranian opposition interpreted this as a smokescreen attempt by the government to disguise the fact that an assassination team had been discovered by the Iraqi regime, which had arrested a certain Sayyid Muhammad Rūhānī as principal accomplice. In other words, it was a discovered Iranian plot.

[13]*Khabarnāmah*, Farvardīn 1351 H. Sh./1972.

[14]*Iran-i Āzād*, Tīr-Murdād 1350 H. Sh./1971.

[15]Rūhullāh al-Mūsavī Khumaynī, *Hukūmat-i Islami* (Najaf: n. p., 1391 H. Q./1971). The text is in Persian.

[16]On the matter of *valāyat-i faqīh*, see fn. seven to chapter two.

[17]"Nazarāt-i Āyatullāh al-'Uzmā Khumaynī Dar Mawrid-i Shāyi'ah-yi Hukūmat-i Rūhānīyat va Shirkat-i Zanhā Dar Umūr-i Kishvar," *Khvāndanīhā*, XXXIX, 6 (29 Mihr 1357 H. Sh./1978), p. 19.

[18]"Payyām-i Hazrat Āyatullāh Khumaynī bi Millat-i Sharīf-i Iran," 12 Safar 1398 H. Q./1978, reprinted by the Anjuman-i Islāmī-yi Dānishjūyān-i Āmrīka va Kānādā.

[19]"Payyām-i Qā'id-i Buzurg-i Islam Imām Khumaynī bi Millat-i Sharīf-i Iran dar Mawrid-i Jināyyāt-i Shah va Tashkīl-i Jumhūrī-yi Islāmī dar Iran," 4 Dhī Hajjah 1398 H. Q./1978, reprinted by the Nihzat-i Āzādī-yi Iran Khārij az Kishvar.

[20]"Payyām-i Imām Khumaynī bi Millat-i Iran," 23 Dhī al-Qa'dah 1398 H. Q./1978, reprinted by the Nihzat-i Āzādī-yi Iran Khārij az Kishvar.

[21]Lucien George, "Iran: Les dernières émeutes sont les prémices d'une gigantesque explosion," *Le Monde*, 6 May 1978.

[22]As revealed in an interview with the correspondent of the French newspaper, *Le Figaro*, reprinted in the *Iran Times*, 20 October 1978 (in Persian).

[23]Paul Balta, "La Crise iranienne," *Le Monde*, 12-13 November 1978.

[24]*Iran Times* (in Persian), 16 June 1978.

[25]*Ibid.*, (in Persian), 2 June 1978.

[26]*Ibid.*, (in Persian), 8 September 1978.

[27]Letter of 30 August 1978 by Āyatullāh Sharī'atmadārī to the Islamic Association of Iranian Students in Europe, the United States and Canada, 8 Shahrīvar 1357 H. Sh./1978, reprinted by the Anjuman-i Islāmī-yi Dānishjūyān-i Āmrīkā va Kānādā.

[28]*Iran Times* (in Persian), 8 July 1978.

[29]Jean de al Guérivière, "L'Iran à la côte de l'alerte," III, *Le Monde*, 9 June 1978.

³⁰Letter of 30 August 1978.
³¹*The New York Times,* 4 December 1978.
³²*The Economist* (London), 29 July 1978, p. 57.
³³Balta, "La Crise iranienne."
³⁴Proclamation of Āyatullāhs Muhammad Rizā al-Mūsavī al-Gulpāygānī, Sayyid Muhammad Kāżim Sharī'atmadārī, and Shihāb al-Dīn al-Husaynī al-Mar'ashī al-Najafī, dated 21 Murdād 1357 H.Sh./1978, reprinted by the Anjuman-i Islāmī-yi Dānishjūyān-i Āmrīkā va Kānādā.
³⁵*Iran Times* (in Persian), 22 September 1978.
³⁶*Ibid.* (in Persian), 1 September 1978.
³⁷*Khabarnāmah: Zamīmah-yi Difā'ī,* Bahman 1350 H. Sh./1972.
³⁸Fischer, *The Qum Report,* p. 16.
³⁹Balta, "La Crise iranienne."
⁴⁰Fischer, *The Qum Report,* p. 17. His data show the Āzarbāyjānī contingent to be approximately 17.5% of the total, but if we exclude the foreign students (about 170), plus the nearly 400 students for whom no province of origin is shown, the proportion of Āzarīs out of the total becomes 19%.
⁴¹*Ittilā'āt,* 30 Mihr 1357 H. Sh./1978. The list of names was not in alphabetical order. It is possible that the ranking of the names in ordinal fashion was related to the degree of influence exerted by each individual. On the other hand, it may have nothing to do with it. The following is the list in order of signing. It will be noted that the *mulavallī* of the Marvī *madrasah,* Āyatullāh Bāqir Āshtīyānī, is missing.

Signatories of the October 1978 Telegram
to Āyatullāh Khumaynī in France

1. Abū al-Qāsim Falsafī
2. Muhammad Rizā al-'Alavī al-Tihrānī
3. Mustafā Masjid-i Jāmi'ī
4. 'Alī Nūr Muhammadī
5. Muhammad ibn 'Alī al-Husaynī 'Ilm al-Hudā
6. Sayyid 'Alī Bithā'ī Gulpāygānī
7. Sayyid Javād Mīr 'Azīmī
8. Ismā'īl Ibrāhīm Nizhād
9. Abū al-Qāsim Musāfirī
10. Bahā' al-Dīn 'Ilm al-Hudā
11. Husayn Mufīd
12. Hasan 'Alī Karbāsī
13. Sayyid Javād Pīshvā'ī
14. Sayyid Mahmūd Hāshimī
15. Intishārī Najafābādī
16. Sayyid Hāshim Hamīdī
17. Muhammad Rizā Karīmī
18. Masīh Masjid-i Jāmi'ī
19. Muhammad Rizā Mu'ayyadī
20. 'Alī Muhammadī
21. Sayyid 'Alī Muqaddam
22. Husayn Ashrafī
23. Mansūr 'Āsimī
24. Sayyid Husayn Abtahī
25. Muhammad Taqī Vahīdī
26. Muhammad Sādiq Vahīdī
27. Sayyid Abū Tālib Mahmūdī
28. Sayyid Muhammad 'Alī Sayyid Jalālī
29. 'Alī Muqaddasī
30. Mihdī Hā'irī Tihrānī
31. Sayyid 'Abd al-Ilah Taqavī Shīrāzī
32. 'Alī Sayyid Sharī'atmadārī
33. Hasan Sa'īdī

The initiator of this telegram was Āyatullāh Muhammad Rizā al-Mūsavī al-Burūjirdī. The preacher, Falsafī, played an active role in the Bahā'ī crisis in the mid-fifties, it will be recalled. Mihdī Hā'irī Tihrānī is one of the sons of Shaykh 'Abd al-Karīm Hā'irī Yazdī, who had received his doctorate at McGill University in Montreal, has published a book about Āyatullāh Muhammad Husayn Nā'īnī, and was a professor at the Faculty of Theology of the University of Tehran at the time. As to the telegram's content, it wished Khumaynī triumph in his new exile and allied the signatories to his cause. It was, for that time, a brave act, despite the relaxations of the Sharīf-Imāmī regime in the context of release of political prisoners.

[42]This amazingly crass effort to mobilize opinion against Āyatullāh Khumaynī was only the last in a long series of efforts by the regime. One of the strangest of these involved the murder, in mysterious circumstances, of Āyatullāh Shamsābādī of Isfahān in mid-May 1976. The Iranian press claimed that the alleged assassins had been inspired by a book written by a certain Shaykh Ni'matullāh Sālihī Najafābādī entitled *Shahīd-i Jāvīd*, published in Qumm in 1350 H. Sh./1971. This individual, described by the press as a "hidebound clergyman" (*rūhānī-yi qishrī*—'Alī Sharī'atī's favorite pejorative), denied the divine knowledge and infallibility of the *imāms*. This in itself is an implausible conjunction of factors, since it would be highly unlikely that such a work could find a publisher in Qumm! The book viewed Imām Husayn's struggle against the *Sunnī* Caliph, Yazīd, in terms of Husayn's quest for power, position, status and control. In consequence, Imām Husayn had no knowledge of his coming martyrdom. The same argument is applied to Imām 'Alī, who was assassinated without any prior idea of his impending death. The press insinuated that Āyatullāh Khumaynī was an accomplice in the act of Shamsābādī's murder by stating that Najafābādī was an adherent of the Āyatullāh, and the four arrested suspects had acted in response to these murky ideas. Shamsābādī had been singled out for punishment because he had led the campaign against the offending book. For this episode, see *Kayhān*, 25 Urdībihisht 2535/1976; and *Ittilā'āt* of the same date. Many believe that Shamsābādī's murder was arranged by provocateurs within SAVAK.

[43]According to Marvin Zonis's reputational elite analysis, *The Political Elite of Iran* (Princeton: Princeton University Press, 1971), Jalāl al-Dīn Tihrānī emerged as the second most political influential *āyatullāh* in the mid-sixties (next to Khumaynī, of course).

[44]"Proclamation of Ayatullah Khomeini Concerning the Formation of the Council of the Islamic Revolution," 13 Safar 1399 H. Q./12 January 1979, in English; reprinted by the Muslim Students' Association of the U.S. and Canada.

[45]Material in the last four paragraphs is based on the interview with Āyatullāh Sharī'atmadārī by one of the Tehran dailies and reprinted in the *Iran Times* (in Persian), 9 February 1979.

[46]This meeting took place on 19 June 1979 and was reported in the major newspapers.

[47]*Iran Times* (in Persian), 25 May 1979.

[48]*Ibid*. (in Persian), 8 June 1979.

[49]*Ibid*. (in Persian), 25 May 1979.

[50]*Ittilā'āt*, 20 Khurdād 1358 H. Sh./1979.

[51]*Iran Times*, (in Persian), 16 March 1978.

[52]*Kayhān*, 27 Isfand 1357 H. Sh./1979.

[53]*Iran Times* (in Persian), 11 May 1979.

[54]*Kayhān*, 27 Isfand 1357 H. Sh./1979; *Ittilā'āt*, 20 Khurdād 1358 H. Sh./1979. During this speech, Falsafī eulogized the late Āyatullāh Sayyid Abū al-Qāsim Kāshānī, thus presumably preparing the way for his rehabilitation among those clergymen who had been offended by his blatant politicking in the early fifties. Falsafī, it will be remembered, had closely identified himself with Kāshānī's anti-Bahā'ī activities and had also participated in the vanguard of anti-Bahā'ī actions in the mid-fifties. The prospect of Kāshānī's rehabilitation has greatly disturbed elements of the National Front. One of its principals, 'Alī Asghar Hājj Sayyid Javādī, was moved to attack the late Kāshānī in the following manner: "... with full knowledge and purely out of self-serving motives, careerism and rumor-mongering, he sold out the adherents of the Iranian nationalist movement and Dr. Musad-

diq to the Shah, the Court and British imperialism . . .'' Not surprisingly, Javādī thereupon received telephone death threats. Cf. *Kayhān*, 8 Farvardīn 1358 H. Sh./1979. Falsafī's charge that Musaddiq split with Kāshānī over the former's alleged designs against Islam met with sharp challenge elsewhere, as well. Kāshānī's political mistakes were recounted as follows: (1) he sided with Riżā Khān (later, Riżā Shāh) in the latter's struggle against Sayyid Hasan Mudarris in the early 1920's and was thereby duped by the Sardār-i Sipah along with Imām Jumʿah Khūʾī, Mīrzā Hāshim Āshtīyānī and Sayyid Muhammad Imām Jumʿah; (2) he allowed himself to be obsessed with political careerist ambitions at the time of the oil nationalization crisis and accepted the Speakership of the Majlis at a time when clergymen were rejecting political posts; (3) he sided with the Shah over Musaddiq. Moreover, Kāshānī was saved by a letter written by Āyatullāh Hājj Sayyid Abū al-Fazl al-Mūsavī Zanjānī to Āyatullāh Burūjirdī which testified that the new military government that had overthrown Prime Minister Muṣaddiq's government intended to defrock Kāshānī. If it had not been for Zanjānī—who was a staunch supporter of Musaddiq—all would have been over for Kāshānī. Consequently, Falsafī had better tend to setting the record straight rather than disseminating misleading ideas about the putative role of Kāshānī as purely one of defending Islam against the Godlessness of Dr. Musaddiq; and should he choose to disbelieve this, he had only to read the appropriate documents that still existed at the home of Āyatullāh Zanjānī. For this attack on Falsafī's conception of Kāshānī's role, see *Ittilāʿāt*, various issues between 21 Khurdād and 31 Khurdād 1358 H. Sh./1979.

[55]Cited in the manifesto of the Mujāhidīn-i Khalq, as published in *Ittilāʿāt*, 20 Khurdād 1358 H. Sh./1979.

[56]*Ittilāʿāt*, 23 Khurdād 1358 H. Sh./1979.

[57]Of these individuals a number belonged to the Council of the Islamic Revolution. Although that body's membership had never been publicly revealed, the left-wing journalist, Ralph Schoenman, who had travelled to Iran in February 1979, released the names of individuals he alleged were the Council's members. His list is suspect in certain respects, because Āyatullāh Murtazā Mutahharī— identified as Chairman of the Council by the press at the time of his assassination in early May—was not listed by Schoenman. The following individuals were identified in the latter's list: Lāhūtī Rūdsarī, Hujjat al-Islam Hāshimī Rafsanjānī (also attacked and wounded by the same group that had assassinated Mutahharī—i.e., the Furqān, about which see below), Muhammad Rabānī Shīrāzī, Muhammad Bihishtī, Hujjat al-Islam Muhammad Mufattih, Āyatullah Anvārī, and, of course, Khumaynī himself. *Iran Times* (in Persian), 30 March 1979.

[58]The figure cut by Khalkhālī evidently disturbed a variety of religious spokesmen. After hundreds of individuals had been executed by the Revolutionary Court under sentences signed by him, Foreign Minister Ibrahīm Yazdī, whose ties to Āyatullāh Khumaynī were well known, declared that Khalkhālī not only had not been the head of the Court but had not even been a member. Subsequently, he went on an alleged fact-finding and peace-keeping mission to Khūzistān to mediate unrest on the part of the ethnic Arab inhabitants of that province. Yet, a statement from the Bureau of Āyatullāh Khumaynī was issued denying that Khalkhālī had been dispatched at Khumaynī's behest. Eventually, it was announced that Khalktālī had become the new leader of the Fidāʾīyān-i Islam. For this series of events, see *Iran Times* (in Persian), 25 May 1979, 1 June 1979.

[59]The compromise may have been helped along by Dr. Yadullāh Sahābī, Minister of State for Revolutionary Planning. For the Persian text of the draft constitution, see *Iran Times*, 22 June 1979; the English text appears serially in the three issues of the same newspaper dated 22 and 29 June and 6 July 1979.

[60]*Iran Times* (in Persian), 11 May 1979.

[61]*Āyandigān*, 19 Urdībihisht 1358 H. Sh./1979.

[62]*Kayhān*, 24 Urdībihisht 1358 H. Sh./1979.

[63]*Ibid.*, 15 Isfand 1357 H. Sh./1979; *Iran Times* (in Persian), 25 May and 8 June 1979.

[64]*Ittilāʿāt*, 28–31 Khurdād 1358 H. Sh./1979.

Notes to Chapter Seven

[1] Warren Ilchman and Norman Uphoff, *The Political Economy of Change* (Berkeley: University of California Press, 1969), p. 257.

[2] Arjomand, "Religion, Political Action and Legitimate Domination," *passim;* this important article was published by the *Archives européenes de sociolgoie,* Vol. XX (1979), pp. 59–109.

[3] Kāshānī's current supporters have released the text of a letter, allegedly in his handwriting, which the *mujtahid* had written to Musaddiq warning him of the imminence of a coup d'état that General Zāhidī was about to launch against him. This letter is cited as evidence that nationalist followers of Prime Minister Musaddiq in 1979 can be expected to show the same contempt for the personalities of the 1979 clergy leadership as Musaddiq had allegedly shown for Kāshānī.

The nationalists, in their turn, have complained directly to Āyatullāh Khumaynī for insisting upon a "unity of words" that amounts to "only one person having the right to speak." And the Director of the National Iranian Oil Company, Hasan Nazīh (who was simultaneously the head of the Lawyers' Syndicate) compared Khumaynī disclaimer (issued on 30 January 1979) that the *marāji'-yi taqlīd* did not intend to govern with his subsequent behavior. "Today, your orders are being swiftly implemented, without regard to the principles which you yourself had mentioned. Not only are you directly intervening in the administration of the country, but you are intervening in questions relating to other countries. You believe in the coexistence of religion and politics. But a clergyman cannot accept the haggling [*chand va chunhā*] of politics, which is against God's will. In this manner are people deprived of freedom. Is this not tyranny?" Such a direct attack on Āyatullāh Khumaynī immediately prompted Sayyid Muhammad Bihishtī, member of the Council of the Islamic Revolution, to demand that Nazīh be brought to trial before the Revolutionary Court on charges of treason. For these developments concerning the open letter by the National Democratic Front to Āyatullāh Khumaynī attacking his concept of unity of words and the incident involving Nazīh and Bihishtī, see *Iran Times* (in Persian), 8 June 1979.

NAME INDEX

SUBJECT INDEX

ʿAbbāsids
and relation to practical political traditions of
medieval Shīʿism, 6
passing of caliphate to Ottoman Turks, 9
ʿAbdullāh Khān (madrasah), tawlīyat over, 130
Administrative Statute on Endowments (1935),
and consequences for ʿulamāʾ, 57-58
Āghā (madrasah), student enrollment in, 129
ahl al-bayt, tradition of martyrdom among, 12
AIOC, fatvās decreeing nationalization of, 60
Akhbārīs, rejection of mujtahids' role by, 11
Akhbārī-Usūlī conflict
as backdrop to ʿulamāʾ social action, 25
results of as key to contemporary Shīʿī theology, 121
"ākhūndism", as pejorative term utilized
against ʿulamāʾ by Furqān, 178-79
amirate by seizure, as symptom of caliphate's
decline, 8
al-amr bi al-maʿrūf wa al-nahy ʿan al-munkar
as linchpin of Shīʿī theory of government, 12
as powerful precept for political action, 120
Bāzargān's stress on political implications of,
113
stress by Āyatullāh Khumaynī upon as doctrinal grounds for action, 164
anjumans, Bāzargān's caveat against daily political activity of, 114
ʿaql, as source of Shīʿī jurisprudence, 121
ʿĀshūrā
as occasion for regime harassment in 1929, 44
massive anti-Shah demonstrations during in
1978, 168
ʿavvām zadigī, as negative feature of Shīʿism according to reformers, 127
awqāf
indications of illegal appropriations of under
Muhammad Riżā Shah, 132-34
nationalization of in Turkey, 18
under Qājārs, 55-56
Āyandigān, exposition of politics of Furqān by,
177, 178

Āzarbāyjānīhā (madrasah), tawlīyat exercised
over by Āyatullāh Khusrūshāhī, 24
Azhar, al-
Egyptian government control of, 17, 18
reforms of 1961 concerning, 21
Bāb, as incarnate in Sayyid ʿAlī Muhammad
Shīrāzī, 76
Bahāʾism
and campaign against, 76-87
as a charge against educational innovators, 33
Bahāʾullāh's conversion to, 76
global message of, 77
origins of, 76
Baʿthist regime (Iraq), pressure on Āyatullāh
Khumaynī by, 135
Bātinī Shīʿism, insistence on absolute monarchy
by, 9
"branches" of Islam, political implications of,
114
brotherhoods, see guilds
Bureau of Religious Affairs, as successor to
Ministry of Religious Affairs in Turkey, 19
Buwayhids, tolerance of Shīʿah by, 3
caliphate
abolition of by Ataturk, 18
as alien to prophetic mission according to ʿAlī
ʿAbd al-Rāziq, 21
censorship, regime policy on, 159
Censorship Law (1922) and ʿulamāʾ control over
publications, 37
Chīzar, as site of new madrasah near Tehran,
129-30
Christianity, Ittilāʿāt's view of, 106, 107
Community of Islam, as embodiment of social
and political life, 4
Conscription Law (1925), consequence of for
ʿulamāʾ, 37
Constituent Assembly
Āyatullāh Khumaynī's orientation toward,
176
Āyatullāh Sharīʿatmadārī's orientation toward, 176

249